Repugnant Laws

CONSTITUTIONAL THINKING

Jeffrey K. Tulis and Sanford Levinson, *Editors*

Repugnant Laws

JUDICIAL REVIEW OF ACTS OF

CONGRESS FROM THE FOUNDING TO

THE PRESENT

Keith E. Whittington

 University Press of Kansas

© 2019 by the University Press of Kansas
All rights reserved

Published by the University Press of Kansas (Lawrence, Kansas 66045), which was
organized by the Kansas Board of Regents and is operated and funded by Emporia
State University, Fort Hays State University, Kansas State University, Pittsburg State
University, the University of Kansas, and Wichita State University

Library of Congress Cataloging-in-Publication Data

Names: Whittington, Keith E., author.
Title: Repugnant laws : judicial review of acts of Congress from the founding to the
present / Keith E. Whittington.
Description: Lawrence, Kansas : University Press of Kansas, 2019. | Series: Constitutional
thinking | Includes bibliographical references and index.
Identifiers: LCCN 2018058631
  ISBN 9780700627790 (hardback)
  ISBN 9780700627806 (ebook)
Subjects: LCSH: Judicial review—United States—History. | Constitutional history—
United States. | BISAC: POLITICAL SCIENCE / Constitutions. | POLITICAL
SCIENCE / Government / Judicial Branch. | POLITICAL SCIENCE / Government /
Legislative Branch.
Classification: LCC KF4575.W474 2019 | DDC 347.73/12—dc23
LC record available at https://lccn.loc.gov/2018058631.

British Library Cataloguing-in-Publication Data is available.

Printed in the United States of America

10 9 8 7 6 5 4 3 2 1

The paper used in this publication is recycled and contains 30 percent postconsumer
waste. It is acid free and meets the minimum requirements of the American National
Standard for Permanence of Paper for Printed Library Materials z39.48-1992.

Certainly all those who have framed written constitutions contemplate them as forming the fundamental and paramount law of the nation, and consequently the theory of every such government must be, that an act of the legislature, repugnant to the constitution, is void.

—*Chief Justice John Marshall,* Marbury v. Madison *(1803)*

CONTENTS

Figures

Tables

The first thing readers of Keith Whittington's remarkable book should notice is its subtitle: *Judicial Review of Acts of Congress from the Founding to the Present.* What he has done is to carefully read and evaluate 1,308 cases decided over the entire history of the US Supreme Court from its beginning to the end of the 2017 term in the spring of 2018, all of which involve judicial review of acts of Congress. Whittington does not consider any of the myriad cases—including the most famous, *Brown v. Board of Education*—invalidating state legislation. Oliver Wendell Holmes famously opined, "I do not think that [the] United States would come to an end if we lost our power to declare an Act of Congress void. I do think the Union would be imperiled if we could not make that declaration as to the laws of the several States." In some ways, Whittington's book is a wonderful examination of the validity of Holmes's assertion with regard to acts of Congress.

Three hundred forty-five of these cases "invalidated or limited statutory provisions [based on a desire to avoid a constitutional conflict], and 963 upheld federal legislation against constitutional challenge." I have been teaching constitutional law for more than forty years, and I confess that I have not read the multitude of cases surveyed by Whittington; an unscientific check with colleagues who teach the same subject leads me to believe that I am not an outlier. The late University of Chicago law professor David Currie is famous for having read every case while writing his multivolume study of the Constitution as interpreted by the Supreme Court, but he may well be unique. And, as much to the point, he was not testing hypotheses in the way the social scientist Whittington is.

Whittington's book is almost certainly unprecedented in its scope and ambition. In addition to Currie's virtually idiosyncratic enterprise, authors of "period" histories of the Supreme Court may have read all the cases occurring within some relatively brief interval. But none of the comprehensive one-volume general histories can claim the authority Whittington evokes on almost every page. It is unimaginable that any professional academic, whether teaching law, political science, or American political history, will not treat this book as an indispensable source. Fortunately, it is also written in a manner that makes it accessible to the general reader who wants to know how important the Supreme Court has been throughout American history.

One often reads stories in the press—and occasionally in the academic literature—proclaiming, for example, that Sandra Day O'Connor and later Anthony Kennedy were the most important political decision-makers in America. In their role as "median justices" on the Court, they often provided the swing votes in 5–4 decisions that were otherwise evenly split between four highly predictable conservatives and four equally predictable liberals. For those who unthinkingly quoted Tocqueville's observation in the 1830s that all political issues in America ended up being legalized and ultimately decided by the judiciary, this meant that what the Supreme Court did was surpassingly important and that the "median justice" was especially important. Tocqueville's first observation may have been true: Americans *do* have a tendency to treat political issues as raising questions about constitutionality—about what the Constitution permits or prohibits. But he was almost certainly wrong in his second observation. Many extraordinarily important issues never come before the Supreme Court, or, should a lawyer be so bold as to bring a case, it is likely to be dismissed on a variety of grounds, allowing the Court to avoid making a decision. As Frederick Schauer notably demonstrated well over a decade ago in the august pages of the *Harvard Law Review*, the issues that are the principal sources of Americans' concern and anguish rarely come before the judiciary, including, most vividly, basic issues of war and peace and "solutions" to problems posed by a globalized economy or global warming. Even if many more constitutional challenges are filed simply because Congress, at least until recently, has passed so many more laws, this does not mean that the Supreme Court will be receptive to such challenges or even grant them the dignity of a full hearing. The Court has steadily been reducing the number of cases it is willing to decide, and in recent years it has issued opinions in only about seventy-five cases, many of them of interest only to the litigants or to specialists in arcane areas of the law.

As Whittington demonstrates, echoing an earlier analysis by the late Charles Black, the principal role of the Supreme Court over its history has been to legitimate actions, particularly by the national government, rather than to strike them down. My own beloved mentor, the late Robert G. McCloskey (whose classic book *The American Supreme Court,* originally published in 1960, I have endeavored to update and keep alive in multiple editions since 1994), once wrote, "the essential business of the Supreme Court is to say 'no' to government." For better or worse, this is almost certainly false, especially if by "government" one means the national government, the focus of Whittington's attention. It may be true that the significance of the legitimation obtained by the Court saying "yes" depends on the possibility of receiving a McCloskeyan "no" instead, but one should not confuse that possibility with the overall likelihood of judicial action.

It is also worth asking under what circumstances the Court can successfully legitimate governmental actions that are opposed by significant sectors of the public. The Court itself once noted that Abraham Lincoln did not sue for a judicial declaration that secession by South Carolina was illegal—a conclusion shared, incidentally, by his predecessor, the hapless James Buchanan. The reason, presumably, was simple: even if one could imagine a federal court issuing such a decree in 1861, it was unimaginable that South Carolina would honor it, any more than Lincoln chose to honor the declaration by Chief Justice Roger Taney in *Ex parte Merryman* that he lacked the unilateral power to suspend habeas corpus (a power not even enjoyed by the British monarch, and granted to Lincoln by Congress only in 1863). If anything, Lincoln's example—and the veneration accorded our sixteenth president—has served to delegitimate Taney and to legitimate presidential power. "Legitimacy" is a complex process, especially when we realize that it requires actual acceptance by target populations rather than what James Madison might have dismissed as a "parchment barrier" of a judicial decision per se.

In some ways, Whittington couches his book as a test of Robert Dahl's famous propositions (1) that the Supreme Court must be understood as a basically political institution and (2) that one must therefore strive to understand the special circumstances under which the Court will invalidate a congressional act. After all, no one joins the Court without the approval of the dominant political coalition at the time, consisting of the president nominating and the Senate confirming. Thus, Dahl suggested that invalidation was most likely when a Court representing a new coalition was considering legislation passed some years ago by the ruling coalition then exercising political hegemony. By definition, the invalidation of recent legislation would be rare unless there was a "regime lag," whereby the Court was still dominated by veterans of the now-supplanted coalition who tried valiantly, if often unsuccessfully, to stave off the reality that elections really do have consequences. Perhaps it is not surprising that Whittington demonstrates serious flaws in Dahl's argument, given that Dahl's article, now well over half a century old, was the first serious attempt to offer an empirical analysis of the circumstances under which the Court would invalidate acts of Congress.

Even if Whittington demonstrates that the Court is more of an active political player than Dahl suggested, he nonetheless reinforces the position taken by Gerald Rosenberg in his classic book *The Hollow Hope*, which maintains that political activists should not expect the Court to deviate very much from the general drift of American public opinion or, perhaps more to the point, the views of political elites who dominate the American political system by winning elections and taking office. Rosenberg was writing specifically about Progressive forces who hoped the Court would be an all-important ally and therefore make it far less important to actually win political victories. But his point applies equally well to conservatives, who hoped in the 1930s that the Court could prevent New Deal reforms or, more recently, that the Court would strike down the hated Affordable Care Act, which, among other things, threatens to entrench medical care as an "entitlement" similar to Social Security, one of the key pieces of New Deal legislation. Other targets of conservative ire, including the use of racial preferences in a variety of contexts and the protection of reproductive choice, have much more to do with *state* legislation and the meaning of the Fourteenth Amendment than with national legislative power. Perhaps the ascent of Brett Kavanaugh to replace Anthony Kennedy on the Court will invalidate the premise of this last sentence, but Whittington's own analysis allows us to wonder, especially given potential election results.

So it would be a mistake—one that Whittington certainly does not make—to dismiss the Supreme Court as unimportant. That would be carrying revisionism much too far! What is crucial, both for the academic scholar and for the general reader simply trying to better understand the American political system, is to get a well-founded sense of when the Court has acted in a fairly determinative manner with regard to other political forces and when, on the contrary, it has basically refused to engage in fights that it believes it cannot win. Here, Whittington is invaluable.

In addition to the grand theme of how the Court has navigated potential conflicts with Congress over the past 225 years, Whittington offers a host of valuable insights along the way. First, there is the hoary story that *Marbury v. Madison* "created" judicial review and then, after that 1803 decision, the Court did not engage in another such act until the notorious *Dred Scott* case in 1857. Both are untrue. Whittington notes that there were several cases before *Marbury* that presupposed the Court's power to invalidate congressional acts that violated the Constitution, even if the Court came up with the "happy ending" that no such invalidation was required in the case at hand. *Marbury*, of course, was different, although it is essential to note that the invalidated statute was remarkably unimportant, save for the political actualities of the moment. The real question was whether the Court would order Secretary of State James Madison to deliver a judicial commission to William Marbury in defiance of President Thomas Jefferson's determination not to do so. The nascent Court could scarcely countenance open defiance or, just as ominously, the prospect of Jeffersonian impeachment efforts as a means of disciplining an out-of-control Federalist Court that was determined not to recognize the so-called Revolution of 1800 that had displaced the prior Federalist hegemony. It was easier to declare that the Court had no power to order the delivery of the commission because the statute allegedly giving it such power was unconstitutional. And a week later, as Whittington notes, the Court almost laconically upheld the ability of the Jeffersonian Congress to purge the federal judiciary of a number of Federalist judges simply by repealing the act, passed in the waning days of the Adams administration, that had created an intermediate tier of federal circuit courts, whose members had been quickly appointed and confirmed by the lame-duck Federalist Congress.

But what about the period 1803 to 1857? Building on the valuable insights of Mark Graber (with whom Whittington coedited, along with Howard Gillman, a pathbreaking casebook on American constitutional development), Whittington demonstrates that, in a number of cases involving statutory interpretation, one can understand the interpretation only against the background assumption that a contrary interpretation would have rendered the law unconstitutional, whether or not the Court actually used such language. Many professors will have to revise their lectures in light of Whittington's scholarship. But he also demonstrates that there were relatively few occasions for judicial review, under any definition, because Congress just was not passing that much legislation to review. The cases Graber and Whittington rely on are known to very few academics because, frankly the substantive issues raised are not considered important. But as sources of genuine illumination of judges' thinking during this period, they are invaluable. As Whittington writes, "The practice of judicial review was built up through the resolution of more mundane cases [than those emphasized by most scholars] in which the political stakes were relatively low."

In addition to Dahl, Whittington assesses the all-too-influential argument of Yale Law School professor Alexander Bickel that the Court's exercise of judicial review is "counter-majoritarian"—that is, unelected judges substitute their judgment for that of the ostensible majority. It is worth quoting Whittington at some length, for it is a decisive rejoinder to the more simplistic statements of Bickel's thesis, which rests on the clearly counterfactual assumptions that any act that receives a majority of votes in Congress necessarily represents the strong endorsement of those voting "aye," let alone that of their constituents. Many cases, Whittington writes,

> could benefit an individual litigant and clean up the processes of government, but they had few larger policy ramifications. They spoke to no serious ideological or partisan disputes and disadvantaged no important political interests. They illustrated how the justices brought their lawyerly expertise to bear in resolving complex legal disputes. In doing so, they filled out the constitutional rule book and took note of when Congress stepped over the lines into foul territory. But such exercises of judicial review were countermajoritarian only in the most formal sense of scrutinizing the work product of elected legislators and correcting its deficiencies, and of hearing the complaints of individuals who were dissatisfied with how the government had treated them.

Harvard political scientist Kenneth Schepsle famously suggested in 1992 that Congress is a "they," not an "it." What this means is that political coalitions usually consist of members with multiple viewpoints who might vote together on a given piece of legislation; for some members of the coalition, however, the affirmative vote is more a matter of being a good team player, or being the recipient of a logrolling benefit with regard to legislation they *really* care about, than a statement of deep principle. This, in effect, gives the Court some significant leeway to strike down even relatively recent legislation passed by the same coalition that placed the justices on the bench, provided the legislation does not reflect a truly strong party position. This is another genuine insight that will require the rewriting of lecture notes and the revision of published textbooks that adopt a more holistic view of ostensibly dominant coalitions. This point is especially powerful with regard to the cleavages within the Democratic Party over passage of an income tax, notoriously declared unconstitutional by the Court in 1894.

Still, as Whittington notes, even these relatively "routine cases of judicial review were most likely to favor the government." Constitutional challenges were rarely successful. "The Court accommodated the expanded legislative agenda rather than obstructing it." And yet, "the most striking feature of the Court's exercise of judicial review vis-à-vis Congress is how mundane it was. History remembers the highlights—the income tax cases, *E. C. Knight*, the child labor case—but this was only a small part of the Court's work and leaves a misleading impression of how judicial review was exercised."

As one would expect (and demand), Whittington incudes full discussions of the "highlights," including the epic struggle between FDR and the Court over the constitutionality of New Deal measures. But he is convincing in his overall thesis, which, simply put, is that we overemphasize the frequency of such cases and thus overestimate the extent to which the exercise of judicial review has genuinely been controversial. At any given moment, as political scientist James Gibson has argued, it is highly probable that a majority of the population will support any given decision. For example, 35 percent of the population is likely to ideologically support the result reached by the Court (this was probably true even during the New Deal shoot-out, given that Kansas governor Alf Landon received 36.5 percent of the popular vote during FDR's landslide victory in 1936); another 20 to 25 percent of the population might accord the Court what political scientists call "diffuse support," which boils down to this position: "I really don't know anything about the Constitution, and I trust the Supreme Court to know what it is doing when it declares something unconstitutional [or constitutional]." That leaves only a probable minority that offers truly enthusiastic support to the substance of a Supreme Court decision. There may be some exceptions. Roughly 90 percent of those polled have registered their opposition to the Court's 2010 decision in *Citizens United,* which invalidated a century-old limitation on corporations' ability to participate directly in political campaigns, but efforts to overturn the decision have gone nowhere. It is possible that *Citizens United* is an exceptional case in terms of judicial review, even though it has received far more scholarly attention than more mundane cases.

Whittington concludes his magnum opus by writing:

> The Court has rarely stood for universally embraced and historically enduring political principles, in part because there are few such principles—or at least few such principles that must be deployed to invalidate an action of Congress. Congress rarely violates universally embraced and historically enduring political principles. Congress does, however, routinely violate principles that are more contested and less enduring but that nonetheless command substantial political support within a given historical era. When the Court intervenes to vindicate those principles against an errant national legislature, it is often doing the political work that political leaders want it to do. It is acting as a player within democratic politics, not simply as a constitutional guardian standing outside of democratic politics.

Inevitably, readers may quibble with some of Whittington's specific judgments, particularly what might be termed the "objective importance" of certain instances of judicial invalidation (or the upholding of questionable, albeit highly popular, legislation). But that does not abate my enthusiasm for the book or lessen my encouragement that anyone interested in the actualities of the American political system read it and ponder its findings carefully. The series within which Whittington's book appears is devoted to innovative approaches to constitutional thinking. It fully deserves its place in the series and our unequivocal admiration for its deep scholarship. That it may also generate further argument is added testament to its importance.

Sanford Levinson
Coeditor, Constitutional Thinking

I have been working on this book (off and on) for an embarrassingly long time. It arose from a conversation with Fred Woodward, then director of the University Press of Kansas, who thought a book on the history of judicial review of federal laws would be useful. I had been thinking something similar. In an earlier book, I explored how constitutional meaning and practices have been politically constructed over time.[1] Because I was interested in emphasizing the contributions nonjudicial actors made to that process, I self-consciously avoided examining judges' actions. In a subsequent book, I considered how judicial review can serve the interests of political leaders and how the courts' authority to give meaning to the Constitution has been encouraged by the very political actors who were apparently under judicial supervision.[2] It now seemed appropriate to approach the issue from a different angle and consider things from the judges' perspective. Such a project was timely, since the Supreme Court stood accused of being the most activist in history for its record of striking down congressional statutes.[3] It also seemed like a fine time to update Robert Dahl's classic study of the Supreme Court's invalidations of federal laws, which had helped inspire the growing literature on "regime politics" in the courts and the development of constitutional law.[4]

I initially thought this would be a little book that could be written fairly quickly. It probably could have been, but that is not the book I wound up writing. As I started to sketch out the content of the book, I realized that I had a fairly good sense of the highlight reel of judicial review—the cases that wind up in the constitutional law casebooks—but I had less of a sense of the ordinary business of the Court. I naïvely thought I should brush up. But this posed a problem. Although there is a conventional list of cases in which the Supreme Court struck down a law of Congress, there is no comparable list of cases in which the Court upheld a law of Congress against constitutional challenge.[5] Would I be missing half the story? More annoyingly, there have been suggestions that the conventional list of cases invalidating statutes is incomplete.[6] Would I be telling an accurate story? So I resolved to start from scratch. I would need to assemble a list of all the cases in which the Court has substantively reviewed the constitutionality of a federal statutory provision. That list would provide a skeleton for what I thought of as a large-N, qualitative study of the political history of judicial review. Maybe the book could not be written so quickly after all. And then other things got in the way, including the production of a historically oriented constitutional law casebook. That project provided more opportunity to think about these issues but less time to write this book.[7]

This is not the book I initially set out to write, and undoubtedly it is not exactly the book I would have written had it been completed in a timely manner. But I hope the result is better for the years it spent simmering on the back burner. In addition, the delay now seems fortuitous, allowing me to speculate in the final chapter on the effect of Anthony Kennedy's departure from the Court. Kennedy has long been a pivotal vote on the Court, and the reconstitution of the bench without him will be a critical moment in the Court's history. The Rehnquist and Roberts Courts were rarely able to strike down a provision of a federal statute without Kennedy's agreement, and he was often willing to join the more liberal justices as well as the more conservative ones. Kennedy's retirement will likely leave the Court with a more reliably conservative majority. Presumably, the liberals on the Roberts Court will find it more difficult in the coming years to strike down the laws they find objectionable. It is not so clear that Kennedy was holding back the more conservative justices from invalidating laws they viewed as unconstitutional. It remains to be seen whether a more conservative Court will become more or less active in striking down federal legislation in the twenty-first century.

The debts accumulated while working on such an extended project are too numerous to count, but I am extraordinarily grateful to all those who spurred my thinking over the years. I am grateful to the University of Texas School of Law, where I spent a very pleasant year and first began the research for this book, and Princeton University, where I completed it, as well as the librarians, colleagues, and staff at both institutions. I particularly appreciate the long conversations with Howard Gillman and Mark Graber on American constitutional history, and I'm sure the good ideas expressed here are as much theirs as mine (the bad ideas are probably all mine). I had the opportunity to present parts of this project at various workshops and conferences, and I appreciate the many faculty and students who took the time to push my ideas around and try to steer me on a better course. I appreciate the efforts of several graduate and undergraduate students who provided research assistance for this project. I am very grateful to Fred Woodward for nudging me to do this book and then harassing me, until his retirement, to finish it. I have always had great appreciation for my friends at the University Press of Kansas, and I regret that I repaid them with a very tardy book.

Some components of the book appeared previously and are used here by permission. My thanks to the *Georgetown Law Journal, Boston University Law Review, Notre Dame Law Review,* and *Constitutional Studies.*

The Politics of Judicial Review

We live in an interesting time in the history of judicial review. A hundred years ago there were serious and lively debates over whether courts should even have the power to strike down acts of elected legislatures. Those debates are largely in the past. Courts now routinely, almost casually, invalidate legislation. But the reaction judicial review now provokes is rather different. Few argue that judges should abandon the power to review and invalidate the deliberate acts of other government officials. Instead, the contemporary argument is largely over *which* acts should be struck down. Courts should be restrained from doing the wrong thing, but they should be active in doing the right thing. Of course, there is little agreement on what counts as the wrong thing or on how courts ought to exercise the power they wield.

Politicians regularly alternate between praising and condemning the Supreme Court for striking down laws. In 2013 President Barack Obama declared, "I applaud the Supreme Court's decision to strike down the Defense of Marriage Act," a 1996 statute passed by a Republican Congress and signed by the previous Democratic president, Bill Clinton. The Court had "righted that wrong," and Obama welcomed its decision.[1] Just the year before, however, as the Court deliberated on the constitutionality of Obama's own signature policy accomplishment, the Affordable Care Act, the president made a round of press interviews calling on the Court to embrace the virtue of "judicial restraint." He explained, "I am confident that the Supreme Court will not take what would be an unprecedented, extraordinary step of overturning a law that was passed by a strong majority of a democratically elected Congress." Unlike the overwhelmingly popular Defense of Marriage Act, the Affordable Care Act had only narrowly made it through Congress on a largely party-line vote. Nonetheless, earlier conservative critics of the Court had been correct, Obama suggested, in complaining that "an unelected group of people would somehow overturn a duly constituted and passed law."[2] Judges would err, and would be improperly "activist," if they "ignored the will of Congress, ignored democratic processes, and tried to impose judicial solutions instead of letting the process work itself through politically."[3]

Of course, President Obama is hardly the only politician or political activist to be of two minds about judicial review. His predecessor, President George W. Bush, was quick to "applaud the Supreme Court's historic decision today confirming what has always been clear in the Constitution: The second amendment protects an individual right to keep and bear firearms," regardless of the District of Columbia's prohibition on the possession of handguns.[4] But he had an equally rapid, and hostile, response to "activist judges" overthrowing legislative bans on same-sex marriage.[5] Whether judges are condemned as lawless activists or praised as fearless heroes often depends on whose political ox is being gored.

Both sides of the partisan and ideological divide in modern American politics simultaneously fear and lust after the power to nullify laws. Former assistant attorney general Walter Dellinger concluded that President Obama "may be more concerned about avoiding a Court that would strike down progressive legislation than he is with achieving a Court that will enforce its constitutional views on the other branches," while Democratic representative Gerald Connolly complained, "what they [conservatives] cannot win in the legislative body, they now seek and hope to achieve through judicial activism."[6] The left-wing People for the American Way's Jamin Raskin denounced the "illegitimate interference by the Court in the processes of political democracy," while the right-wing National Organization for Marriage's Brian Brown condemned "a lawless ruling that contravenes the decisions of over 50 million voters and their elected representatives."[7] While praising the nomination of Justice Sonia Sotomayor, Democratic senator Patrick Leahy argued, "We do not need more conservative activists second-guessing Congress and who through judicial extremism override congressional judgments."[8] A few years earlier, while criticizing the nomination of Chief Justice John Roberts, Leahy was primarily concerned that Roberts hold to "a judicial philosophy that appreciates the vital role of the judiciary in protecting the rights and liberties of all Americans" and the "bedrock principle of judicial review."[9] When conservative legislators introduced a resolution denouncing a federal circuit court decision upholding a school board's policy, Democratic representative Barney Frank enjoyed the irony and expressed the hope that "we will stop pretending that we are upset about activism when what you are really upset about is judicial pacifism." "Clearly," he continued, "people are not opposed to judicial activism. . . . [T]hey are opposed to the lack of judicial activism."[10]

Even the justices have difficulty avoiding the modern confusion over their power. Justice Anthony Kennedy, sometimes regarded as the keystone to judicial activism on the recent Court,[11] surprised many when he lectured to Pennsylvania law students, "any society that relies on nine unelected judges to resolve the most serious issues of the day is not a functioning democracy." Perhaps he clarified his point when he went on to claim that a real democracy would be able to "solve these problems before they come to the Court" through respectful discourse. Judges cannot be expected to stay their hand or defer to the democratic process when politicians have failed to solve political problems in a reasonable way.[12] Justice Ruth Bader Ginsburg has sounded a more conciliatory note, claiming, "we trust the democratic process, so the Court is highly deferential to what Congress does." But such trust is not always in evidence, and she simultaneously complained that the Roberts Court is "one of the most activist courts in history" and that she needs to remain on the bench to rein in her colleagues.[13] The late Justice Antonin Scalia certainly would have questioned whether Ginsburg's continued presence would advance that particular cause. From his perspective, the modern Court had become unmoored from any sense of self-restraint. When "the Power to Do Good came into every judge's hands—or at least the hands of every judge empowered to override legislative acts," we entered the age of "judicial hegemony."[14] In fact, Scalia and Ginsburg had an almost identical history of voting to strike down legislation. They differed, of course, on when such a vote should be cast.[15]

Political leaders have developed a love-hate relationship with judicial review, which creates both challenges and opportunities for judges. It is the nature of judicial review to take power and policy choices out of the hands of elected politicians and place them in the hands of judges. If judges were to systematically stand in opposition to the will of united majorities, their political situation would likely become untenable.[16] Alexander Hamilton promised that the judiciary would be the "least dangerous branch" because of judges' limited resources for effectuating their wills.[17] Courts might hope to exercise independent judgment, but their status as a powerful political institution is always dependent on the goodwill of others.[18]

The central concern of this book is how the justices of the Supreme Court have navigated these opportunities and challenges. How have they managed to exercise judicial review for more than 200 years, and how have they chosen to make use of this significant power? Judicial review is generally viewed as a fundamentally obstructionist force within democratic politics, but how obstructionist has the Supreme Court actually been? Whose agenda has been blocked, and whose agenda has been promoted, by the Court's exercise of this power?

The Problem of Judicial Review

A variety of normative debates have swirled around the power of judicial review. The most persistent focuses on the individual decisions handed down by the Court and asks whether they were rightly decided. The possibility that the justices got the law wrong or misused their power has been raised after nearly every controversial constitutional decision rendered by the Court. Criticisms of the Court raise the issue of how the justices should go about the process of understanding the terms of the Constitution and what principles ought to guide their decisions.

Such arguments over how the Court ought to resolve cases have frequently (especially in the twentieth century) fed into accusations of judicial activism—a charge that is notoriously slippery and often indicates little more than that the critic dislikes the Court's decision.[19] At heart, the accusation of judicial activism suggests that the justices have not merely erred in their decision but also abused their power. The problem of judicial activism speaks to the judicial role and goes beyond the specifics of any particular case or constitutional doctrine. "Activism" suggests that the Court is inappropriately striking down laws and thus acting more like a "superlegislature" than a court, acting willfully rather than judiciously.

If the concept of judicial activism is crude and unavoidably political as it is understood in common discourse, it has been treated more consistently in the empirical literature on the behavior of courts. The approach there has been to reduce the idea of judicial activism to something that is measurable, relatively objective, and comparable across contexts. In such studies, the term "judicial activism" refers to the relative frequency of judicial invalidation of statutory provisions because they are inconsistent with constitutional requirements. Activist courts strike down many statutes; restrained courts more rarely declare legislation unconstitutional. There are normative implications to such judicial activity, but mere activism itself in this sense is not normatively freighted.[20] This is the sense in which judicial activism is used in this work.

Perhaps the most enduring and vexing normative debate surrounding the power of judicial review is its possible conflict with democratic values. At the end of the nineteenth century, the Populists and their allies raised a new challenge to the courts and to the power of judicial review. Upset with the conservative courts' obstruction of newly passed Populist measures, political insurgents reacted by charging that judicial review was inconsistent with democratic ideals.[21] Populist presidential candidate James B. Weaver praised courts that could remain "pure" and "incorrupt[ible]," but he thought that "elective control is the only safeguard of liberty," and in his view, American courts had inappropriately seized "the kingly prerogative" of setting aside duly enacted laws.[22] Abusive legislatures that were willing to pass unconstitutional laws were better corrected at the ballot box than at the judge's bench. Distinguished Harvard law professor James Bradley Thayer sounded a somewhat more cautious note, warning that courts should strike down laws only when the legislature had made a "clear mistake," when there was no rational argument to justify what the legislature had done. This "remarkable practice" of judicial review should not encroach on the "vast and not definable range of legislative power and choice."[23] Such complaints continued through the New Deal era, when eminent historian Henry Steele Commager complained of "the failure to confront the real issues presented by judicial review"—namely, its inconsistency with democracy.[24] As Progressive judge Learned Hand asked at midcentury, was the United States to be governed by the people and their elected representatives or by a "bevy of Platonic Guardians"?[25]

The complaint assumed its canonical form early during the reign of the Warren Court. Yale's Alexander Bickel spoke for one set of New Deal liberals in announcing that judicial review posed a "counter-majoritarian difficulty." The "ineluctable reality" was that "judicial review constituted control by an unrepresentative minority of an elected majority" and necessarily "thwarts the will of representatives of the actual people of the here and now." In sum, "judicial review is undemocratic."[26] Bickel set the agenda for many constitutional scholars, who have spent decades puzzling over whether and how such an undemocratic practice can be justified within a democracy. The answers to this puzzle have varied. Relatively few scholars (one being political theorist Jeremy Waldron) have concluded that judicial review is, in fact, unjustifiable.[27] But there is little doubt that the "difficulty" identified by Bickel remains the starting point for normative arguments about judicial review. What actually happens, according to Bickel, is that courts armed with the power of judicial review necessarily and routinely obstruct the will of the majority.

Evaluating this concern is one of the goals of this book. Bickel's argument rests on the deceptively simple empirical assumption that, by striking down laws, courts are significantly obstructing the functioning of democratic institutions. When a law is struck down, the product of an elected legislature is obviously nullified. What is less clear is whether the invalidated law reflects the significant political commitments of the "representatives of the actual people of the here and now." Bickel relies on a vision of a heroic court, a court that is willing and able to stand athwart democracy yelling "Stop." If courts regularly give voice to the desires of political minorities, they pose one kind of challenge to democratic values (and open the door for one kind of defense of judicial review). But the empirical foundations for this line of normative argument are hardly well established. As we shall see, the actual relationship between the US Supreme Court and political majorities is more complicated than the countermajoritarian difficulty implies.

The Puzzle of Judicial Review

There are a number of empirical puzzles surrounding the exercise of judicial review. Some have examined the extent to which the power of judicial review significantly affects policy outcomes and under what conditions it does so.[28] Others have used judicial review as a vehicle for exploring more general theories of judicial behavior. The particular context of judicial review sheds some light on the extent to which judges simply act on their core preferences when deciding cases (and to a significant extent, they do).[29] Similarly, judicial review is a particularly interesting context for thinking about the extent to which justices strategically shy away from conflicts with potentially hostile political actors (and it appears that they do).[30]

Of particular interest is to what extent courts actually behave in a countermajoritarian fashion. For normative theorists like Bickel, judicial countermajoritarianism is self-evident. For some, the countermajoritarian quality of judicial review is a virtue. For others, an antidemocratic court is a problem that requires justification or amelioration. For empirical scholars, the possibility of a countermajoritarian court is a puzzle that requires explanation.

The great democratic theorist Robert Dahl posed a particularly incisive challenge to this vision of a heroic court. Dahl was quite skeptical of the idea that any government institution within a democratic polity would systematically protect "the policy preferences of minorities" against the will and interest of political majorities. Such a body would be "an extremely anomalous institution from a democratic point of view."[31] Like most political scientists, Dahl assumed that the US Supreme Court is a political institution tasked with elaborating legal rules that have important policy implications within a highly charged political environment. The central drivers of constitutional decisions in the Supreme Court (where most of the cases are "hard," in the sense that the legal questions are novel and the accepted legal answers are unclear) are the political viewpoints of the justices. To the extent that the justices disagree about how a case should be decided, their disagreement tends to reflect systematic differences of opinion on what the constitutional law *should* be. If the justices "choose among controversial alternatives of public policy" when rendering their decisions and developing constitutional law, they are necessarily thrown back onto "their own predispositions or those of influential clienteles and constituents."[32] In the United States, such differences are often, but not exclusively, organized by political parties and can be arrayed along conventional ideological lines. It should come as no surprise that Whigs and Democrats, New Dealers and Reaganites come to systematically different conclusions about what the Constitution requires.

This perspective suggests more than the significance of political attitudes in determining judicial behavior. It also suggests that it would "be somewhat naïve to assume that the Supreme Court either would or could play the role of Galahad."[33] The interesting question is how such policy-oriented justices are situated within the political environment. For Dahl, the combination of a politicized appointment process and partisan divisions over constitutional issues means that the Court as an institution can be counted on to rubber-stamp the policy decisions of elected officials, except for rare and fleeting moments when the composition of the Court lags behind the rapidly chang-ing electoral fortunes of legislative coalitions.

Dahl's fundamental insight is that courts are more likely to serve as part-ners and allies with those in power than as antagonists and gadflies. The "policy views dominant on the Court are never for long out of line with the policy views dominant among the lawmaking majorities of the United States," and it would be "unrealistic" to expect the Court to be a serious obstacle to the ambitions of political leaders.[34] This assessment of the fed-eral judiciary gave rise to a set of specific hypotheses for which Dahl sought evidence in the history of the US Supreme Court's review of federal statutes. Dahl expected to find two things: first, that the Court rarely struck down statutes, and second, that the statutes struck down were of low political sa-lience or relatively old, such that current political leaders had little stake in them. The sincere expression of judicial policy attitudes would mostly be cashed out, with the justices giving their blessings to legislative actions.

Although Dahl found some support for his hypotheses in the judicial rec-ord through the mid-twentieth century, his specific argument had some weaknesses.[35] Notably, it seemed to underpredict the incidence of judicial review. Dahl emphasized the extent to which the Court would be a con-gressional lapdog, calling judicial review "largely irrelevant" and stating that "lawmaking majorities generally have had their way."[36] And yet, the Court *does* routinely strike down laws, as the critics of judicial activism can attest.

The active exercise of judicial review poses a puzzle from two distinct per-spectives. From a Dahlian perspective, we might expect judges and legisla-tors to be on the same page; thus, judges would rarely have any desire to strike down laws passed by their similarly minded colleagues in the legisla-ture. Judges defer not because they are deferential but because they are gen-erally in agreement with legislators. Dahl indicated that judicial selection is the crucial mechanism for keeping courts in line with broader political sensibilities, but there might be a wider range of social influences that lead judges and politicians to share a similar outlook.[37] From a strategic perspective, we might expect judges to defer to powerful politicians who have the tools to retaliate against unwelcome court decisions or who might not enforce those decisions. Given the relative weakness of courts compared with other social and political institutions, the maintenance of judicial independence itself is a notable puzzle. The active exercise of judicial review is a prominent metric of independence, raising the question of how judges are able to invalidate laws over time.[38]

There are many reasons why judges might choose to stay their hand, but often they do not. A central puzzle for the study of judicial review is identifying how judges are able to exercise the power of judicial review so successfully and so often. This requires that we make sense of both the Dahlian point that judges and legislators are often of the same mind and the strategic point that judges are often operating from a position of political vulnerability. In brief, why would judges want to strike down laws, and how do they get away with it?

The argument in this book focuses on how courts fit into the larger political system. Fissures routinely exist within political majorities, and American political institutions are fractured. Both these features of the American political system provide opportunities for judges to exert influence. The active exercise of judicial review does not necessarily indicate that judges are free from constraints or choose to play Galahad; rather, it indicates that judicial review can be exercised in a way that is consistent with the goals of other powerful political leaders. Courts make headway by advancing their own preferences within the band of indifference established by other political actors. Charging headlong into battle with other government officials—what Chief Justice John Marshall once characterized as "butting against a wall in sport"—holds few attractions for a court that hopes to retain power and influence over the long term.[39]

Dahl's simplified model of American politics captures important aspects of how the justices relate to politicians, but the limitations of his model also point to the reasons why the Court is more active than he expected. In particular, three conditions of Dahl's model are worth noting: the assumptions of unified political parties, stable partisan majorities, and shared policy preferences.

Mark Graber made a crucial contribution to the development of a theory of regime politics by pointing out that fractured coalitions—what Dahl thought of as "weak" majorities—are the norm rather than the exception in the American party system.[40] Dahl anticipated that the Court would have more room to maneuver, and would necessarily be less inclined to march in step with legislators, when majorities were splintered. When the Court's legislative allies disagree among themselves, the Dahlian logic of judicial passivity begins to fall apart. Moreover, party leaders often find it helpful to shift policy decisions out of the political arena precisely when their political allies cannot agree on the issues.[41] Politicians might actually *want* judges to strike down legislation, allowing the courts to take the blame for controversial decisions and circumventing stubborn legislative logjams.

Like much of mid-twentieth-century political science, Dahl's discussion of the Court's role in the political system takes for granted the existence of stable majority parties. The New Deal experience seemed to illustrate how the American party system worked, with electoral realignments periodically elevating a new majority party that could expect to dominate politics for a generation or more.[42] But the New Deal example turned out to be misleading. Parties often struggle to win successive electoral victories and regularly fail to capture complete control of the fragmented set of American political institutions. The legislative landscape does not simply reflect the will of a single political party, and the composition of the Court does not smoothly transition into a reliable partnership with a dominant group of political leaders. The justices may be coalitional partners, but the ability of any coalition to put its stamp on the polity is limited.

Dahl suggested that judges, or at least Supreme Court justices, were little more than legislators in robes, and many empirical political scholars have followed his lead. Undoubtedly, Dahl was right that presidents are unlikely to appoint a justice "whose stance on key questions was flagrantly at odds with that of the dominant majority" or "hostile" to the president's own views.[43] It is likewise frequently the case that political parties develop distinctive and coherent constitutional ideologies that are shared by both judges and legislators.[44] But that still leaves substantial room for judges to develop and hold distinctive views that might diverge from those of their legislative allies. Internal divisions within political parties might be expressed in judicial selections.[45] Some constitutional questions are of little interest to legislators.

Some matters of principle may receive lip service from elected politicians but be difficult to consistently preserve in the rough-and-tumble of daily politics. Some commitments might be of greater import to judges than to politicians.

James Madison thought democratic legislatures were an "impetuous vortex"; in a republic, power could be expected to gravitate to the people's house.[46] It would be surprising if any institution of government, including the US Supreme Court, could resist the pull of that vortex for an extended period. Nonetheless, the Court does actively exercise the power of judicial review to nullify the work of the legislature. Unpacking the circumstances in which the power is exercised can clarify how and to what extent the exercise of judicial review is countermajoritarian and the degree to which the justices can be seen as reliable partners of government officials rather than their scourge.

Why Focus on Congress?

To examine these issues, this book concentrates on judicial review of federal statutes. Cases involving the review of congressional legislation occupy only a portion of the Court's constitutional docket. It also routinely evaluates the constitutionality of judicial and executive actions, and the judicial review of state statutes has historically absorbed more of the Court's time than the review of federal statutes. State cases have also often generated substantial political controversy, sometimes on a national scale. Cases such as *Lochner*,[47] *Brown*,[48] and *Roe*[49] highlight the significance of the federal review of state laws to the history and politics of judicial review. Nonetheless, judicial supervision of the constitutional boundaries of congressional authority is both substantively important and analytically illuminating.

Historically, the power of the Court to review acts of Congress has been more controversial than its power to review state statutes. Jacksonian jurist John Gibson, for example, questioned whether courts could wield what he characterized as a "political power" to nullify the acts of a coordinate branch of government, but he had little doubt that judges could enforce the requirements of the federal Constitution against the "inferior obligation" of state law.[50] Even as he offered his vision of a limited power of judicial review, Harvard scholar James Bradley Thayer proposed that federal review of the states was "a different matter in hand" than judicial review of a coordinate legislature. The federal courts had a clear obligation, he thought, to maintain "the paramount government" against state transgressions, but they played a much more modest role in monitoring the constitutional fidelity of Congress.[51] Justice Oliver Wendell Holmes disclaimed such "nostrums" as the indispensability of judicial review. "I do not think the United States would come to an end if we lost our power to declare an Act of Congress void. I do think the Union would be imperiled if we could not make that declaration as to the laws of the several States." Holmes thought that "national views" must prevail over "local policy," but he had more faith in national majorities.[52] In the midst of World War II, historian Henry Steele Commager distinguished between judicial review "as a harmonizer of the federal system" when applied against the states and judicial review against Congress, a supposed "check upon democracy."[53]

Even accepting the Court's basic authority to delimit congressional power, the actual exercise of that authority has repeatedly given rise to controversy. From *Dred Scott*[54] in the antebellum period to the *Income Tax Cases*[55] at the turn of the twentieth century to the struggle over the New Deal to the campaign finance decisions of the modern era, the nullification of a federal statutory provision has been followed by complaints that the Court both misinterpreted the Constitution and abused its power. As Commager framed the issue in the aftermath of the New Deal, "the crucial question is not so much whether an act does or does not conform to the Constitution, but who shall judge regarding its conformity?" He thought that, based on the historical evidence, "Congress, not the courts," is the more consistent guardian of constitutional commitments. Judicial review of Congress is mostly "a drag upon administrative efficiency and upon democracy."[56]

Examining the horizontal constitutional review by judges of a coordinate branch of government puts the countermajoritarian difficulty clearly in focus. The vertical review of lower levels of government by the US Supreme Court poses numerous complications for any assessment of how antidemocratic the Court might be in practice. The policies of state governments that come under federal judicial scrutiny may enjoy popular support, but the possibly antidemocratic quality of judicial review in such cases is always mixed up with issues of federalism. State laws pose the question of not only *whether* the political majority should get its way but also *which* political majority should get its way.[57] When confronting localities, the federal courts may represent a national perspective on the contested issues. The most salient feature in many of these cases is not that the Court is unelected but that it is national. Analyzing the judicial review of Congress reduces the dimensions of conflict. In such cases, the Court pits its own authority against that of another national actor. The most salient differences between those institutions are reduced to the juridical nature of the Court and the democratic credentials of Congress. If the Court is countermajoritarian, the evidence should be clearer in the Court's record of reviewing acts of Congress.

Challenging Congress also puts the Court's power and authority to a stiffer test than challenging local officials. National, not local, officials decide who will occupy the seats on the US Supreme Court. Congress, not state legislatures, has the tools to sanction the Court. Presidents, not governors, have the greatest capacity to render a judicial decision a dead letter. Federal judges can lean on the authority and might of the federal government when taking action against states and localities. When they decide to act against Congress, they stand exposed. The strategic environment within which the Court operates is at its most hazardous when the justices must consider whether to confront Congress.

Why Exercise Judicial Review?

It would be useful to clarify what we mean by the power of judicial review. Judicial review as it has been exercised in the United States is different from similar systems of constitutional review developed in other countries (primarily in the twentieth century). In one common model of constitutional review, a specialized constitutional "court" is responsible for evaluating, upon request, the constitutionality of legislation (and sometimes even proposed legislation).[58] In some ways, such abstract constitutional review more closely resembles the early presidential veto than American-style judicial review.

American judicial review has two essential components that were emphasized by even the earliest commentators on the practice. First, American judges are armed with the authority to interpret the state and federal constitutions as normal instruments of law. Second, judges are authorized—perhaps even required—to refuse to give legal effect to statutory provisions that violate constitutional requirements, so interpreted. That is, judges are authorized not only to "say what the law is," by reading and elaborating the terms of the Constitution, but also to declare "null and void" the contrary commands of lesser legal authorities. At its heart, the exercise of judicial review vis-à-vis the legislature involves determining whether a statutory provision has exceeded the scope of the legislature's authority and refusing to enforce or give legal effect to those provisions that are outside the constitutional limits of the lawmaking body.

There is a reason why we settled on calling this practice "judicial review." Neither the US Constitution nor the various state constitutions name this power, and for many decades, lawyers and commentators had no particular term for the authority to refuse to apply unconstitutional legislation. By the end of the nineteenth century, the practice was too pervasive and politically important to go unnamed, and a variety of terms were floated as possibilities. Many emphasized features of the practice from which its advocates had long tried to distance themselves. From the early days of the republic, proponents of this judicial power denied that it implied judicial superiority to the legislature or involved judges in the fundamentally legislative action of repealing duly enacted laws.[59] Terms such as "judicial supremacy," "judicial veto," and "judicial nullification" implied exactly such a power (and were often favored by critics of the courts). "Judicial review," by contrast, invoked a familiar judicial authority to evaluate whether governmental bodies were operating within their legal mandates.[60] In the administrative context, this meant examining whether executive agencies were acting in accord with applicable statutes. In the constitutional context, this meant examining whether the power exercised by a variety of government officials—from legislators to presidents—was constitutionally authorized. The Europeans (and the American Populists and Progressives) might have been right in thinking that interpreting fundamental law is inescapably political, but the conceit of American-style judicial review is that the texts of constitutions establish legal rules that can be interpreted and applied in much the same way as other types of legal rules—and that the parties in legal disputes are entitled to have judges take into account *all* the applicable legal rules (including constitutional rules) when disposing of their cases and determining their rights and duties.[61]

The judicial treatment of unconstitutional legislation is undoubtedly the paradigmatic case of judicial review and poses the hardest questions about the Court's authority. Nonetheless, its power with regard to unconstitutional legislation is of a piece with its power related to the actions of other government officials and, significantly, its power with regard to constitutionally valid legislation as well.[62] As the anti-Federalist writer Brutus pointed out during the constitutional ratification debates, the new federal judiciary would have the authority not only to declare laws unconstitutional and invalid but also to declare laws consistent with the Constitution and valid.[63] When combined with the precedent-following logic of a judiciary within a common-law system, decisions that are favorable to Congress, he warned, could have ramifications well beyond an individual case or a particular statute. The judicial imprimatur could burn away the fog of doubt surrounding the scope of congressional authority and clear the way for more aggressive exertions of national legislative power. The justices themselves quickly moved beyond thinking about how constitutional rules affected the legal posture of individual litigants and began to focus on the rule of constitutional law announced in a case. Judicial review might be justified in terms of how preexisting constitutional rules affect dispute resolution and the rights of individual parties, but for the US Supreme Court, judicial review operates as a policy-making tool by which the justices establish the constitutional rules that will shape the future exercise of government power and guide future judicial decisions giving effect to government action.

In practice, the exercise of judicial review varies substantially across cases. Some cases that reach the Supreme Court primarily challenge the constitutionality of a legislative provision. Others, especially in earlier periods of American history, raise constitutional questions almost incidentally. Once the Court shifted to a largely discretionary docket that allowed it to control the cases it heard, the legal questions to be argued and resolved became narrower. Previously, when the Court heard primarily cases on appeal, the justices were often at the mercy of the litigating attorneys, who might offer wide-ranging arguments that could potentially advance the cause of their clients. Likewise, the justices have some discretion over how they address constitutional claims. Often, constitutional arguments are irrelevant to the justices' resolution of a case, and they either ignore or explicitly set aside these arguments (such cases are not considered here). At other times, constitutional claims are relatively minor matters that the justices might address briefly while explaining the ultimate disposition of the case (this is more likely to occur when the Court upholds a statute). Of course, the judicial opinions that have received the most attention over time are those that address constitutional arguments at some length and in a manner that is critical to the holding.

Cases of judicial review also vary in terms of how the Court treats the constitutionality of a provision of federal law.[64] In the modern context, the Court is sometimes called on to evaluate so-called facial challenges to a law, which it has characterized as "the most difficult to mount successfully, since the challenger must establish that no set of circumstances exists under which the Act would be valid."[65] More often, the Court is asked to evaluate a statute that is already being applied and can be considered within a specific factual situation. In any case, the justices use the record before them to reach one of three conclusions about a statutory provision. Most often, the Court upholds a statute against a constitutional challenge. The decision to uphold a statute, however, is always a decision to uphold its particular application in the case at hand. The justices may conclude that the litigant is not entitled to have the effects of the statute set aside in the specific case before the Court, but that does not necessarily mean that there are no circumstances under which the statute's application would be constitutionally defective. The justices may not be inclined to hear another challenge to a statutory provision they have upheld earlier, but at least implicitly, the justices are always determining whether a statute is valid in the case in front of them.

Alternatively, the justices may conclude that a statutory provision is constitutionally invalid, at least as applied in the circumstances of the case before them. Such as-applied invalidations effectively narrow the scope of a statute but do not necessarily render a judgment about all its possible applications. That is, the opinion leaves open the possibility (perhaps only a hypothetical one) that in some circumstances the statute's application could be constitutional. Any such alternative scenario would have to be separately litigated to reach a definitive understanding of constitutional validity. As Richard Fallon has helpfully explained, the meaning of statutes "frequently must be *specified* through case-by-case applications; the process of specification effectively divides a statutory rule into a series of *subrules*; and in most but not all cases, valid subrules can be *separated* from invalid ones, so that the former can be enforced, even if the latter cannot."[66]

Finally, the justices might determine that there is no valid application of the statute, in which case they will strike it down in its entirety. Such a ruling might be appropriate when the rule laid out in the statute is relatively simple (such that any permutations in its application are clear from a single case), when the case involves a core application of the statute (such that any potentially valid applications are marginal and likely to be ignored), or when the case involves an application of the statute that cannot be readily distinguished from other likely applications (such that, in Fallon's terms, the subrule at issue is not separable from other possible subrules). Such cases might or might not be presented to the Court as facial challenges arising from the first application (or even potential application) of a statute, but in the Court's treatment of the statute, the law is voided in its entirety rather than being severed from the invalid application or simply narrowed in scope. Both types of invalidations—as applied and in their entirety—are considered here.[67]

The logic for exercising judicial review is somewhat different from a legal and a political perspective. From a legal perspective, courts should exercise judicial review whenever the consideration of constitutional arguments might affect the disposition of the case before them. More broadly, perhaps, courts should stand ready to monitor potential incursions of constitutional boundaries by government officials. From a political perspective, the case for exercising judicial review is less straightforward. Judges might be formally armed with this power, but politics speaks less of duty than of preference. Judges might be expected to exercise their power of judicial review when doing so advances their policy preferences (including, perhaps, their preferences related to constitutional policy or the content of constitutional rules), but not necessarily out of a high-minded interest in neutrally defending against constitutional violations. The political logic of judicial review might work differently in three basic situations, outlined below.

Judicial Review of Politically Divergent Legislation

Most political science theories posit that judicial review is most likely to occur in the context of politically divergent legislation, and this context gives rise to much of the normative theorizing about the legitimacy of judicial review. When the justices are confronted with legislation passed by their political foes that advances policies with which the justices disagree, they can be expected to use the power of judicial review to strike down those laws. Dahl thought such situations would be rare because the same political officials who pass federal statutes also appoint Supreme Court justices. Others have focused less on the causes and likelihood of divergence between the judicial and legislative branches of the federal government, but they too cite divergence as the most likely circumstance in which laws would be struck down.[68] Conservative courts should be expected to strike down liberal laws, and liberal courts should be expected to strike down conservative laws. Congress should not expect a friendly hearing from a hostile Supreme Court.

Judicial Review of Politically Convergent Legislation

Judicial review by friendly courts poses a thornier analytical problem. Dahl thought friendly courts should not exercise the power of judicial review at all—or, to the extent they do, they should use it simply to legitimate the policies promoted by their political allies in the legislature. To the extent that judicial review is primarily a negative power, a capacity to obstruct legislation, it has little utility when the same party occupies both the judiciary and the legislature.

We can make some progress in solving the puzzle of judicial review by friendly courts by introducing some additional elements to the stylized model of judicial-legislative interaction. First, we should appreciate that the judiciary is a collective institution, not a unitary actor. While the scholarly focus has often been on the US Supreme Court, it is worth recalling that the Court is *supreme* because it sits atop a judicial hierarchy that includes both lower federal courts and state courts. Even if a majority of the justices are friendly to the nation's elected leaders, other judges within the far-flung American judicial system might not be. In that context, it is worthwhile for the Court to take up cases to uphold statutes rather than strike them down. By exercising its power to uphold laws against constitutional challenge, the Court is facilitating the policy-making authority of its legislative allies by signaling lower courts to refrain from exercising judicial review (and perhaps setting favorable precedents that might affect the decision-making of future, less friendly Supreme Court justices).

Second, we should appreciate that legislatures and political parties are not unitary actors. Intracoalitional disagreements are common in American politics, so even a politically allied Court may find itself pressured by competing demands from its own coalition partners. When members of a political coalition are unable to agree, they can neither generate a shared expectation of how allied judges will use their powers nor constitute a reliable pool of like-minded lawyers from whose ranks judges can be drawn. Jurists may be confronted with legislation passed by their putative legislative allies that the judges see as problematic and a departure from constitutional orthodoxy.[69] Moreover, in such circumstances, coalition leaders often encourage judges to enforce ideological principles by striking down laws passed by fractious and unreliable legislators.[70] When electoral or coalitional pressure forces legislators to pass statutes that compromise their principles, they may decide that judicial restraint in the pursuit of justice is no virtue.

Third, we need to recognize that the body of law has been built up over time, and judicial review is often intertemporal and not just contemporaneous. If the judiciary dealt only with legislation adopted by its coalitional allies, perhaps it would have little call to strike down statutes. But a newly elected legislature does not immediately bend the entire corpus of law to its will. The law governing the citizenry at any given moment represents a layering of legislative decisions over time—some made by legislators of a like mind to those who currently hold office, and others made by different political coalitions. American-style judicial review does not operate as a constant monitor of bills moving through the legislative process; judges do not have the option of vetoing proposed legislation, forcing all legislation through the filter of their own particular preferences. Instead, judges might be asked to evaluate a statute—or the particular application of a statute—years after it was adopted, and often long after the statute's legislative sponsors have passed from the political scene or lost interest in the details of their handiwork. Such politically antiquated statutes might be vulnerable to judicial invalidation even by a friendly court. Such cases also highlight the varying consequences of judicial invalidation. In some cases, judicial invalidation is likely to be a substantial roadblock to the pursuing the underlying policy. In other cases, the Court's action might channel legislative policy-making down a more constitutionally acceptable pathway. The Court's invalidation might simply invite Congress to revisit and amend the statute to bring it into compliance with the judicial decision, rather than tell Congress that its policy goal is constitutionally off-limits.[71] If Congress and the Court largely agree on political objectives, the Court might nudge Congress in the right direction, pointing out the best way to achieve them.

Judicial Review of Politically Indifferent Legislation

As Dahl pointed out, presidents are unlikely to appoint individuals to the bench who "flagrantly" disagree with presidential priorities on the "key questions" of the day.[72] Across American history, the major political parties have routinely taken up competing positions on major constitutional questions, whether because the constitutional issue has independent political salience or because the favorable resolution of the question is a precondition to advancing some separate matter of public policy.[73] But the parties do not attempt to cover the entire landscape of constitutional law and have no reason to do so. Politicians are motivated to care about constitutional issues that have significant political and policy consequences. They are likely to be indifferent to how constitutional questions are resolved if they do not rise to the level of affecting the outcomes of elections or obstructing core policy commitments.[74] In such circumstances, judges receive less guidance on how cases should be resolved and have more leeway to act independently.

It makes little sense to think that all constitutional questions have ideological valence. Some questions are simply technical—or not yet salient enough to generate ideological division among political actors. However, just because a constitutional question is politically insignificant does not necessarily mean that it is legally inconsequential. Such questions might matter to the resolution of actual disputes within the court system, and lawyers and judges might develop their own preferences as to how they should be resolved. Other issues might tend to systematically divide politicians and judges, but if the political salience of those issues is sufficiently low, judges might have the space to take action that separates them from their political allies. Most obviously, the integrity and power of the judiciary itself and the judicial processes are of prime concern to judges but normally of little concern to politicians and political activists. But judges may also develop independent interests in other, more substantive areas such as criminal justice, free speech, or economic regulation.[75]

The Supreme Court inescapably exercises judicial review in a political context. On some occasions, voiding laws means obstructing the cherished ambitions of robust political coalitions. On other occasions, striking down a law means pleasing political allies or simply flying below the radar of political operatives. The logic of the countermajoritarian difficulty rests largely on the assumption that judicial review takes place only or primarily in the first circumstance, with the Court adopting a hostile posture to the legislative majority. Such a picture is too simple, however, mischaracterizing both the nature of legislative politics and policy-making and the relationship of the Court to the larger political system. If we are to assess how countermajoritarian the Court might be, we must be sensitive to how and when the Court exercises the power of judicial review, not merely that it strikes down laws.

The Lost History of Judicial Review

Studies of the history of judicial review tend to have one of two objectives. They generally focus on either the origins of the power to strike down laws or how that power has been abused over time. Judicial review is a controversial topic; the identification of its origins has been contentious, and the record of its use has been the subject of ongoing quarrels.

This book has a different focus. Here, the concern is not the birth of judicial review or the misdeeds of the Court but the Court's routine, day-to-day exercise of the power of judicial review over the past two centuries. Judicial histories and constitutional casebooks contain the judicial highlight reel, but even these highlights tend to be reconstructed over time to meet the perceived needs of the moment.[76] The most politically important and legally relevant decisions are remembered, while others fade into obscurity and may be forgotten completely. One task of this work is to recover the lost history of judicial review.

Even the incidence of judicial review across American history is a matter of some uncertainty and dispute. In the early twentieth century, there was substantial disagreement among political activists and scholars over when and how often the Court invalidated legislation. The answer to the latter question ranged from often to hardly ever. Constitutional scholar Edward Corwin largely put an end to that debate in the mid-twentieth century. At the behest of Congress, Corwin produced what quickly became a canonical list of US Supreme Court cases that had invalidated provisions of federal statutes, as well as a similar list of cases invalidating state statutes. The list has subsequently been maintained by the Congressional Research Service (formerly the Legislative Reference Service).[77]

Despite the aura of authority that surrounds the Corwin list, even these semiofficial catalogs have been revised over time. The Legislative Reference Service dropped some cases that Corwin had initially included, on the grounds that the statutes in question were not found to be "unconstitutional in their entirety and therefore [wholly] inoperative."[78] Corwin himself significantly revised a list created by the Legislative Reference Service in the early twentieth century, adding some cases and subtracting others. More recently, Mark Graber has been particularly diligent in identifying obscure cases in which the exercise of judicial review was not notable to either contemporaries or historians and the justices themselves were not always clear about the significance of their actions. As Graber has observed, the justices sometimes hid in plain sight simply by refraining from uttering the "magic words" that a law is hereby declared unconstitutional, null and void.[79] There is value in taking a fresh look at the sources rather than accepting received wisdom.[80]

Beyond being underinclusive, the Corwin list obviously presents a one-sided history of judicial review. It makes no attempt to identify those cases in which the Court upheld federal statutes against constitutional challenge. It is no surprise that when Congress turned its attention to examining the Court's exercise of judicial review, it focused on those cases in which a law had been invalidated. From the beginning of its history, Congress has been interested in receiving timely information about court-identified constitutional defects in federal statutes and the courts' refusal to apply them. When a constituent reported to the Second Congress that a panel of federal judges had refused to take action on his case because the federal law in question was unconstitutional, the congressional recorder observed, "the novelty of the case produced a variety of opinions with respect to the measures to be taken on the occasion." At length, Representative William Murray "urged the necessity of passing a law to point out some regular mode in which the Judges of the Courts of the United States shall give official notice of their refusal to act under any law of Congress, on the ground of unconstitutionality."[81] As is so often the case, however, Congress failed to act on the proposal, and no method of official notification of judicial invalidation was ever adopted.

Populist and Progressive critics who complained about the incidence of judicial review were most aggrieved when the Court obstructed legislative action. Although cases in which the Court approved politicians' actions sometimes provoked controversy, they attracted less attention than instances of invalidation.[82] Analytically and politically, cases in which the Court explicitly considers the constitutional scope of Congress's legislative authority and consciously and deliberately upholds federal policy against constitutional challenge are distinct from run-of-the-mill cases of statutory interpretation and are themselves exercises of the power of judicial review.[83] Understanding how the power of judicial review developed over time and has been used politically requires that cases in which the Court has invalidated provisions be placed in context with cases in which it has upheld the application of legislation.

In considering how the power of judicial review developed and has been exercised, we should not overlook those cases in which the Court refrained from simply and explicitly declaring a constitutional provision void but nonetheless used its authority to enforce constitutional limitations on Congress. Justice Joseph Story captured a certain early nineteenth-century sensibility when riding circuit in Massachusetts:

> Whenever it becomes our duty to decide on the constitutionality of laws, sound discretion requires that the Court should not lightly presume an excess of power by the legislative body; nor so construe the generality of words, as to extend them beyond its lawful authority, unless the conclusion be unavoidable. . . .
>
> As little reason could there be to imagine the Legislature would voluntarily transcend its constitutional authority. The language must be very clear and precise, which would impose on the Court the duty of declaring the solemn act of the Legislature to be void. The Court could never incline so to construe doubtful expressions, much less to seek astutely for hidden interpretations, which might darkly lead to such a result.[84]

Story is not proposing that the courts reserve the constitutional question for the future or defer to legislative judgment on a contested constitutional point. He is not foreshadowing either Louis Brandeis[85] or James Bradley Thayer.[86] For Story, the question is merely one of the forms by which courts enforce constitutional limitations on legislative authority. If the statute is "clear and precise," the courts may have to declare it void. If the statute is less clear, the courts may be able to announce that the proposed application of the law exceeds the power of Congress and that such application will be regarded as off-limits and not judicially enforceable. Such a strategy may allow the courts and others to maintain that the legislature has not "voluntarily transcend[ed] its constitutional authority," even as judges enforce constitutional limitations against the legislature and refuse to apply laws on constitutional grounds in the cases before them. As one prominent antebellum commentator noted, "statutes are sometimes void," but courts can sometimes bend statutes so "as not to infringe these [constitutional] principles," on the assumption that legislatures intended their acts to be constitutional.[87] The laws may be unconstitutional as applied in a particular case and related cases, but they are not void in their entirety, and perhaps the legislature did not have such unconstitutional applications in mind when it passed the statute. The political conflicts created with the legislature may (or may not) be less severe when the judiciary exercises its power to enforce constitutional limitations without declaring laws void, but this has an equivalent effect of signaling to litigants that the courts will engage in constitutional interpretation and free parties from the immediate burden of statutes that cannot be constitutionally justified. We seriously misunderstand how courts have exercised the power of judicial review if we overlook the myriad ways in which judges are willing to enforce constitutional limitations and set aside statutory commands.

Because of possible omissions in the historical record, it is necessary to reconsider all instances in which the Court has exercised the power of judicial review. The starting point for this book is the Judicial Review of Congress (JRC) database, which was built from the ground up (see the appendix). The JRC database catalogs every case across American history in which the US Supreme Court substantively reviewed the constitutionality of a federal statutory provision, whether the Court ultimately invalidated the statute or upheld it. The database focuses on the legislative authority of Congress (as distinct from Congress's investigatory power or the constitutional authority of the president or the states) and cases in which the Court has been called on to determine whether a statutory provision can be constitutionally applied against a party before it. The database excludes cases in which the Court declined to issue a definitive interpretation of the Constitution or made only a trivial reference to the constitutional authority of Congress. Of paramount interest are cases in which explicit constitutional challenges to federal legislation have been raised, deliberated, and resolved. The result is an inventory of 1,308 cases decided by the US Supreme Court from 1789 to 2018, from the appointment of Chief Justice John Jay to the retirement of Associate Justice Anthony Kennedy. In that period, the Court upheld the application of a statute in 963 cases and struck down or constitutionally narrowed a statutory provision in 345 cases.

Judicial Review of Congress

Before delving into the details of particular cases and their political contexts, it is useful to provide an overview—an examination of the larger patterns related to the Court's exercise of judicial review across history. There has been substantial variation over time, and central features of the historical practice of judicial review are still unclear (or even misrepresented), given the incomplete catalog of cases in which the Court has exercised the power.

Figure 1-1 shows how often the US Supreme Court has evaluated the constitutionality of federal statutes over the course of its history. The figure distinguishes between cases upholding statutory provisions against constitutional challenge and cases invalidating or narrowing statutory provisions on constitutional grounds. For ease of presentation, the figure depicts a centered, five-year moving average of the annual number of cases decided by the Court.[88]

Several features of this figure are worth noting. First, the Court has upheld laws against constitutional challenge far more often than it has struck them down. Across its history as a whole, the Court has upheld acts of Congress in just under three-quarters of the cases in which it resolved a constitutional challenge to a federal law. The rate of invalidation has varied over time, but the raw numbers emphasize that the Court has more often been a handmaiden to the congressional exercise of power than an obstruction. Invalidations are not rare, but invalidation is not the most likely outcome when the Court agrees to hear a case involving a constitutional challenge to a federal law.

Notably, the tendency to uphold laws has held true throughout the Court's history. Even during periods of relative activism, when the Court struck down laws in an unusually large number of cases, it was still more likely to uphold a law than to strike it down. Likewise, whether the Court was hearing many challenges or working with a relatively small caseload, decisions upholding laws predominated.

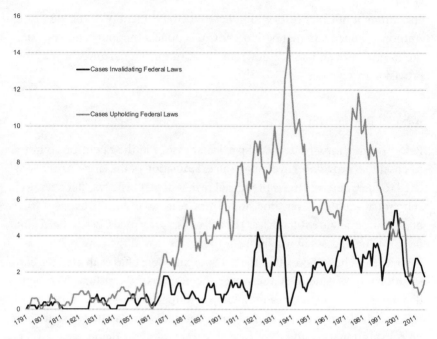

Figure 1-1: Judicial Review of Acts of Congress by the US Supreme Court, 1789–2018. *Note*: Centered, five-year moving average of annual count of cases upholding and striking down federal statutory provisions.

The prevalence of cases upholding laws against constitutional challenges has persisted through the twentieth century, despite operational changes that might have reduced the number of such cases. Until early in the twentieth century, the Court had a largely mandatory jurisdiction, and it was obliged to hear all appeals that met statutory and constitutional requirements. As a result, the justices heard numerous "easy" cases in which the law was relatively settled and clear and the dispute had been adequately resolved by the lower courts. In the early twentieth century, the justices persuaded Congress to change the Court's appellate responsibilities and shift to a largely discretionary docket that permitted the justices to choose which cases to hear.[89] As a result, the justices could focus on "hard" cases in which the state of the law was unsettled. As a practical matter, the justices also weighted their docket with more interesting cases, which often meant more constitutional cases and fewer tax and bankruptcy cases.[90]

Cases involving the constitutionality of federal statutes occupied a consistently larger proportion of the Court's docket in the twentieth century than in the nineteenth. Prior to passage of the Judge's Bill of 1925, which granted the Court a largely discretionary docket, cases challenging federal statutes constituted a mere 2 percent of its docket. Since 1925, such cases have accounted for 8 percent of the docket—a large increase, even if such cases still make up only a small proportion of the Court's overall workload. Even after shuffling the docket to exclude easy cases, the Court continued to uphold statutes more often than it struck them down. That basic pattern did not reverse itself until the end of the twentieth century, when the Court began to take very few cases in order to uphold a law. Compared with the norm since passage of the Judge's Bill, the Roberts Court has decided somewhat fewer cases striking down federal laws but dramatically fewer cases upholding laws.[91] Since the late Rehnquist Court, the justices have reversed their historical pattern, with a larger proportion of judicial review cases resulting in invalidation.

Judicial review has been a persistent feature over the course of American history, but not a stable one. The history of judicial invalidation of federal laws can be divided into three broad periods.[92] From the founding through the Civil War, the Court reviewed laws at a low rate and somewhat sporadically. Nonetheless, the judicial enforcement of constitutional law quickly became a familiar, if not exactly common, part of the American political landscape. The Court struck down federal statutory provisions at a rate of less than one every two years (and state statutes at a slightly higher rate) in the decades prior to Reconstruction. During that time, it was not uncommon for the Court to go years without invalidating a statutory provision. Judicial review, however, was common, and the Court never went more than two years without resolving some constitutional question in the nineteenth century.

The time between the Civil War and World War I was distinct from earlier and later periods. Although the number of cases upholding laws climbed during this period, the number of cases striking down federal laws stabilized at a new plateau. The Court struck down federal statutory provisions at a rate of nearly one case per year during these decades—more than twice the rate in the decades preceding Reconstruction. Judicial invalidation of state statutes followed a similar pattern but reached an even higher plateau of nearly four cases per year.[93] The Court occasionally concluded a term without striking down a federal law, but when the Roberts Court failed to resolve *any* constitutional challenge to a federal statute in 2009, it was the first time this had happened since 1864. The judicial resolution of doubts about the constitutional validity of legislation had become a routine part of American governance.

The years since World War I constitute the third period, with the Court striking down federal laws in nearly three cases per year and state laws in nearly ten cases per year. The Court occasionally goes a year without striking down a federal law, but this has become a once-in-a-decade event. The judicial nullification of federal law was once shocking to political observers and was considered a grave intervention into the workings of American democracy. Now demonstrators gather around the Supreme Court building several times a year, calling for the justices to overturn what legislatures have done. When the Court concludes its term and begins its summer recess, the question is no longer whether it has struck down any laws but rather how many it has struck down and how important they were.

There are still peaks and valleys of activism within these broad trends. In some ways, the modern Court is more activist than the Court of the late nineteenth century—striking down more laws, on a more regular basis, and in a higher percentage of cases—but the historical tendency sets a baseline of political expectations. A normal year of judicial activity in the twentieth century would have been an outrageous amount of activism in the nineteenth century. Although this long-term trend is interesting, it is more useful to think about fluctuations within a given historical period. Within their own time, Courts are more or less activist in comparison with their near contemporaries, not their ancient ancestors.

Figure 1-2 illustrates these ebbs and flows of activism within period norms. It charts the annual deviations from the period average in US Supreme Court cases that invalidated federal and state laws. Years of relative activism rise above the x-axis, and years of relative restraint drop below it, with the length of the bars reflecting the absolute distance between the period average and the actual count.[94] The size of the bars is of less interest than their density and direction. We might imagine the Court randomly oscillating around its period average, and this was largely the case in the nineteenth century, when years of relative activism were interspersed with years are relative quiescence.

The twentieth century ushered in more distinct cycles of activism within the context of an overall greater level of activity. The Court entered an extended period of striking down laws—both state and federal—in the 1920s

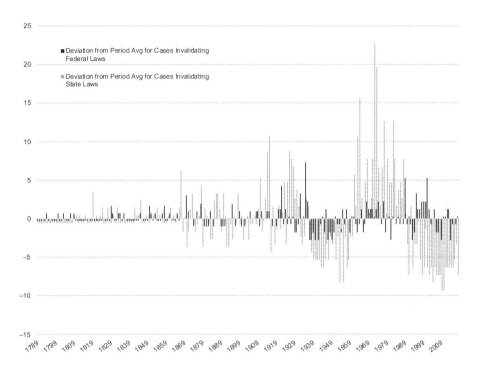

Figure 1-2: Judicial Activism and Restraint by the US Supreme Court, 1789–2018.
Note: Absolute deviation from period average in annual count of invalidating cases.

and early 1930s. In 1937 the Court beat a hasty retreat, establishing a new pattern of relative restraint that lasted through the 1950s. In the 1960s the Warren Court launched a new period of extended activism that continued into the Burger Court, exceeding in length and intensity the activism of the Taft Court. This, in turn, was followed by a dramatic but often unnoted period of restraint by the Rehnquist and Roberts Courts.[95] Notably, the Rehnquist Court exhibited a brief period of divergence in its handling of state and federal laws, showing sharp restraint in cases involving state laws but an intensification of the Burger Court's activist posture toward federal laws. No Court since the early republic has committed to a principle of wholesale deference to legislatures,[96] but since the early twentieth century, the Court has vacillated between periods of relative activism and periods of relative deference. Even in its more deferential phases, the modern Court still regularly strikes down laws at a historically torrid pace (it struck down federal laws in nearly twice as many cases in the "restrained" 1940s as it did in the "activist" 1880s, for example).

The count of the cases reflected in figures 1-1 and 1-2 is subject to some qualifications that should be noted. One obvious qualification is that these figures treat cases as interchangeable units, as if every case (and statute) were functionally equivalent. That is, of course, a simplification, although a conventional one within the quantitative literature. In reality, not all cases are alike. Some are more legally consequential or more politically salient or more conceptually surprising than others. We care more about *Obergefell v. Hodges*, which struck down bans on same-sex marriage,[97] than *Reed v. Town of Gilbert, Arizona*, which struck down a city ordinance favoring signs by non-profit groups.[98] Such differences are explored in more detail in subsequent chapters, but generally, the number of cases decided and the number of consequential cases decided tend to move in tandem.

It is also true that the Court exercises the power of judicial review in a context created by the legislature. Courts have nothing to review if legislatures are not active in passing laws.[99] Of course, the legislative activity of Congress has not been static across its history. One might contextualize the judicial review of acts of Congress by taking into account the number of bills actually passed by Congress.[100] Not all statutes are equally likely to be reviewed, and one useful filter is to focus on public bills (acts that create general legislation) and ignore private bills (acts that are designed to affect a particular individual or a small set of individuals). But the Court is not confined to reviewing statutes as such, and Congress has altered how it packages legislation over time. In the week of March 7, 1904, for example, Congress passed seven public bills that occupied a mere six pages in the legislative record. This was early in the meeting of the Fifty-Eighth Congress, which was notably productive and adopted several hundred pieces of legislation. But the work of that week was typical, consisting of such measures as P.L. 58-40, which established a federal district court in Marietta, Indiana; P.L. 58-44, which granted several acres of federal land adjacent to the University of Montana to the state for use by that institution; and P.L. 58-47, which granted permission to a Minnesota power company to build a dam across the Mississippi River. Such was the mundane business of a busy national legislature at the turn of the twentieth century. A century later, Congress would either pass off such decision-

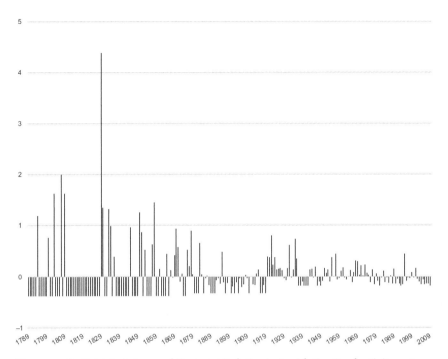

Figure 1-3: Judicial Activism and Restraint Relative to Legislative Productivity, 1789–2017. *Note*: Absolute deviation from period average in annual count of invalidating cases divided by annual count of statutory pages times 100.

making to administrative agencies or bundle dozens (or hundreds) of such proposals into larger pieces of legislation. How constitutional challenges to congressional output arise and how they are evaluated by the courts do not turn on whether such measures are moved individually through the legislative process or packaged together in larger statutes.

More useful than the number of public bills passed by Congress is the number of pages of statutory language adopted by Congress, for all those pages have the potential to generate constitutional problems, regardless of whether bills are packaged singly or multiply. The annual number of public bills passed by Congress peaked in the mid-twentieth century and has gradually declined since then, as Congress has relied more on omnibus bills, but the number of pages in *Statutes at Large* has continued to increase. Figure 1-3 shows a five-year moving average of the annual number of cases invalidating federal statutory provisions over the annual legislative output of Congress as

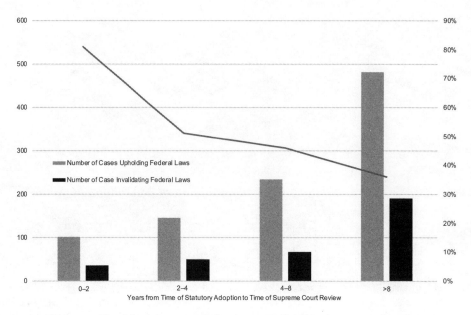

Figure 1-4: Time from Statutory Adoption to Judicial Review, 1789–2018

represented by the number of pages taken up by that legislation in *Statutes at Large*.[101] From this perspective, the Court has become progressively less activist over time, as the output of Congress has far outstripped the judicial review activity of the Supreme Court. Figure 1-3 is particularly helpful in offering a new perspective on the activism of the Burger and Rehnquist Courts. Their spurt of invalidations is overshadowed by the mountain of legislation produced by Congress at the end of the twentieth century. Relative to congressional productivity, however, the Court's activism of the 1850s through 1870s and 1920s through 1930s stands out as quite notable.

Dahl suggested that striking down older statutes would be less politically challenging than striking down newly adopted ones, but he had little evidence to assess how long the litigation process actually takes. Figure 1-4 organizes cases based on the time between a statutory provision's adoption or latest revision to its review by the Supreme Court. Cases are divided between those that upheld a statute and those that struck one down and are organized into intervals denoting how many years passed before review. It is clear that most cases involved statutes that were relatively old.[102]

More than half the cases reviewed statutory provisions that were more than eight years old. Just over 10 percent reviewed statutory provisions less than two years old, and roughly a quarter were reviewed within four years—a time frame that Dahl thought was particularly meaningful as a metric of politically salient legislation. Somewhat surprisingly from a Dahlian perspective, there is relatively little difference in the rate of invalidation between recent statutes and older statutes. But the judicial review of contemporary statutes is only a small part of the Court's business; much of the Court's actual exercise of the power of judicial review involves considering statutes that have been in place for some time. The routine exercise of judicial review is not concerned with evaluating—and potentially obstructing—the work of contemporary majorities. Although striking down an older statute can be politically risky, since older statutes sometimes still have political force behind them, judicial review of legislation that is years or even decades old tends to undercut Bickel's claim that the very nature of judicial review is to thwart "the will of representatives of the actual people of the here and now." A great deal of judicial review by the Supreme Court is concerned with thwarting the will of long-gone political majorities. The prospect of judicial review generally does not hover over congressional deliberations.

Not all invalidations are the same, however. Cases in which the Court defines and enforces constitutional limits on the legislative authority of Congress can be divided into those that strike down a statutory provision in its entirety and those that strike down a proposed application of a statute and restrict its constitutionally acceptable scope. As figure 1-4 indicates, in a large percentage of cases in which the Court invalidated a statute in its first years, it involved a blanket nullification of the provision. As statutes age, invalidations more often restrict the scope rather than reject the terms of the statute itself. Broad-based challenges to the very language and purpose of a statute tend to be brought before the Court and resolved relatively quickly (or at least those that successfully cut against congressional authority are resolved quickly). However, a long tail of constitutional doubts may be raised about statutes over the course of their lengthy lifetimes, but these are more likely to shrink the scope of legislation rather than cut it down entirely.[103]

Cases vary not only by what the Court does but also by what is at stake. Constitutional challenges can take more or less time to reach the Court, and they may be resolved by broader or narrower rulings. But cases can also involve more or less important statutes. There is no singular way to identify the political and policy importance of a statute across American history, and such features of legislation are best considered within their own detailed context. Nonetheless, a rough proxy can be constructed to make an initial cut at the data. Stephen Stathis, a specialist at the Congressional Research Service, identified "landmark legislation" passed by every Congress through 2012 and provided a brief abstract of each statute.[104] That list roughly divides legislation into important federal statutes passed each year and less notable acts that make up the bulk of the annual congressional output (and it has the advantage of covering all of American history with a single consistent metric). Moreover, the abstracts help identify whether a particular provision being challenged is an especially important component of a landmark statute or an ancillary feature.

Important statutes occupy much of the Court's attention in judicial review cases.[105] Even though such landmark statutes represent only 2 percent of all the public bills passed by Congress, nearly half the cases evaluating the constitutionality of a statutory provision involve legislation on Stathis's list. Although relatively minor pieces of legislation occupy a fair amount of the Court's attention, a disproportionate share of the constitutional docket is taken up by the most important congressional acts. But not every provision of a landmark statute is itself significant; less than half the constitutional challenges involving landmark legislation are related to key provisions of those statutes. This is not to say that these other cases are inconsequential; however, when considering important statutes, the Court is more likely to be nibbling around the margins rather than examining the key pillars. For example, the Court's decision in *Califano v. Goldfarb*[106] was legally significant in terms of applying the equal protection doctrine to gender, and it involved an important statute (the Social Security Amendments of 1950), but the gender-based eligibility defaults were hardly at the statute's core. Important statutes and their key components are not especially likely to be upheld. When they are invalidated, there is no significant distinction in whether the Court strikes at the provision in its entirety or as applied.[107]

What Is to Come?

The remainder of the book traces the politics of the US Supreme Court's exercise of judicial review of congressional legislation over the course of American history. Although some legal context and ramifications of the Court's decisions are noted, this book is not primarily a history of the evolution of constitutional law. Rather, it is a political history of the Court's use of the power of judicial review to define and enforce limits on congressional power. Each chapter focuses on a particular period and situates the Court and its actions within the political and intellectual context of that era. Several themes are developed in the following chapters.

- First and most fundamentally, there has been far more judicial review of federal laws than has generally been appreciated. Behind the most notable cases stand dozens of less memorable decisions that helped define the scope of congressional authority and establish the Court's significance as a regular participant in constitutional debates.
- Second and relatedly, an important aspect of the Court's work in exercising judicial review has been in upholding laws against constitutional challenge. The Court's ongoing effort to silence critics of congressional power is a crucial part of how the Court advances a common project of governance with its allies in the elected branches.
- Third, over much of its history, the US Supreme Court has acted as a nation builder, helping to craft government institutions and procedures and knit together a diverse and far-flung country. While the Court's work as an obstructionist defender of minority interests against majoritarian political leaders is often the most visible aspect of its history, that is ultimately a much smaller function than its role as an arm of the national state.
- Fourth, the Court's basic approach to its task has undergone substantial development over time. The power of judicial review did not emerge full blown from the Philadelphia Convention of 1787. The construction of judicial power and constitutional rules has been an ongoing political project to which both the justices and elected officials have contributed.
- Fifth, the justices participate in an often partisan process of constructing a set of constitutional values, principles, and rules that can command support from the political leaders and activists who dominate the political arena at the time. The constitutional debates and the contours of the accepted constitutional answers have shifted over time, as the nation has struggled with new social and political problems, and as the competing parties have formulated approaches to address those problems and identify new aspirations for the community.
- Sixth, the justices are part of the national political scene, but they also stand apart from it. They pursue their own priorities and a distinct set of interests and values within the bounds set by the larger political context in which they operate.

• Finally, judicial review operates within a political context composed of fractious political coalitions, strategic political leaders, and numerous interests. The common Bickelian image of a heroic (or villainous) Court standing against the will of a united people, as expressed through legislative majorities, is deeply misleading. Although such a description is sometimes apt, more often the Court is navigating a far more complex political environment and working in conjunction with allies elsewhere in the political system.

Before delving into the details of the cases that make up the JRC database, chapter 2 begins with a brief sketch of the origins of judicial review. Impressive work has been done in recent years to expand our understanding of the early development of judicial review in the United States, and this chapter draws liberally from that research.

Chapters 3 and 4 examine how the Court exercised judicial review of Congress from its creation through Reconstruction. These decades cover the first period of judicial review highlighted in figure 1-1. Chapter 3 covers the first seven decades of the Court's existence, when it was surprisingly active in applying constitutional rules to federal legislation. Chapter 4 examines a much briefer period during the Civil War and Reconstruction, when the power of judicial review faced significant challenges and the foundations for a new era of judicial activism were laid.

Chapter 5 examines the period covering the postbellum years and the Progressive Era. Although this time is best remembered for the Supreme Court's activism in striking down state laws regulating economic relations, these decades also saw some of the Court's most controversial invalidations of federal laws and pitched battles over the power of judicial review itself.

The final two chapters focus on the twentieth century. Chapter 6 examines the period dominated by a liberal Court, from the New Deal battles to the struggles over the Warren Court. Chapter 7 analyzes the return of a more conservative Court, from the ascendance of the Burger Court through the Roberts Court.

Chief Justice John Marshall once intoned that the Supreme Court was burdened with the "awful responsibility" of identifying the constitutional boundaries within which government officials must operate and insisting that they stay within their proper bounds.[108] It was the Court's role to determine which acts of Congress are "repugnant to the Constitution" and to set such laws aside as unenforceable.[109] Such declarations threatened to set the justices above other government officials. The Court has long implied that it is situated outside the world of politics, located at some Archimedean point from which it can stand in judgment of those who play the political game. Of course, there is no such vantage point. The justices too must operate within the political world, and politics helps determine which ideas move the Court and how constitutional rules are constructed and maintained. The power of judicial review has been meaningful in American history not because the Court stands against politics but because of how the Court operates within politics.

2

The Road to Judicial Review

It was once commonplace to assert that Chief Justice John Marshall's opinion in the 1803 case *Marbury v. Madison* "established"—or at least definitively "settled"—the power of judicial review for American courts.[1] But *Marbury* was not so important. Marshall's opinion did, however, nicely encapsulate the thinking of political and legal elites in the early republic on the subject of the judiciary's authority to evaluate the constitutionality of laws and the legal status of statutes that were in conflict with clear constitutional requirements.[2] Marshall's rhetorical prowess—and his coterie of Federalist acolytes interested in advancing his reputation—eventually made *Marbury* the standard authority on the power of judicial review, but that was largely because of what *Marbury* said, not what it did. Marshall knew how to turn a phrase, and the *Marbury* decision was very readable.

Marbury was not the origin of the power of judicial review, so the story of the history of judicial review should not start there. The US Supreme Court's exercise of judicial review to assess the constitutionality of acts of Congress built on earlier theoretical and political developments. Those earlier developments laid a foundation on which the Court could build, but they also set expectations that helped define how the early Court approached the task of judicial review. The courts' authority to review the validity of acts of Congress was not the primary focus or implication of those earlier developments, but the Supreme Court's authority was a natural outgrowth of them.

Judicial review can be conceptualized in two distinct ways. One perspective is primarily political. From this perspective, constitutional review by courts is part of a scheme of checks and balances in which various political institutions are armed with weapons to resist the encroachments of other government officials. Lodging a power to examine whether legislative actions violate constitutional rules is a potentially effective mechanism of constitutional maintenance. The second perspective is primarily legal. From this perspective, the written constitution is incorporated into the larger body of law, which judges have a duty to interpret and apply as appropriate.[3] When called on to reconcile conflicting legal requirements, judges should necessarily favor those that stand higher in the legal hierarchy, which means that statutory directives must give way to constitutional mandates. Both types of arguments were familiar to Americans forming new governmental institutions in the late eighteenth and early nineteenth centuries.

English and Colonial Backdrop

In the years leading up to the American Revolution, American lawyer James Otis tried to persuade Massachusetts colonial courts to declare laws of Parliament null and void. He had no immediate success but raised the question of what powers English common-law courts should possess in the late eighteenth century. In an effort to crack down on smuggling, Parliament empowered colonial customs officers to conduct searches for contraband in the Boston area. Writs of assistance were issued to facilitate these searches, but the writs allowed customs officials to search private property at their own discretion. Otis, among others, objected that writs of assistance violated the traditional requirement for search warrants that called for a showing of probable cause and authorized only a specified search. Otis went further than most, however, in arguing that the colonial court should refuse to issue writs of assistance because "no Acts of Parliament can establish such a writ; though it should be made in the very words of the petition, it would be void. An act against the constitution is void."[4] Governor Thomas Hutchinson, who presided over the colonial court, later reported that he had to persuade his colleagues not to go along with Otis's suggestion. Hutchinson thought it self-evident that the logic of Otis's argument—that a statute against "the peculiar rights of Englishmen is *ipso facto* void"—was a recipe for anarchy. Such a theory "must be fatal to all Government." Parliament was "beyond dispute the supreme legislature of the British dominions," and judges had no choice but to take its legislative acts as "legally right."[5]

Otis appealed specifically to the authority of *Bonham's Case*, an English decision rendered by the influential Sir Edward Coke a century and a half earlier. Dr. Thomas Bonham sued the College of Physicians after it convicted and punished him for practicing medicine without a license. Coke held that Parliament had not empowered the college to license, judge, and punish individuals who practiced medicine. More significantly, he suggested that Parliament *could not* have given the college the power to act as both accuser and judge in such a case. It was sometimes true, Coke contended, that "the common law will controul Acts of Parliament, and sometimes adjudge them to be utterly void; for when an Act of Parliament is against common right and reason, or repugnant, or impossible to be performed, the common law will controul it, and adjudge such Act to be void."[6]

Especially as seen through the lens of Otis and the subsequent development of judicial review in the United States, Coke's remarks have been the subject of extended interpretive disputes.[7] It seems likely that in his own context, Coke was thinking about statutory interpretation and the internecine rivalries of the English courts rather than a form of modern judicial review in which courts could declare statutes null and void. Certainly, later English judges did not take Coke's assertions to be so bold as James Otis (or John Marshall) claimed.[8] Most significantly, William Blackstone set out the conventional English thinking of the mid-eighteenth century in his influential legal treatise (which appeared in print just after Otis made his argument in Massachusetts) and came down firmly on the side of parliamentary supremacy. He concluded plainly: "So long, therefore, as the English constitution lasts, we may venture to affirm, that the power of parliament is absolute and without control."[9] In particular, Blackstone insisted, judges were not "at liberty to reject" even unreasonable laws, "for that were to set the judicial power above that of the legislature, which would be subversive of all government."[10]

The Americans tended to be more comfortable with Otis's argument than the English were in the 1760s and 1770s. Otis himself, with an assist from a young John Adams, amplified his argument from the writs of assistance case in a later pamphlet defending the colonial cause.[11] He continued to argue that "even the authority of the parliament of *Great-Britain* is circumscribed by certain bounds, which if exceeded, their acts become those of meer *power* without *right*, and consequently void . . . *acts against the fundamental principles of the British constitution are void.*"[12] At least some judges agreed. The judges of the county court in Northampton County, Virginia, formally resolved that they would not comply with the Stamp Act and require payment of the tax, "inasmuch as they conceive the said Act to be unconstitutional."[13] Likewise, Caroline County, Virginia, judge Edmund Pendleton, who became a leading state judge after the Revolution, wrote to James Madison that his "oath to determine according to the law" precluded him from complying with the Stamp Act because Parliament did not possess the necessary "constitutional authority" to impose such a tax on the colonies.[14]

The crucial theoretical foundation for the American position was the rejection of Blackstone's claim that Parliament was the most basic sovereign power and thus held a legislative authority that was literally without bounds. Blackstone admitted that "Mr. Locke, and other theoretical writers," had contended that the people themselves held a supreme power over the legislature, but in the jurist's opinion, "however just this conclusion may be, in theory, we cannot practically adopt it, nor take any *legal* steps for carrying it into execution," so long as the government continued to exist. For as long as Parliament endured, it had "sovereign and uncontrollable authority" and "can, in short, do everything that is not naturally impossible," up to and including "change and create afresh even the constitution of the kingdom."[15] In his popular American edition of *Blackstone's Commentaries*, St. George Tucker pointed out how American political theory departed from the English theory Blackstone laid out. The revolutionaries had "shaken off" the "received maxims" of the Old World. "*In our own republic at least*," what Blackstone had dismissed as the fancy of theoretical writers had been settled by the practical action of constitutional bodies acting on behalf of the people. John Locke's theories had been made real in America.[16] "In the United States this absolute power is not delegated to the government: it remains with the people, whose safety requires that the government which they have themselves established, should be limited."[17] Legislatures in the United States, Tucker contended, "have no rights, nor authority, nor even an existence, but from the People," and the powers entrusted to those legislative agents are few and limited.[18] Under these circumstances, the legislature has neither the power nor the authority to violate the terms of the constitution, and any acts that attempt to do so are without legal effect.

The boundaries of parliamentary authority had become a particularly salient question in the lead-up to the American Revolution, but the North American colonists had other experiences with limited government on which to draw. From their founding, the colonies had operated under their own limited constitutions.[19] The colonial charters were written legal documents that defined how political power was to be organized within the colony and circumscribed that power. In many of the colonies, only the lower chamber of the legislature was directly accountable to the colonists themselves, magnifying the perceived gap between the government and the people. But all colonial officials, whether elected by the people or not, were legally constrained by the colonial charters.

The charters included two kinds of significant limits on governmental power. The first was essentially federal. The charters limited the scope of the governing authority of the colonial governments. Within the British imperial system, the colonies were granted some limited autonomy over a variety of subjects of domestic concern, but the imperial government in London retained authority over subjects of mutual concern, such as colonial trade and foreign policy.[20] Ultimately, it was friction between the scope of colonial authority over all matters "within the said province and territories" (as the Frame of Government of Pennsylvania put it) and the scope of Parliament's authority "to make laws and statutes of sufficient validity to bind the colonies and people of America . . . in all cases whatsoever" (as Blackstone put it) that drove the constitutional arguments of the American Revolution.[21] Until the revolutionary break itself, it was well accepted that the "subordination of the colonies, and the authority of Parliament to preserve it," was an essential feature of the imperial constitutional system.[22] The legal authority of the colonial governments was limited.

The second limit on the power of the colonial governments was related to individual rights. Some rights were specifically protected in detailed provisions of the colonial constitutions. The Massachusetts Body of Liberties of 1641 is the most well known, with a lengthy enumeration of "rights, liberties and privileges concerning our churches and civil state, to be respectively, impartially, and inviolably enjoyed and observed throughout our jurisdiction for ever." Those liberties included a guarantee that every person within its jurisdiction "shall enjoy justice and law that is general for the plantation . . . without partiality or delay" and a prohibition against husbands laying

"bodily correction or stripes" on their wives "unless it be in his own defense upon her assault."[23] Other rights were secured by general provisions
that guaranteed colonists the traditional legal rights of British subjects. The
1732 charter of the Georgia colony was typical in affirming that "all and every
person which shall happen to be born within the said province, and every of
their children and posterity, shall have and enjoy all liberties, franchises and
immunities of free denizens and natural born subjects, within any of our
dominions, to all intents and purposes, as if abiding and born within this
our kingdom of Great-Britain." The charters encouraged immigration by assuring new arrivals that they would retain the rights and liberties they would
have enjoyed in Britain. They would be no less free in Boston or Williams-
burg than they would have been in London or Manchester.

In effect, the colonial charters created legally enforceable limits on the
power of local government officials. Those limits could be enforced in a variety of ways. Most immediately, governors were expected to control the
colonial legislatures through their power to veto legislation. Laws that contradicted British liberties or British imperial policy would be checked by the
British representative in the governor's mansion. Failing that, imperial authorities expected all colonial policies to be transmitted to London for review by the king's Privy Council. This quasi-judicial body would ensure that
the colonial legislatures did not exceed the scope of their charters. Finally,
judges treated these charter arrangements as relevant law and were expected
to prioritize charter requirements over legislative acts. As the British Board
of Trade noted, "All these colonies . . . by their several constitutions, have
the power of making laws for their better government and support, provided
they be not repugnant to the laws of Great Britain, nor detrimental to the
Mother-Country."[24]

As a result of this background, revolutionary Americans were quite familiar with the practice of a functioning system of limited government and
legally enforceable constitutional restrictions. The system of legislative supremacy in England described by Blackstone did not resemble the political
systems of North America. Mary Sarah Bilder, who has extensively examined the restrictions associated with colonial charters, notes that this imperial constitutional system "helps explain the rapid acceptance of federalism
and judicial review of state legislation," for the new states under the Constitution of the United States were in much the same legal position as the

colonies had been under English rule.[25] The judicial duty to nullify acts that were "repugnant" to the terms of corporate charters was widely accepted in English law, even when those corporations took the form of colonial governments.[26] Philip Hamburger has detailed how colonial judges sometimes struggled with their legal duty to uphold British law and rights in the face of conflicting local statutes. The colonial charters, including the 1633 Rhode Island charter, generally asserted that local statutes must "be not contrary and repugnant to, but, as near as may be agreeable to the laws of this our realm of England, considering the nature and constitutions of the place and people there." Such language left room for local officials to distinguish the needs (and liberties) of colonists from those of the average British subject. As one dissenting judge in South Carolina contended, the colonial legislature was required to follow British law only "as near as conveniently as may be."[27]

Colonial officials were familiar with the practice of declaring legislative acts to be repugnant to the constitution, but they did not necessarily like it. Colonial legislatures tried to obstruct and evade review of their actions by other institutions, and they often objected when their legislation was struck down. Nonetheless, the principle that legislatures are subordinate to written constitutions became a familiar one. As Bilder points out, however, this history also suggested "profound theoretical problems with judicial review of congressional action."[28] The colonial charters were designed to enforce the colonial governments' subordination to the central government. After the Revolution, Congress could reasonably see itself in the position of the British Parliament rather than a colonial legislature. Courts might be expected to keep the subordinate state governments in line, but not Congress itself. The founding generation was knowledgeable about the instrument of judicial review, but the appropriateness of its application to Congress required the embrace of the logic of popular sovereignty and individual rights more than the logic of federalism.

Developments in the States

The newly formed states of the independent United States were the first to experiment with horizontal judicial review—courts' constitutional review of the coordinate legislatures of the same government. After independence, state judges did not appeal primarily to the subordination of state legislatures within the federal system. Rather, initial American arguments over judicial review emphasized the authority of the people to impose legally binding constraints on even elected government officials and to impose legal duties on judges asked to interpret and apply the acts of state legislatures. That argument about popular sovereignty and its legal consequences was as applicable to Congress as it was to state legislatures. As Hamburger has observed, it was a "lopsided debate," with critics of the emerging power of judicial review making little headway in stemming the tide.[29]

In the years immediately following the Declaration of Independence, judges up and down the Atlantic coast proclaimed their authority to review the constitutionality of legislative acts. In an early review of these state court decisions, Charles Grove Haines concluded that the search for a single decisive case that established the power of judicial review and drove subsequent developments was misguided. "It seems rather that a series of precedents with a cumulative effect, along with a common sentiment in practically all of the colonies, led men to the acceptance of certain ideas and consequences," and this resulted in judicial review's emergence "as a well-settled principle of constitutional law" by the time of the federal convention in 1787.[30]

The earliest state cases tended to involve statutes that impinged on the judicial process itself. Among the most prominent was a case from Rhode Island challenging a statute that precluded jury trials for defendants who had refused to accept the state's paper money as legal tender. Rhode Island was unusual, in that it did not have a written constitution on which the courts could rely in evaluating statutes. In this case, the court did not publish an opinion reporting its decision, but the case gained prominence when the lawyer for the defendant published a pamphlet containing his argument criticizing the law and justifying judicial action.[31] The North Carolina legislature was even more aggressive in interfering with traditional legal rights when it adopted a statute directing judges to dismiss suits over land titles if the defendant could produce evidence of acquisition through state forfeiture of the land of a Loyalist. Unlike in Rhode Island, the parties in North Carolina could point to a specific constitutional provision that conflicted with the statute. But like the Rhode Island case, this one gained national prominence when the lawyer made his appeal in public writings.[32] The lawyer happened to be James Iredell, perhaps the most notable Federalist lawyer south of Virginia and a future member of the US Supreme Court. Iredell argued that judicial review was the natural application of revolutionary principles. The Revolution had been fought "against the abuse of unlimited power, which was not to be trusted, without the most imminent danger."[33] The revolutionary movement would come to naught if American legislatures simply picked up the parliamentary mantle of unlimited power.

Virginia proved to be a particularly friendly environment for judicial review. In the summer of 1782, three individuals were convicted of treason and sentenced to death for assisting British troops. The state's Treason Act allowed a pardon only when both chambers of the legislature concurred (in this case, only the lower chamber had voted for a resolution of pardon), and it barred the governor from issuing a pardon. The state constitution, however, specified two options for a pardon: by the governor or (if so stipulated by statute) by the lower legislative chamber alone. The prisoners argued that the Treason Act violated that constitutional provision by giving the upper chamber a role in the pardoning power. Soon after the state senate declined to pardon the men, state attorney general (and future US attorney general) Edmund Randolph wrote to James Madison, informing him that he expected the courts to confront the question of their willingness to strike down a law as "contrary to the constitution."[34] By the time the case was heard in the fall by the Virginia Court of Appeals, it had become a cause célèbre among Virginia's legal elite, and John Marshall was one of those who crowded the courtroom to hear the arguments.

When the court convened, it was widely assumed that it had the power to strike down the statute. Even though he was charged with defending the state's position in the case, the attorney general immediately conceded that "every law against the constitution may be declared void" by the court.[35] Given social disagreements about how political power should be exercised and to what ends, a constitution was an essential "touchstone" for preventing the abuse of power. Only the constitution could indicate "how far the people, the fountain of power, have chosen to deposit it in the hands of their legislative servants."[36] Randolph attempted to save the statute by arguing that the conflict between its terms and those of the state constitution were more apparent than real, although it is unclear whether even Randolph himself was persuaded by this argument. In addition to the lawyers for the two sides, the court heard amici arguments from three distinguished members of the bar, including St. George Tucker.[37] Only one of the three doubted the power of the court to strike down unconstitutional statutes. Tucker thought it evident that the courts had the ultimate responsibility to determine, in individual cases, "what is or is not Law, and consequently (I should presume) on the validity or nullity of different Laws contradicting each other." Moreover, the constitution is "the first law by which they are bound," for "the Constitution [is] not lyable to any alteration whatsoever by the Legislative, without destroying that Basis and Foundation of Government."[38] As he would later emphasize in his notes on *Blackstone's Commentaries*, Tucker insisted that the Americans had abandoned the English model of parliamentary sovereignty. The British constitution was traditional and always subject to parliamentary reimagination, whereas the American constitutions were "express" and composed of solemn promises made to and by the people themselves.[39] The court ultimately ruled against the prisoners, but only one of the eight judges expressed doubts about the court's power to strike down a law, if necessary.[40] Chancellor George Wythe, a signatory to the Declaration of Independence, was particularly vocal: "If the whole legislature, an event to be deprecated, should attempt to overleap the bounds, prescribed to them by the people, I, in administering the public justice of the country, will meet the united powers, at my seat in this tribunal; and, pointing to the constitution, will say, to them, here is the limit to your authority; and, hither, shall you go, but no further."[41] In his notes, presiding judge Edmund Pendleton simply observed that Wythe had "urged several strong and sensible reasons . . . to prove that an Anti-constitutional Act of the Legislature would be void."[42]

If the litigation over the Treason Act came to a somewhat anticlimactic conclusion, other cases questioning the validity of Virginia laws that conflicted with the state constitution soon followed. Just a few months later, the executive council (of which John Marshall was a member) refused to implement a statute that authorized it to investigate state judges, announcing that the law "is repugnant to the Act of Government, contrary to the fundamental principle of our constitution." Edmund Randolph was less certain that it was proper for an executive body to declare laws void and unenforceable, but the action stood.[43] A few years later, the judges of the court of appeals informed the legislature that they would not comply with a new statute requiring them to take on additional trial court duties. They were in agreement that "the constitution and the act are in opposition and cannot exist together; and that the former must control the operation of the latter." They thought the "supremacy of the constitution" was self-evident and, in any case, had been repeatedly recognized "in the opinion of the legislature themselves."[44] A few years after that, the Virginia judges again asserted their independence to defy judicial reorganization by the legislature, and again, the judges were unified in claiming that statutes violating the constitution could not be enforced.[45] Judge Thomas Nelson emphasized that a constitution "is to the *governors*, or rather to the departments of *government*, what a *law* is to individuals" and sought to normalize the power of judicial review.[46]

> I do not consider the judiciary as the champion of the people, or of the Constitution, bound to sound the alarm, and to excite an opposition to the legislature—But, when the cases of individuals are brought before them judicially, they are bound to decide.
>   And if one man claim under an act contrary to the Constitution, that is, under what is *no* law . . . must not a court give judgment against him?[47]

There was nothing novel about the task of examining potential conflicts of law and determining whether legal directives "*be in force* or *not in force*, or in other words, whether it be a *law* or *not*."[48] Spencer Roane, who would later become a leading figure in Jeffersonian politics in Virginia, insisted that "if the legislature may infringe this Constitution, it is no longer fixed; it is not this year what it was the last; and the liberties of the people are wholly at the mercy of the legislature." If legislatures "have not power to change the fundamental laws," then "would you have [judges] to shut their eyes against the law which is of the highest authority of any."[49]

Unlike Rhode Island, Virginia had a written constitution. Several Virginia judges, when called on to evaluate the constitutionality of a legislative act, emphasized the importance of the fixed terms of the constitution as a barrier to legislative manipulation. The judges still faced a potential complication, however, since Virginia's 1776 constitution had been adopted by the revolutionary state assembly rather than by a distinct constitutional convention. Thomas Jefferson pointedly argued that this origin rendered the constitution defective, stripping it of its fundamental status above the legislature and ordinary law and suggesting that an "ordinary legislature" could make or alter the constitution.[50] Such concerns might suggest that new statutes conflicting with the old constitution should simply be regarded as amendments, rather than repugnant acts that could be declared void. The judges paused to consider such objections but decided the constitution was best understood as fundamental, not ordinary, law. The revolutionary legislature itself was not an ordinary legislature; rather, it was "a spontaneous assemblage of the people of Virginia . . . to consult for the good of themselves, and their posterity." They adopted not only a constitution "evidently designed to be permanent" but also a bill of rights "purporting to appertain to their posterity." Most important, even though the constitution was not formally ratified, it "is sanctioned by the consent and acquiescence of the people" over the course of many years and was treated by both the people and the legislature itself as a law "of superior authority to any opposing act of the legislature."[51] The state constitution had attained the status of a fundamental law, even if those who drafted it "were new and unexperienced, in the science of government."[52]

In the years after independence, state courts across the country assumed that unconstitutional statutes were void and that judges had the proper authority to declare this to be the case.[53] Sometimes, as in Virginia, the arguments on behalf of judicial power and the limits on legislative authority were made explicitly and at length. Elsewhere, the idea of judicial review nearly went without saying. In Pennsylvania, the state attorney general defended a municipal ordinance before the state supreme court by arguing that the judges should give "every legal presumption . . . in favor of the constitutionality of the acts of the legislature" and strike down laws only in a "clear case." The judges cut him off and urged him to move along to other points, observing that the "law is clearly so" with regard to the standard that must be met before "we can declare a law void."[54] In South Carolina, the court noted, "It is clear, that statutes passed against the plain and obvious principles of common right, and common reason, are absolutely null and void, as *far as they are calculated to operate against those principles.*" By declining to apply the act in question to the party in that case, the court avoided doing "so much injustice" to the legislature by not supposing "it was their intention" to violate fundamental principles of law and justice.[55] The new state of Kentucky was unusual in specifying within the text of its constitutional declaration of rights that those rights "shall forever remain inviolate; and that all laws contrary thereto, or contrary to this constitution, shall be void."[56] The Kentucky Supreme Court quickly found several statutes related to juries and otherwise "clearly unconstitutional" and therefore void.[57] In New Hampshire, a county court explained that a statute that purported to overturn the result of a court decision was unconstitutional and therefore "ineffectual and inadmissible" in court.[58] The new state courts, bolstered by both formal and practical independence from the legislature and faced with a fundamental law that was understood to bind the legislature itself, repeatedly concluded that they had a responsibility to regard statutes passed in violation of constitutional requirements as "void" and "ineffectual" and unenforceable in any courtroom.

Constituting a New National Government

By the summer of 1787, when the Philadelphia Convention met to draft a new federal constitution, the judicial power to interpret written constitutions and set aside conflicting legislative acts was widely, if not universally, assumed. That is not to say that the power of judicial review was widely or well understood or regarded as a relatively important part of the American constitutional scheme. So far, many of the judicial declarations of such a power had been low-visibility affairs, and in some cases the judicial opinions had not even been reported. Judges were most often asked to assess the constitutionality and applicability of laws when the statute in question directly interfered with the judicial process itself and the legal rights of the parties that came before the courts. They had not exercised a wide-ranging veto over general matters of public policy.

Nonetheless, across the twentieth century, debates raged over whether the power of judicial review was intended by the constitutional framers or whether it was a later usurpation by an ambitious Supreme Court. In particular, scholars and activists have pointed to the rather thin record of discussion of any such power at the Philadelphia Convention as an indication that the judicial power to declare laws unconstitutional and void was unanticipated by those who drafted and ratified the Constitution and should not be understood as part of its original design. At the turn of the twentieth century, Progressive lawyer Joseph P. Cotton asserted that "the existence of [a judicial power to declare acts of Congress unconstitutional] was denied by every other branch of the government and by the dominant majority of the country," and "no such power had been clearly anticipated by the framers of the constitution."[59] Socialist activist Louis B. Boudin concluded that a "careful examination of all the evidence on the subject now extant leads to the conclusion that the Constitution was adopted by the Philadelphia Convention, and ratified by the people of the states, without any belief, without even a suspicion on the part of the great majority of those voting for it . . . that it contained any such implications."[60] As the Warren Court was being formed, iconoclastic University of Chicago Law School professor William Crosskey revived the thesis and argued at great length that "the situation seems very clear: judicial review was not meant to be provided generally in the Constitution, as to acts of Congress."[61]

Such doubts were met with an extended response, and even many critics of the Court's exercise of judicial review acknowledged that the historical evidence favored the existence of such a power embedded in the constitutional scheme. Even so, the case in favor of judicial review is not entirely straightforward. Edward S. Corwin admitted, "it seems fairly certain that the framers of the Constitution did not expressly confer upon the federal courts the power to question the validity of federal legislation." But he thought the power was implicit in "a certain theory of government, embodied in the Constitution itself," and "the logic of a certain way of looking at the relation of the individual to government."[62] William M. Meigs more boldly concluded, "it was expected and intended, both by the Federal Convention and the opinion of publicists of the day," that the Court would exercise the power of judicial review against Congress.[63] Charles Beard mounted an effort to identify the views of each member of the constitutional convention, and he concluded that a majority were aware of and favored the power of judicial review delegated to the Supreme Court—a result he found clearly consistent with the antidemocratic, pro-property orientation of the Federalists.[64] Harvard Law School's eminent Henry M. Hart was less polite in responding to Crosskey's effort to resuscitate the Progressive-Era argument, dismissing the "Don Quixote of Chicago" as having "constructed a never-never world of his own" that was "rendered plausible only by a confident tone, nice printing, and an abundance of notes and appendices."[65] In the aftermath of the Crosskey imbroglio, Alexander Bickel concluded, "it is as clear as such matters can be that the Framers of the Constitution specifically, if tacitly, expected that the federal courts would assume a power . . . to pass on the constitutionality of actions of the Congress and the President, as well as of the several states."[66]

The goal here is to acknowledge but not to rehash that debate.[67] On the whole, the conclusions to be drawn from the historical evidence largely depend on how to interpret silences (there were no serious objections to the language or design of the Constitution from those who might have doubted the power of judicial review) and inferences from structure, purpose, and conceptual background (the belief in a limited government constrained by a constitutional text was widespread). The immediate problem confronting the framers was how to control the states, and on that issue, they were fairly explicit in empowering judges to strike down state laws that were inconsistent with the requirements of the new federal constitution. The problem of unconstitutional laws that might emerge from Congress was less pressing and therefore less discussed, but there is little reason to think that judicial review was not among the contemplated solutions to that problem as well.

References to judicial review at the Philadelphia Convention were relatively few.[68] Edmund Randolph, who had helped usher in judicial review in the state courts of Virginia, introduced the Virginia Plan, which launched the convention's deliberations on a new constitutional scheme. William Paterson's notes on the convention debates include an intriguing entry about the introduction of the Virginia Plan, separating the proposal for creating a national judiciary under the heading "Checks upon the Legv. And Ex. Powers."[69] Judicial review is not the only way the delegates could have understood the courts' role in checking the legislature, but the reference at least suggests that the initial presentation of the Virginia Plan implied judicial review.[70]

More substantive were the discussions surrounding the Virginia Plan's proposal to create a council of revision. The council would consist of the president and a number of judges, and it would have a qualified veto power over proposed legislation. When this part of the plan was taken up for debate, it met with significant opposition. It was in this context that several members objected that judges should not participate in a body that could veto laws because judges were *already* empowered to strike down laws that were unconstitutional or infringed on judicial power. Elbridge Gerry of Massachusetts explicitly referred to examples of judicial review that had already occurred in the states and noted that judges "will have a sufficient check agst. encroachments on their own department by their exposition of the laws, which involved a power of deciding on their Constitutionality."[71] Rufus King of New York likewise thought the power to "stop the operation" of laws that violated the Constitution was implicit in judges' duty of "expounding . . . those Lawes."[72] Luther Martin of Maryland was similarly explicit in arguing that the "Constitutionality of laws" would "come before the Judges in their proper official character," and putting judges on a council of revision would be redundant and give them "a double negative."[73] Notably, the rebuttal by proponents of the council of revision did not question whether judges would void unconstitutional laws. Instead, they argued that the qualified veto by the council of revision was broader than judges' authority in their judicial capacity and would serve as additional security against legislative abuses. James Wilson of Pennsylvania (and a future Supreme Court justice) pointed out that judicial review as such would provide no protection against laws that were "unjust . . . unwise . . . dangerous [or] destructive, and yet not be so unconstitutional as to justify the Judges in refusing to give them effect"; the council's veto power would "prevent the passage of an improper law" and not merely "declare it void" sometime after passage.[74] George Mason and James Madison backed Wilson's argument.[75] The idea of a council of revision was eventually abandoned, and the qualified veto over legislation was transferred to the president acting alone. The delegates preferred to keep the executive and the judiciary completely independent and not to involve judges in the role of policy-maker, evaluating which legislative proposals would be imprudent and which would be beneficial.

The mixed discussion of a council of revision and judicial review illuminates how the power of judicial review was conceptualized at the time. The council of revision was an explicitly political body designed to act as a constitutional check on Congress. As such, it was seen as a way to block ill-considered policy proposals and to arm the other branches against legislative encroachments on their proper powers and institutional prerogatives. By contrast, the power to invalidate unconstitutional laws was characterized not as a special power or right of the judiciary but as an intrinsic feature of its work in "expositing" the law. In determining what the law is and applying it to individual cases, judges would necessarily have to set aside statutes that purported to repeal or amend parts of the Constitution or otherwise contradicted constitutional requirements. Getting the law right means, in part, keeping the effective law consistent with the terms of the Constitution. Saying what the law *is* entails reconciling apparent contradictions in the law and subordinating statutory provisions to constitutional provisions.

This legal orientation toward the power of judicial review was further emphasized when the convention later turned its attention to other features of the Constitution.[76] When William Johnson of Connecticut proposed adding cases arising under "this Constitution" to the jurisdiction of the Supreme Court, Madison objected that this might imply that the Court would be "expounding the Constitution in cases not of [a Judiciary Nature]."[77] The delegates nonetheless unanimously approved the change, with the understanding that it applied only to cases of a judicial nature. Whether the Court would interpret and apply the Constitution along with other federal laws was not in dispute; the only question was whether the Court might be asked to interpret the Constitution in mere political controversies. In considering the proper ratification procedures for the proposed Constitution, Madison was insistent that ratification be by "the people themselves" in popular conventions rather than by state legislatures, as the Articles of Confederation had been. A "treaty" like the Articles of Confederation could be unmade by the same body that had adopted it in the first place; if a state legislature passed a law in contradiction to a measure it had previously adopted, courts would give effect to the new law. By contrast, if the Constitution were adopted by the people, later legislatures would have no authority to contradict it. Such conflicting statutes "would be considered by the Judges as null & void."[78] When considering whether to include a prohibition of ex post facto laws, Oliver Ellsworth of Connecticut thought an explicit prohibition was unnecessary because such laws were "void of themselves" and thus would not be accepted as valid legislation by any competent court. North Carolina's Hugh Williamson pointed out that his state's constitution included such a provision, and it had proved useful "because the Judges can take hold of it."[79] Both seemed to think that judges would necessarily set aside ex post facto laws as invalid, but Williamson believed an explicit textual provision might embolden judges to stand up to an errant legislature.

The inclusion of the supremacy clause in the Constitution should also be noted. The Virginia Plan included a proposal that Congress have the power "to negative all laws passed by the several States, contravening in the opinion of the National Legislature the articles of Union."[80] Although Madison thought such a veto power was essential to the success of the union, the proposal proved controversial and was voted down. The debate soon exposed the fact that most delegates thought the courts already had such a power. As Roger Sherman of Connecticut put it, the proposal implied that a state law that was contrary to the Constitution would, "if not negative, be valid &

operational." But if the system were functioning properly, as Pennsylvania's Gouverneur Morris noted, such a law would be "set aside by the Judiciary department" without the need for Congress to take any action.[81] Rather than Madison's national veto, the delegates preferred Luther Martin's supremacy clause, which simply made explicit the common assumption that state and federal judges were bound to apply federal law where appropriate, "any thing in the respective laws of the individual States to the contrary notwithstanding."[82] As the final version of the supremacy clause made even clearer, state laws that were inconsistent with the Constitution would be declared void by the courts as part of their routine duties of correctly identifying and applying valid law to the cases before them. Although the convention delegates more explicitly addressed judicial review of state laws under the federal Constitution, the logic of their discussion of the supremacy clause was of a piece with their understanding of the judicial power vis-à-vis congressional statutes. The implications of adopting a written constitution for the judicial resolution of ordinary cases that had been elaborated by state court judges was well understood by the delegates to the Philadelphia Convention as well.[83]

The events after Philadelphia did little to counter the assumption that judicial review of the constitutionality of federal statutes was built into the constitutional design. Outside the convention, courts' authority to evaluate the constitutionality of federal laws was assumed—and promoted—by Federalists and anti-Federalists alike.[84] In North Carolina, James Iredell was promoting the idea of judicial review to the state courts and also trying to convince skeptical convention delegate Richard Spaight. Spaight feared the claimed power would operate as essentially an absolute veto on the legislature. Iredell responded, "[it] really appears to me, the exercise of the power is unavoidable, the Constitution not being a mere imaginary thing, about which ten thousand opinions may be formed, but a written document to which all may have recourse, and to which, therefore, the judges cannot willfully blind themselves."[85] In Virginia, John Marshall assured anti-Federalists that if Congress exceeded its delegated powers, "it would be considered by the judges as an infringement of the Constitution . . . [and they] would declare it void."[86] When anti-Federalists doubted the effectiveness of the courts' check on Congress, James Wilson reassured them that when a federal law inconsistent with the Constitution came to the courts to be applied to a citizen, the judges would find that "it is their duty to pronounce it void."[87] In

Connecticut, Oliver Ellsworth explained, "[if] the United States go beyond their powers, if they make a law which the Constitution does not authorize, it is void; and the judicial power, the national judges, who to secure their impartiality are to be made independent, will declare it to be void."[88] Of course, in New York, Alexander Hamilton penned his famous *Federalist* essay both explaining the power of judicial review and quieting fears of judicial abuse by assuring skeptics that the judiciary would be the "least dangerous branch." His antagonist, "Brutus," likewise assumed that the Court would exercise the power of judicial review but feared that the result would only increase congressional power.[89]

The First Congress expected the courts to assess the constitutionality of its actions. Thomas Jefferson had urged James Madison to embrace a Bill of Rights for the new federal constitution because of "the legal check which it puts into the hands of the judiciary."[90] Language such as that in the First Amendment declaring that "Congress shall make no law" fed directly into the explicit prohibitions on legislative action that proponents of judicial review had argued would trigger a judicial duty to void repugnant acts.

Perhaps even more important was passage of the Judiciary Act of 1789, organizing the federal courts and establishing their jurisdiction. The statute created a federal court system capable of engaging in judicial review and enforcing and expanding on its constitutional decision-making.[91] Of particular relevance for how judicial review was imagined and accepted at the time of the founding was section 25 of that statute. Section 25 was intermittently controversial during the first few decades of the country's existence because it allowed appeals from the state supreme courts to the US Supreme Court, thereby casting the state supreme courts in the role of inferior courts within an overarching national judicial system and authorizing the US Supreme Court to reverse decisions by the states' high courts. An older Spencer Roane, who had helped established judicial review in Virginia and likely would have been Thomas Jefferson's choice to fill John Marshall's seat on the Supreme Court, was particularly vocal in his denunciations of section 25.[92] But more specifically, section 25 gave the US Supreme Court jurisdiction to hear cases in certain circumstances:

[When a state supreme court had] drawn in question the validity of a treaty or statute of, or an authority exercised under the United States, and the decision is against their validity; or where is drawn in question the validity of a statute of, or an authority exercised under any State, on the ground of their being repugnant to the constitution, treaties or laws of the United States, and the decision is in favour of such their validity, or where is drawn in question the construction of any clause of the constitution, or of a treaty, or statute of, or commission held under the United States, and the decision is against the title, right, privilege or exemption specially set up or claimed by either party, under such clause of the said Constitution, treaty, statute or commission.[93]

The statute, chiefly drafted by Oliver Ellsworth in the Senate, presumed the practice of judicial review of both state and federal laws under the new US Constitution. Congress wanted to ensure that decisions striking down federal laws as unconstitutional (as well as decisions upholding state laws against federal constitutional claims) had their final resolution in the US Supreme Court, not in a state supreme court. The statute assumed that the state courts would be exercising judicial review over federal laws, and it authorized the US Supreme Court to do the same (at least in a particular set of circumstances). Moreover, the statute recognized that when the Supreme Court heard such cases, they could be "reversed or affirmed"; that is, upon reexamining the state court's decision, the US Supreme Court might either uphold *or strike down* a federal or state statute on federal constitutional grounds. Elbridge Gerry made the implications clear when he spoke on behalf of the measure in the House of Representatives: "When we have established the courts as they propose. . . . Will they not attend to the Constitution as well as your laws? The Constitution will undoubtedly be their first rule; and so far as your laws conform to that, they will attend to them, but no further."[94] No one in Congress appeared to disagree with the basic point that the courts would consider the constitutionality of federal statutes and set aside those that violated the terms of the Constitution.[95]

Similar assumptions were made outside of Congress. James Wilson was one of the first justices of the US Supreme Court, and shortly thereafter, he was also appointed the first law professor at what would become the University of Pennsylvania. In a series of published lectures, he instructed his students that, in "our system of jurisprudence," it was "incontrovertible" that the Constitution was the "supreme law" and subjected the legislature to its control. If the "legislature should pass an act, manifestly repugnant to some part of the constitution; and . . . the operation and validity of both should come regularly in question before a court," it would be "the right and it is the duty of the court to decide upon them" and determine what is to be "the law of the land." It would necessarily be the case that the "contradictory rule" issued by "a subordinate power" (Congress) would be "void, and has no operation." As a result, "every transgression of those [constitutional] bounds shall be adjudged and rendered vain and fruitless. What a noble guard against legislative despotism!"[96] The federal circuit courts quickly got to work striking down state laws that conflicted with their understanding of the requirements of the US Constitution.[97] The most famous of these cases was *Vanhorne's Lessee v. Dorrance*, which involved a Pennsylvania statute that attempted to settle a land dispute.[98] The case stood out in large part because Justice William Paterson (while performing his circuit duties) issued instructions that directed the jury to find in favor of the plaintiff, and those instructions were published by the Supreme Court reporter. Paterson's instructions focused on the unconstitutionality of the Pennsylvania statute. He explained to the jurors at great length that legislatures in the United States did not possess the "absolute and transcendent" power of the English Parliament but were instead bound by the "permanent will of the people" as represented in the "fundamental law" of the Constitution, which is "paramount to the power of the legislature."

> The constitution is the work or will of the people themselves, in their original, sovereign, and unlimited capacity. Law is the work or will of the legislature in their derivative and subordinate capacity. The one is the work of the creator, and the other of the creature. The constitution fixes limits to the exercise of legislative authority, and prescribes the orbit within which it must move. In short, gentlemen, the constitution is the sun of the political system, around which all legislative, executive and judicial bodies must revolve. Whatever may be the case in other countries, yet in this there can be no doubt, that every act of the legislature, repugnant to the constitution, is absolutely void.[99]

Paterson's explanation of the power of judicial review and the courts' duty to void statutes that violate the Constitution was among the most cited authorities on the subject in the early nineteenth century, often eclipsing *Marbury* itself.[100]

Vanhorne's Lessee and section 25 of the Judiciary Act of 1789 are useful reminders that the constitutional logic that supported the judicial power to review state laws was not sharply separated from the constitutional logic of horizontal review of a coordinate legislature. For the Federalists who mobilized to reform the Articles of Confederation in the 1780s, the problem of states ignoring their responsibilities and commitment to the federal constitution was one of the central threats to the stability and independence of the republic. For that reason, imposing some controls on the states to better enforce federal constitutional requirements was a priority. Even so, it quickly became apparent to those who were engaged in such matters that the adoption of written constitutions resting on the firm foundation of popular sovereignty would empower judges to monitor and correct legislative abuses. As judges went about their business of expositing the law, they could not help but note when a statute was "unconstitutional and repugnant to the Law of the Land."[101] As an attorney in Rhode Island argued in the year of the Philadelphia Convention:

> Have the Judges a power to repeal, to amend, to alter laws, or to make new laws?—God forbid!—In that case they would become Legislators—Have the Legislators power to direct the Judges how they shall determine upon the laws already made?—God forbid!—In that case they would become Judges.—The true distinction lies in this, that the Legislative have the incontroulable power of making laws not repugnant to the constitution: — The Judiciary have the sole power of judging of those laws, and are bound to execute them; but cannot admit any act of the Legislative as law, which is against the constitution.[102]

3

Exercising Judicial Review before the Civil War

There is a standard story about the exercise of the power of judicial review by the US Supreme Court before the Civil War. In that story, the Court was focused on establishing the Constitution's, the federal government's, and the federal judiciary's supremacy over the states. It was a time for contracts, commerce, and limitations on state power. Judicial review of Congress was exceptional and idiosyncratic. There was *Marbury v. Madison* in 1803, Chief Justice John Marshall's great maneuver to establish the power of judicial review,[1] and then there was *Dred Scott v. Sandford* in 1857, Chief Justice Roger Taney's great folly that attempted to impose a pro-slavery reading on the Constitution and instead became the Court's "self-inflicted wound."[2]

The standard story is wrong. The US Supreme Court was more active in exercising its power to interpret the Constitution and limit the legislative authority of Congress than is conventionally recognized. *Marbury* and *Dred Scott* were the tips of the iceberg of federal judicial review, not the entire edifice. They were, to be sure, among the most politically contentious uses of that power by the Court during the early republic and thus among the most historically memorable. But the highlight reel is not the game itself.

Current accounts of the political development of judicial review of Congress are somewhat schizophrenic. On the one hand, they emphasize a "big bang" theory of the establishment of judicial review, in which the wily Chief Justice John Marshall "created" or "established" the power of judicial review in the single case of *Marbury v.*

Madison. On the other hand, current accounts suggest that the judicial power to check the other branches of the federal government went unused for two generations until the Court foolishly attempted to impose a pro-slavery settlement on the territory question and was repudiated at the polls in 1860.

Neither account is true. The power of judicial review developed gradually during the first half of the nineteenth century, facilitating the goals of national political actors and consolidating the Court's claimed ability to define the institutional limits of congressional power. This chapter advances recent efforts to understand how the power of judicial review has been politically constructed through the back-and-forth dialogue between the branches over time, rather than through one-time, unilateral doctrinal assertions by the Court.[3] *Marbury* was not the big bang, and *Dred Scott* was not a bolt from the blue. The process of institutionalizing the power of judicial review could not be achieved in a day, and it could not be achieved by the unilateral dictate of the Court. Judicial review by the US Supreme Court was routinized long before *Dred Scott.*

Understanding the extent to which the federal courts had become a forum for raising and resolving constitutional objections to federal legislation by the 1850s clarifies how *Dred Scott* occurred, whereas conventional narratives do not. *Dred Scott* was unusual on some dimensions. For instance, the Court ruled against congressional power in a high-profile and politically salient case, which had not been its general pattern during this period. But the Court *had* established itself as an institution engaged in the task of constitutional interpretation and the enforcement of constitutional limitations against Congress. There is no doubt that political actors were deeply engaged in constitutional interpretation in the early republic, but we would be wrong to conclude that the Court played no role in that process.[4]

The Jacksonian Democrats are regularly portrayed as hostile to judicial power and deeply committed to political rule by popular majorities. Given these assumptions, *Dred Scott* looks all the more anomalous. The Taney Court is seen as departing from its ideological commitment to judicial deference to advance the contingent interests of the slave power by striking down the federal ban on slavery in the western territories. But the Jacksonian Democrats were not so deeply committed to judicial deference, and the Taney Court was not so unfamiliar with the Court's power to strike down legislation.[5] The apparent judicial activism of *Dred Scott* was prefigured by an extended antebellum engagement with the possibility of using the federal courts to advance constitutional objectives.

The *Marbury* and *Dred Scott* pairing is misleading in other ways as well. Both cases have generally been presented within a political narrative that is familiar from the twentieth century. John Marshall is portrayed as a lonely Federalist standing firm against Jeffersonian political majorities, while loyal Jacksonian Democrat Roger Taney is depicted as striking out against the ascending Republican insurgency. The Supreme Court of the first decades of the nineteenth century is characterized as the same kind of partisan, countermajoritarian institution the Populists and Progressives railed against in the first decades of the twentieth century. Its judicial activism might have occurred as isolated events, but it is thought to reflect the Supreme Court's basic nature.

Neither Court should be understood in such partisan countermajoritarian terms. As Mark Graber has emphasized, for much of its existence the Marshall Court was more National Republican than Federalist. Rather than inexplicably surviving as a Federalist fragment within a Jeffersonian political world, the Marshall Court found numerous allies within the Jeffersonian coalition, particularly after the War of 1812, as the Jeffersonians splintered into more and less orthodox factions. John Marshall spent his judicial career more as the friend of Jeffersonian John Quincy Adams than as the avatar of Federalist John Adams, and this made both a political and a constitutional difference.[6] Neither the Marshall nor the Taney Court exercised judicial review primarily by launching itself against the legislative policy achievements of partisan foes. Neither stood as a significant veto point that was likely to obstruct the legislative efforts of unified political majorities. Both Courts exercised the power of judicial review, but they usually did so in ways that defied partisan labels.

There were sixty-two cases between 1789 and 1861 in which the US Supreme Court substantively evaluated the constitutionality of a federal statutory provision. The Court struck down or imposed constitutional limitations on the applicable scope of the federal law at issue in 32 percent of those cases. This is actually a somewhat higher percentage of invalidation in cases involving a constitutional challenge than is true for the Court's history as a whole (26 percent). Defining and enforcing the scope of congressional legislative authority was a routine part of the Court's business from early in the nineteenth century.

The early Court, however, heard fewer constitutional cases involving the authority of Congress than did later Courts, and the cases in which the Court limited congressional power generally had less political salience and substantive importance than in subsequent eras. It is not entirely surprising that the Court exercised judicial review against Congress less often in this early period. Both Congress and the Court were less active in the early decades of American history than they would become in later decades. The legislative output of Congress was lower, and the Court's docket was smaller. However, the Court actually struck down a higher percentage of federal statutory provisions in those early years than it would in the twentieth century (see figure 1-1). Nonetheless, judicial review cases occupied a small proportion of the Court's docket, and the relatively small number of such cases meant that the Court might go years without even hearing a challenge to a federal law, let alone striking one down. Even so, once the Court was fully operational and hearing cases on a regular basis, it resolved multiple cases every decade, and in only a single decade did it fail to strike down a law. In the 1810s the Court heard only three challenges and did not rule against Congress in any of those cases—a streak that continued through much of the 1820s. From the perspective of the late Jeffersonian period, one might be forgiven for thinking that judicial review of Congress was a negligible aspect of the constitutional scheme and mostly a thing of the past. In the Jacksonian years, however, such a conclusion would seem quite outdated.

The Court heard and decided constitutional challenges to federal legislation throughout the period from its inception through secession. Instances of the Court invalidating or narrowing statutory provisions were interspersed with decisions upholding provisions. Even so, the pace of judicial review increased over time. Prior to the 1820s the Court, on average, decided less than one case per year in which it reviewed the constitutionality of an application of a federal law. After that, the Court averaged one case per year, and this increased after the 1840s. The Court's invalidation and narrowing of statutes followed a similar pattern. At the beginning and end of the period, the Court held applications of the law unconstitutional in a higher proportion of cases than it did in the middle of the period. But even in those years, the Court upheld federal laws more often than not. The Taney Court exercised the power of judicial review more often, but on the whole, it was not more or less deferential than its predecessors.

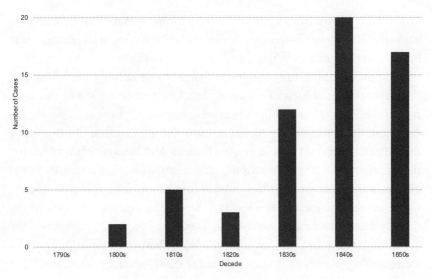

Figure 3-1: Cases of Judicial Review of Congress by Lower Federal Courts, 1789–1859

A similar story is told in figure 3-1, which reports the number of federal circuit court and district court cases explicitly evaluating the constitutionality of a federal law. The record here is less comprehensive, not least because lower court decisions were less reliably reported than Supreme Court opinions. It is also true that the same issue might generate multiple decisions in the lower courts, as different judges in different circuits and different levels of the judiciary struggled with a question. Two features of figure 3-1 are particularly notable. First, cases involving the lower courts' review of federal legislation emerged quite early. Lawyers challenged the constitutionality of applying federal law to their clients, and federal judges felt obliged to address those challenges in formal opinions. The number of cases raising such issues in the Jeffersonian period was small, but they attempted to resolve a number of questions, including the constitutionality of the Jeffersonian embargo,[7] the scope of congressional authority to grant patents,[8] the enlistment of minors in the US Navy,[9] and the fugitive slave acts.[10] Second, the number of cases rose dramatically in the Jacksonian period. The lower courts were active across a range of issues during this period, but they found themselves entangled in heated controversies over the constitutionality of the fugitive slave law[11] and bankruptcy law provisions.[12] Although federal judges in the lower courts almost always upheld congressional power in these cases, by the time of *Dred Scott*, the federal judiciary had already spent two decades as an active battleground over the constitutional limitations on Congress, including a fairly organized effort by antislavery advocates to draw the courts into antebellum slave politics.

The Supreme Court's review of the constitutionality of federal legislation occurred in the context of an early and expanding theory and practice of judicial review of state legislation. Judges in more than thirty cases in the state and federal courts had concluded that the statutes before them were unconstitutional prior to the 1803 *Marbury* decision.[13] Judicial review in the states spread and grew in the first decades of the early republic.[14] Influential political actors were supportive of a judicial power to restrict legislative power in the name of upholding constitutional constraints.[15] The US Supreme Court soon became quite active in enforcing constitutional limits on the states, and this particular use of judicial review was both politically salient and valued by national political elites in the early republic.[16] Nonetheless, the standard account is that the Supreme Court generally refrained from evaluating the constitutionality of the acts of the national legislature during this period. It is certainly the case that the Court began to review federal laws more frequently and to issue more politically salient invalidations after the Civil War, but litigants and commentators understood throughout the early republic that the Court could and did enforce constitutional limitations against Congress.

Judicial Review before *Marbury*

The US Supreme Court was asked to consider the constitutional limitations on congressional power to make legislation in a handful of cases in the 1790s, and it was willing to hear those challenges and impose limits on congressional authority. Nearly all these cases involved questions affecting the judiciary itself—its powers and jurisdiction under the Constitution—but they were not limited to such cases, and the Court gave no indication that its power to interpret the Constitution and evaluate the constitutionality of federal laws depended on whether the cases raised such issues. But in these early cases, the justices provided little explanation or justification for their exercise of this power to interpret the Constitution and refuse to apply laws in circumstances that, in their opinion, exceeded the constitutional authority of Congress. Constitutional issues simply arose and were disposed of in the course of ordinary litigation, without special comment. The constitutional rulings were not always prominent to the case or of substantial political significance. In no case in the Federalist era did the Court mount a frontal challenge to congressional policy. It either upheld congressional authority against the challenge of political opponents or made marginal adjustments to statutes that left plenty of room for Congress to achieve its policy objectives. In doing so, the Court both built up the power of the national state and protected the independence and authority of the judiciary within the state.

The first case in which the US Supreme Court apparently resolved a constitutional question involving the legislative authority of Congress went unreported. The Court concluded that the statutory provision at issue was constitutionally invalid and that any actions taken under it were void. The decision in *United States v. Yale Todd* was not unexpected, and the suit itself was an amicable one designed simply to resolve the legal matter so the government could get on with the task of settling its accounts.[17]

Yale Todd stands at the end of a series of federal court decisions involving the Invalid Pensions Act of 1792 and its 1793 revisions.[18] The Invalid Pensions Act established benefits for veterans who had been injured in service during the American Revolution and created a procedure for claimants to apply for benefits through the federal circuit courts. The circuit court judges would investigate claims and make recommendations to the secretary of war, who would confirm whether an injured individual had in fact served in the military and decide whether to enter the claimant's name on the pension rolls. The rolls would then be forwarded to Congress for action. The circuit judges, including the Supreme Court justices serving in their respective circuits, decided that, consistent with the Constitution, federal judges qua judges could not perform this duty.[19]

Most famously, the circuit court in Philadelphia refused to carry the act into effect in *Hayburn's Case*, but it declined to issue a decision and opinion in that case. Instead, the judges and justices expressed their constitutional objections to President George Washington in a formal letter, as other circuit courts had done. They observed that the "business directed by this act is not of a judicial nature. It forms no part of the power vested by the Constitution in the courts of the United States." Under the act, the decision of the circuit court judges could be "revised and controlled by the legislature, and by an officer in the executive department. Such revision and control we deemed radically inconsistent with the independence of the judicial which vested in the courts."[20] Although the Philadelphia judges refused to process veterans' claims, the judges in some circuits, including Connecticut, agreed to act in their private capacity as "commissioners."[21] Perhaps rankled by press criticism that the "humane purposes of Congress" were being thwarted by the constitutional objections of well-fed judges who did not appreciate the condition of the "feeble, war-worn veteran," even Justice James Iredell in the southern circuit reconciled himself to "doing invalid business out of Court."[22] Attorney General Edmund Randolph petitioned the Supreme Court to take action in *Hayburn's Case*, but the Court held it over without issuing an opinion, giving Congress time to revise the statute.[23] With the justices united on the unconstitutionality of the original statutory provision and generally unwilling to implement the act, Congress modified the law to remedy the constitutional objection. The Supreme Court never took up the attorney general's motion in *Hayburn's Case* or rendered a judgment.

In 1793 Congress repealed the offending provision of the 1792 act, but it added a new provision preserving the validity of any rights established under the old procedures. Since some of the circuit court judges had initially agreed to serve in their private, voluntary capacity as pension "commissioners," some petitioners' claims had been processed under the 1792 act, and Congress directed the secretary of war and the attorney general "to take such measures as may be necessary to obtain an adjudication of the supreme court of the United States on the validity of any such rights claimed under the act."[24] By 1794, Attorney General William Bradford figured out how to get the issue before the Supreme Court. In 1792 Yale Todd had successfully petitioned the commissioners for the district of Connecticut to add his name to the pension rolls. In an "amicable action," the United States sought to recover the $172.99 Todd had received thus far from the government. The Court unanimously ruled in favor of the government's action, holding invalid the process by which Todd had established his right to the pension.[25] Although the opinion was not recorded, Chief Justice Taney drew the likely inference decades later: "The power proposed to be conferred on the Circuit Courts of the United States by the act of 1792 was not judicial power within the meaning of the Constitution, and was, therefore, unconstitutional, and could not lawfully be exercised by the courts."[26] Congress concluded the affair by enrolling Todd and other "unfortunate claimants" who had been "rejected solely for a defect in point of form, and . . . [are] again compelled to incur the expense of supporting their claims before another tribunal," on the pension rolls.[27]

There is little question that the justices as a group regarded the Invalid Pensions Act of 1792 as unconstitutional and not legally binding on them. The *American Daily Advertiser* contemporaneously reported that *Hayburn's Case* marked the "first instance in which a Court of Justice had declared an act of Congress to be unconstitutional," the "novelty" of which produced quite a bit of unreported debate in Congress on how best to respond.[28] The circuit courts' action on the pension law led some emerging proto-Republican papers to hail the "wise and independent" members of the judicial branch in exercising their "noble prerogative" of "declaring an act of the present session of Congress, unconstitutional" and to hope that those judges would next turn their attention to "any existing law of Congress which may be supposed to trench upon the constitutional rights of individuals or of States," such as the National Bank bill recently adopted over the strong opposition of James Madison and Thomas Jefferson.[29] Regardless of the "merits of the particular question," the judges' actions were pleasing to the Jeffersonians simply because they effectuated "another resource admitted by the Constitution for its own defense, and for the security of the rights which it guarantees to the several States and to individual citizens."[30] Although some Federalists such as Fisher Ames complained that the pension law decisions, "generally censured as indiscreet and erroneous," would only embolden the "States and their Courts" in their lack of respect for the "authority of Congress," the judicial actions were readily accommodated.[31] Yale Todd and his fellow veterans still got their pensions.

Ultimately, because there is no record of an opinion in *Yale Todd* itself, it can only be inferred that the Court's grounds for its holding were the constitutional arguments elaborated by the justices two years earlier. Chief Justice Taney accepted that inference when he took note of the case.[32] *Hayburn's Case* and *Yale Todd* are the first two cases listed in the quasi-official table of cases holding federal statutes unconstitutional in the appendix to the 131st volume of *U.S. Reports*.[33] Some later commentators, including Justice Samuel Miller and Solicitor General William Marshall Bullitt, readily integrated the two cases as standing for the constitutional rule that Congress cannot impose a nonjudicial duty on federal judges.[34] James Bradley Thayer, however, dismissed as "inaccurate" the view that *Yale Todd* was decided on constitutional grounds, concluding instead that the case involved the statutory question of whether circuit court judges could process pension claims as "commissioners" (an office that was not mentioned in the statute), given their refusal to process them as judges.[35] Others have followed this interpretation, finding it plausible that the Court avoided the constitutional issue and resolved the case on the lesser statutory issue.[36] This interpretation was certainly consistent with the pleadings, which asked whether "Said judges of S^d Circuit Court Sitting as Commissioners and not as a Circuit Court had power & Authority by virtue of S^d Act So to order and adjudge," as well as with the attorney general's later opinion that pension claims processed by the district judge for Maine, who had "conformed himself" to the act, were valid.[37] Ultimately, Todd's claim could have been saved if the Court had been willing to accept the judges' actions either as "commissioners" (stretching the statute) or as circuit court judges (stretching the Constitution), but it would do neither. *Yale Todd* ruled out any constitutional application of the 1792 statutory provisions in the circuit courts.[38] We cannot know what the justices might have said from the bench in 1794, but, taken as a set, the pension cases clearly show that the justices were determined to assert the institutional autonomy of the courts and refuse, on constitutional grounds, to implement federal policies that violated those foundational rules.

Equally unusual, but for different reasons, is *Penhallow v. Doane's Administrators*.[39] This case—the earliest in which the Court *upheld* a constitutional power of Congress—involved an act under the authority of the Articles of Confederation (and even before). In 1780 the Confederation Congress created a Court of Appeals in Cases of Capture, which took over the Commissioners of Appeals' jurisdiction to hear appeals from state courts of admiralty. At issue was Congress's authority "to institute such a tribunal with appellate jurisdiction in cases of prize"—specifically, to take an appeal from a case originating in New Hampshire. The New Hampshire courts had awarded a captured British ship to a group of New Hampshire citizens, but the federal Court of Appeals had reversed this ruling and given the prize to an out-of-state group. Writing seriatim, the justices in 1795 upheld congressional power in this regard. To Justice Paterson, the "powers of Congress [at that date] were revolutionary in their nature, arising out of the events, adequate to every national emergency, and co-extensive with the object to be attained." This particular power "grows out of the nature of the thing" and met with "the approbation of the people."[40] If New Hampshire objected, it could have withdrawn from the confederacy and gone its own way. Justice Iredell thought this was a more difficult case, not least because the arguments on behalf of Congress tended to suggest that "Congress had unlimited power to act at their discretion so far as the purposes of the war might require," and Iredell was unwilling to take that approach.[41] The decisive principle for him was the states' uniform consent to the powers exercised by Congress and the fact that, at the time, the states—including New Hampshire—had given their "express authority" to the exercise of this power. Justice Blair chose to emphasize that the early Congress "acted in all respects like a body completely armed with all the powers of war," and he opined that "a single expression, used perhaps in a loose sense" in the Articles of Confederation, should not create an "inference so contrary to a known fact"—namely, that the states did not truly "retain their sovereignties" prior to ratification of the articles (or the Constitution).[42] Justice Cushing objected to this denigration of the states' status, but he thought the specific matter of prize cases had been settled by prior practice.[43]

The justices had no doubt that "constitutional points" of "great importance" were at issue in this case.[44] The establishment of the Court of Appeals was a matter of substantial controversy during the war, as Congress was cross-pressured by geostrategic concerns voiced by George Washington and foreign states about gaining control over privateers and captures and by states that jealously guarded their own prerogatives to handle this profitable and emotional aspect of war.[45] The 1780 resolution was a compromise measure, creating a court that had no real enforcement powers but had nonetheless proved useful. The losing parties in such cases often carried on their political and legal battles for years, and in the post-Confederation period, national government officials were particularly eager to establish the principle that foreign policy was a national domain and that the determination of such legal rights was firmly in the hands of the courts.[46] When New Hampshire sent a memorial to Congress asking it to intervene, that petition was sent to a committee until after *Penhallow* was decided, at which point James Madison reported that the entire subject was "wholly judicial" in character and had already received a "final decision by the Supreme Court of the United States," precluding any further congressional inquiry in the matter.[47] Even so, justifying this exercise of congressional power was tricky, as the tensions among the justices evidenced. Later, National Republican commentators would pick up on the themes of Paterson's opinion as early authority for a strong national union. In 1829 Nathan Dane added an appendix to his popular abridgment of American law, responding to what he saw as Jeffersonian heresies in the form of emerging doctrines of state nullification. The national government, he argued, was established first, "on *revolutionary* principles"; only afterward were the state governments constituted in *"acknowledged subordination."*[48] This essential narrative was embraced by others, including Joseph Story and James Kent.[49] But in the politics of the 1790s, those in the national government were not about to cast doubt on the appropriateness of national judicial control over maritime cases.

The next year the Court upheld congressional authority in two more cases. *Hylton v. United States* was the first reported case of Supreme Court review of a federal statute passed under the authority of the US Constitution.[50] Moreover, it involved a contemporary case of national political significance. The pension cases were of political interest because they highlighted the power of judicial review and because of the public's sympathy for the injured war veterans affected by the controversy, but the constitutional question of whether judges could be given such duties was not a matter of political debate, and its resolution did not pose serious obstacles to achieving the legislative policy aim. There were immediate financial interests at stake in *Penhallow*, but in the 1790s there was no serious political debate over the federal power to resolve prize cases. *Hylton*, by contrast, was a partisan case, though one of only minor importance.

When asked for the first time to resolve a partisan dispute over the scope of congressional power, the Court did not hesitate to side with Congress and uphold its taxation authority. Doing so strengthened the government's hand and its newly granted power to tax, and it kept the judiciary out of potential disputes over tax policy. James Madison and the proto-Republicans in Congress objected to the adoption of a federal tax on carriages, which happened to be owned primarily by southern planters.[51] They argued that such a tax on personal property was a "direct tax," which the Constitution required be apportioned among the states by population. Despite such objections, the carriage tax passed as a stand-alone bill in a divided vote in 1794.[52] In a friendly suit designed to win an opinion from the Court to settle the controversy, the justices lent their support to the Federalist administration.[53] Although the justices admitted that the meaning of "direct tax" was obscure, and they even disagreed among themselves about its definition, they were willing to approve of the carriage tax. Reading the direct tax qualification to the federal taxing authority so broadly as to encompass the carriage tax, they argued, would be impractical and bring back the difficulties of collecting revenue from state governments.[54] As promised, the Virginians ended their tax protest and took the particular issue of the carriage tax as settled, though it remained a black mark against the Federalists and their penchant for latitudinarian constructions in the minds of the Jeffersonians.[55]

The other case that year involved a controversy arising not from the legislature but from the application of a federal law. Here, the Court upheld the use of admiralty courts to enforce embargo statutes and limited the right to a jury trial for those accused of smuggling. In 1794, as part of the effort to keep the United States out of the European war, Congress extended its general arms embargo and deemed that ships smuggling guns and materiel were subject to forfeiture.[56] When a French privateer was caught running guns to the West Indies in violation of the embargo, the government launched forfeiture procedures against the schooner *La Vengeance*. The government won in district court, but the circuit court reversed on appeal. Justice Samuel Chase, sitting in circuit, treated the case as one of admiralty jurisdiction, which meant that the district court's factual conclusions were subject to review, and he reversed the trial judge. Providing little guidance, Congress had merely indicated that such forfeitures should be tried in the "proper" court, which should "hear and determine the cause according to the law."[57] To sustain the original conviction, Attorney General Charles Lee was placed in the awkward position of arguing that Congress could not have authorized the circuit court to take the action it did. He contended that the embargo law was a criminal law regulating an offense that was necessarily committed "part[ly] on land." As a consequence, the Sixth Amendment imposed a constitutional limitation on Congress's ability to authorize courts to exercise admiralty jurisdiction and reconsider the facts in such cases. Thus, he concluded, the "judgment of the District Court is final."[58] The Supreme Court was unpersuaded, cutting off argument to briefly assert that "no jury was necessary" in such a case. The violation of the embargo was "entirely a water transaction," and forfeiture of the vessel was a civil action, not a criminal prosecution putting the life or freedom of a person at risk. Therefore, the Constitution posed no obstacle to treating this as a matter of admiralty jurisdiction.[59]

Lee tried again as a private attorney a decade later, when he made the constitutional claim more explicit. He had argued in *La Vengeance* that admiralty jurisdiction was defined by English law, and in *United States v. The Schooner Betsey and Charlotte*, he upped the ante. Article III of the US Constitution gave admiralty jurisdiction to the federal courts, "and under that clause of the constitution," Congress "could not give . . . courts jurisdiction of a case which was not of admiralty and maritime jurisdiction at the time of the adoption of the constitution." Making a familiar originalist argument, he contended that the scope of admiralty jurisdiction was defined by the "understanding of the people of the country at that time," and forfeiture proceedings could not be pulled into that jurisdiction. In the case of *Schooner Betsey and Charlotte*, the government had charged the owners with violating the Jeffersonian embargo against St. Domingo, and now the government was insisting that enforcement of the embargo was a matter for admiralty courts and not for juries. Lee pleaded with the Court that *La Vengeance* "was not so fully argued as it might have been," but Justice Chase cut him off: Even though the attorney general's argument in the earlier case "was no great thing, the Court took time and considered the case well." Such important cases should not "be left to the caprice of juries."[60] In his brief opinion for the Court, Chief Justice Marshall noted that the constitutional issue of jury trials was the "only doubt which could arise," but "the case of the *Vengeance* settles the point."[61] Congress could constitutionally authorize the courts to exercise admiralty jurisdiction when enforcing the embargo statutes.

At stake in *La Vengeance* and *Schooner Betsey and Charlotte* were federal foreign policy and revenue, and the Court refused to allow these critical issues to fall under the sway of local juries that might disagree with national policy on these matters. At this early stage, the Court was determined that the strengthened federal government created by the US Constitution would not be held hostage to local prejudices, as it had been under the Articles of Confederation.[62] The cases had an immediate payoff for the Jefferson administration, as Congress would shortly pass the first of the general embargo acts, which were immensely unpopular but could be enforced in significant measure in admiralty courts, without interference by potentially obstructionist juries.[63]

In 1800, three years before *Marbury*, the Supreme Court under Chief Justice Oliver Ellsworth invalidated an aspect of the Judiciary Act of 1789 for the first time. The Court under John Marshall would later reaffirm and elaborate that decision. The Judiciary Act of 1789 defined the jurisdiction of the federal circuit courts, stating in section 11 that this included "all suits of a civil nature at common law or in equity, where the matter in dispute exceeds, exclusive of costs, the sum or value of five hundred dollars, and the United States are plaintiffs, or petitioners; *or an alien is a party*, or the suit is between a citizen of the State where the suit is brought, and a citizen of another State."[64] Although this section of the Judiciary Act generally tracked and limited the diversity jurisdiction given to the federal courts in Article III of the US Constitution, its reference to "an alien" as a party did not match any language in the Constitution's jurisdictional grant.[65] When a British merchant named Higginson filed suit in federal court against Mossman, the executor of an estate, to collect an old debt, Mossman's citizenship was not established in the record. On its face, the record established that an alien (Higginson) was a party, but nothing else. As Higginson's lawyers pointed out, this was sufficient under the Judiciary Act. Mossman's lawyer objected that Congress "cannot amplify, or alter" the provisions of the Constitution by statute and that the "constitution no where gives jurisdiction . . . in suits between alien and alien." The Court agreed, recognizing that the Judiciary Act could not be applied in a manner inconsistent with the Constitution. The "legislative power of conferring jurisdiction on the federal Courts is . . . confined to suits between citizens and foreigners"; the Court would allow such suits only when it was established that at least one party was a citizen, the text of the Judiciary Act notwithstanding.[66]

Nearly a decade later, former attorney general Charles Lee represented a British subject attempting to sue merchants "late of the district of Maryland," contending that this was a sufficient jurisdictional basis under section 11 of the Judiciary Act. Chief Justice Marshall dismissed the case with a brief opinion: "Turn to the article of the constitution of the United States, for the statute cannot extend the jurisdiction beyond the limits of the constitution. . . . The Court said the objection was fatal."[67] In 1829 the Court was again asked to accept a case under this provision of the Judiciary Act, and again the Court was obliged to explain that the statute had to be interpreted and applied "in conformity to the constitution of the United States." This meant that a case could not be entertained in the federal courts "unless a citizen be the adverse party," requiring the Court to reverse the decision of the circuit court for want of jurisdiction.[68] In the latter cases, the Supreme Court set the text of the law against the text of the Constitution and found the statute to be lacking, without reference to the earlier decision in *Mossman*.

Early commentators recognized the implications of the Court's actions in these cases. Treatise writers at the time understood the constitutional significance of these cases, which placed the statute "in subordination to the constitution."[69] "In legislating upon this subject" of the jurisdiction of federal courts, Congress had, in "a very few instances, inadvertently transcended the limits imposed by the constitution," and in such cases, the Supreme Court had refused to implement the law as Congress had written it.[70] As one writer observed, "The inferior federal courts possess no powers whatever except those included in the terms of statutes passed in pursuance of the Constitution. . . . If the power be statutory, it is still a nullity if it transcends the scope of the constitutional grant."[71] In light of such constitutional concerns, lawyers were advised that the citizenship of at least one of the parties had to be clearly established in the record; otherwise, the federal courts would be obliged to decline jurisdiction over the case.[72] In the opening of his 1827 *Digest of the Laws of the United States*, Thomas Gordon observed, "An act of congress, contrary to the constitution of the United States, is void—and courts of justice are bound so to declare it, or to modify the law according to the constitution, if the case admit such modification." His authorities for this proposition included both *Mossman* and *Hodgson*, the two section 11 cases decided to that date.[73] Judges likewise noted the judicial review quality of *Mossman* and its successors. On circuit, Justice Samuel Nelson observed that, "from its language," the Judiciary Act was "defective in respect to the jurisdiction conferred upon the circuit courts." Nelson glossed over this difficulty by assuming that "the meaning intended by congress" was more significant than the actual language of the statute, and that the courts were required to construe the statute "in connection with the provision of the constitution," citing *Jackson v. Twentyman* as support.[74] Other judges were less delicate. They simply pointed out that the "language of the judiciary act . . . must be restrained within the terms of the constitution."[75] The Constitution was, after all, "the superior law," and courts and litigants were obliged to "look . . . farther" than the statute itself to determine the legitimate jurisdiction of the federal courts.[76]

There is so little information about the legislative history of the Judiciary Act of 1789 that it is hard to say whether this jurisdictional provision was the result of a drafting error or a conscious choice by Congress.[77] Bad draftsmanship on the part of its principal sponsor, future chief justice Oliver Ellsworth, is certainly possible. Soon-to-be attorney general Edmund Randolph complained that the jurisdictional provisions of the statute were "inartificially, untechnically and confusedly worded," and he wondered why Ellsworth had not simply repeated the language of the Constitution itself.[78] In any case, although the more pressing issue was the relatively limited scope of authority given to the lower federal courts, the Supreme Court was not going to allow Congress to use a mere statute to expand the federal courts' jurisdiction beyond constitutional limits.[79] Congress brought the text into conformity with judicial practice by simply adopting the constitutional language when overhauling the judiciary statute in 1875.[80]

By the end of the Federalist era, the Supreme Court had already been asked repeatedly to evaluate the constitutional limits of Congress's legislative authority and consider whether the apparent demands of a statute could trump the alleged requirements of the Constitution. Moreover, the justices had already shown twice that they were unwilling to give effect to the terms of a statute if doing so would exceed the constitutional authority of Congress as the justices understood it. In none of these cases, however, did the Court provide an elaborate explanation of the power of judicial review of the type offered by Justice Paterson sitting in circuit or by the judges of the Virginia high court.[81] Rather, like many state courts, the Supreme Court simply exercised the power to evaluate the constitutionality of federal laws, without any explanation of where such a power might come from. In those cases in which the substantive constitutional issue in dispute was politically controversial, the justices upheld legislative authority. Where the justices balked—in pension cases and alien jurisdiction cases—the constitutional difficulty was easily resolved, of little substantive congressional concern, or both. Congress cared about taxing carriages and handling prize cases; it did not care about suits between two aliens. The Court upheld congressional authority when it mattered, but it also insisted that Congress could not extend the justices' workload beyond constitutionally prescribed limits. If the pension cases made High Federalists such as Fisher Ames nervous, they were soon mollified by the carriage tax case, and Federalists in general were soon lauding the federal courts as the only proper place for resolving contested constitutional issues in the midst of the Sedition Act controversy.[82]

Marbury and the "Jeffersonian Crisis"

The political environment in which the Court operated changed dramatically in 1798, and even more so in 1800. With tensions between the United States and the European powers increasing in the 1790s, and American sympathies torn between France and England, the Federalists became less tolerant of internal dissent. The Alien and Sedition Acts of 1798 imposed new restrictions on the emerging Jeffersonian party and its supporters. In doing so, the Federalists drew the federal courts into the partisan fray.[83]

During the last years of the eighteenth century, the Jeffersonian Republicans came to see the federal courts as a hostile political force. Just a few years earlier, the Jeffersonians had looked to the courts to enforce constitutional boundaries against Federalist ambitions. Thomas Jefferson had urged James Madison to advance a constitutional Bill of Rights precisely because he hoped the courts would be emboldened to protect individual rights from government abuse. When federal judges first indicated that they would not give effect to unconstitutional federal statutes, the Jeffersonians hoped the courts would set their sights on Alexander Hamilton's most controversial and ambitious policy achievements. The Supreme Court's willingness to uphold the carriage tax in 1796 began to undermine those hopes, and the situation rapidly deteriorated from there. Federal judges took the lead in enforcing the Sedition Act, fining and imprisoning Jeffersonian editors and politicians. Justice Samuel Chase distinguished himself with his aggressive implementation of the act. While riding circuit in 1800, Chase oversaw the sedition trial of Jeffersonian newspaper editor Thomas Cooper in Philadelphia, recommended that a Delaware grand jury bring an indictment against a local printer who had published criticisms of the justice's own conduct, and presided over the sedition trial of another Jeffersonian editor, James Callender, in Richmond. Hoping to find a friendly jury in Virginia, Callender's lawyers tried to argue that the Sedition Act was unconstitutional, but Chase cut off their arguments and issued prepared instructions to the jury stating that the constitutionality of statutes was a matter for judges to decide and announcing that this legislation was in fact consistent with the Constitution.

Chase had taken similar steps while overseeing the treason trial of John Fries back in Philadelphia, blocking his attorneys from making an argument that the tax protester's actions did not meet the constitutional definition of treason. Chase explained to Callender's attorneys, "the judicial power . . . is the only proper and competent authority to decide whether any statute made by congress . . . is contrary to, or in violation of, the federal constitution." Although the justice recognized that "Congress may, from inattention or error in judgment, pass a law prohibited by the Constitution," the Sedition Act was evidently not such a law.[84] Reacting to their overwhelming defeat at the polls in 1800, the Federalists in Congress passed a new judiciary bill that expanded the jurisdiction of the federal courts and added numerous judicial seats for the lame-duck president John Adams to fill. This act cemented the Jeffersonian view that the federal courts had been reduced to little more than a partisan Federalist stronghold. The federal judiciary was "filled with men who had manifested the most indecorous zeal in favor of the principles of the Federal party," and "from that battery all the works of republicanism are to be beaten down and erased."[85]

Having soured on the federal courts as a fair interpreter of the Constitution and a barrier against constitutional violations by Congress, the Jeffersonians took power in 1801 with a primary goal of declawing the Federalist courts. In 1798 the Jeffersonians had convinced the two state legislatures they controlled to adopt resolutions denouncing the Alien and Sedition Acts as unconstitutional, and James Madison had penned a report for the Virginia legislature in 1799 defending that action and criticizing the courts as an inadequate protection against congressional abuses. One of the first orders of business of the newly elected Jeffersonian Congress was to repeal the Judiciary Act of 1801, returning the federal judiciary to its previous size and structure. Adams's "midnight appointments" were out of a job. Within months, Justice Chase was targeted for impeachment, and he narrowly avoided removal by the Senate in 1805. Chase's acquittal largely ended the Republicans' overt hostility to the Marshall Court, and in his second term of office, President Thomas Jefferson was able to appoint three new justices to the Court, which was expanded to seven members in 1807. Nonetheless, some Jeffersonians, such as Judge Spencer Roane in Virginia and Thomas Jefferson himself, nursed that distrust for years.

It was in those heated moments of the first years of the "Revolution of

1800" that the Supreme Court was called on to evaluate what the Jeffersonians had done. It was during this period that the Court itself first offered an elaborate explanation of the power of judicial review and made strong claims for the judicial authority to interpret the Constitution. The Court used the power to interpret the scope of congressional legislative authority primarily to endorse what Congress had done and to elaborate on the expansive powers at the national legislature's command. When it found that Congress had exceeded its authority, as it did in the later alien jurisdiction cases already noted, the consequences for Jeffersonian policies and congressional power were modest at best.[86]

Chief Justice John Marshall was not implicated in the worst abuses of the Federalist judges, but the Jeffersonians still did not trust him. Marshall was serving in Congress and then in the executive branch when Chase was conducting his sedition trials, and his appointment to the Court was not the result of the Judiciary Act of 1801. Marshall's political leanings were more moderate than those of the unpredictable Justice Chase, but he nonetheless had little love for the Republican insurgency.

The Court decided only two cases involving the judicial review of Congress during Jefferson's first term of office, but both were highly politicized. As a practical matter, the more important of the two was *Stuart v. Laird*, decided a week after *Marbury*. When facing a confrontation with the Jefferson administration, the Court ducked. In *Stuart*, ducking meant at least partly upholding congressional authority to take hotly contested actions (while avoiding the deeper issues raised by the legislation). The case arose out of the Jeffersonian repeal of the Judiciary Act of 1801.[87] That act (which had set up a new layer of separate circuit courts and expanded the jurisdiction of the federal courts) had outraged the Jeffersonians, who saw it as saddling the nation with a host of life-tenured patronage appointees who might make mischief from their new positions. The repeal eliminated those circuit courts and dismissed the judges appointed to them.

In *Stuart*, former attorney general Charles Lee asked the justices to make a frontal assault on the Jeffersonian Congress. He sought a ruling that would have struck down the repeal act as unconstitutional. Citing James Madison on the importance of judicial tenure during good behavior, and contending that the repeal deprived the courts of "all their power and jurisdiction" and displaced "judges who have been guilty of no misbehavior in their offices," Lee argued that the repeal act was an unconstitutional assault on the judiciary.[88] The Court largely ignored this generalized complaint about the repeal, since at stake in *Stuart* was the right of parties litigating in the federal courts, not the right of the judges hoping to hear such cases. In reviewing this more modest issue, the Court observed that there were "no words in the constitution to prohibit or restrain the exercise of the legislative power" to rearrange the courts and transfer cases among them.[89] Relative to the rights of the parties bringing cases in the federal judiciary, there was nothing unconstitutional about requiring litigants to present their cases to the circuit courts as they were constituted by Judiciary Act of 1789, as opposed to those as briefly constituted by the Judiciary Act of 1801. Lee wanted to try the broader political and constitutional issues implicated by the repeal act, but John Laird's legal rights and the ability to enforce his judgment in federal court were fully satisfied if Congress could successfully transfer his case from one court to another. Focusing on this issue made it relatively easy for the Marshall Court to dodge the political and constitutional challenges looming in the background. Unusually, the chief justice allowed someone else, William Paterson, to write the opinion in this critical case. The Court's decision to go along with the Jeffersonian revolution in *Stuart*, not its impotent carping in *Marbury*, was the more important episode of judicial review arising from the electoral transition.

Unlike *Stuart*, *Marbury* was not brought to the Court to challenge the constitutionality of a statute. William Marbury brought his case with the goal of winning his commission as justice of the peace of the District of Columbia. Marbury was a minor functionary in Federalist political circles in Maryland and Washington when his patrons persuaded outgoing president John Adams to appoint Marbury to one of the new judicial offices.[90] Incoming president Thomas Jefferson regarded all such appointments, "crowded in" by the lame-duck Adams "after he knew he was not appointing for himself," as "mere nullities."[91] Upon his inauguration, Jefferson directed his secretary of state to withhold any commissions left undelivered by his predecessor John Marshall, who had been overwhelmed by the deluge of paperwork produced in the last frantic hours of the Federalist administration. With Marshall now sitting on the Supreme Court, Marbury sought a writ of mandamus from the justices that would command the secretary of state to deliver his commission, regardless of the president's order.[92]

Marbury's suit might have seemed like an opportunity for Chief Justice John Marshall, but it eventually became a problem. Marshall might well have been among the Federalist operatives who encouraged Marbury to file his suit (the ubiquitous Charles Lee agreed to represent Marbury). When the petition was filed in December 1801, the case seemed to be a prime vehicle for embarrassing the new administration for its lawless withholding of valid commissions from their rightful owners and for asserting the judicial power to supervise how the executive branch conducted its duties. By the time the case was decided in February 1803, the Republican Congress had repealed the Judiciary Act of 1801 over the vocal objections of the Federalist minority, and the House was considering impeachment charges against a federal judge sitting in New Hampshire. Believing the Court had no role to play in the internal business of the executive branch, the Jefferson administration did not even acknowledge the judicial proceedings, and it was possible that the administration would refuse to comply with any judicial order to deliver the commission. It was not a propitious time to test the strength of the Court against that of the White House.

The constitutionality of federal legislation was, at best, incidental to Marbury's case, and the issue was neither raised nor contested during oral arguments. Marbury's petition relied on the Judiciary Act of 1789 to establish the US Supreme Court's jurisdiction to hear the case first. It was on this point that the case ultimately turned. According to Court, receipt of the petition raised a question about the power of Congress to alter the duties of federal judges, in this case by arguably expanding the original jurisdiction of the Supreme Court to hear such a case. Chief Justice Marshall, writing for the Court, demurred, of course. To the extent that Congress, via the Judiciary Act of 1789, sought to give the Supreme Court an authority that "appears not to be warranted by the constitution . . . it becomes necessary to enquire whether a jurisdiction, so conferred, can be exercised."[93] The Court's answer was "no, it could not." Such a purported act could not "become the law of the land" to be implemented by the courts.[94] *Marbury v. Madison* was the sixth case in which the Court substantively reviewed the constitutionality of federal legislation and the third in which it refused to apply a statutory provision in a manner that was inconsistent with the Constitution.

The textual conflict between the Judiciary Act of 1789 and the Constitution was less clear in *Marbury* than it had been in *Mossman*, and there is no reason to think that the Court was obstructing the intentions of Congress in the former case, any more than it had in the latter.[95] Unlike *Marbury*, however, *Mossman* effectively rewrote the statute to salvage a class of constitutionally viable cases without requiring legislative action. Cases in which a citizen sued an alien could still move forward under the statutory provision allowing federal jurisdiction in cases in which "an alien is a party," even if cases involving two aliens could not. *Marbury* emphasized the idea that an "act of the legislature repugnant to the Constitution is void,"[96] rather than the idea that it must be applied "in conformity to the constitution,"[97] but the effect was comparable. Section 13 of the Judiciary Act described the original and appellate jurisdiction of the Supreme Court and granted the "power to issue . . . writs of mandamus, in cases warranted by the principles and usages of law, to any courts appointed, or persons holding office, under the authority of the United States."[98] The Court in *Marbury* denied that this provision could confer original jurisdiction where the Court did not otherwise have it. A class of possible, if unlikely, applications of the statute was constitutionally prohibited. But there remained a class of constitutionally permissible applications for this statutory provision, which Congress made explicit when it revised the relevant passage of the Judiciary Act.[99]

Marbury was also distinctive in that it defended the power of judicial review in a way that earlier Supreme Court cases had not. In doing so, Marshall "wrote as if the question had never arisen before," even though the "issue of judicial review was by no means new."[100] Although the *Marbury* Court's actions in exercising the power of judicial review were not particularly distinctive, Marshall's argument on behalf of judicial review would become a reference point in later debates over whether this power could be justified. When arguing about or teaching the theory of judicial review, the opinions in *Hylton* and *Mossman* are not especially interesting. Marshall's opinion in *Marbury* is.[101]

It is not apparent that the exercise of judicial review in *Marbury* was itself controversial, politically salient, or contrary to the preferences of other powerful political actors. By reading the mandamus provision of the Judiciary Act as unconstitutionally expanding the original jurisdiction of the Supreme Court, Marshall was able to issue a jurisdictional ruling that engendered no strong feelings in order to avoid ruling on an issue that was more controversial. Voiding the mandamus provision allowed Marshall to avoid deciding whether to issue a mandamus to the Jefferson administration—a writ that likely would have been ignored. Jeffersonians objected to Marshall's tongue-lashing of the administration over the treatment of William Marbury, but they did not object to his claim of authority to review the constitutionality of federal laws or to the fate of this statutory provision.[102]

The Court's decision that its original jurisdiction could not be expanded to include mandamus cases had potentially troubling implications, which the Court soon smoothed over. In *Ex parte Bollman*, it reminded all concerned "that it disclaims all jurisdiction not given by the constitution, or by the laws of the United States." The Jefferson administration had taken no position on the question raised in this case: whether habeas corpus petitions fell within the Court's original jurisdiction under the Constitution and thus ran afoul of the recent precedent of *Marbury*. Happily, Marshall thought not. The writ of habeas corpus could be distinguished from the writ of mandamus because the former necessarily involved a possible "revision of a decision of an inferior court, by which a citizen has been committed to jail." It thus fell within the appellate jurisdiction, a constitutionally permissible outcome.[103] *Marbury* would not be read to impede the Court from receiving that important stream of cases.

By the time the Court was asked to review another act of Congress, Jefferson had been reelected president, the Federalists had lost even more seats in Congress, and the first Republican had been seated on the US Supreme Court. Conservative Federalists could no longer cling to the hope that Jefferson's presidency was merely a temporary interruption of their own natural leadership of the young American republic. But by Jefferson's second term, the revolutionary zeal of the first term was fading, and his coalition was fracturing; those who had pushed the attacks on the federal judiciary were falling out of favor and growing increasingly impatient with the more moderate Jeffersonian leadership.[104]

Only two years after *Marbury* and *Stuart*, the Court again agreed to review the constitutionality of a federal law, for the first time considering the scope and meaning of the constitutional enumeration of powers. This time, the Court would be evaluating a Federalist-era statute of little political significance. *United States v. Fisher* involved statutory provisions giving the federal government priority over other claimants in the settlement of debts in cases of bankruptcy. Here, Chief Justice Marshall previewed the argument that would later garner far more attention in *McCulloch v. Maryland*. Provisions of this type were common in federal law, and Jefferson's US attorney had no difficulty finding constitutional authority for them. He did not shy away from judicial review but embraced it: "The constitution is the supreme law of the land, and not only this court, but every court in the union is bound to decide the question of constitutionality." Even so, US attorney Alexander Dallas cited *Hylton* for the proposition: "If the question be doubtful the court will presume that the legislature has not exceeded its power" and will refrain from finding the act "unconstitutional."[105]

Following the US attorney's lead, Marshall began by switching the emphasis from his recent ruling in *Marbury* (which was not cited by either counsel or the Court): "To the general observations made on this subject, it will only be observed, that as the court can never be unmindful of the solemn duty imposed on the judicial department when a claim is supported by an act which conflicts with the constitution, so the court can never be unmindful of its duty to obey laws which are authorized by that instrument." The question at hand was whether the statutory preference for the federal government was "necessary and proper to carry into execution the powers vested by the constitution in the government of the United States."[106] Prominent Philadelphia Federalist Jared Ingersoll argued that a general power to give the United States priority in the collection of debts was neither necessary to the execution of any particular power nor proper in a government that respected the rights of other contracting parties.[107] On this, Marshall thought "it would be incorrect and would produce endless difficulties, if the opinion should be maintained that no law was authorized which was not indispensably necessary to give effect to a specified power. . . . Congress must possess the choice of means, and must be empowered to use any means which are in fact conducive to the exercise of power granted by the constitution." No one could deny that giving the government priority in collecting on debts owed to itself would facilitate the government's ability "to pay the debts of the union," and (ignoring Ingersoll's concern that these statutory provisions interfered with previously contracted property rights) this tool was not barred to the federal government.[108] Case closed. Without the nationalist trappings, and with a slightly less developed formulation, Marshall laid out in *Fisher* his core views on the necessary and proper clause, which he would later repeat in *McCulloch*. The purpose and effect were the same. The Court upheld the specific policy currently favored by the Republican administration and the broad scope of congressional discretion in making policy and building the capacity of the national state. At the same time, it sheltered the judiciary from having to render judgments on the necessity or propriety of the legislature's policy choices.

Building the Courts

In the decades after the Jeffersonian crisis had passed, the Court considered one group of cases that involved the scope of judicial power itself. The US Constitution delimited the jurisdiction and power of the federal courts, but much was left to the discretion of Congress. As indicated in cases like *Mossman* and *Marbury*, the Court insisted that Congress could not authorize the exercise of federal judicial power in a manner that conflicted with the terms of the Constitution. As a result, parties frequently argued that federal judges did not possess the constitutional authority to rule against them, even if they had the statutory authority to resolve the case. At times, the Court worked hand in hand with Congress to extend the jurisdiction and power of the federal courts. At other times, the Court pushed back against congressional actions that impinged on what the justices considered legitimate judicial power. Across the range of such cases, the justices clarified the constitutional authority of the courts, empowering Congress to empower the courts and limiting how Congress might hamper the judiciary.

The first case arose out of a congressional act importing the civil procedures of the Louisiana state courts into the federal courts. The Louisiana legal system, based on French civil law, was unique, as elsewhere in the United States the English common-law tradition was followed. A Louisiana statute included a provision that allowed appellate courts to review the factual record heard in trial courts. Such a proceeding would not be allowed "in any court of the United States, sitting in any other state in the union than Louisiana," but the federal statute seemed to require it in cases arising in Louisiana. The Court balked. "The trial by jury is justly dear to the American people," and the Seventh Amendment to the Constitution required it in all federal suits "which are not of equity and admiralty jurisdiction, whatever may be the peculiar form which they may assume to settle legal rights. . . . The only modes known to the common law to re-examine such facts are the granting of a new trial."[109] In dissent, Justice McLean argued that, in Louisiana, "the principles of the common law are not recognized. . . . They have a system peculiar to themselves." Congress was appropriately adapting "the principles of government to the moral and social condition of the governed" by directing the federal courts to follow the local law in this matter. In effect, McLean wrote, "this is not a suit at common law, and therefore does not come strictly within the provision of the article [the Seventh Amendment]."[110] Justice Story, for the majority, disagreed. Directing the federal courts to depart from common-law forms in civil suits arising in Louisiana would "involve a violation, however unintentional, of the constitution." Congress did not have the authority to "create so important an alteration in the laws of the United States, securing the trial by jury," and as a result, "it would not be competent for this court to reverse the judgment for any error in the verdict of the jury at the trial." The courts should proceed as if there were an implicit exception in the federal statute for Louisiana state proceedings that were at odds with the requirements of the Constitution.[111]

Four years later, the Court took the same approach to a different statutory requirement. Under the Duty Act of 1799, it was "the duty of the court" to grant judgment on suits filed by the government to collect unpaid customs duties from a posted bond. If the defendant claimed an error in the calculation of the duties owed, then "if the court be satisfied, that a continuance . . . is necessary for the attainment of justice, and not otherwise, a continuance may be granted until the next succeeding term and no longer."[112] When the US attorney brought suit against Anson Phelps and his associates to collect unpaid duties totaling $1,678.70, the defendants objected that their goods had been misclassified by the customs officers and that they owed only $331.07. After receiving a continuance until the next term, the defendants were still not prepared to prove their case because they needed the testimony of a witness in Liverpool, and they moved for another continuance. The United States objected, and as the attorney general argued to the Supreme Court, the "imperative command of the law" required the court to enter a judgment for the government at that point in the proceedings (the trial court had granted the defendants' motion). Although Chief Justice Marshall recognized, in a brief opinion for the Court, that the law was designed to secure "the prompt collection of duties," an "opportunity to obtain evidence . . . according to the circumstances of the case, must be given."[113] A reported interjection by Justice McLean, and the arguments of counsel, made the basis for that conclusion more apparent: "Congress had exercised a power beyond the authority given by the constitution. It would be depriving the party of his right to a trial by jury."[114] Again, a constitutionally necessary exception had to be read into the federal statute.

The Court upheld statutory provisions despite constitutional objections to congressional actions affecting the remedies available to parties in litigation. When Congress supplemented the powers of judges in the territorial courts of Arkansas, it opened new avenues of appeal for some litigants. When it was objected that the retroactive application of the law to preexisting cases was effectively an exercise of the judicial power by Congress, overturning settled judgments and destabilizing vested rights, the Court disagreed. The law provided "new remedies" but did not otherwise "affect the right" of parties in any existing case. It "organizes a tribunal with power to entertain judicial proceedings," but it was not itself an exercise of judicial power. Such effects were commonplace and unobjectionable.[115]

Like the Marshall Court, the Taney Court was willing to uphold restrictions on the jurisdiction of the federal courts. An 1839 statute required customs collectors to deposit all revenue, including that collected under protest, directly in the federal treasury so that it might be appropriated as needed, without waiting for a judicial resolution of the dispute. The secretary of the treasury was then responsible for repaying overcharges. The effect of the statute, according to Chief Justice Taney, was to preclude lawsuits against the customs collectors to recover overcharges. Over vigorous dissents from Story and McLean, the majority of the Court upheld the legislative maneuver as a constitutionally valid assertion of sovereign immunity.[116] The Court upheld the original Judiciary Act's restriction on the diversity jurisdiction of the circuit courts. The Constitution left to the discretion of Congress the jurisdiction to be vested in the inferior courts, and Congress could choose to vest in them less than the Constitution allowed.[117] Courts-martial, existing outside the context of Article III, were constitutionally valid.[118] The Court elaborated on the validity of the political departments' determination of the national boundary between the United States and Spain, precluding judicial review of legislative decisions affecting legal rights on this subject.[119] It upheld the finality of the judgment of surveyors of waterfront lots under an 1811 act relating to the Louisiana territory; judicial jurisdiction over disputes arising from such surveys was not constitutionally required.[120] However, Congress could provide for appeals from land commissioners for the California territory to district courts, so long as it was "regarded as an original proceeding"—a "transfer" rather than a true "appeal."[121]

The Taney Court also heard challenges to federal statutes that allegedly interfered with judicial processes, and like the Marshall Court, the Jacksonian Court upheld congressional actions against such challenges. One somewhat difficult case involved an act of Congress that declared designated bridges crossing the Ohio River to be "lawful structures in their present positions and elevations, and shall be so held and taken to be, anything in the law or laws of the United States to the contrary notwithstanding."[122] That declaration followed a Supreme Court determination that the bridges were obstructions to navigation on the river and had to be removed or altered.[123] The Court observed that Congress could not "annul the judgment of the court already rendered," and congressional action would have been unavailing had the remedy in the case "been an action at law, and a judgment rendered in favor of the plaintiff for damages." But the primary aspect of the Court's earlier judgment had been "a continuing decree" "directing the abatement of the obstruction." Once Congress, exercising its power to regulate interstate commerce, rendered the bridge "no longer an unlawful obstruction," then clearly "the decree of the court cannot be enforced." There would no longer be an interference with any public right and nothing more for the Court to do in this case, and the congressional action did not interfere with or supplant the judicial power to adjudicate the case.[124]

The Court also approved a reorganization of the Treasury Department that authorized auditors to issue "distress warrants" imposing liens on the property of debtors. Justice Curtis argued that the initial question—whether this was an exercise of a "judicial" power by an executive officer—could best be answered by examining whether this procedure denied an individual of "his liberty or property, 'without due process of law,' and, therefore, is in conflict with the fifth article of the amendments of the constitution." Curtis concluded that such procedures were, in fact, commonplace in both state and federal law and antecedent British law as well. "This legislative construction of the constitution, commencing so early in the government, when the first occasion for this manner of proceeding arose, continued throughout its existence, and repeatedly acted on by the judiciary and the executive, is entitled to no inconsiderable weight upon the question of whether the proceeding adopted by it was 'due process of law.'"[125]

In a series of cases in the late 1840s and early 1850s, the Taney Court also extended the admiralty jurisdiction of the federal courts into the interior of the country, removing cases from state jurisdiction and placing them under federal authority. The Judiciary Act of 1789 conveyed the constitutional grant of admiralty jurisdiction to the federal courts, and in each case, the Court and the parties cited constitutional objections to reading the federal law as endowing the federal courts with admiralty jurisdiction. A suit in admiralty was filed in a Louisiana district court, claiming damages from a collision between two ships in the Mississippi River well north of the port of New Orleans. The respondent protested that the constitutional scope of the admiralty jurisdiction was tied to the English rule that admiralty extended only to where the tide ebbs and flows. Congress could not authorize the federal courts to reach further upriver than that. Justice Wayne, for a divided Court, firmly rejected this view. "We think we may very safely say, such interpretations of any grant in the constitution, or limitations upon such grants, according to any English legislation or judicial rule, cannot be permitted. At most, they furnish only analogies to aid us in our constitutional expositions."[126] To do more "would be a denial to Congress of all legislation upon the subject. It would make, for all time to come, without an amendment of the constitution, that unalterable by any legislation of ours, which can at any time be changed by the Parliament of England."[127] The understanding that had developed in North America by the time of the founding, he argued, included a more expansive scope for admiralty, and all such jurisdiction was meant to be transferred to the federal courts. Besides, a more expansive rule than that which might be appropriate for a small island was "more congenial with our geographic condition" and the nature of the mighty Mississippi.[128] The Court elaborated in a separate case that "the question has become settled" by "the practical construction that has been given to the Constitution"; that is, "a more enlarged" admiralty jurisdiction was now accepted, whatever "the true construction" of the original constitutional grant might have been. Federal admiralty jurisdiction could, therefore, reach a carrying contract for goods that were to be borne partway on water but "land-locked the whole way" (and ultimately lost in a shipboard fire).[129] Finally, in 1852, Chief Justice Taney wrote for the Court in a case considering the 1845 statutory extension of federal admiralty jurisdiction over the Great Lakes. Although Taney thought the commerce clause might give the federal government partial authority over shipping in the lakes, the statute in question did not fit the bill and would be unconstitutional on those grounds. Taney likewise called attention to the geographic differences between England and the United States. "The lakes are in truth inland seas," and "certainly it was not the intention of the framers of the Constitution" to deny to those citizens who live near the lakes the benefits enjoyed by those citizens who live near the Atlantic Ocean.[130] In England, "tide-water and navigable water are synonymous terms," and that might have been true of the original thirteen states as well, but it was no longer true. Therefore, the Constitution should not be read to impose "purely artificial and arbitrary as well as unjust" distinctions when it could be read otherwise.[131]

The Taney Court proved to be quite open to the extension of federal power, but it drew the constitutional line in *People's Ferry Company of Boston v. Beers and Warner*. Attempting to collect on an unpaid debt for labor and materials used in constructing a ferryboat, Beers and Warner made use of the Judiciary Act's grant of admiralty jurisdiction to file suit in federal court. The district court allowed the suit to proceed under the "more enlarged" "rules and principles of the admiralty law" in the United States (compared with the more restrictive English rules, from which the Supreme Court had previously departed).[132] The Supreme Court disagreed, however, finding that the "question presented involves a contest between the State and Federal Governments" and noting that the "latter has no power or jurisdiction beyond what the Constitution confers."[133] The congressional grant of jurisdiction had to be limited by the constitutional authorization as it was understood at the time of the founding: "what was meant by it then, it must mean now; what was reserved to the States, to be regulated by their own institutions, cannot be rightfully infringed by the General Government." A contract "made on land, to be performed on land," could not be brought under federal authority.[134] As contemporary commentators noted, the courts were relatively expansive when it came to congressional authority to vest admiralty jurisdiction over locality, but they were relatively restrictive on the subject matter of contracts.[135]

Building the Nation

An additional set of Supreme Court cases might best be understood as facilitating the process of nation building. In the first decades under the US Constitution, all the institutions of the federal government were struggling with the ongoing project of pulling a diverse nation together and establishing their own autonomy and supremacy as governmental actors advancing national interests. This nationalist project cut across partisan lines. Federalists and Jeffersonians, Whigs and Jacksonians might differ on how far and how fast national institutions should grow, but national politicians across the ideological spectrum embraced a patriotic ideal of a unified United States with a robust federal government capable of identifying and advancing national interests against disintegrating pressures. As Thomas Jefferson assumed the presidency in 1800, he worried about the prospect of a partisan, Federalist judiciary working to subvert Republican policies. As time passed, the critique of the Court as a partisan actor fell away. Critics of the Court in later decades were more likely to worry about its nationalist character. When South Carolina's John C. Calhoun dismissed the Court as inadequate for resolving the constitutional disputes of the Jacksonian period, he did not point to the justices' partisanship as disqualifying. In some ways, his objection was more basic. He rejected the idea of the neutrality of a Supreme Court *of the United States*, established under the Constitution and staffed by justices appointed and confirmed by national political leaders, when resolving constitutional questions that turned on the scope of federal power itself. Calhoun's complaint was that the Court was a political partner of Congress and the president, not that the Court was the ally of any particular political coalition. "The judges are, in fact, as truly the judicial representatives of this united majority, as the majority of Congress itself, or the President, is its legislative or executive representative; and to confide the power to the Judiciary to determine finally and conclusively what powers are delegated and what reserved, would be, in reality, to confide it to the majority, whose agents they are, and by whom they can be controlled in various ways."[136] As Calhoun recognized, the Court was a partner in the nationalist project of strengthening the federal government, often at the expense of the state governments and local interests.

As might be expected, the Court took advantage of opportunities to solidify its own power by upholding the acts of Congress that defined and extended federal judicial power. The Constitution had left essential aspects of federal judicial power in the hands of Congress, which alone had the statutory power not only to create judicial positions but also to regulate the flow of judicial business. The justices could do little but advocate on their own behalf when Congress refrained from granting them the full scope of their constitutional power (as it often did in the early nineteenth century). But when Congress chose to push the envelope and extend more controversial powers to the federal courts, the justices had the opportunity to act more directly by adding their imprimatur to what Congress had done and insisting on its constitutional legitimacy.

The Court upheld congressional grants of authority to the federal judiciary vis-à-vis the states against constitutional challenge. Most famously and significantly, the Court validated the constitutionality of section 25 of the Judiciary Act of 1789, which allowed the US Supreme Court to hear appeals from the state courts. Spencer Roane was a leader of the orthodox Jeffersonian faction in Virginia, and for many years he was one of the most distinguished jurists in the state courts. After extended deliberation, he issued an opinion for the Virginia high court declaring that there "is no iota of expression in the constitution" that supports the congressional authority to grant the US Supreme Court the power to review the actions of a state supreme court.[137] Justice Story took the first crack at the federal response in *Martin v. Hunter's Lessee*. In insisting that the Court could exercise appellate jurisdiction over the Virginia Court of Appeals, Story emphasized that "there is nothing in the constitution which restrains or limits" the power of Congress to designate the federal appellate jurisdiction. It "is plain that the framers of the constitution did contemplate that cases within the judicial cognizance of the United States not only might but would arise in the state courts, in the exercise of their original jurisdiction," and the Supreme Court could readily review the actions of the state judicial tribunals when exercising that federal jurisdiction.[138] John Marshall had his turn in *Cohens v. Virginia*, when the Court again chided the Virginia Court of Appeals. Marshall looked on with disbelief at arguments suggesting "that the constitution of the United States has provided no tribunal for the final construction of itself . . . but that this power may be exercised in the last resort by the Courts of every State in the Union. That the constitution . . . may receive as many constructions as there are States; and that this is not a mischief, or, if a mischief, is irremediable." But "no government ought to be so defective in its organization, as not to contain within itself the means of securing the execution of its own laws," and "there is certainly nothing in the circumstances under which our constitution was formed; nothing in the history of the times, which would justify the opinion that the confidence reposed in the States was so implicit as to leave in them and their tribunals the power of resisting or defeating, in the form of law, the legitimate measures of the Union."[139] Chief Justice Roger Taney would come to the same conclusion in *Ableman*.[140] Although Judge Roane was apoplectic at the Supreme Court's treatment of the state courts through its section 25 jurisdiction and continued to argue that section 25 was unconstitutional, mainstream Jeffersonians in the national government were not convinced.[141] There was a simple expedient available to states' rights advocates, but proposals for legislative repeal of this statutory provision during the Jeffersonian and Jacksonian eras went nowhere.

In addition to recognizing federal judicial authority over the states, the Court recognized Congress's power to extend that authority into the states. The Marshall Court upheld the authority of Congress to confer federal jurisdiction over cases involving the Bank of the United States. The judicial power was "co-extensive" with the legislative power, and Congress could direct that its instruments (which included the federal bank) be able to sue and be sued in federal courts. Moreover, it was sufficient if the bank as a party created cases "under" federal law, even if the substance of the dispute raised other legal issues that were not particularly federal.[142]

Three years after handing a defeat to states' right champion Roane in *Martin*, the Court returned to the question of enumerated powers in *McCulloch*. The case is sufficiently well known that little time is spent on it here.[143] In defending its punitive tax on the Bank of the United States, the state of Maryland claimed that Congress had exceeded its constitutionally delegated powers in chartering the bank in the first place. This gave Marshall a chance to elaborate on the themes he had first developed in *Fisher*, but in a much more politically consequential case. The Court struck down Maryland's tax as an unconstitutional interference with an instrument of federal policy, while upholding the congressional authority to charter a bank as an appropriate means of fulfilling the constitutional responsibilities of the federal government.[144]

Three points should be noted about *McCulloch*. The first is that *McCulloch* was an emphatic assertion of judicial authority to resolve contested constitutional issues. In the post–New Deal context, *McCulloch* is often taken to stand for "judicial deference to the plausible interpretive acts of Congress," but Marshall was insistent that the constitutional bounds of legislative policy discretion were to be established and enforced by the Court.[145] Given the contentious interests involved and the history of tensions surrounding the bank, Marshall asserted, "By this tribunal alone can the decision be made. On the Supreme Court of the United States has the constitution of our country devolved this important duty."[146] Politicians should debate the best method for financing the government, but the Court was the best and paramount forum for determining the constitutionality of Congress's actions.[147]

Second, the Court was able to assert its interpretive authority because it could count on the support of political leaders. By 1819, the power of Congress to charter a bank was no longer controversial. Madison and Jefferson had sharply challenged the constitutionality of the charter of the first bank in 1791, and the Republican Party in the 1790s took the bank to be a prime example of the Federalists' willingness to ignore constitutional restraints. But the War of 1812 persuaded many Jeffersonians of the necessity of a bank, and President Madison signed the charter for the second Bank of the United States. Circumstances had changed, rendering a bank "necessary and proper" where it had once been merely expedient. Madison also argued that the bank controversy had been settled by precedent. Over the course of nearly a quarter century, the "general will of the nation" had shown its acceptance of the validity of the bank.[148] Jeffersonian attorney general William Wirt defended the bank's constitutionality in *McCulloch* during the Monroe administration. The behavior of bank branches in the states was locally controversial, but in 1819 the charge that the power to incorporate the bank was beyond the constitutional competence of Congress was the territory of extremists and a fallback position for the states trying to defend their anti-bank policies. In upholding the congressional power to charter a bank, the Marshall Court was simply endorsing the reigning political consensus.[149]

Third, Marshall's explanation of why the bank was constitutional was immediately controversial with the Jeffersonians, and the bank itself would become controversial again a decade later when Andrew Jackson reopened the issue. As a result, although the decision in *McCulloch* went with the political grain and received widespread support, its broad interpretation of the necessary and proper clause fell on deaf ears and had little influence in the pre–Civil War period. Jefferson, Madison, and Roane all complained that Marshall's opinion went far beyond what was necessary to uphold the bank and had "stricken off" the constitutional limits on Congress.[150] The Jeffersonians turned to "sound arguments" directed "to Congress & to their Constituents" to bury *McCulloch*.[151] Both the Jeffersonians and the Jacksonians elaborated a narrower reading of the necessary and proper clause as constitutional orthodoxy.[152] In political practice, *McCulloch* was a dead letter. Once a majority of Jacksonian justices joined the Court, it was widely believed that they needed only an appropriate case to formally reverse *McCulloch*.[153] With strict constructionists controlling the flow of legislation through Congress, however, such a case never arose. A Jacksonian Congress would not pass a statute that pushed the boundaries of federal power and had to lean on the support provided by the *McCulloch* precedent. As a result, *McCulloch* remained on the books to be cited and revived by nationalists after the Civil War.

The Taney Court was likely hostile to the broad view of enumerated powers sketched out by Marshall, but only one minor case raising such issues came before it, and the necessity and propriety of the federal law in question could not have been more straightforward.[154] States' rights devotee Justice Peter Daniel wrote the unanimous opinion for the Taney Court upholding federal power in *United States v. Marigold*. Peter Marigold had been convicted of the federal crime of passing counterfeit coins "brought into the United States, from a foreign place." At least since the Jeffersonian embargo, Daniel thought there was no question that the federal government could prohibit the importation of certain goods as part of its power to regulate international trade. Moreover, the power to ban counterfeit coins was a necessary incident of the congressional power to coin money, a power that "would be useless" if Congress could not protect what it had created. *Marigold* gave no occasion to reconsider *McCulloch*, and Daniel somewhat grudgingly admitted that the Court could not "withhold" from Congress a power "necessary to the execution of expressly granted powers, and to the fulfillment of clear and well-defined duties."[155]

Jacksonian dominance of the political arena meant that the Taney Court was rarely called on to evaluate the constitutionality of the Whig program.

The most constitutionally dubious legislation, from a Democratic perspective, was blocked by presidential vetoes and political mobilization. There is reason to believe that a Jacksonian Court would have reversed *McCulloch* and struck down a renewed national bank, given the chance.[156] But in the cases most likely to involve partisan divisions, the Taney Court upheld federal power as it had been exercised by the Whig Congress. The majority in *Searight v. Stokes* carefully limited the issue to whether the federal government could spend funds to maintain a road used by the postal service—a position the Jacksonians had come to accept—and avoided the more ideologically contested question of whether the government could construct such roads in the first place. The basic question of the constitutionally proper use of federal appropriations for internal improvements and the general welfare was left to congressional debate and presidential veto.[157] The Whig-backed Bankruptcy Act of 1841, responding to the fallout from the Panic of 1837, altered the British rule by allowing debtors to initiate bankruptcy proceedings to shield themselves from creditors. It was soon assailed as not meeting the constitutional definition of a "bankruptcy" law (which was asserted to follow from the British practice regnant at the founding) and was instead construed as a reviled debtor-relief law. Some judges embraced this argument, including a Democratic federal district court judge and some state court judges, and they refused to enforce the law.[158] By a procedural quirk, however, the majority of the justices concluded that there was no way to bring a case involving the bankruptcy law before the Supreme Court (Catron dissented from this jurisdictional determination). In lieu of a formal opinion, the Court ordered that an "opinion delivered by Judge Catron in his judicial district" (while he was riding circuit) be published in *U.S. Reports* as "being of general interest."[159] Catron's opinion in *In re Klein* was a vigorous defense of the constitutionality of the bankruptcy law (a defense he repeated in his published dissent to the jurisdictional holding). Applying the contracts clause to the states and empowering Congress via the bankruptcy clause were intended not to create a general prohibition on debtor relief but to ensure that states could not exploit out-of-state creditors and that the proper accommodation of debtors' and creditors' interests was decided in Congress, where "the entire people are equally represented, and have the power to protect themselves against hasty and mistaken legislation."[160] The Bankruptcy Act, with its innovative provision for debtor-initiated proceedings, reflected that national policy accommodation. Nonetheless, the Bankruptcy Act was repealed by the new Democratic majority less than a month after the Court issued its opinion, so there was little opportunity for the lower courts to respond to the Court's unorthodox action. The next term, Catron admitted that the Court's approach had been "extra-judicial," but he agreed with his brethren that "a more imposing application, requiring an opinion, could not have been presented," given how many cases could be affected by a single renegade district judge if he could not be corrected by the Court.[161] The Court wanted judges to get the message that the law was constitutionally valid and to fall in line.

As it had been in *McCulloch*, the Court was sometimes called on to uphold the constitutional validity of federal action as part of its inquiry into the constitutionality of a conflicting state action. *McCulloch* was an unusual instance of such a conflict, which more routinely occurred in the context of federal authority to regulate commerce. Thus, in overturning New York's steamship monopoly in *Gibbons v. Ogden*, the Court had to briefly consider whether federal authority to license ships could extend to the navigation of interstate waterways. The Constitution "contains an enumeration of powers expressly granted by the people to their government. It has been said, that these powers ought to be construed strictly. But why ought they to be so construed? Is there one sentence in the constitution which gives countenance to this rule?" Marshall thought not, and he likewise thought it obvious that the congressional power to regulate interstate commerce "comprehends navigation, within the limits of every State in the Union; so far as that navigation may be, in any manner, connected with 'commerce with foreign nations, or among the several States, or with the Indian tribes.'" Federal licenses, as applicable to the navigation of this waterway, were constitutional.[162] Once this had been established, Justice Story could likewise find for the Court that Congress could regulate the salvage of shipwrecks above the high-water line as part of its power to protect commercial waterways; this avoided any factual entanglements over whether particular items had been scavenged from above or below the high-water line.[163] This larger provision, bolstered by federal responsibility for foreign affairs, supported the federal government's exclusive authority to regulate trade with Indian tribes.[164]

The Taney Court was willing to give the federal government room to exercise discretion when operating within the states. The Court had little difficulty turning back a constitutional challenge to the federal government's

leasing, rather than selling, mining lands it owned within the states, despite
local policy against the maintenance of such a "body of tenantry." The federal government had long been understood to retain public lands it did not
explicitly transfer to the states, and the mode of "disposal must be left to the
discretion of Congress" under the federal power "to dispose of . . . property,
belonging to the United States."[165] In *Searight v. Stokes and Stockton*, Justice
Daniel insisted, in dissent, on denying a congressional "power to construct
roads, or any other description of what have been called internal improvements, within the limits of the states."[166] The other justices, including Chief
Justice Taney writing for the majority, were forced to deny "that the constitutional power of the general government to construct" the Cumberland
Road is involved "in the case before us; nor is this court called upon to express any opinion on that subject." Perhaps Congress did not have the power
to construct the road in the first place, as strict constructionists within the
Democratic Party had long contended, but it surely *did* have the authority,
in the Jackson administration (in which Taney had served), to appropriate
a sum to repair the road and commit it to the states, on the condition that
the United States "shall not thereafter be subject to any expense for repairing
said road." There was no "just ground for questioning the power of Congress" to take that action to prevent "this important line of communication" from falling "into utter ruin."[167] Having accepted that condition during
the Jackson administration, Pennsylvania could not now charge federal mail
carriers tolls for using the road. The majority of the Taney Court was not
interested in unearthing old debates over the constitutionality of internal
improvements, so long as it could get by with validating the compromise
worked out during the Jackson presidency and making Pennsylvania live up
to that bargain.

The Court did not always side with Congress when determining the scope
of federal power relative to the states. On rare occasions, the Court determined that Congress had gone too far. One such case involved a type of
dispute that was common to the period but of little immediate consequence
to the general public. William Pollard was among those who had received a
Spanish land grant in what was then known as Spanish West Florida. There
was a dispute over the legitimacy of Pollard's title, which was particularly
valuable because it involved riverfront land that had become a central part
of the booming port town of Mobile, Alabama. The property was the object

of extended litigation, and in 1836 Pollard's heirs tried to end the dispute by persuading Congress to pass a private bill that declared, "a certain lot of ground situated in the city of Mobile" was "confirmed unto the heirs of William Pollard." The private act, of course, simply spurred more litigation over what it entailed and whether Congress even had the power to take action in the case.

In one of the several times the justices heard arguments involving this "certain lot of ground," they realized that Congress had a federalism problem. The actual occupants of the land (not Pollard or his heirs) had extended it through landfill some distance into the "flowed land" of the Mobile River. Under the 1836 act of Congress, Pollard's heirs claimed this land, which had once been under the high-water mark. But the Court concluded, since Alabama had been admitted to the Union in 1819, "to Alabama [and not the federal government] belong the navigable waters, and soils under them." In *Pollard v. Hagan*, and over Justice Catron's dissent, the Court determined that Congress, in its 1836 act, had exceeded its authority to dispose of land within the states. The Constitution afforded Congress no authority to grant the land in question after the date of statehood, so the 1836 act was void as it applied to the filled land.[168] Once Alabama became a state, Congress could no longer claim ownership of the land, and it could not exercise a power of eminent domain within the states for the purpose of disposing of land.[169] Since Congress had only purported to relinquish the federal government's own claim to the land, voiding the act had consequences primarily for only one leg of the Pollard lawsuit. But in denying Congress's authority to act here, the justices were afforded an opportunity to explain why Congress could not act in a wider range of situations that might arise in the future—and had already arisen in the past but had not reached the US Supreme Court. The holding in *Pollard* echoed the Court's earlier finding in *Mayor of New Orleans v. United States*, which similarly concluded that the United States could not constitutionally retain the quay in New Orleans when Louisiana became a state.[170]

Pollard gave judicial articulation to the "equal footing" doctrine, which held that new states in the West were admitted to the Union with the same rights and authority as the original states. Congress had no greater authority over land and waterways in the new states than in the old. In *Pollard*, the manipulation took the form of a private act attempting to dispose of property, but the decision had broad implications for statutes originating in the territorial period and for statehood enabling acts. Most notably, state courts had treated provisions of the Northwest Ordinance and statehood enabling acts that required the free navigation of rivers as still binding after statehood, and similar questions could be raised about provisions regarding slavery or religious liberty in the states. After *Pollard*, it was no longer obvious that such congressional statutes could be as binding on a state "as its own constitution."[171]

Withers v. Buckley raised similar concerns for the Court. When Congress admitted Mississippi as a state in 1817, the authorizing act included a provision that the Mississippi River and all "navigable rivers and waters leading into the same" would be "common highways, and forever free" to both residents of the state and citizens of the United States. When the state built a canal that redirected water flow and cut off water access to the Mississippi River from the plantation of David Withers, Withers sued, relying in part on the congressional act that prohibited interference with his use of the "common highway." The Supreme Court first distinguished the waterway used by Withers from "navigable rivers and waters," but it did not rely on this statutory interpretation. The decisive point, according to the Court, was the fact that an act of Congress "could have no effect to restrict the new State in any of its necessary attributes as an independent sovereign Government" or "inhibit or diminish its perfect equality with the other members of the Confederacy with which it was to be associated." Congress did not have the constitutional authority to "forbid . . . the power of improving the interior of that State, by means of either roads or canals, or by regulating rivers within its territorial limits, although a plan of improvements to be adopted might embrace or affect the course or the flow of rivers situated within the interior of the State." Mississippi's canal did not violate the Constitution or other US laws because Congress had no constitutional authority to interfere with Mississippi's discretion in this matter.[172] Such decisions did not stop Congress from using statehood enabling acts (and comparable bills) to make declarations about what future states could "never" do, but it was now widely understood that such declarations had no legal force. They were symbolic and hortatory. The courts would not enforce the supremacy of federal law in such cases.[173]

The Court had already determined, before *Withers*, that Congress could not use its separate power to regulate interstate commerce to interfere with improvements a state might make to internal waterways. Maine had granted

a twenty-year monopoly on steamship operations on a section of the Penob-
scot River to William and Daniel Moor in payment for clearing the river of
obstructions, deepening its channel, and building any necessary canals to
make it fully navigable. Steamship operator Samuel Veazie, who possessed
the same sort of federal coasting license that had allowed Thomas Gibbons to
challenge Aaron Ogden's exclusive state license to operate on the New York
border, similarly tried to trump Maine's restrictive law.[174] The Maine Supreme Court was not persuaded, and the Taney Court emphatically agreed.
The Constitution's grant of authority to Congress to regulate commerce
"can never be applied to transactions wholly internal . . . or to a polity and
laws whose ends and purposes and operations are restricted to the territory
and soil and jurisdiction of such community." Such an expansive understanding of congressional authority not only would "paralyze every effort at
internal improvements by the several States" but also would be a "pretension
as far reaching . . . [to] control the pursuits of the planter, the grazier, the
manufacturer, the mechanic, the immense operations of the collieries and
the mines and furnaces of the country." To allow the coastal license to reach
matters that were "essentially local in their nature and extent" would be "an
abuse wholly beyond the object and power of the government granting it."[175]
If the federal power to regulate commerce on the waterways between states
had been upheld in *Gibbons*, extending the implications of a rather innocu-
ous federal statute, it was rejected in *Veazie*, limiting its scope.

Clarifying the Rules

In *McCulloch*, John Marshall observed that, by the Constitution's nature,
"only its great outlines should be marked, its important objects designated,
and the minor ingredients which compose those objects be deduced from
the nature of the objects themselves."[176] James Madison had made a similar
point during the ratification debates, admitting that all laws, including the
Constitution, "are considered as more or less obscure and equivocal, until
their meaning be liquidated and ascertained by a series of particular discussions and adjudications."[177] Some of the Court's early work in answering
constitutional questions about legislative acts was simply a matter of eluci-
dating these "minor ingredients" of the constitutional scheme. While such
cases were generally not as momentous as *McCulloch*, they emphasized the

role of the Court as an arbiter of the constitutional rules and often had short-term significance for the parties immediately involved and long-term significance for the organization of governmental operations.

The Court considered only a handful of constitutional challenges to the application of federal laws on due process grounds prior to the Civil War. The first such case is particularly idiosyncratic, but it harks back to the most basic justifications for the judicial nullification of statutory provisions.[178] In 1798 Congress sought to protect its creation, the Bank of the United States, by making it a federal crime to circulate fraudulent banknotes. In defining the crime, however, the statute stated that no one can represent as true a "false, forged or counterfeit bill or note issued by order of the president . . . and signed by the president." Read literally, the law applied only to notes that were both counterfeit *and* issued and signed by the president of the Bank of the United States. Zebulon Cantril was indicted and convicted in Georgia for attempting to pass off a "forged and counterfeit paper . . . purporting to be a bank bill of the United States for ten dollars." The defense moved to have the verdict quashed on the grounds that the indictment was insufficient to meet the statutory definition of the crime (the purported bank bill had not actually been signed by the bank president); moreover, the statute Cantril had been convicted of violating was "inconsistent, repugnant, and therefore void." The circuit court was divided on the issue and certified the question for the Supreme Court's review. Marshall's opinion was not reported in detail, but it agreed with the motion and directed the lower court to arrest the judgment.[179] The Court could have readily looked past the literal terms of the statute and interpreted it as Congress had clearly intended, but instead it chose to assert that the judiciary could void such a statute for repugnancy.[180] Although repugnancy can be understood as a canon of statutory interpretation, later courts have recognized that in the American context, it has constitutional implications.[181] A repugnant statute fails to give adequate notice of legal obligations or adequate guidance for its consistent application.[182] Congress had corrected the statutory error before the Court handed down its order, so the decision was of little policy consequence.[183]

In 1829 the Court heard the first of a series cases involving problems associated with land grants and raising issues about the constitutional authority of Congress. The complexity of sorting out land grants in the early nineteenth century occupied a substantial part of the Court's agenda during the late Marshall and early Taney periods. Cases that raised questions about constitutional limitations on Congress most often involved issues of property rights. In these cases, the principles the Court had enunciated in *Fletcher v. Peck*, stretching the contracts clause to prevent Georgia from retracting vested property rights, were extended and applied against the federal government.[184]

The first case in which the Court invalidated a grant arose from one of the earliest land grants. Duncan M'Arthur claimed a military land warrant from the state of Virginia in recognition of his service during the Revolutionary War. The patent was issued in 1812 for land in the state of Ohio that had been reserved for that purpose by Virginia when it ceded the Northwest Territory to the federal government in 1784. Meanwhile, John Reynolds purchased an overlapping parcel of land that had originally been sold by the federal government in 1813. The problem arose in part because the US and Virginia governments disagreed about the precise boundary of the state's reserved lands, and the federal government had sold the same parcel of land a decade earlier, but the original purchaser had defaulted on the contract. M'Arthur sued in Ohio to have Reynolds ejected from the land, and the state court agreed, rejecting Reynolds's claim under federal law.

On appeal, the US Supreme Court affirmed the judgment of the state court and, in doing so, asserted that a federal statute cannot be constitutionally enforced. The most direct constitutional issue arose from an 1818 statute whereby Congress had declared that an 1802 surveyor's line would be "considered and held to be" the true boundary of the Virginia military reserve "until otherwise directed by law," even though Virginia had disputed this line, and earlier acts of Congress on the subject had left the issue somewhat open.[185] The land in question was on the federal side of the disputed boundary, and Reynolds argued that the law voided Virginia's putative sale of the land. Attorney General William Wirt intervened on Reynolds's side, but he was indisposed at the time of oral arguments and unable to participate. The Court refused to give the 1818 law the "retrospective operation" desired by Reynolds and the federal government. To do so would be to allow Congress "to look back to titles already acquired" and to unilaterally "declare by law" what the terms of the Virginia cession meant. Such a retroactive law would "adjudicate in the form of legislation . . . [and] would be an exercise of a judicial, not of a legislative power." If taken as a legislative act, it would deny the vested property rights of M'Arthur. If taken as a judicial act, it would encroach on the judicial power to interpret the law. Neither outcome was constitutionally permissible, so the act had to be read as prospective only and irrelevant for Reynolds. The Court also noted, "There is undoubtedly much force in the argument suggested at the bar" that Congress had neither retrospective nor prospective power over the land in question once Ohio had been admitted to statehood, but it was "unnecessary to pursue this inquiry" because Reynolds's claim had already been defeated on grounds of retrospective operations.[186] The case obviously raised concerns on other grounds—separation of powers, due process, federalism, property rights— but as we shall see, it is of a piece with other cases related to how Congress can deal with property that, from a judicial perspective, has vested in an individual.[187] Despite the government's effort to give retrospective effect to the legislative determination of property holdings, *Reynolds* foreshadowed the judicial determination in numerous courts that such laws cannot constitutionally extend to interfere with vested rights.[188]

A second case, decided four years later, involved Spanish grants in the Florida Territory. Don Juan Percheman, a Spanish military officer, claimed 2,000 acres in Florida under an 1815 grant from the Spanish governor, four years before the treaty that transferred the territory to the United States. The treaty included a provision protecting private titles to lands in the ceded territories, but Chief Justice Marshall declaimed any reliance on that provision because the "whole civilized world" knew that "cession of a territory is never understood to be a cession of the property belonging to its inhabitants. The king cedes only what belongs to him."[189] The proper interpretation of the treaty was irrelevant. Constitutionally protected property rights were what mattered. The difficulty was determining who owned what property in the ceded territory. Following the terms of the treaty, the federal government set up a process (over time, several processes) to "ratif[y] and confirm" the grants issued under Spanish authority. An 1822 statute "for ascertaining claims and titles to land within the territory of Florida" supplanted and extended several earlier statutes and provided for a board of commissioners to examine land claims and recommend to Congress which ones should be ratified as valid. Congress established a small window for filing claims with the commissioners, and any claims that missed the deadline would "be deemed and held to be void and of none effect."[190] By 1830, Congress had confirmed all claims approved by the commissioners under the 1822 and subsequent acts, but it had also asserted that the courts had jurisdiction to hear disputes over the commissioners' conclusions only in cases involving more than 3,500 acres, and then for only a limited time before being "forever barred" from any action "in any court whatever."[191] The congressional preference when absorbing foreign territories, rarely realized in practice, was to reach a final determination on the legal claims of existing titleholders as quickly as possible in order to keep squatters at bay and clear the way for a more regular system of land sales and settlement.[192] Refusing fraudulent claims was a higher priority than validating legitimate claims, and the cumbersome pace of the commissioners led many original claimants to sell out to speculators, who in turn lobbied for more generous terms from Congress.[193] Percheman's claim had been rejected by the commissioners, and his parcel was too small to qualify for a judicial hearing under the law. Nonetheless, the trial court accepted the case and rejected the federal government's claim to the land.

Before the Supreme Court, Percheman's counsel emphasized that his right to the land had vested long before the treaty transferring the territory; therefore, Congress was not "competent" to authorize "any tribunal under its authority to invalidate such a title." Congress was obligated to respect Percheman's title to the land, not to question it, and certainly not to nullify it. Attorney General Roger Taney claimed the land in question for the United States, emphasizing that Congress had gone to great lengths over the past eleven years to achieve a "final settlement to land claims in Florida" and that the only body appointed by Congress to arbitrate Percheman's claim had heard and rejected it.

The Marshall Court would have none of it. Despite the apparent language of the treaty and the subsequent acts of Congress implementing it, the Court could not accept that "the security of private property" was contingent on "some future legislative act." Vested property rights could not constitutionally be left to the discretion of Congress, and that fundamental principle "must enter into our construction of the acts of congress on the subject." With that principle in view, "it is impossible to suppose that congress intended to forfeit real titles" based on parties' failure to comply with the ramshackle procedures established by these statutes. "Is it possible that congress could design to submit the validity of titles, which were 'valid under the Spanish government, or by the law of nations,' to the determinations of these commissioners?" Perish the thought. The commissioners "appear not to have proceeded with open doors, deriving aid from the arguments of counsel, as is the usage of a judicial tribunal," and their mode of appointment and the procedures for filing claims militated against taking them to be "a court exercising judicial power and deciding finality on titles."[194] The federal government could not divest Percheman of his property in this manner, and the Court affirmed the ruling of the trial court and upheld Percheman's claim against the government.

The government won more often than it lost such cases. Two cases mirrored the land disputes just reviewed. In one case, Daniel Webster represented the plaintiffs before the Court in 1829. Their title to land just east of the Mississippi River derived from a Spanish grant made in 1804, and they were seeking to eject the defendant, who was actually in possession of the land. The defendant argued that the United States, not Spain, was in lawful possession of that territory after the Louisiana Purchase, and an act of the Spanish governor created no legal right that the United States was obliged to respect.[195] The act forming the Louisiana Territory in 1804 had asserted that any grants made by Spain in the disputed territory, "under whatever authority transacted or pretended," were "from the beginning, null, void, and of no effect in law or equity." After the United States acquired the Florida Territory (and "East Louisiana") from Spain, it continued to assert this view and argued that it was consistent with the language of the Florida treaty. In this instance, the Court was unprepared to defend allegedly vested property rights against the federal government:

> In a controversy between two nations concerning national boundary, it is scarcely possible that the courts of either should refuse to abide by the measures adopted by its own government. . . . The judiciary is not the department of government, to which the assertion of its interests against foreign powers is confided and its duty commonly is to decide upon individual rights, *according to those principles which the political departments of the nation have established.* If the course of the nation has been a plain one, its courts would hesitate to pronounce it erroneous. We think then, however individual judges might construe the treaty . . . it is the province of the Court to conform its decisions to the will of the legislature, if that will has been clearly expressed.[196]

The treaty did not say, "those grants are hereby confirmed"; it merely said that valid Spanish grants would be confirmed and ratified. Congress had created a procedure for doing so—the land commissions the Court would encounter again in *United States v. Percheman*. In *Foster and Elam*, the Court deferred to those commissions, stating that the "Court is not at liberty to disregard the existing laws on the subject." The plaintiffs had not even submitted their claims to the commissions, let alone had them confirmed. "Congress had reserved to itself the supervision of the titles," and it had not given the federal courts blanket jurisdiction to vindicate such titles.[197]

One might have thought that the result in *Foster and Elam* would be decisive in *Percheman*, but by the time of the latter case, the Court claimed that the Spanish-language version of the treaty provided a different perspective on the agreement, stating that the Spanish titles "*shall remain* ratified and confirmed." This reading was consistent with the "usages of the civilized world," and it would now "enter into our construction of the acts of congress on the subject," leading to a different result.[198] Percheman's attorneys put before the Court not only the Spanish-language version of the treaty but also an extensive record of the negotiations behind the provisions, which suggested that Secretary of State John Quincy Adams meant to exclude only a very small set of Spanish grants from American recognition. The *Foster and Elam* litigation involved land next to the Mississippi River that was of critical concern to the United States from the time of the Louisiana Purchase onward. By contrast, Percheman's land was deep in the Florida Territory, and if the Jackson administration succeeded in ousting him, few Spanish titles would be secure from political influence. Normal constitutional protections for property rights would come into play there.[199]

Between *Foster and Elam* and *Percheman*, the Court changed its approach toward the rights conveyed by the Spanish cession. The Court likewise altered its thinking about the 1836 act granting federal relief to William Pollard's heirs. In 1809, when the Spanish government granted Pollard land at the mouth of the Mobile River, Spain's authority over that territory was contested by the United States (which claimed it was part of the Louisiana Purchase). When the United States gained clear possession of the territory (along with additional land in Florida) by treaty a decade later, it pledged that all proper grants would "be ratified and confirmed" and held valid in accordance with Spanish law. In December 1819 Congress admitted Alabama (where Pollard's land was located) into the Union. Some years later, the Supreme Court held that, with regard to the disputed Spanish territory, confirmation of a valid title was not automatic but required positive action by Congress (as if the land had belonged to the United States all along).[200] Even though Pollard's claim to the land had been rejected by the commissioners Congress had assigned to investigate such claims, at the request of Pollard's heirs, Congress confirmed the claim by private act in 1836. In the earlier case, the Alabama trial court had refused to instruct the jury that the 1836 act settled the matter and instead instructed the jury that it could conclude that the congressional act was void. The US Supreme Court found this instruction to be in error. Writing for a unanimous Court in *Pollard's Lessee v. Files*, Justice Catron argued that Congress had properly confirmed Pollard's claim, which the Court characterized here as pending and awaiting validation in the land office; therefore, it predated an 1824 statute waiving all federal interest in riverfront lots that had not been "sold or confirmed to individuals . . . and to which no equitable title exists." Claims traced to the 1824 act could not extend to the Pollard property, and therefore the 1836 act could not interfere with any preexisting property rights.[201] Against claims of competing property rights, the relief act was constitutional.[202]

The Taney Court upheld its own property claim against the federal government in *Lytle v. Arkansas*. In 1830 (supplemented by an 1832 act) Congress gave the occupants of cultivated public lands in the Arkansas Territory the preemption right to purchase the land and gain valid title to it. In 1832 Congress gave the territorial governor of Arkansas the authority to select 1,000 acres of land adjoining Little Rock, initially for the construction of public buildings, but later for sale to private individuals to fund public buildings. Acting under this authority, the governor selected and sold a parcel of land that had previously been claimed by settlers under the preemption act but not yet validated by the land office (and never would be). Whereas the settlers challenged "the competency of the United States to thus appropriate the land in controversy," the government contended that Congress was free to redirect the land to other purposes at any time, regardless of the preemption rights of the settlers. The state supreme court had ruled against the settlers' preemption rights, but a closely divided US Supreme Court disagreed. The minority, led by Justice Catron, rejected the settlers' claims as too tenuous and ultimately adverse to the public interest. If such preemption rights were upheld, the act granting land to the governor "would have been without value, as the whole grant might have been defeated by occupant claims, and the seat of government transferred to private owners." Indeed, all sorts of reservations of federal land by the president for "public use," whether reserved for public works, lead mines, or ship timber, would be defeated by the nebulous and overly expansive preemption rights of local "villager[s]." It was preferable for the Court to defer to the "accumulated intelligence and experience of those engaged in the administration of the Department of Public Lands" than to tie the government's hands with weakly grounded property rights. For the majority (which Chief Justice Taney joined), the "claim of a preemption is not that shadowy right which by some it is considered to be." "National feeling" favored the "adventurous pioneer," and his rights could not simply be shoved aside. The land claimed by the settlers had to be excluded from the land granted to the governor; the second grant was, to that extent, void. To do otherwise would be to allow Congress "to impair vested rights."[203]

The Court also sought to clarify how the constitutional separation of powers should work. The Marshall Court heard the earliest cases challenging statutes as unconstitutional delegations of legislative power. In each case, the Court upheld the challenged provision, finding that it did not cross the line into a prohibited delegation. First to be challenged was the Non-Intercourse Act of 1810. In 1809 Congress repealed the comprehensive and much-hated Jeffersonian trade embargo that banned all commercial shipping to and from American ports and replaced it with the Non-Intercourse Act, which barred trade only with warring England and France, and only until they altered their policies toward neutral American shipping. The 1809 act expired at the end of the congressional session, but Congress revived it with the 1810 act. The revival was conditional, however, on a presidential finding and proclamation that each country to which the act applied had not altered its policies. When the brig *Aurora* was caught importing goods from Liverpool in violation of the 1810 act, lawyer Joseph Ingersoll asked a basic question: "Whoever heard of a conditional penal law?" "Congress could not transfer the legislative power to the President. To make the revival of a law depend upon the President's proclamation, is to give to that proclamation the force of a law."[204] Writing for the Court in 1813, Justice William Johnson did not bother to examine the constitutional question in detail. He simply informed the parties that the justices "can see no sufficient reason, why the legislature should not exercise its discretion in reviving the act . . . either expressly or conditionally, as their judgment should direct."[205]

Next to be challenged on nondelegation grounds was the antipiracy statute of 1789. Daniel Webster argued in an 1820 case that Congress had not
bothered to define the crime of "piracy" and was "not at liberty to leave it
to be ascertained by judicial interpretation."[206] Justice Story would not play
along. Webster took "too narrow of a view of the language of the constitution" in giving Congress the power "to define and punish piracies." Congress
was free to use "a term of a known and determinate meaning," just as it was
free to use "an express enumeration of all the particulars included in that
term." The Court knew what Congress meant by piracy, so there was no delegation of legislative power to the courts to make criminal law.[207]

Five years later, the Court turned back an objection that the Judiciary
Act of 1789 had unconstitutionally delegated legislative power to the states.
Under that act, "the laws of the several States," except where otherwise provided, "shall be regarded as rules of decision in trials at common law, in
the Courts of the United States." Chief Justice Marshall was unconcerned.
Congress could not compel state officers to take any actions, but "Congress
may certainly delegate to others, powers which the legislature may rightfully
exercise itself," and piggybacking on the judicial procedures the states had
already put in operation was only prudent.[208] Likewise, Congress could delegate the details of the judicial process to the judges themselves. Such judicial processes were merely "ministerial," not truly "legislative," and Congress
could delegate such matters as it thought "expedient."[209] The Court was not
going to tie up the legislative process by requiring Congress to specify all
the details of federal policy. Congress could make use of the flexibility and
expertise of others, from presidents to judges to state legislatures, to better
accomplish national goals.

In 1820 the Court revisited the constitutional rules of federal taxation. In
Loughborough v. Blake, the Marshall Court considered whether "Congress
[has] a right to impose a direct tax on the District of Columbia." The case
raised questions about both the constitutional restriction on direct taxes
(that they be apportioned "among the several states" by population) and the
"great principle which was asserted in our revolution, that representation is
inseparable from taxation." Marshall dismissed the first objection with the
assertion that direct taxes could be imposed elsewhere than in the states, so
long as they adhered to the principle of proportionality. More difficult was
the second objection, but Marshall escaped this as well. The problem of taxa-

tion without representation during the colonial period derived from the lack of "common feelings" between Britain and the North American colonies, but it was "too obvious not to present itself to the minds of all" that those who chose to live in the District of Columbia had "voluntarily relinquished the right of representation, and had adopted the whole body of Congress for its legitimate government." A legislative representative for the district "might be more congenial to the spirit of our institutions," but its absence did not exempt its inhabitants "from equal taxation" by the "ordinary revenue system."[210]

Congressional authority in newly formed states was at issue in two cases that involved the Appellate Jurisdiction Act of 1847 and the transition from territory to statehood. After Florida's admission to statehood in 1845, Congress created a federal district court for the state, but no judge was appointed to fill the seat for more than a year. In the meantime, the territorial court that had been erected in Florida in 1828 continued to hear and decide cases that fell within federal jurisdiction (the Florida state courts had assumed cases of local jurisdiction). At the time of statehood, no provision had been made to transfer cases pending in the territorial court to the federal district court. In 1847 Congress tried to rectify the situation by providing that any case still pending in the territorial court would be transferred to the district court, and any ruling made by the territorial court after statehood could be appealed to the US Supreme Court. Weeks after Florida's admission to the Union, Joseph Porter sued Hiram Benner and others in the territorial court for recovery of the value of supplies he had provided to a ship docked in Key West, under the admiralty jurisdiction of the federal courts. Benner denied that the territorial court had jurisdiction over the case. Nonetheless, the territorial judge ruled in favor of Porter, and on appeal, the US Supreme Court annulled the actions of the territorial court, concluding that the 1847 statute could not salvage the jurisdiction of the territorial courts. Congress could not constitutionally extend the life of any part of the territorial government once the territory had been converted into a state.[211] Only Article III judges could exercise federal judicial power within a state.

A variation on this problem arose after Wisconsin was admitted to statehood in May 1848. At the time, Congress provided for the transfer of any pending cases that fell under federal jurisdiction from the territorial court to the federal district court. *McNulty v. Batty* originated in the territorial court as a suit to recover a debt, normally a matter of state law. An appeal from the territorial supreme court to the US Supreme Court was pending at the time of Wisconsin's transition to statehood. In February 1848 Congress had extended the 1847 appellate jurisdiction law to all territories (not just Florida), with the understanding that the US Supreme Court would retain jurisdiction of appeals from the territorial courts pending at the time of statehood. The Supreme Court refused to accept jurisdiction in the *McNulty* case, however. Congress could not constitutionally authorize the Supreme Court to hear cases that otherwise did not fall within federal jurisdiction just because territorial status ended. Moreover, the newly formed district court did not have jurisdiction to receive any order entered by the Supreme Court, since the district court could not otherwise hear such a local case. Ultimately, *McNulty* came to rest in whatever condition it was in at the time of Wisconsin's admission to the Union, and Congress did not have the constitutional authority to extend its life.[212] After this "embarrassment" over the question of federal jurisdiction and the transition to statehood, Congress adopted a new scheme in future statehood enabling acts that passed constitutional muster.[213]

Confronting Slavery

The Court did not come all at once to the slavery question in the *Dred Scott* case in 1857. The judiciary had largely escaped the growing slavery controversy during the early years of the republic, but by the fourth decade of the nineteenth century, the Court, like the rest of the country, was firmly entering what would become known as the antebellum era.[214] It should come as no surprise that the justices were not particularly sympathetic to antislavery arguments when they heard cases that challenged slavery laws. Despite the growing antislavery sentiment and increasingly well organized and influential antislavery movement, national political leaders throughout this period were committed to policies that were friendly to slave owners. Until the very end of the antebellum period, building a national coalition that could seriously compete for control of the institutions of the federal government meant having a working relationship with the pro-slavery interests that dominated the electoral votes and congressional seats of the South. None of the major political parties was willing to adopt an antislavery stance, and antislavery politicians were relegated to noisy factions within the major parties (such as the Conscience Whigs) or to third parties (such as the Liberty Party, the Free-Soil Party, or the more successful Republican Party). The justices chosen by presidents who had negotiated that obstacle course were not inclined to embrace radical antislavery doctrines. The mainstream of American politics was pro-slavery throughout this period, and the justices reflected mainstream sensibilities.

The Taney Court's constitutional decisions on slavery were also prefigured by congressional decisions on how to organize the Court. Congress defined the size of the Supreme Court. Informal norms regulated the pool of potential nominees for individual seats on the Court. In the early nineteenth century, each justice was responsible for a geographic circuit and was expected to personally participate in circuit court decisions, which often required the application of local law. Justices exercising such responsibilities were expected to hail from the circuits they would oversee, meaning that the drawing of circuit boundaries had significant consequences for the composition of the Court itself. If a circuit encompassed only the New England states, then only a lawyer from New England would be nominated or confirmed to fill that seat.

When the Jacksonians came to power, they broke the political logjam that had delayed the Court's growth to accommodate the western states. The Judiciary Act of 1837 redrew circuit boundaries and expanded and reorganized the Court.[215] Andrew Jackson had two new seats to fill on the Court, and the western states were organized into three new circuits, with the states created from the antislavery Northwest Territory making up only a single circuit. The result was a Court tilted toward areas of Jacksonian strength, which also meant a nine-member Court with five seats situated in slave states. The geography of party politics tilted the Court away from the main sources of antislavery agitation. It is not surprising that Republican editor Horace Greeley dismissed the Taney Court as "five slaveholders and two or three doughfaces."[216]

Three times before secession, the Supreme Court heard cases involving the constitutionality of federal provisions under the fugitive slave clause, and each time the Court upheld the statutory arrangement. First, and most elaborately, Justice Story considered the claim that the Fugitive Slave Act of 1793 "is unconstitutional, because it does not fall within the scope of any of the enumerated powers of legislation confided to that body; and therefore is void." Story thought the act was "clearly constitutional in all its leading provisions," with the possible exception of the one directing state governors to act (this provision was not at issue in *Prigg* but was later struck down in *Dennison*). Congress had the necessary authority to pass laws not only to carry out its own enumerated powers but also "to carry into effect rights expressly given, and duties expressly enjoined" in the Constitution.[217] Second, in 1847 the Court took the time to rehearse Story's argument at length and reaffirm the power of Congress "to do justice" to the requirements and to "fulfill the duty incumbent on us towards all the members of the Union" embodied in the "compromises of the constitution" as it exists with regard to slavery.[218] Third, in 1859 the Taney Court lent its authority to the deeply controversial Fugitive Slave Act of 1850. Without offering any reasons for its opinion, the Court thought it "proper to say that, in the judgment of this court, the act of Congress commonly called the fugitive slave law is, in all its provisions, fully authorized by the Constitution of the United States."[219] Therefore, state resistance to the enforcement of that law should immediately cease.

Finally, the problem of federal regulation of slavery made an appearance in two cases framed in part by issues involving states' rights. The most familiar is *Dred Scott v. Sandford*, striking down a provision of the Missouri Compromise that sought to exclude slavery from some of the federal territories. As the Court construed the issue, the congressional ban on slavery in a territory raised two difficulties. First, it was inconsistent with the "principle upon which our Government rests and upon which alone they continue to exist, [that the United States] is a union of States, sovereign and independent within their own limits in their internal and domestic concerns, and bound together as one people by a General Government, possessing certain enumerated and restricted powers." Congress could not "obtain and hold colonies and dependent territories, over which they might legislate without restriction," and hold true to those principles. In dealing with the territories, Congress was obliged to promote "the interests of the *whole* people of the Union" when disposing of or regulating the "property held in common by the confederated States."[220] Congress could not discriminate against the interests of the slave states in favor of the interests of the free states when managing their common property in the western territories. Second, Congress was barred from "assum[ing] discretionary or despotic powers which the Constitution denied to it," which included the power to discriminate against "the right of property of the master in a slave"—a right recognized in the Constitution—while respecting other forms of property that were similarly situated.[221] Congress did not have the same broad discretion over how it defined property rights in the territories as the states had within their own domains. Both federalism principles and individual property rights precluded the federal government from emancipating slaves in the territories.

After some initial hesitation, the justices determined that the "distracting question" of slavery in the territories "*must* ultimately be decided by the Supreme Court."[222] They made a bid to do so with *Dred Scott*. They had previously intervened to bolster congressional authority to pass fugitive slave legislation. Those decisions might not have ended antislavery agitation, but they lent support to nationalist politicians who sought to reconcile the competing pressures.[223] As John Marshall had been in the *McCulloch* case, the majority in *Dred Scott* was convinced that the Court alone could bring political peace and quash the dangerous antislavery agitation that was rending the political system and the nation. To a much greater degree than Marshall in the Bank of the United States case, however, the *Dred Scott* Court had the support of the political establishment in its determination that judicial intervention was necessary. The Marshall Court had done what Jeffersonian leaders wanted in striking down state obstructions to the Bank of the United States, but there was no raging controversy over the power of Congress to charter the bank. By contrast, there was no more contested issue in the late antebellum era than the question of slavery in the territories, and mainstream political leaders were desperate for the Court to step in. Congressional and party leaders had repeatedly ducked the issue and invited judicial resolution from the late 1840s until *Dred Scott* in 1857.[224] As perennial Whig presidential candidate Henry Clay declared in 1850, "Now what ought to be done more satisfactory to both sides of the question . . . [is] to leave the question of slavery or no slavery to be decided by the only competent authority that can definitely settle it forever, the authority of the Supreme Court of the United States."[225] Democratic president James Buchanan likewise used his inaugural address on the eve of the *Dred Scott* decision to urge the citizenry to recognize that slavery was "a judicial question, which legitimately belongs to the Supreme Court of the United States"; he encouraged Americans "to suppress this agitation" and set aside all "differences of opinion" and "cheerfully submit" to the judicial resolution, whatever it might be.[226] Sectional agitators, whether from the North or the South, were more reluctant to leave things in the hands of the justices, but party leaders who hoped to build or sustain national coalitions were willing to take their chances with whatever the Court might do.[227] Moreover, given the southern tilt to antebellum politics, a pro-slavery outcome would hardly have been unwelcome or inconsistent with dominant interests, and political observers considered the 1856 election, which had brought Buchanan to the White House, to be a mandate for pro-slavery politics.[228] The Court was invited to intervene in the slavery issue, but it was not directly pressured to rule in a particular way. The justices took up the invitation, as they had done before. In this case, they used the opportunity to strike down a defunct statutory provision from the Missouri Compromise rather than uphold a current one as Marshall had done in the bank case.

A different constitutional problem arose in Ohio in the midst of the secession crisis. The Fugitive Slave Act of 1793 stated, "it shall be the duty of the Executive authority of the State" to arrest and render up fugitives.[229] The statutory language seemed plain; it asserted a federal "power to command and to coerce obedience" of state government officials under the authority of carrying out the provisions of the Constitution's fugitive slave clause. But, Chief Justice Taney argued, "we think it clear, that the Federal Government, under the Constitution, has no power to impose on a State officer, as such, any duty whatever, and compel him to perform it; for if it possessed this power, it might overload the officer with duties which would fill up all his time . . . and might impose on him duties of a character incompatible with the rank and dignity to which he was elevated by the State."[230] This provision of the Fugitive Slave Act was not constitutionally enforceable against the governor of Ohio, who refused to arrest or extradite Willis Lago, a free African American man who had been indicted in Kentucky for aiding the escape of slaves in that state. This was not a crime that Ohio was prepared to recognize in 1861, the governor concluded; nor was the incoming Lincoln administration likely to disagree with that assessment. This refusal was a matter of interstate comity, the Taney Court concluded, and Congress could not intervene to commandeer the officials of the Ohio state government. Justices and commentators had long predicted this outcome if the provision were ever put to a constitutional test.[231] The language of statutory "duty" was exclusively used by the early Congress to express commands to inferior officers, and there was little reason to imagine that the Fugitive Slave Act of 1793 was any different in its design, although the duties imposed were not always ministerial and readily subject to a writ of mandamus.[232] The Court did not void the entire statutory scheme by which governors might satisfy their constitutional obligation to deliver up fugitives; it voided only the enforceable duty. The congressional declaration that governors *should* turn over fugitives without delay was an important message that the Court endorsed. Moreover, the statute had originally been written to empower state executives who were looking for procedures to follow when extraditing fugitives and lacked any such guidance or authority from their own state legislatures.[233] The law could still serve these functions, even if Congress could not commandeer the governor to act against his wishes.[234]

The handful of Supreme Court cases challenging the constitutionality of federal laws relating to slavery were among the most politically controversial the Court has ever heard. *Dred Scott* overshadowed anything else the Court had done up to that time, and it put the Court firmly in the sights of Republican Party activists who saw the justices as little more than handmaidens to the slave power. From the perspective of history, the Court was consistently on the wrong side of the slavery question. From the perspective of contemporary politics, the Court consistently aligned itself with the political leadership of the federal government. The justices made their peace with slavery as a distasteful but essential part of the compromises that kept the Union together, and they closed ranks with the bipartisan political consensus that defended the institution in the antebellum years. When that consensus finally fell apart, the justices were exposed to the same opprobrium that stained other national figures.

Conclusion

Judicial review of Congress in the early decades of the nation's history largely took place in the shadows, and as a result, it has been easily forgotten. Only occasionally did the Court venture into the limelight and issue constitutional judgments on politically contentious legislation or in politically charged disputes. The practice of judicial review was built up through the resolution of more mundane cases in which the political stakes were relatively low. The justices made it clear early on that the Constitution was among the laws that needed to be interpreted and applied during the resolution of legal disputes in the federal courts. Even so, it was accepted that the Constitution was a superior law that took precedence over the ordinary statutes passed by the national legislature operating under the authority of the fundamental law. The judicial duty when conflicts became apparent was clear. Statutory provisions could be applied in the courts only in a manner that was consistent with the requirements of the Constitution. When the commands of Congress seemingly exceeded its constitutional mandate, they lacked legal force. While the justices preferred to avoid saying that Congress had intentionally violated the Constitution, they were confident in their own power to adhere to the terms of the Constitution as they understood it, regardless of what Congress had done.

On those occasions when the Court was called on to answer more controversial questions, it almost invariably upheld congressional authority. From the Sedition Act to the carriage tax to the Bank of the United States to the Fugitive Slave Act, the Court threw its support behind federal lawmakers. The most famous cases were also the most unusual. In *Marbury*, the Court voided an uncontroversial provision of the Judiciary Act to escape a risky confrontation with the newly elected president. In *Dred Scott*, the Court voided the defunct Missouri Compromise in a bid to undercut a political insurgency that threatened the antebellum political order. The Court miscalculated the Republican Party's strength, however, and found itself at odds rather than aligned with the new political majority, placing the Court in a hazardous position as the nation entered the secession crisis.

More often, the Court was confronted with constitutional questions in the course of resolving more ordinary litigation. In such cases, neither the litigant nor the Court was interested in a frontal assault on important federal policies. The concern was how the law applied to the case at hand. Depending on the statutory language, this could require disallowing a certain class of applications of the statute, requiring implicit exceptions to its application, or effectively rewriting the statute to accomplish constitutional objectives while excluding the unconstitutional ones. Regardless of how the justices approached the task, both the Court and commentators recognized that the judiciary was imposing constitutional limits on the legislative power of Congress in such cases, and it was rendering parts of federal statutory law legally unenforceable. In some cases, the dubious statutory text covered a complex set of applications, some constitutional and some not. Consistent with *Marbury*'s logic—that is, that the power of judicial review is grounded in the judge's authority to decline to follow a statutory command that would lead to an unconstitutional outcome in the case before the bench—the Court refused to allow the law of Congress to supersede the law of the Constitution in individual cases, but it frequently left in place the law itself, if there were other potential applications that were not before the bench.

The fact that the Court was willing to hear constitutional arguments on the limits of congressional power did not make it an important player in the biggest constitutional disputes of the period. It largely remained a bystander in the great constitutional debates of the early republic. Congress and the executive branch largely debated and resolved the critical issues of separation of powers, federalism, and individual rights in the late eighteenth and early nineteenth centuries. Even when the federal judiciary spoke to these issues, it was a secondary player, and it certainly did not settle them.

As the Court used its power to interpret the Constitution to void congressional actions, trim or redirect legislative actions, and validate or construct federal policy, it contributed above all to the process of nation building. It reaffirmed national priorities and helped protect and sustain the institutions needed to advance those priorities. It projected national power—such as it was in these early days—into the international arena, into the states, and into the frontier. It supported the flexibility of the governing institutions of the new constitutional system while fleshing out the features, jurisdiction, powers, and prerogatives of the federal judiciary and carefully laying down markers to outline how Congress could and could not legislate over the courts. It announced what Congress could do, and it corrected Congress when it went astray. In doing so, the Court used judicial review to work with, rather than against, Congress to construct a new national government. Before the Civil War, the Court never created serious obstructions to important policies favored by active majorities when reviewing federal laws. The Court established the power of judicial review by using it. But the Court used it to validate congressional actions or correct congressional errors, not to block what Congress was trying to accomplish.

4

Review of Congress during the Civil War and Reconstruction

The American constitutional system was transformed during the Civil War and Reconstruction. The Reconstruction Amendments to the US Constitution formally abolished slavery and secured new political and civil rights for the freedmen and, in doing so, reworked the federal constitutional scheme in ways that are still being explored today. Meanwhile, new precedents for the exercise of presidential power during wartime were being laid down, and long-unsettled constitutional issues, such as the right of states to secede from the Union, were laid to rest.

The judiciary's power to review the constitutionality of statutes likewise emerged from these years a different practice. The addition of the Fourteenth Amendment, in particular, gave the federal courts expansive new authority to review the constitutionality of state legislation and opened a rich new vein of federal constitutional jurisprudence on individual rights. The addition of new constitutional text had fewer implications for the judicial review of Congress, yet the US Supreme Court became markedly more active in reviewing federal statutes. In the two decades prior to the Civil War, the Court resolved an average of just over one constitutional challenge to a federal statute per year, and it struck down a law at the rate of one every other year. Over the last two decades of the nineteenth century, the Court heard constitutional cases at five times that rate and struck down a federal law nearly once per year.

Part of the increase in judicial review simply reflected Congress's greater productivity in drafting statutes to be reviewed. The Su-

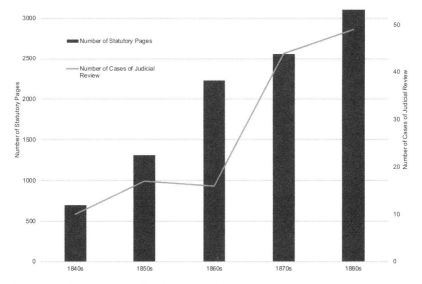

Figure 4-1: Legislative Productivity and Judicial Review, 1840–1890

preme Court more often and more regularly evaluated the constitutionality of congressional statutes as Congress more regularly produced them. The Thirty-Fourth Congress, which met in 1855, filled about 250 pages of the statute books with public acts. The Thirty-Ninth Congress, which met ten years later, filled more than twice as many pages. The government was becoming bigger and more complex. The national legislature was busier than ever writing new laws. Constitutional puzzles followed apace. As figure 4-1 indicates, as the number of statutory pages grew during the middle decades of the nineteenth century, the number of cases in which the Court evaluated the constitutionality of a federal statutory provision also increased.

The growing volume of judicial review was accompanied by a shift in its nature. Figure 4-2 shows the number of cases prior to 1862 in which the Supreme Court reviewed the constitutionality of federal statutory provisions produced by each Congress, and figure 4-3 does the same for cases decided between 1862 and 1885. The figures show which Congresses produced laws that generated judicial review, and together they show which Congresses received judicial scrutiny in the cases considered in chapter 3 and constitutional scrutiny in the cases considered in this chapter.

The figures clearly illustrate a transformation in how judicial review was

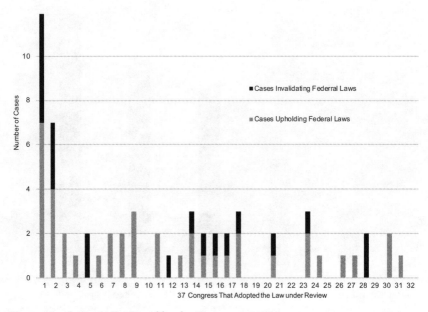

Figure 4-2: Congress Reviewed by the Court, 1789–1861

exercised. As observed in the previous chapter, in the first several decades of its existence, the Court was more active in exercising judicial review than is usually recognized, and the pace of that activity picked up in the antebellum years. But as figure 4-2 emphasizes, the Court often found itself returning to the work of the earliest Congresses, which had laid down much of the basic framework that gave form to the new government and structure to its policies. These complex laws were frequently invoked in litigation. In particular, the judiciary's own power and jurisdiction were defined in legislation such as the Judiciary Act of 1789, and the Court frequently had to explain the constitutional bounds within which Congress could work in setting up the federal courts, as Chief Justice John Marshall famously did in the *Marbury* case. Although the Marshall and Taney Courts sometimes examined the constitutionality of relatively contemporaneous statutes, they were often working with older legislative material.

By contrast, the Court under Chief Justices Salmon Chase and Morrison Waite turned its attention resolutely toward more contemporaneous policies when exercising the power of judicial review. The Court in the 1860s and 1870s sometimes found itself answering constitutional questions about earlier stat-

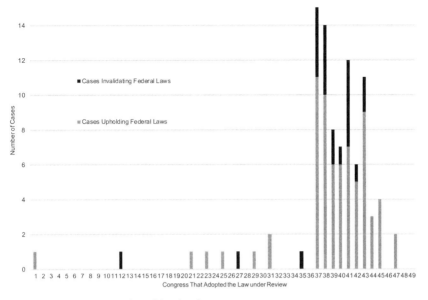

Figure 4-3: Congress Reviewed by the Court, 1862–1885

utes, but most of its work involved laws passed by the Thirty-Seventh Congress (the first to meet after the secession crisis) and its successors. The prospect of judicial review gained a new immediacy and political relevance. The Court was generally a distant consideration in the early republic, but it became a more hovering presence as the nation slid into Civil War and Reconstruction.

That the Court would be in a position to keep up with Congress and interrogate the legislature's constitutional authority to make policy was hardly obvious as the war began. The Taney Court had tried to put a dagger in the heart of the new Republican Party with its decision in *Dred Scott*. The Court had aligned itself with the antebellum political mainstream on the slavery question, but it had made no friends among the insurgent Republicans who held political power after the 1860 elections. As the secession crisis turned to war, the Taney Court represented the ancien regime, and the justices were met with skepticism. Abraham Lincoln had come to national prominence denouncing the Court as a tool of the slave power, and he did not let up upon winning the White House. The administration treated *Dred Scott* as a dead letter and ignored its implications for black civil rights. When war broke out and the military started to detain civilians, the administration simply ignored Chief Justice Taney's writ of habeas corpus. Lincoln's attorney general later explained that the president is not "subordinate" to the Court, and the executive need not recognize any "legal superior possessing the power to revise and reverse its action."[1] Legislative leaders were inclined to think that the "sovereign power in this republic is in [the] Congress of the United States," and the possibility that they might violate the Constitution should not be "presumed, even for the purpose of argument."[2] Republican legislators toyed with the idea of eliminating the power of judicial review entirely, and they took steps to shield key features of Reconstruction from judicial review.[3] Republican lawmakers gave more credence to their own authority to reshape constitutional meaning than to the Court's.

The Court managed to weather the storm and emerged from the 1860s as powerful as it had ever been. Theorist Robert Dahl might have anticipated an immediate upswing in judicially voided statutes as the newly elected Republican legislators ran headlong into their partisan foes entrenched on the bench. Such was not the case. As the Republicans enacted their policy agenda and prosecuted the war, the Court did not exert itself. As figures 4-1 and 1-3 indicate, the Court did not become unusually activist in the 1860s. Even as Congress ramped up its legislative efforts, the Court stayed its hand.

The Republican politicians did their part to render the Court friendlier and more passive. Congress briefly considered dissolving the Taney Court, on the grounds that it had "lost public confidence" and the incumbent justices belonged to the party that "has now gone out of power," but cooler heads prevailed.[4] It was more productive to simply reorganize the federal judiciary. A series of statutes redrew the federal judicial circuits to (eventually) give the Court a firm northern majority, while immediately adding a tenth seat to be filled by President Lincoln. Timely deaths and resignations facilitated the rapid creation of a pro-administration majority on the bench. Needless to say, Lincoln took care to select justices known to be sympathetic to the Union cause.

Dahl would tell us that the predictable result should have been a Court lulled into quiescence. But the justices did not remain quiescent for long. Through the war years, they resolved essentially no constitutional disputes— an unusual gap, even for the mid-nineteenth-century Court. Congress was left to its own devices until the victory on the battlefield had been secured. Even then, the Court was slow to rule against the constitutionality of federal statutes. Not until the Ulysses S. Grant administration did the Court begin to issue constitutional rulings at an accelerating pace. By the 1870s, even though the Court was firmly in the hands of Republican appointees, the justices were reviewing Republican-sponsored statutes—and striking them down—at an unprecedented rate.

The Chase and Waite Courts of the 1870s and 1880s were both constitutionally activist and politically convergent. How were they able to sustain that posture, and why would they want to do so? These decisions might seem more explicable if the justices had been focusing their attention on prewar Jacksonian legislation, but as figure 4-3 indicates, they were predominantly considering statutes that had been adopted by Republicans since the start of the war. What were they doing? As figure 4-3 illustrates, they were mostly upholding Republican statutes against constitutional challenges. The justices were asked again and again to explain how Congress's actions aligned with the requirements of the Constitution, and they generally rose to the challenge. In doing so, they painted a portrait of a Constitution that was flexible enough to accommodate even dramatic new federal initiatives. They began to construct a Republican Constitution that was more capacious than the one the Jeffersonians and Jacksonians had envisioned.

But they also found occasion to strike laws down. In doing so, they both revealed and exploited divisions within the Republican coalition. The Republican Party was a rapidly assembled conglomeration of former Whigs, abolitionist activists, and war Democrats that was struggling to consolidate a national electoral majority. There were, to be sure, many points of agreement, but even in the legislative arena, the areas of disagreement were often on display as the party debated war policy and Reconstruction. If such fundamental disagreements were suppressed on the Court when they mattered most, intraparty disagreements over secondary and tertiary issues were waiting to be expressed. Once the immediate pressure of the war was over, the justices had more room to disagree among themselves and to disagree with their partisan allies in the legislature.[5]

In the rapidly changing world of the Civil War and Reconstruction era, the timing of judicial review mattered. In the midst of crisis, the Court sat on the sidelines as the politicians struggled to determine the best course of action. Once the crisis had passed, the party fissured and pulled back from some of its earlier commitments. In that postbellum environment, the Court was able to shape the constitutional order. The Court did not set itself against the deeply held commitments of robust political majorities. It exercised judicial review by navigating among the party's conflicting commitments. The Court exercised power not *against* the majority but *within* the majority.

Matters of War

The first and highest priority for the Lincoln administration was, of course, winning the war. The Court could have gotten in the way—and forced a confrontation with the elected branches—but ultimately it did not. In the spring of 1861 Chief Justice Taney, while riding circuit, questioned Lincoln's authority to suspend the writ of habeas corpus, but the administration preferred to avoid complying with the writ while dodging litigation that might have brought the issue before the full Court for resolution.[6] Taney drafted an opinion denouncing the military draft as unconstitutional, but the Court never heard a case that tested its resolve to issue such an opinion.[7] When the Court did get an opportunity to rule on the constitutionality of the congressional exercise of war powers, the crisis had largely passed, and it proved to be generally supportive.[8]

The exception was perhaps the most momentous use of judicial review against Congress in the Court's first century of existence, and the result was humiliation and an immediate judicial retreat. The suspension of the gold standard and the issuing of greenbacks did not mobilize the army on the battlefield, but it was among the most important war measures adopted by Congress. The Civil War stretched Union resources thin, and the government had to get creative to pay its bills. The Legal Tender Act of 1862 authorized the issuance of paper money as legal tender and suspended the necessity of repaying public or private debts in gold or gold-backed currency. Relying on fiat currency to sustain itself, Congress was able to mobilize resources for the war without having to incur ruinous indebtedness or raise taxes.

Government leaders had doubts about their constitutional authority to require private individuals to accept paper currency as legal tender, but the perceived necessity in the emergency trumped constitutional scruples. In 1862 House Ways and Means Committee chairman Elbridge Spaulding struggled to get the votes needed to pass the legal tender proposal. Hoping to overcome the constitutional objections raised by numerous Republican legislators, Spaulding asked Attorney General Edward Bates to provide an opinion on its constitutionality. Bates would not go that far, but he authorized Spaulding to tell his colleagues that, "as a private man," Bates thought legal tender was not "forbidden to Congress" by the Constitution—a statement that did not sway many committee members.[9] Secretary of the Treasury Salmon Chase "regret[ted] exceedingly that it is found necessary to resort" to legal tender, but he bowed to the need "to meet existing necessities in the mode most useful and least hurtful to general interest."[10] Spaulding tried to place the bill in its proper context: it was "a war measure, a measure of necessity, and not of choice," but in "extraordinary times . . . extraordinary measures must be resorted to in order to save our Government."[11] Only the threat to the country's continued existence could render legal tender necessary and proper.

Once the war had been won, the party splintered over what to do about legal tender. Wall Street was eager to return to a hard currency and end the inflationary boon to debtors. Debtors, of course, preferred to continue paying back their loans in depreciated dollars. As a practical matter, the government was in a difficult position as it tried to disassemble the massive financial scaffolding that had been built on paper currency. The Grant administration's go-slow approach left millions of dollars of greenbacks in circulation. It was in this environment that creditors pushed the issue by trying to have legal tender declared unconstitutional. A badly divided Court accepted the invitation to intervene.

This important case came before the Court in less than ideal circumstances. The Court was understaffed. It had consisted of ten members at the time of Lincoln's assassination—five of them appointed by Lincoln, including his final appointment, which had moved Chase from Treasury to become chief justice. After Democrat John Catron died, Congress eliminated three seats on the Court rather than letting President Andrew Johnson send up a nomination. Democrat John Moore Wayne's death left the Court with only eight members (and one of them, Democrat Robert Grier, had been debilitated by multiple strokes) when it heard arguments on the constitutionality of the Legal Tender Act. Congress had already passed a statute restoring the Court to nine seats, but President Grant had not yet announced his nominee to fill the vacancy. Nonetheless, Chase put together a five-person majority (including Grier, who retired shortly thereafter) to hold the act unconstitutional.

Writing for that transitory majority, Chase reflected, "amid the tumult of the late civil war [when] apprehensions for the safety of the Republic [were] almost universal . . . the time was not favorable to considerate reflection upon the constitutional limits of legislative or executive authority." Excessive power "was assumed under patriotic motives," and "many who doubted yielded their doubts" in the face of constitutional views that had "never before [been] entertained by American statesmen or jurists." With the "return of peace, and under the influence of calmer times," those doubts that had been swallowed in the face of national necessity should now be voiced, and the Court had to recognize that the law had not been "fully sanctioned" by the Constitution.[12]

In expressing his concerns about the constitutionality of legal tender, Chief Justice Chase ironically revived John Marshall's *McCulloch* opinion, which had been ignored while the Jacksonians controlled the Court. Although *McCulloch* was generally understood to be a sweeping grant of power to Congress, Chase focused on Marshall's interpretation of the limits implicit in the necessary and proper clause. Namely, for a law to be necessary and proper for carrying out an enumerated power, the means chosen by Congress to pursue constitutionally legitimate ends had to be neither prohibited by the text of the Constitution nor inconsistent with its "letter and spirit."[13] Even if paper currency was "an appropriate and plainly adapted means for the execution of the power to declare and carry on war," which Chase doubted, it ran afoul of Marshall's twofold qualification on the necessary and proper clause. Chase thought that, in barring the federal government from taking "private property without process of law," the Constitution effectively prohibited Congress from requiring "all citizens to accept, in satisfaction of all contracts for money, half or three-quarters or any other proportion less than the whole of the value actually due." Forcing creditors to accept depreciated greenbacks to settle a debt was as much an "arbitrary privation of property" as forcing a contracting party to accept fifty acres of land instead of the hundred acres for which he had paid. Moreover, Chase believed that the constitutional prohibition against states impairing the obligations of a contract represented a "cardinal principle" of justice, the spirit of which pervaded the entire document. Even without the due process clause explicitly forbidding the federal government from depriving individuals of their property, the "spirit" of the Constitution rendered such instruments inappropriate.

The backlash to the Court's decision was immediate and vociferous. Moreover, Grant swiftly announced nominees to fill the two vacancies on the Court, and the remade Court ordered new hearings on the legal tender issue. Just over a year after the *Hepburn* decision, the Court reversed it by a five-to-four majority in the *Legal Tender Cases*. Newly appointed Justice William Strong made quick work of Chase's opinion. Strong reemphasized Spaulding's conclusion that extraordinary times called for extraordinary measures and that the Constitution had to be sufficiently flexible to accommodate such crises. Thus, Strong began by noting that it "would be difficult to over-estimate the consequences which must follow our decision." At stake was the "entire business of the country," the "possible continued existence of the government," and whether the government "is without those means of self-preservation which, all must admit, may, in certain contingencies, become indispensable." The Constitution must be understood to be adequate to any contingency, which meant giving Congress a free hand to act when need be. The "whole history of the government and of congressional legislation," Strong contended, has shown that even in tranquil times, Congress had been entrusted with "very wide discretion . . . to carry into effect the great objects for which the government was framed." That discretion must necessarily be even more unfettered in times of crisis. As for the Constitution's implicit and explicit prohibitions on legal tender cited by Chase, Strong concluded that, since "Congress is empowered to regulate money," the general constitutional principle that the government cannot interfere with contracts or property did not apply. Contracts involving "a tender of legal values" rested on the back of whatever decisions Congress made about the definition of "lawful money," and any losses a creditor suffered as a consequence of congressional decisions were akin to the natural fallout from any policy choice.[14] The Constitution did not protect individuals from injuries or losses arising from the normal exercise of legitimate congressional regulatory powers.

The initial legal tender case shook the country, and the sudden reversal shook it again for different reasons. Although the decision to uphold the legal tender law brought the Court into alignment with the Republican leadership, the decision to overrule *Hepburn* mere months later suggested to many that the Court, and thus the Constitution, had become a political plaything.

The short-lived decision in *Hepburn* marked the Court's most significant obstruction of congressional policy between secession and the Gilded Age.

Even though the Court did not take up the constitutionality of war measures until well after Appomattox, the justices were generally supportive of Congress's actions. There were myriad constitutional difficulties associated with the Civil War, but the Court contributed little toward solving them and was content to simply cement the victory.[15]

One of the unusual aspects of the congressional exercise of war powers in the context of the Civil War was the infliction of punishment on the Confederates. In general, the persons and property of enemies in wartime are entitled to little constitutional protection; however, the military enemy in the Civil War consisted of American citizens, which created innumerable political and constitutional complications. The Court imposed some limits on how Congress could treat these foes, but it was generally accommodating toward the exercise of political power that might advance the war effort. Most notably, the Court limited the effect of the "Ironclad Oath," which required federal employees, officials, and lawyers to swear not only that they would defend the Constitution in the future but also that they had never provided "a voluntary support to any pretended government, authority, power or constitution within the United States, hostile or inimical thereto."[16] Augustus Hill Garland had served in the Arkansas state house, and he represented that state in the Confederate senate during the war, even though he had voted against disunion at the Arkansas secession convention in 1861. After the war ended, Garland was among those who sought to reintegrate the state into the Union, and he quickly sought and received a pardon for his wartime actions from President Andrew Johnson. Garland had been sworn into the federal bar to argue cases before the US Supreme Court prior to secession, and he petitioned the Court to resume his federal practice, despite the congressional ban. Despite the attorney general's argument that Congress had complete discretion to establish the qualifications for any lawyer to practice before the courts constituted by federal statute, a majority of justices, most of them appointed before the war, concluded that the statute as it applied to Garland could only be understood as a form of legislatively imposed punishment for past behavior. As such, it not only violated the constitutional strictures against punishment by statute but also impinged on the judicial authority to assess the qualifications of those admitted to practice in the courts and the presidential authority to grant a full pardon, which shielded individuals like Garland from prosecution or punishment. Garland went on to a distinguished career not only as a litigator in the federal courts but also as a governor, a US senator, and eventually a US attorney general in the first postbellum Democratic administration. The Court's ruling signaled that the judiciary was willing to respect the blanket pardons Johnson handed out after the war.[17]

Not long thereafter, in a less contentious case, the Court tried to smooth over the more punitive features of a different war measure. In the early days of the war, Congress imposed a hefty direct tax that was apportioned among the states based on the value of land. Since the Confederate states were unlikely to collect their share of that revenue and forward it to the federal government, Congress further provided that in any state in which the collection of the tax was obstructed "by reason of insurrection or rebellion," the tax fell directly on individual landholders, along with a draconian penalty. In addition, a lien would be imposed on the property "without any other or further proceeding whatever," and the title would subsequently be forfeited to the United States. Tax commissioners were appointed to take possession of such land and sell or lease it to loyal citizens, unless the original owner was willing to appear before the commissioners "in his or her own proper person," take a loyalty oath, and pay the taxes, fines, and other associated expenses to recover the land.[18] When the tenants of a parcel of land in Alexandria County, Virginia, tried to pay the tax, the commissioners refused the payment and sold the land. After the war, the son of the original owner sued to recover the land, but the attorney general insisted that there were no constitutional limitations on Congress's authority to seize such land by "summary proceedings." The Court quailed at the implications and chose to construe the statute as a "revenue" measure, although it admitted that Congress was seeking to raise revenue in extraordinary circumstances and that its directives for disposing of the seized land "had reference to the suppression of rebellion rather than to revenue." As the Court pointedly observed, the suggestion that "the title of a citizen to his land can be divested by forfeiture and vested absolutely in the United States" with no real judicial process ran afoul of established constitutional principles. The Court was unwilling to admit that Congress sought to make "an act of sovereignty so highly penal," and it insisted that, "as a law for raising revenue," the conventional legal processes must apply, including the right of "some friend or agent" of the owner to pay the assessed tax prior to any sale.[19] The tax commissioners could not, under these circumstances, "make a valid sale for taxes," although the Court refrained from calling Congress out for seizing land contrary to the due process of law. As the Court later explained, since the commissioners had announced a "general rule," in keeping with apparent congressional policy in that statute and subsequent ones, that the tax could be paid only by the owner in person, the courts were obliged to assume that any subsequent land sales were invalid. The "legal presumption" had to be that the tax would have been paid, if only the constitutionally appropriate procedures had been followed.[20]

More generally, however, the Court upheld the authority of Congress to take aggressive action against the rebels through the exercise of its war powers. The justices were emphatic that the congressional war powers were sweeping and fully at play in the context of the Civil War. "The measures to be taken in carrying on war and to suppress insurrection are not defined. The decision of all such questions rests wholly in the discretion of those to whom the substantial powers involved are confided by the Constitution." That authority encompassed more than the power to achieve "victories in the field and the dispersion of the insurgent forces"; it extended to the power "to guard against the immediate renewal of the conflict, and to remedy the evils which have arisen from its rise and progress."[21] The Court had little problem, for example, upholding the Confiscation Acts, which allowed the government to seize property that was being used to aid the rebellion. All the justices agreed that these statutes were properly "an exercise of this war power" and not "mere municipal regulations for the punishment of crime," although there was less agreement about what counted as enemy property in the exceptional circumstances of civil war.[22] Similarly, the justices had no objection to Congress imposing regulations related to importing cotton from the insurrectionary states. It was the "undoubted right" of Congress to prohibit, tax, or regulate trade with Tennessee (or to delegate that power to the executive branch) "as incident to the power to declare war and to carry it to a successful termination," even if such regulations could not be sustained if imposed against a state in other circumstances.[23] While the Court was more skeptical of wartime legislation that threatened to warp the peacetime legal order, it had no interest in denying Congress extraordinary powers to fight the war itself.

The Task of Reconstruction

The Civil War raised complicated constitutional challenges precisely because it involved American citizens and American political jurisdictions, blurring the line between the home front and the battlefield. But at least the power to wage war was well understood. The Reconstruction that followed the war was terra incognita. The rebellious territory had been formally pacified, but the return to normalcy—or to the "Union as it was, and the Constitution as it is," as the Democratic Party pledged—was not immediately forthcoming.[24] The Reconstruction Amendments, ending slavery, extending federal civil rights, and prohibiting racial discrimination in voting, wrought their own perplexing constitutional changes that Congress and the Court had to work out. The congressional policy of extended Reconstruction of the former Confederate states rested on innovative and highly controversial constitutional theories.

Undoubtedly, the most significant threat posed by the Court's judicial review of Congress, other than obstructing the war itself, was obstructing Reconstruction. The impeachment of President Andrew Johnson in 1868 showed how far congressional Republicans were willing to go to clear impediments to Reconstruction. Venturing into this territory was risky, and the justices wanted no part of it. Augustus Garland, freshly restored to the Supreme Court bar, helped orchestrate the most direct constitutional challenge to Reconstruction by seeking an injunction that would prevent the president from enforcing it. For the Court, Chief Justice Chase firmly refused to reach the merits of the case. The Court was unwilling to enjoin the president from performing actions "purely executive and political," and it openly speculated that the president might ignore any such injunction or might even be impeached if he complied with the Court's judgment. The Court was not prepared to set up such a "strange spectacle" and "collision" among the three coordinate branches.[25] In 1866 the chief justice was not prepared to stake the Court's future on the political fortunes of Andrew Johnson. The Court ducked again when it had another opportunity to rule on the constitutionality of the Reconstruction Acts, this time in the midst of President Johnson's impeachment trial. The Court let the habeas petition of William McCardle, a newspaper editor detained by Union troops in Mississippi for his anti-Reconstruction editorials, sit on its docket until Congress could pass a statute stripping the Court of jurisdiction to hear the case. The Court promptly upheld the Repealer Act and dismissed the habeas petition, saying nothing about the constitutionality of continued martial law in the South.[26] When it came to Reconstruction, silence was golden.

The situation changed after the fires of the 1860s cooled down. As President Grant was leaving office, Union troops were being withdrawn from the South, and the Republican Party was conceding "redemption and home rule" to the former Confederate states, the Court began to consider the implications of the Reconstruction Amendments.[27] In particular, the Court was presented with a series of cases testing the scope of the enforcement clauses of the Fourteenth and Fifteenth Amendments, which gave Congress the "power to enforce this article by appropriate legislation." In deciding these cases, the Court chipped away at congressional civil and voting rights statutes, while endorsing the federal courts' core authority to intervene in cases involving this new set of constitutional rights.

Notoriously, in the mid-1870s the Court stifled more ambitious efforts to extend federal protection to freedmen in the South. The Enforcement Act of 1870 imposed federal penalties on anyone who, on account of race, hampered a qualified citizen from voting. The law inserted the federal government into state and local elections to an unprecedented degree in an effort to enforce the new constitutional requirement that no citizen be denied the right to vote in any election on account of "race, color, or previous condition of servitude." But the constitutional text included two potentially important qualifications: the right could not be "abridged by the United States or by any State," and the right to vote could not be abridged specifically on account of race. The Fifteenth Amendment had created a "new constitutional right which is within the protecting power of Congress," but the question was whether Congress had exceeded its mandate to enforce this right with "appropriate legislation." The Court first objected that a provision of the Enforcement Act "does not in express terms limit the offence of an inspector of elections, for which a punishment is provided, to a wrongful discrimination on account of race, &c." As a result, the law worked a "radical change in the practice" of administering state elections, but it did so in ways that introduced ambiguity as to when state officials could be held criminally liable for their actions. Any indictment handed down would be consistent with the plain language of either the statute or the Constitution, but it could not simultaneously be consistent with both. The justices complained that if Congress was going to create new criminal offenses, "it should express its will in language that need not deceive the common mind," and it should avoid writing statutory text that seemed to manifest no "intention to confine its provisions to the terms of the Fifteenth Amendment."[28] The situation was just as bad with another section of the statute, which punished conspiracies to abridge the right to vote but neglected to limit itself to criminalizing actions by government officials. The Reconstruction Amendments authorized Congress to protect citizens from their state governments, but the states alone were responsible for protecting them from "their fellow-citizens."[29]

For the Court to bring the statute in line with the Constitution, it would have to write in the necessary qualifications and limitations, which would be to "make a new law, not . . . enforce an old one." Congress needed to revise the statute itself to render it compliant with the Constitution.[30] The trouble was that, by time the Court issued its ruling, the House of Representatives was in the hands of the Democratic Party, and Congress was gridlocked on the subject of civil rights legislation. Moreover, the facts on the ground were quickly outstripping what the Reconstruction Amendments, as construed, were designed to remedy. As posited by the Court, the Reconstruction Amendments protected freedmen from the sort of legislative "black codes" the Confederate states had tried to adopt immediately before Reconstruction, but it offered them little protection against the Ku Klux Klan, which arose at the end of Reconstruction. For defense against that threat, the Court suggested, the freedmen would have to turn to their state legislatures, not to Congress, because the Reconstruction Amendments were not malleable enough to adapt to the new situation.

That the Court was not inextricably opposed to the Reconstruction project can be seen in subsequent decisions upholding important aspects of those laws. Those cases were of three types. One set revolved around racial discrimination by government officials. Not long after the Court had identified constitutional problems in the congressional civil rights acts, it was asked to review the constitutionality of federal prosecutions that fell within the "protecting power of Congress." The so-called *Ku Klux Klan Cases* tested whether Congress had adequate constitutional authority to punish conspiracies to "intimidate any citizen in the free exercise or enjoyment of any right or privilege secured to him by the Constitution or laws of the United States" or to prevent a qualified citizen from voting in a *federal* election.[31] The Court thought it obvious that "a government whose essential character is republican" had the power to protect the election of its officers from "the influence of violence, of corruption, and of fraud." In the case of a gang of white Georgia men who had beaten an African American man for voting in a congressional election, the justices emphasized that the federal government would not be at the mercy of "those who respect no right but brute force."[32] In the case of a county judge in Virginia who had excluded all African Americans from the jury pool, a divided Court likewise argued that the Reconstruction Amendments were designed "to raise the colored race from that condition of inferiority and servitude in which most of them had previously stood, into perfect equality of civil rights with all other persons within the jurisdiction of the States," and they gave to Congress the "means to compel the execution" of that new constitutional duty.[33]

A second set of cases revolved around the general exertion of federal authority over federal elections. When Albert Siebold was convicted for stuffing the ballot box for a congressional election while serving as an election judge in Baltimore, Maryland, his lawyers objected to Congress adopting such incomplete election regulations. Here, the Court was willing to emphasize that it "seems to be often overlooked that a national constitution has been adopted in this country, establishing a real government therein," and that local officials owed a duty to the United States as well as to their own state governments when administering federal elections.[34] When it came to federal elections, Congress had discretion over the degree to which it displaced state election rules and supplemented or bolstered them. In this context, Congress could rely on the original Constitution, not just the Reconstruction Amendments, for its authority to act, but the justices did not overlook the myriad reasons why Congress might want to be more vigorous in supervising elections after the Civil War.

A final set of cases revolved around the extension of federal judicial authority over a wider range of cases. Since the early republic, Congress had carefully limited the jurisdiction of the federal courts and had left the resolution of most legal disputes to the state courts, without federal interference. After the Civil War, Congress found new reasons to channel the flow of litigation into the federal courts. If federal civil rights were to be adequately protected, parties had to be able to get a hearing before a federal judge and not have to rely on the tender mercies of the state judiciary. As a consequence, the Republican Congress worked to expand the scope and powers of the federal courts, and when those unprecedented measures were challenged, the US Supreme Court stood ready to uphold them as fully authorized by the Constitution. When a landowner sued the mayor of Nashville for trespass, the mayor claimed he had been acting under military orders and sought to have the case heard in federal court. The justices were happy to oblige, asserting that it "is the right and the duty of the national government to have its Constitution and laws interpreted and applied by its own judicial tribunals." Anything else would leave the government in a state of "pitiable weakness."[35] When a federal tax collector in Tennessee was charged with murder for shooting (allegedly in self-defense) a bootlegger in the line of duty, the justices were open to allowing a federal judge to try the case. If the federal government could not adequately protect its own officers, it could hardly "preserv[e] its own existence."[36] The Court upheld expanded federal jurisdiction in a series of cases that otherwise might have been heard in state courts, for Congress was free to determine that, when "prejudice and local influence, against which the Constitution intended to guard," were likely to prevent a party from receiving justice, those cases should be brought "into a national court."[37]

Taxes

The newly empowered Republicans in Congress busily built up a national state capable of winning the war and advancing Republican political objectives. A key feature of that state-building project was raising revenue. The antebellum federal government had relied on tariff revenue and land sales to pay the public expenses. The war disrupted both of these traditional revenue sources while adding extraordinary new demands on the public purse. Congress scrambled to cover the gap. As the legal tender issue indicated, those efforts at resource extraction were creative and dramatic and reached well beyond taxation. But Congress also acted to diversify the federal government's tax base and to fully exploit all available opportunities to fill the government's coffers. As Congress became more innovative in imposing taxes, taxpayers became more aggressive in pushing back in court. Beginning in the mid-nineteenth century, the Court began to reveal that the Constitution contained an intricate web of rules about how Congress could tax its citizens. Given the financial incentives for fully exploring those rules, the Court heard numerous cases questioning the constitutionality of federal taxes. Although such suits were sometimes successful, the Court spent most of its time explaining why the new taxes were constitutionally permissible.

Across the Court's history, an extraordinary number of constitutional challenges to federal statutes involved tax cases. Early cases of this type included challenges to the Federalist carriage tax and the Jeffersonian tax on the inhabitants of the District of Columbia; however, they did not become a regular feature of the Court's constitutional jurisprudence until after the Civil War.[38] Perhaps the frequency of tax cases is appropriate in a country founded in large part on a tax revolt, but it is also a reminder of the extent to which the US Constitution is an economic document. From the Civil War through the Progressive Era, disputes about money and property gave shape to the Court's constitutional jurisprudence.

Despite the volume of such suits, taxpayers had only a few, relatively minor victories. As Congress placed the Union on a war footing, it adopted the first federal income tax in the summer of 1861. These taxes were extended and increased over the next several years. Only a small fraction of the population with relatively high cash income was taxed, but those taxpayers were geographically concentrated and highly critical of the levy. The emergency tax measure was finally repealed in 1872. Among those subjected to the tax was a county probate judge in Massachusetts, who objected that his salary was constitutionally exempt from federal taxation. The Court agreed. The Court had previously decided that state governments could not tax the instrumentalities and officers of the federal government, for such taxes could interfere with the successful execution of federal policy.[39] Faced with a federal tax on state officers, the Court found that the states were similarly situated. In this regard, the states were constitutionally equal to the federal government and equally immune to federal interference with their instruments.[40] Soon thereafter, the Court extended the same logic to cover the interest revenue on municipal bonds.[41] It was not a foregone conclusion that the Court would extend to the states the same immunity from taxation it had previously extended to the federal government, but the decisions had only a limited effect on federal policy.

Far more often the Court waved away potential constitutional objections to the assessment of a federal tax. Like the taxes that the Court evaluated, the constitutional rules that Congress was accused of violating were various. Litigants were not attempting to develop an overarching theory of constitutional limitations; they were just trying to reduce their tax bills. Likewise, the cases rarely amounted to a frontal assault on the federal tax structure. More often, litigants objected to quirky applications of the federal tax code or to relatively minor features of the revenue acts. Even so, the justices emphasized the legislative freedom to choose how to raise revenue and closed the door on possible avenues of tax avoidance.

The most general constitutional challenge involved the new federal income tax. In 1866 a young, well-to-do Democratic lawyer in Illinois objected to the tax imposed on his princely income of $50,799. By the time the Court heard the case, William Springer had been elected to Congress, and the federal income tax had been repealed. Springer argued that the federal tax on income was a direct tax, and the Constitution required that direct taxes be apportioned among the states according to population. Although the justices admitted that the meaning of "direct" taxes was obscure, they thought it was best confined to capitation taxes and taxes on real estate.[42] Anything else was an indirect tax and, as a result, was not subject to the constitutional rule of state apportionment.[43] The door was open for Congress to reinstitute the tax.

Other challenges were more marginal. For example, the Court was asked to determine whether an 1862 tariff act that imposed higher duties on goods originating from "beyond the Cape of Good Hope" that first passed through ports closer to home effectively violated the constitutional requirement that Congress not distinguish among American ports. An East Coast importer who was forced to pay the higher rate on Chinese and Indian silk that made its way to the United State by way of Liverpool complained that Congress had effectively advantaged ports on the Pacific coast, where importers could obtain the same silk directly from China and pay a cheaper import duty. The Court thought "the answer to the objection is obvious and conclusive"; the Constitution prevented Congress from distinguishing among American ports, not from distinguishing among foreign exporters in a way that might have incidental consequences for American importers.[44] In another case, the Court ruled that Congress could retroactively impose tax obligations, so long as they did not "operate to disturb rights vested or acquired before their enactment."[45] Congress could also impose a tax based on the productive capacity of distilleries without violating the constitutional requirement that excise taxes be uniform.[46] The Court found that mandatory identification stamps on tobacco intended for export did not amount to a constitutionally prohibited export tax.[47] In addition, Congress had wide discretion in designing taxes for the District of Columbia.[48]

Regulating the Economy

The Civil War and Reconstruction were the distinctive congressional projects of this turbulent period, but they were not the only projects pursued by the newly empowered Republicans. Former Whigs made up the core of the Republican Party, starting with President Abraham Lincoln himself, and they had long strained at the constitutional limits on national power celebrated by the Jacksonian Democrats. Unsurprisingly, with the Democrats vanquished into a potentially temporary minority by the secession of the South, the economic program of the former Whigs came to the fore. This put new pressure on inherited constitutional norms, resulting in litigation testing the validity of congressional acts.

Congress was also responding to changes in the American economy. The United States witnessed a surge in industrial production during the latter half of the nineteenth century, only temporarily slowed by the Panic of 1873. Technological innovation fed industrial development. Labor began an extended shift from agriculture to manufacturing, and railroads rapidly expanded to knit the country together. Not surprisingly, these economic transformations placed demands on Congress to provide adequate legal and institutional supports for economic actors and a regulatory framework to guide economic development. Economic developments had an influence on the statute books, just as they did on the American landscape.

As Congress flexed its economic muscles, constitutional challenges arose. These did not, however, resemble the great ideological contests that mobilized the Jeffersonians against the Hamiltonian financial system or the Jacksonians against Henry Clay's American System. These constitutional questions about economic policy were not at the center of the policy agenda; they did not structure partisan debate or mobilize voters. Constitutional doubts about legislation were particular and idiosyncratic, rather than general and systemic, and they were raised on the margins. And, for the most part, these constitutional challenges were unsuccessful. The Court accommodated the expanded legislative agenda rather than obstructing it.

When striking down a small handful of laws, the Court was previewing bigger battles yet to come. In 1867 Congress tried to ban the sale of illuminating oil mixtures containing naphtha, which was particularly combustible and more dangerous than kerosene. Although the prohibition was buried within a revenue measure, the justices found that "it is plainly a regulation of police." But as such, it "can only have effect where the legislative authority of Congress" can constitutionally extend, and it "can have no constitutional operation" within the states. The Court thought the point was so obvious that no extended consideration was necessary.[49] Of greater substantive importance was the emerging field of trademarks. In 1876 Congress passed a bill specifically designed to protect trademarks, but once again, when several individuals were arrested in New York and Ohio for possessing counterfeit packaging for trademark-protected brands of champagne and whiskey, the Court pointed out that, "like the great body of the rights of person and property," the property in trademarks "rest[s] upon the laws of the States . . . for security and protection."[50] Although the justices canvassed several possible provisions of the Constitution that might authorize Congress to criminalize counterfeit goods, they were all inadequate to the task at hand. "If its main purpose be to establish a regulation applicable to all trade, to commerce at all points, especially if it be apparent that it is designed to govern the commerce wholly between citizens of the same State, it is obviously the exercise of a power not confided to Congress."[51] Economic transactions within a state were beyond Congress's constitutional ability to regulate. In the next session, Congress adopted a revised trademark statute that explicitly limited federal protection to trademarks "used in commerce with foreign nations, or with the Indian tribes."[52]

It would be a mistake to infer that the Court was a serious obstacle to the economic policies Congress was adopting in the mid-nineteenth century. Like judges, legislators were aware that regulation of the internal commerce of the states was the states' exclusive domain. Federal statutes such as the original Trademark Act were the exception rather than the rule, and they were generally attributable to inartful draftsmanship rather than a conscious desire to push constitutional boundaries. The Court was more than happy to give its imprimatur to acts that had a better jurisdictional hook to the congressional powers enumerated in Article I. Congress could regulate the sale of "spirituous liquor" to an Indian, even if the transaction occurred between individuals outside of Indian territory and completely within the confines of a state.[53] It could regulate telegraphs, even though such an instrumentality of interstate commerce was unknown at the time of the founding.[54] It could improve navigable rivers,[55] regulate bridges,[56] inspect steamships,[57] require that the sale of ships be recorded with the customs collector,[58] regulate the coastal trade,[59] and require railroads to establish sinking funds.[60] It could exclude obscene materials from the mail[61] and extend copyright protection to photographs.[62] The Court insisted that the Constitution was flexible enough to accommodate changing economic and political conditions, but the core principle remained: activities that were wholly interior to the states were not subject to federal authority.

Housekeeping

As Congress became more active and produced a wider variety of legislation, constitutional questions inevitably arose as those statutes were interpreted and administered. The details of governance had always generated constitutional issues to be resolved by the courts, but the pace of government activity in the first decades of the republic meant that those cases arose only sporadically. At the time of the secession crisis, the federal government employed just over 2,000 people in the nation's capital. Twenty years later, the government employed more than six times that number. Across the same period, federal expenditures jumped fourfold. The government that emerged from the fires of the Civil War was bigger and more ambitious than the one the Jacksonians had constructed in the antebellum era. Governmental size and complexity induced a steady undercurrent of constitutional litigation, which was supplemented by the occasional legislative innovation.

When Congress ran afoul of constitutional rules, it was often in familiar ways. With the West still being settled, Congress continued to be called out for mishandling disputes over land titles.[63] As Congress reorganized and expanded the federal courts, it sometimes made missteps in creating pathways of litigation.[64] Legislators were sometimes sloppy in drafting penal statutes[65] or in handling property claims.[66] Such cases could benefit an individual litigant and clean up the processes of government, but they had few larger policy ramifications. They spoke to no serious ideological or partisan disputes and disadvantaged no important political interests. They illustrated how the justices brought their lawyerly expertise to bear in resolving complex legal disputes. In doing so, they filled out the constitutional rule book and took note of when Congress stepped over the lines into foul territory. But such exercises of judicial review were countermajoritarian only in the most formal sense of scrutinizing the work product of elected legislators and correcting its deficiencies, and of hearing the complaints of individuals who were dissatisfied with how the government had treated them.

Such routine cases of judicial review were most likely to favor the government. Occasionally the Court put its stamp of approval on more contentious policies that were worthy of public attention, quieting potential protests about congressional actions. The Court was asked to weigh in on civil service reform[67] and on federal efforts to stamp out Mormon polygamy,[68] but the justices shared the political consensus on how Congress could approach such matters. More often, the Court was asked about mundane details of federal policy and its administration, and the Court generally endorsed congressional authority on a range of questions, such as the proper transition from territory to statehood,[69] the federal exercise of eminent domain within the states,[70] the alteration of the terms of a federal charter,[71] and the rank of a retired military officer.[72]

The power of judicial review arises out of the Court's role as an interpreter of applicable laws and a resolver of legal disputes. As Chief Justice Marshall emphasized at the opening of the nineteenth century, the Constitution is one of the laws judges are charged with interpreting and applying in the course of their duties. But most legal disputes are routine; they may be of great interest to the parties involved, but they are of only limited interest to the broader public or even to the legislators who adopted the statutes in question. As the exercise of judicial review became more routine in the middle decades of the nineteenth century, these ordinary cases were the staple of the judicial diet. The routine resolution of such disputes highlighted the ordinary and apolitical nature of the Court's work. Constitutional questions were simply on the continuum of legal questions posed by the ordinary cases disposed of by the courts. These ordinary cases provided the background against which the occasional constitutional challenge to congressional Reconstruction or legal tender was spotlighted. The constitutional puzzle might be plain on the face of a statute or revealed only in the course of its administration, but the underlying question was always the same: Can Congress validly do this? The answer was usually, but not invariably, yes.

Conclusion

From an attitudinal perspective, Chief Justice Taney, a holdover Democrat, might have been expected to rally his remaining colleagues to obstruct the policies of the new Republican administration. Instead, the Court laid low during the war years. Equally surprising, the Court became more activist only after it was stacked with Republican appointees. Ultimately, it was a politically convergent Court that set a new standard for the judicial review of federal statutes after the war. The Republicans in Congress found themselves under unprecedented scrutiny by the Supreme Court, but it was a Supreme Court filled with their political allies.

Those allies were content to support congressional war powers and mostly stay out of the way of Reconstruction. But they became active participants in intraparty squabbles over what the postbellum constitutional order would look like. On perhaps the most politically consequential issue the Court was willing to confront—legal tender—its interference with the elected branches was short-lived. Although paper currency had been justified as a war measure, it could not easily be excluded from the peacetime constitutional regime. The necessity that justified legal tender may have passed, but the politicians needed space to unravel the financial knot they had created during the war, and a reconstituted Court gave it to them. The Court found more support when it came to black civil rights. As the Republican Party retreated in the 1870s from its more ambitious efforts to protect the freedmen, the Court mirrored that retreat. The justices were prepared to endorse new national monitoring of federal elections and an expanded role for the federal judiciary, but they were not willing to follow the more radical members of the Republican Party in authorizing federal protection against private racial discrimination. The Court threw its support behind the more conservative members of its own party, and although it left the door open for Congress to resuscitate some of the statutes the Court had struck down, there was little political will to do so.

The Court found a place for itself as an active interpreter of the Constitution and an enforcer of constitutional limits on Congress by staying at the political margins. As Congress became more active in building a more robust federal government, the Court helped flesh out the constitutional details of what Congress could and could not do and how the national legislature could govern. The Court played a more active role not by positioning itself as a countermajoritarian obstruction to Congress but by opening its doors to ordinary litigants who used constitutional arguments to advance their particular interests. The Court found plenty of work to keep it busy as it fine-tuned the constitutional order.

5

Congress and the *Lochner* Court

Remarkably, from midway through the Civil War to midway through the New Deal, the justices of the US Supreme Court hailed primarily from the party of Lincoln. For over three-quarters of a century, the principles, priorities, policies, and commitments of the Republican Party shaped the Supreme Court and, through it, shaped American constitutional law. Democratic administrations under Grover Cleveland and Woodrow Wilson proved to be just brief interludes from Republican control of the White House, and their appointments did little to alter the course of the Court.

Republican dominance in presidential politics, and thereby in judicial appointments, does not imply placidity. These were turbulent years for the United States and for American politics. The last decades of the nineteenth century saw the parties locked in close competition, with the Republicans rarely able to win a popular majority in the presidential election and frequently unable to hold the House of Representatives. Upstart political parties like the Populists, the Greenbacks, the Prohibitionists, and the Socialists siphoned voters away from the two major parties. Internal factions splintered both the Republicans and the Democrats, as the country struggled through transformative industrialization, urbanization, and immigration, and as the state and federal governments built a new administrative apparatus to manage society and the economy.

During these decades, the judiciary's authority to enforce constitutional requirements come under unprecedented challenge. As previously noted, the Court maintained a new level of activism in the years surrounding the turn of the twentieth century. Every term the justices heard new constitutional challenges to federal statutory provisions, and in nearly every term the justices ruled against the constitutional authority of Congress in at least one case. Judicial interpretation and enforcement of constitutional requirements against Congress was becoming a routine feature of American governance. The regular use of the power of judicial review against politically salient legislation focused attention not only on the creativity of the Court's doctrinal innovations but also on the simple fact of judicial activity. The courts came under vocal assault by the political Left. Populist and Progressive politicians and activists denounced the power of judicial review as undemocratic and offered a variety of proposals for reining in the courts. Every blow the Court rained down on the legislature became another occasion to question the legitimacy of judges armed with an absolute veto and, perhaps, of a Constitution that authorized such a practice. In response, conservatives rallied to the defense of the courts. Conservative lawyers formed the American Bar Association to organize support for judicially enforced limits on the popular will, and conservative politicians denounced those who would risk the liberties of Americans by weakening the protections offered by judicial review.

The case of *Lochner v. New York* has generally been taken as emblematic of the era.[1] The doctrine of substantive due process at the heart of *Lochner* reflected the more general commitment of the Court in the late nineteenth and early twentieth centuries to aggressively supervise the actions of political officials.[2] In the face of a new activism on the part of American governments, and in the wake of post-abolitionist sensibilities about the threat legislatures and democratic majorities could pose to individual liberty, the Court was not disposed to heed the Thayerian call for judicial deference to legislatures in constitutional controversies.[3]

The Court was focused on the federal constitutional restrictions on state legislative power in *Lochner* itself, of course, and how Congress fared before the Court during this period is seldom explored. The *Lochner* Court's elaboration of substantive due process and consequent supervision of the states has understandably received the lion's share of attention, but an examination of the judicial review of federal statutes in these years gives a somewhat different perspective on the Court's constitutional jurisprudence. The infamy of *Lochner* has overshadowed the Court's other interests.

This chapter considers the years surrounding *Lochner*, from just after Reconstruction to the end of World War I. As the Court, and the nation, transitioned from Reconstruction to the Gilded Age, it largely left behind debates over the Civil War and its immediate aftermath and embarked on a new set of debates over how to respond to the industrializing economy. After World War I and William Howard Taft assuming the office of chief justice, the Court entered a new phase of activism that would culminate in the battles over the New Deal in the 1930s.

During these years, a largely conservative Court under the leadership of Melville Fuller and Edward Douglass White struggled to keep up with a rapidly growing caseload, and constitutional challenges to federal statutes occupied an important part of its agenda. In doing so, the Court was operating in cooperation, rather than in conflict, with other national political officials. Although the justices occasionally struck down provisions of politically important statutes or limited their scope with constitutional rules, the Court's exercise of judicial review during this period was usually routine, uncontroversial, and normatively unobjectionable. Moreover, the invalidation of federal action rarely, if ever, pitted the Court against a clear majority of elected officials. The Court's constitutional interventions, even in the notorious sugar trust case and income tax cases, did not generally impose heavy political costs on national political leaders. By taking a close look at the politics surrounding the laws the Court invalidated during this period, we can gain a new appreciation of how the activism of the *Lochner* Court emerged and how it was sustained. The Populists who complained from the back benches about an antidemocratic Court proved incapable of winning national elections. The *Lochner* Court worked hand in hand with the conservative political leaders in both parties to realize a common constitutional vision of limited government within a decentralized federal system.

When focusing on the statutes rejected by the courts, it is tempting to view the judiciary as a colossus standing athwart the government and sweeping away a large measure of the legislature's handiwork. The criticisms of judicial review that ring down from the Populist and Progressive Eras suggest that conservative judges were actively blocking reform legislation at every turn. Perhaps with the New Deal struggle in mind, we can easily imagine the Court having ample opportunity to review every congressional action and exercising an absolute veto, unconstrained by the possibility of legislative override or the calculation of electoral consequences. The dominant image of the Court during this period was laid down early by its scholarly Progressive critics, who saw it as a tool of corporate privilege and an "almost despotic" power against the people.[4]

Such a vision is highly misleading. For instance, the courts are rarely as unrelenting as statutory invalidations suggest. But the instances in which the judiciary strikes down government actions, however infrequent, are felt far more keenly than those in which the judiciary upholds government action. Certainly, the veto is most politically salient and attracts the attention of contemporary media and later commentators. Carefully cataloging each rejection of a railroad regulation or a working-hour limitation, histories portray an all-out struggle between the judicial forces of reaction and the popular forces of reform during the *Lochner* era.[5] Judicial historian Charles Warren offered a contemporaneous revision of this emerging standard narrative. He found that between 1887 and 1911, the Supreme Court issued 560 decisions reviewing the constitutionality of state statutes under the Fourteenth Amendment. An examination of these cases as a whole, he thought, "conclusively proves that the alleged evil in the trend of the Court is a purely fancied one."[6] Some recent scholars have made similar observations about the Court's record. As Robert McCloskey wrote, "Most of the important legislative measures that were really demanded by public opinion did pass and did manage to survive the gauntlet of judicial review."[7] Although the Court was more active than it had been earlier in its history, *Lochner* was a mere activist island in a sea of judicial passivity.

While *Lochner* and decisions affecting state legislation were getting all the attention during the Progressive period, the record of Congress before the Court was largely unchanged. Between 1885 and 1919, the US Supreme Court seriously entertained constitutional challenges to federal statutory provisions in more than 200 cases, and it most often upheld the congressional assertion of power. The Court struck down federal action in only 32 of these decisions, giving Congress an enviable success rate of 85 percent. Warren's judgment based on the record of state cases seems equally valid in the context of federal cases: "The actual record of the Court thus shows how little chance a litigant has of inducing the Court to restrict" the power of the federal government.[8]

Over this span, the Court heard a fairly large number of constitutional challenges to the actions of the federal government, with an average of just

Table 5-1: Cases Invalidating Statutes by Type and Party, 1885–1919

	All Statutes	"Landmark" Legislation	Notable Provisions
Passed by Democratic House	9	4	3
Passed by Republican House	23	14	7

less than one legislative provision being struck down by the Court every year. With the exception of a three-year period at the beginning of the 1890s, the Court did not let more than two years pass without nullifying a federal statute. Nonetheless, the Court turned back far more constitutional challenges to federal law than it sustained. In an average year during this period, the Court heard six constitutional challenges to the federal government and upheld the government's position in five of them. No term passed without the Court deciding at least one constitutional case involving a federal law.

Focusing just on the statutes the Court struck down, it is readily apparent that the Court invalidated some important pieces of legislation during this period, often shortly after enactment. These important episodes of judicial review do not fit easily into Robert Dahl's theory that statutes fall victim to a Court that is lagging electoral trends.[9] From a strictly partisan perspective, we might expect the Republican-dominated Court to be largely quiescent as long as its partisans dominated the elected branches of the federal government. We might expect the Court to rouse itself only to invalidate the relatively small number of laws that emerged from Congress when the Democrats briefly captured power behind Grover Cleveland and Woodrow Wilson.

Tables 5-1 and 5-2 provide some perspective on the Court's work with Congress in these decades. The Republicans maintained an effective lock on the US Senate for most of this period, and they had a distinct advantage in

Table 5-2: Cases Invalidating Statutes by Age and Party, 1885–1919

	Less than Four Years Old	More than Four Years Old
Passed by Democratic House	4	5
Passed by Republican House	6	17

the Electoral College as well; however, control of the US House of Representatives was more closely contested. Democratic influence over the content of legislation was undoubtedly at its height when the party of Andrew Jackson controlled both chambers of Congress and the Oval Office, but it exercised at least some influence over federal policy in the somewhat more common circumstances of House control. Table 5-1 shows the number of cases in which the justices invalidated federal statutory provisions: all cases, those on Stathis's list of "landmark" legislation, and notable provisions of those statutes.[10] As the table indicates, the Court did not limit its attention to legislation produced by Democrats; Republican-passed statutes also fell before the Court's constitutional review. Moreover, even important statutes and statutory provisions written by Republican legislators were struck down. Table 5-2 indicates how much time had passed between congressional adoption of a statute and the Court's invalidation of it. Judicial review of statutes within four years of adoption might be regarded as relatively contemporaneous, while older statutes might have less political immediacy. On this dimension, Republicans fared somewhat better, with a smaller proportion of their invalidated statutes meeting their fate at an early stage.[11] But the Republicans hardly escaped judicial scrutiny unscathed.

A closer look at the circumstances surrounding these cases clarifies why and how the Court took this path. The Court did not throw itself headlong against Republican majorities. It worked within the fissures of the dominant political coalitions, nudging Congress to follow the straight and narrow path of conservative constitutionalism but rarely raising insurmountable obstacles to the realization of core policy goals.

Striking Down Important Republican Policies

Only seven cases invalidating federal legislation between 1885 and 1919 involved notable provisions of landmark legislation passed during a Republican government. Assuming Dahl's expectation of shared preferences between the judicial branch and the elected branches of the federal government during Republican control, even this handful of cases is rather surprising. A closer look at these cases provides a more nuanced picture of how the Republican-dominated Court related to important Republican policy initiatives. The basic theme, however, is still one of a relatively friendly Court.

The one instance in which the Supreme Court invalidated an important Republican measure soon after its adoption involved the Employers' Liability Act of 1906, which the Court struck down in January 1908.[12] The legislative and political damage of the Court's action was minimal, however, and Congress quickly responded by passing the Employers' Liability Act of 1908, which satisfied the Court's objections.

Labor unions had long sought changes in the rules affecting employers' liability for workplace injuries suffered by employees. Among these were the common-law doctrines of fellow servant and contributory negligence, which insulated employers from liability when workplace injuries were partly the result of the negligence of the injured worker or a fellow worker. These doctrines had long been contested in statehouses and courthouses, and when sitting as a federal judge, William Howard Taft helped rewrite some of them. During the 1908 presidential campaign, Theodore Roosevelt supported Taft and cited this as evidence of Taft's sympathy for labor.[13] The Employers' Liability Act was intended to override such doctrines and make common carriers operating in federal jurisdictions liable for workplace deaths and injuries, building on earlier statutes passed during the McKinley and Roosevelt administrations. Although Roosevelt often had a prickly relationship with labor unions during his presidency, the adjustment of employer liability undoubtedly fell within the scope of his views stated to senator and former attorney general Philander Knox: "We must not only do justice, but be able to show the wage worker that we are doing justice." If the "friends of property" were to be "shortsighted, narrow-minded, greedy and arrogant," they were inviting an "explosion."[14] To Roosevelt's mind, few actions were more calculated to set the working class against the courts and the rule of law than a judge showing "in an employer's liability or a tenement house factory case . . . that he has neither sympathy for nor understanding of those fellow citizens of his who most need his sympathy and understanding."[15] Roosevelt felt strongly enough about the issue to lobby Justice William Day as the Court deliberated on the *Employers' Liability Cases*, warning, if the "spirit" behind *Lochner*-type decisions were to spread, "we should not only have a revolution, but it would be absolutely necessary to have a revolution, because the condition of the worker would become intolerable."[16] His missive came too late, as the justices had already voted to strike down the law, but his larger hopes were realized as the majority of the justices did not adopt the spirit of *Lochner*.

In his opinion for the Court, Justice Edward White turned back the most fundamental challenges to the act. White assured the government that Congress could readily reach the relationship between employer and employee as an appropriate means of regulating interstate commerce. Congress erred, however, in writing the statute so as to attempt to control "common carrier[s] engaged in trade or commerce in the District of Columbia, or in any Territory of the United States, or between the several States," apparently seeking to regulate those who "engage in interstate commerce" rather than to "regulate the business of interstate commerce."[17] Without further qualification, the statute "includes subjects wholly outside of the power of Congress to regulate"—namely, the purely local activities of businesses that happen to also engage in interstate commerce. The Court declined the invitation of government lawyers to rewrite the statute to limit it to federally cognizable subject matter, but it invited Congress to fix the statute with the proper words of limitation. Given the results of his commerce clause analysis, White thought it unnecessary to address due process challenges, except to note that the Court had previously upheld similar state statutes against such challenges. Day concurred with White, but Peckham, joined by Fuller and Brewer, concurred only in the local activities analysis, while explicitly distancing himself from the claim that Congress could regulate master-servant relationships. Moody noted that although a full dissent would generally not be necessary, given that Congress could easily rewrite the law to fix the constitutional problem, he wanted to go on record to observe that in the actual case before the Court—involving interstate carriers whose employees were in fact engaged in interstate transportation at the time of their deaths—the federal rule would easily be constitutional. He went on to warn his brethren against taking even "well-settled doctrines of law" that reflect "the economic opinions of [the] judges and their views of the requirements of justice and public policy" as having "constitutional sanctity" that could "control legislators."[18] Harlan, McKenna, and Holmes would have interpreted the act to conform to Congress's constitutional limitations, despite the apparent overreach of the statutory language.

Although a five-justice majority struck down the Employers' Liability Act as written, six justices clearly signaled their willingness to uphold a rewritten statute that reflected what Congress had intended all along. Congress responded immediately, and four months later, the president signed the Employers' Liability Act of 1908, which corrected the error and which the Court later upheld, as promised. In his next, and final, annual message to Congress, Roosevelt called for a broader liability statute for all workers squarely within federal jurisdiction that would bring the United States up to "par with the most progressive governments in Europe" and could be a model for the states. In chiding legislators for "slovenly haste and lack of consideration" in producing flawed statutes that were vulnerable to evasion or constitutional objection, the outgoing president referred to the Employers' Liability Law of 1906 as the "striking illustration of the consequences of carelessness in the preparation of a statute." Roosevelt observed that the statute had been "adjudged unconstitutional by a bare majority of the court," even though "six out of nine justices of the Supreme Court held that its subject-matter was within the province of congressional action. . . . It was surely a very slovenly piece of work to frame the legislation in such shape as to leave the question open at all."[19]

The Sherman Anti-Trust Act of 1890 took longer to reach the Court. The Court did not limit its applicability until nearly five years after its passage. Benjamin Harrison, the Republican president who had signed the statute, had long since left the White House, and conservative Democrat Grover Cleveland was serving his second term as president. While the Sherman Act was an important piece of legislation, trust-busting could hardly be regarded as a central Republican commitment in the late nineteenth century.

Since the demise of Reconstruction, Democrats had strongly challenged the Republican hold on the federal government. The GOP had an effective lock on the Senate in the late nineteenth century; however, in 1890 the Republicans held the House of Representatives for only the second time since Union troops had been withdrawn from the South. Moreover, no Republican presidential candidate since Ulysses S. Grant had captured a majority of the popular vote. With the election of Benjamin Harrison, Republicans had only just recovered from the first postbellum loss of the presidency to Cleveland in 1884, and even then, they managed an Electoral College majority but not a popular vote plurality.

Antimonopoly planks were central features of the platforms of several fairly successful (in the context of a closely divided electorate) third parties, including the Greenbacks and the Prohibitionists, which often chose a former Republican to head their tickets. Former Republican congressional leader and 1884 Greenback presidential candidate Ben Butler denounced the Republicans as the "Party of Monopolies."[20] During his first term, Democrat Grover Cleveland tried to harness antimonopoly sentiment for his tariff reform crusade. Protectionist tariffs were a central commitment of the Republican Party, and the Democrats were only too happy to point out that "trusts and combinations are permitted to exist, which, while unduly enriching the few that combine, rob the body of our citizens by depriving them of the benefits of natural competition." They argued that angry voters should blame "unnecessary taxation"—that is, protectionist tariffs—for the problem.[21] For Cleveland's Democrats, free trade was the best federal response to the trust problem.

With the Sherman Act, the Republicans hoped to deflate the trust issue. As Finance Committee chairman, Ohio senator John Sherman explained to his colleagues that trusts were now threatening to subvert "the policy of the Government to protect and encourage American industries by levying duties on imported goods."[22] Although state courts could and did regulate monopolies in restraint of trade within the states, Congress had to pass a statute that authorized federal courts to do the same with "contracts etc. in restraint of commerce between the states."[23] Congress, however, recognized the constitutional and policy difficulties involved. While Sherman himself favored a broad reading of federal power in this area—"as broad as the earth"—others were more skeptical, and the Senate Judiciary Committee rewrote Sherman's bill so that the result "should be clearly within our constitutional power . . . and would leave it to the courts in the first instance to say how far they could carry it." In doing so, the committee dropped all references to "trade and production" in favor of "trade and commerce." Influential Democratic senator James George, who had made the motion to send the bill to the Judiciary Committee and had called Sherman's original bill "utterly unconstitutional," praised the result as "very ingeniously and properly drawn to cover every case which comes within what is called the commercial power of Congress," while admitting there "is a great deal of this matter outside of that."[24] One reason the constitutionality of the Sherman Act did not reach the Supreme Court more quickly was that the Harrison administration was less than vigorous in pursuing prosecutions under the act, and it rarely won an indictment or conviction when it did pursue a case.

The Cleveland administration could not have been disturbed when the

Court limited the Sherman Anti-Trust Act in 1895. In his second inaugural address, Cleveland was careful to qualify his promise to regulate trusts to "the extent that they can be reached and restrained by Federal power."[25] Attorney General Richard Olney was a long-standing critic of the Sherman Act. Although Olney was unable to persuade the administration to adopt the cause, he avoided "prosecuting under a law [he] believed to be no good."[26] Olney initiated no new antitrust cases during his tenure as attorney general. However, as a test case, he moved forward with *E. C. Knight*, a suit against the sugar trust that had been prepared by the previous administration. Many observers thought his prosecution of the sugar trust before the Supreme Court was less than robust.[27] When Cleveland appointee Chief Justice Melville Fuller wrote the opinion sharply limiting the federal government's constitutional power to reach manufacturing, Olney noted that he had "always supposed" this would be the outcome. The president likewise raised no complaint.[28] Instead, in his next annual message to Congress, the president explained that it was "not because of any lack of disposition or attempt to enforce" antitrust measures on the part of the administration that the monopoly problem remained unaddressed. It was simply that "the laws themselves as interpreted by the courts do not reach the difficulty." Following the "decision of our highest court on this precise question" of the scope of federal authority over trusts, the president urged Congress to limit its acts to the proper and narrow sphere of "transportation or intercourse between States" and leave the rest to the states.[29]

Cleveland's second attorney general, Judson Harmon, had some success in that regard. Harmon was under political pressure to bring a suit against a railroad pool, and he thought interstate railroads properly fell under federal jurisdiction. He was willing to file the necessary papers and observed to the US attorney that if the application for an injunction failed, "the responsibility w[ould] be on the court and not on us." After Republican William McKinley took office in 1897, his attorney general never tired of pointing out to those pressing for action against trusts that the administration was "governed only by a sincere desire to enforce the law," but its hands were tied by the "well-defined limits of Federal jurisdiction so clearly laid down by the Supreme Court in cases already decided."[30]

In other cases, the Supreme Court struck down provisions of important statutes after their political support had waned. The Court struck down stray elements of Reconstruction-era statutes in three early twentieth-century cases, well after Reconstruction had been abandoned and Jim Crow had been imposed. In 1887 the Court was asked to revive a civil rights provision to which the justices had previously objected. Just a few years earlier, the Court had concluded that the Fourteenth Amendment did not authorize Congress to punish private individuals whose actions deprived others of the equal protection of the law.[31] When a group of Chinese immigrants sought to use the statute to bring federal charges against a mob that had chased them from their homes in Oregon, the Court reaffirmed that it was unwilling to enforce a statutory provision that indiscriminately swept up acts that fell outside federal jurisdiction as well as those within it. Congress had to shoulder the responsibility for drafting a more narrowly tailored statute that might, for example, specifically punish conspiracies to deny aliens their rights under federal treaties.[32]

In 1903 the Court held that the Force Act of 1870 exceeded congressional authority under the Fifteenth Amendment in reaching the attempted bribery of black voters by private individuals, as opposed to state actors.[33] Following the lead of government attorneys, the Court invited Congress to prohibit bribery in federal elections under its general power to regulate elections, but it averred that the Force Act was not written to do so. Three years later, the Court, over the dissent of Justices John Marshall Harlan and William Day, elaborated that acts by private individuals violating the rights of blacks were not subject to federal jurisdiction. The Court held that black citizens must take "their chances with other citizens in the States where they should make their homes" and seek redress for private wrongs from state officials.[34]

In 1913 the Court swept away the last of the Civil Rights Act of 1875. In a case involving the segregation of black passengers in inferior accommodations on a coastal ship operating under federal jurisdiction, the Court concluded that although Congress had the authority to regulate such ships, the Civil Rights Act was unconstitutional on its face in attempting to establish a uniform regulation across the country.[35] The congressional purpose in the act was invalid, and that invalid purpose was fatal, even if the particular application might otherwise be within congressional authority. As it had done before, the Court left Congress free to revisit the civil rights issue in a more narrowly tailored statute.[36]

Striking Down Important Democratic Policies

During the *Lochner* period, the Court decided three cases invalidating central provisions of important Democratic statutes, all of which were decided soon after the laws' passage. Partisan judicial obstructionism is not the whole story in these cases, however. Closer inspection reveals intracoalitional struggles, as the Court sided with more conservative elements in the Democratic Party against more Populist or Progressive elements.

The Court's invalidation of the income tax provisions of the Tariff Act of 1894 was a remarkable display of judicial aggressiveness, similar to its posture during the New Deal. Free trade had been a central commitment of the Democratic Party since passage of the Compromise Tariff of 1833, during Andrew Jackson's presidency.[37] Democrat Grover Cleveland railed against the protective tariff as an example of government corruption and an injury to consumers, and the Tariff Act was the legislative centerpiece of his second term as president.[38] When Republicans controlled the federal government during the Civil War, they adopted many of the economic policies of their Whig predecessors, including the protective tariff. The protective tariff soon became a key plank in the Republican platform, and the Republicans kept duties on imported goods high whenever they held power, until their conversion to free trade after the Second World War.

In the midst of economic depression and pending budget deficits, tariff reform was a tough sell. Nonetheless, Cleveland was actively engaged in designing a reform bill and pushing it through Congress. During his first administration, Cleveland had been stung by the complaints of northeastern manufacturers who would feel the pinch of radical tariff reform. Thus, his second-term reform bill was mindful of both manufacturing interests and fears of worsening budget conditions. The president worked with William Wilson, chairman of the House Ways and Means Committee, to design a carefully balanced bill, but Populists on the House floor denounced it as a "robber tariff" and little better than Republican measures; they pushed hard for more radical reform.[39] The Populists were generally unsuccessful, but they did manage to add sugar to the list of duty-free imports, and they balanced the revenue loss with an income tax amendment that hit corporate profits, inheritances, and personal income over $4,000. In the Senate and in conference, Cleveland lost control of the bill, which was soon festooned with new protections. Months later, Wilson read a letter from the president on the House floor, admitting that "every true Democrat and every sincere tariff reformer" knew that the bill fell "far short," but it was now "so interwoven with Democratic pledges and Democratic success" that it had to be accepted. Although Cleveland disapproved of the income tax provisions, they did not "violate a fixed and recognized Democratic doctrine," and Cleveland was willing "to defer to the judgment of a majority" if that was the price of tariff reduction.[40] Judging the bill to be a lost opportunity and a perversion of his original goals but nonetheless essential to the health of the nation and his party, a morose Cleveland allowed it to pass into law without his signature a few months before the midterm elections.

The income tax provisions in the bill were harshly denounced as purely sectional class measures, as indeed they were. Nebraska representative William Jennings Bryan, the emerging leader of the Populist wing of the Democratic Party, was a primary sponsor of the amendments. Although the tax was small, it introduced the greatly feared principle of progressive taxation of income (rather than the traditional sources of federal government revenue—consumption taxes and the sale of national resources), and it was expected that the entire tax burden would be borne by the residents of four eastern states: New York, New Jersey, Pennsylvania, and Massachusetts. Two of these states—New York and New Jersey—happened to be important swing states in Gilded Age presidential elections, and New York in particular was essential to Democratic Electoral College calculations.[41] It was the centrality of the state that led to reformist New Yorker Grover Cleveland's Democratic presidential nominations in 1884, 1888, and 1892 and the integration of the Mugwumps (a breakaway group of Republican professionals and businessmen centered in New York) into the Cleveland coalition. Democratic New York senator David Hill warned his Populist colleagues: "The times are changing: the courts are changing, and I believe that this tax will be declared unconstitutional. At least I hope so."[42] The business community in New York was apoplectic over the income tax. While some in the New York City press labeled it a Cleveland tax, others defended the president as an opponent of the tax and a victim of the Populists.[43]

Within just a few months, the income tax was before the Supreme Court. First it struck down the tax on income from real estate and state and local bonds, and a month later a narrow majority struck down the rest.[44] Attorney

General Richard Olney, by all accounts, offered an able defense of the measure, calling on the Court to respect Federalist-era precedent and the appropriate sphere of legislative discretion over the proper exercise of the taxing power. Despite this defense, Chief Justice Melville Fuller, a Cleveland appointee, wrote both opinions striking down the provisions, finding that they violated basic constitutional efforts "to prevent an attack upon accumulated property by mere force of numbers."[45] The decision set off enormous criticism of the Court, led by Bryan, who routed the Cleveland forces to capture the Democratic nomination the next year. The president, however, refrained from joining the din, and his loyalists, in a breakaway party convention, denounced Bryan for his attacks on the judiciary.[46] When income tax dissenter Justice Howell Jackson died just months after the decision, Cleveland replaced him with conservative New York corporate attorney Rufus Peckham, first clearing the nomination with Senator Hill.[47] Peckham would later gain notoriety as the author of *Lochner*.

The situation was somewhat different when the Court made another quick strike against a major piece of Democratic legislation and nullified the Keating-Owen Act, which prohibited the interstate shipment of goods made with child labor. The Democratic Congress passed the child labor bill on the eve of the 1916 election. Both the Republican and Democratic platforms, boasting their Progressive credentials, endorsed federal action on child labor. Nonetheless, President Woodrow Wilson had pushed such measures off the legislative agenda during his first term, in favor of other priorities. Despite his embrace of a "living Constitution," Wilson had written just a few years earlier that judicial approval of federal child labor legislation would require an "obviously absurd extravagance of [constitutional] interpretation," leaving no effective limits on congressional power other than "the limitations of opinion and of circumstance." He admitted that "the very stuff of daily business, forced [such issues] upon Congress," but it was up to "statesmanship" to resist reading the Constitution "arbitrarily to mean what we wish it to mean" and rushing in with "a temper of mere impatience."[48] The Democratic caucus initially gave in to the demands of southern senators, who threatened a filibuster if the Democrats attempted to pass a child labor bill during the election year. The president, under threat from independent-minded Progressives and facing a tough reelection campaign, traveled to the Capitol to emphasize the importance of adhering to the recently adopted party platform.[49] With a flourish, the triumphant president completed the process, holding a public signing ceremony at the White House. The next day he formally accepted the Democratic nomination for president.

The Court heard a test case of the statute within two years of its enactment. The administration aggressively defended the act but lost when a narrowly divided Court ruled against it in *Hammer v. Dagenhart*.[50] Two of Wilson's three appointees to the Court were among the dissenters. The majority, however, bore the strong mark of Wilson's predecessor, William Howard Taft, who had resisted the Progressive wing of his own party. Taft had appointed three of the justices in the majority and was close friends with the opinion's author, William Day.[51] The Wilson administration continued to look for a way around the Court's decision until the end of his term in office. The federal child labor law was popular, but its policy significance was limited. Most states had already adopted such regulations, although enforcement varied, and the ambitions of reformers expanded once they achieved their initial legislative aims.[52] Manufacturers in states with such regulations chafed at competition from states that allowed child labor, and the moral principle of limiting child labor was a winning one. Even so, other legislation that emerged from Congress—notably, the Adamson Act, establishing eight-hour workdays for railroad employees—was judged more newsworthy, and the Court's decision in *Dagenhart* did not provoke anything like the popular reaction to the *Pollock* income tax case.[53]

Striking Down Less Important Measures

With few exceptions, the remainder of the federal provisions struck down during this period were the products of Republican legislatures.[54] None of them had the contemporary political significance of the statutes already considered, and few of them created significant disagreements among the justices. Whereas the *Employers' Liability Cases*, *Pollock*, and *Dagenhart* were closely divided decisions, only two other constitutional invalidations created significant disagreement among the justices. Both involved recently enacted statutes, but it would be difficult to characterize them as serious clashes of the constitutional visions of Congress and the Court. Although the Court's actions in these less politically charged cases reflected the constitutional sensibilities of the majority of the justices, they indicated a Court concerned with upholding deeply rooted jurisprudential principles against a sometimes careless Congress, rather than a politically activist Court.

The Court, in a six-to-three decision, struck down a provision of the Immigration Act of 1907 just two years after its enactment. The 1907 statute was a modest step between the late nineteenth-century Chinese Exclusion Act and the adoption of national origin quotas in the 1920s as part of the Progressive-Era attempt to restrict and control immigration. The primary battle in 1907 was over a proposed literacy test for immigrants and a restriction, favored by President Theodore Roosevelt and others, on the number of Japanese immigrants. Pro-immigration forces led by Speaker Joseph Cannon managed to delay both proposals with a stripped-down bill that created an investigatory commission and an immigrant head tax.[55] Among its other provisions was a measure (anticipating the 1910 Mann Act) forbidding the importation of "any alien woman or girl for the purpose of prostitution, or for any such immoral purpose," and making it a felony to support or harbor such an alien for up to three years after her entry into the United States.[56] Two brothel owners from Chicago challenged the constitutionality of the measure before the Court after their federal conviction for harboring a Hungarian prostitute. Justice Brewer, a relative judicial ally of immigrants, wrote the opinion for the majority in this case. Although he accepted the federal government's authority to prohibit the immigration of such women, he found that the harboring provision, detached from the actual importation, exceeded congressional authority to regulate immigration and encroached on the police powers of the states. Congress had no general police power, and it could not claim the authority "to control generally dealings of citizens with aliens."[57] Justice Oliver Wendell Holmes, often a judicial supporter of immigration restriction, wrote a dissent joined by Justices Harlan and Moody. Though admitting that "a period of three years seems to be long," he was willing to give Congress the leeway to burden citizens with the responsibility to determine the "fact and date of a prostitute's arrival" in order to deter their "cooperation" in her "unlawful stay."[58] Beyond hampering federal raids on houses of ill repute in Illinois, however, the case was of little consequence.

The Court likewise split in a five-to-four decision invalidating a provision of the War Revenue Act nearly three years after its enactment and two years after the Treaty of Paris ended the short-lived Spanish-American War. The affected provision imposed a stamp tax on "bills of lading or receipt . . .

for any goods, merchandise or effects, to be exported from a port or place in the United States to any foreign port or place."[59] Justice Brewer, again writing for the majority, observed that a prohibition on the powers of Congress, just as much as a grant of power, "should be enforced in its spirit and to its entirety." The government argued that it was not taxing the exported goods themselves but merely imposing a "stamp duty on a document not necessarily though ordinarily used in connection with the exportation of goods." The majority found this distinction too fine to be maintained while still respecting the "fidelity to the spirit and purpose" of the constitutional prohibition on export taxes.[60] The principle defended by the Court seems clear enough, but the case generated substantial disagreement among the justices and required an extended discussion by Brewer on the proper degree of deference owed to Congress. Similar taxes had a long history in the United States, and the relevant precedents were somewhat conflicting. As Justice Harlan vigorously argued in dissent, Congress had, without constitutional objection, imposed such a stamp tax on bills of lading for goods for export as early as 1797 (repealed by the Jeffersonians) and again in 1862 (repealed at the end of Reconstruction). Nonetheless, the majority concluded that, "when the meaning and scope of a constitutional provision are clear, it cannot be overthrown by legislative action, although several times repeated and never before challenged." Further, it noted that such judicial challenges may have been unlikely before the "burdens of taxation" were enlarged by the "great expenses of government," making the "objects and modes of taxation . . . a matter of special scrutiny."[61]

No other invalidation of federal law during this period provoked as many as three dissents, and more than half of all the decisions striking down federal legislation were filed without any recorded dissent.[62] The Court unanimously decided all but one of the remaining cases that invalided statutory provisions less than seven years old. The exception was affirmation of the Oklahoma Supreme Court's decision to uphold 1910 state legislation moving the capital from Guthrie to Oklahoma City, which conflicted with a provision of the statehood enabling act designating Guthrie the state capital until at least 1913.[63] Against the federal government's assertions that this was a political question, the Court emphasized that newly admitted states were on an equal footing with preexisting states, and the location of the state capital was an essential state power. Justices McKenna and Holmes dissented without filing an opinion. It appears that other such cases were even easier calls for the Court.

Other relatively new statutes were struck down with little controversy. The Court had no difficulty voiding a provision of the Indian Services Appropriation Act of 1907 by which Congress sought to create a jurisdictional fast track and pay the litigation costs for a suit questioning the constitutionality of earlier statutes affecting land titles. The Court found that this did not comport with the judicial power to hear actual cases and controversies.[64] Similarly, the Court recognized that a congressional directive to expropriate a lock and dam from a private company without compensating it for the lost income from tolls was an unconstitutional taking that inappropriately sought to preclude a full judicial determination of just compensation.[65] Furthermore, a congressional directive to approve a disputed lease in possible violation of the terms of a previous cession of the land by treaty was an interference with the judicial determination of vested property rights.[66] The congressional effort to revoke the tax-exempt status of lands previously allotted to the Choctaw and Chickasaw tribes was readily rejected as an unconstitutional taking of a vested property right.[67] The Court likewise rejected a particularly harsh provision of the Chinese Exclusion Act of 1892 that subjected illegal aliens to confinement at hard labor without a jury trial, even though it had earlier upheld other, more central elements of the act that authorized the summary deportation of resident aliens.[68] The Court unanimously clarified that its earlier decision exempting the Philippines, as a held possession, from the full coverage of the Constitution could not be extended to territories fully integrated into the United States, such as Alaska. Therefore, despite the assistant attorney general's pleas that the Sixth Amendment could not possibly apply "to this barren and desolate region, peopled as it is by savages and an alien race," the Court invalidated the provision of a congressional code for Alaska that allowed criminal defendants to be tried with only a six-person jury.[69]

Those laws invalidated more than six years after enactment displayed a similar hodgepodge of constitutional infirmities and were likewise of limited political salience. Sometimes it was unclear how much real support the disputed measures had ever enjoyed. In *Adair v. United States*, decided in 1908, the Court nullified a provision of the 1898 Erdman Act.[70] As a liberty-of-contract case striking down a federal prohibition on the railroads' use of "yellow-dog" contracts barring union membership and union blacklists, *Adair* was the closest thing to a congressionally targeted *Lochner*.[71] The Court extended the protection of yellow-dog contracts to the states a few years later, and soon thereafter it authorized the use of injunctions against unions seeking to organize employees who had signed such contracts.[72] The Erdman Act was the legislative response to the infamous Pullman strike four years earlier, which the Cleveland administration had broken up through court injunction and military force. The heart of the act was the establishment of an arbitration system to resolve labor disputes in the railroad industry. Section 10, however, "was less than peripheral to the political conflicts" that gave birth to the statute.[73] The policies contained in section 10 had been suggested by the US Strike Commission, formed after the Pullman strike, and had been incorporated by Attorney General Richard Olney into the bill that eventually became the Erdman Act. These policies, however, received virtually no attention in Congress and were considered unimportant and virtually unenforceable by labor leaders.[74] More generally, the act was a largely symbolic measure that provided the first statutory sanction for labor injunctions, and it was bitterly denounced by mainstream labor leaders such as the American Federation of Labor's Samuel Gompers and his congressional allies. When section 10 was finally invoked and struck down by Justice Harlan and a majority of his brethren a decade later, the Erdman Act as a whole was largely moribund, and there was little concern in Congress or the administration over the fate of this side provision.[75]

Other invalidated statutory provisions were not so rooted in a particular political moment, and they were of no great political interest to current majorities.[76] For instance, the Court struck down the conviction of Albert Heff for selling alcohol to Native American John Butler. By virtue of earlier legislation, Butler had become a full citizen and was no longer under the special guardianship of the federal government; therefore, Heff's conviction encroached on the exclusive police powers of the states.[77] A 1909 case evaluated the code for the District of Columbia, which allowed the government to appeal errors in criminal trials, although acquittals could not be overturned. The solicitor general argued that such appeals could usefully clarify the law, but the Court rejected the code provision as inappropriately seeking an advisory opinion from the courts.[78] In another case, the government argued that the Constitution did not require jury trials in the District of Columbia, but the justices believed that such a position would do "violence to the letter and spirit of the constitution."[79] In two separate opinions, the Court struck down additional provisions of the 1898 War Revenue Act as indirectly seeking to tax exports.[80] In 1899 the Court nullified a provision of the federal criminal code relating to those accused of receiving stolen property of the United States. Under the code, the separate conviction of those charged with the theft was considered conclusive evidence that the goods were in fact stolen. The Court found that such a rule denied defendants the right to confront their accusers.[81] The Court also held that a Civil War Congress's efforts to compel businesses to disclose their books in tax disputes ran afoul of constitutional protections against unreasonable searches. "It is not the breaking of his doors, and the rummaging of his drawers, that constitutes the essence of the offense; but it is the invasion of his indefeasible right of personal security, personal liberty, and private property."[82]

Upholding Congressional Power

The Fuller and White Courts resolved an extraordinary number of constitutional challenges in favor of congressional power. As the Court emerged from Reconstruction, the judicial docket was increasingly crowded. Congress expanded the jurisdiction of the federal courts, allowing corporations and others to have their disputes heard by federal rather than state judges.[83] Congress generated more laws and began to build the institutions of the national state, making federal governance more visible and creating more federal law to be interpreted and applied. As the economy nationalized and society became more complex, litigants poured into the courts. With a mandatory docket, the justices found themselves flooded with cases to review. Constitutional claims mixed readily with more mundane arguments over statutory interpretation. As figure 5-1 illustrates, the surge in the number of constitutional challenges being resolved by the Supreme Court resulted in a historically low invalidation rate of federal statutes. As litigants pressed the justices to hear more challenges to the constitutional authority of Congress, the justices responded by turning back those challenges and emphasizing congressional authority. When the *Lochner* Court was asked to review the constitutionality of federal laws, the justices generally upheld them.

While many of those cases involved relatively unimportant statutes, the

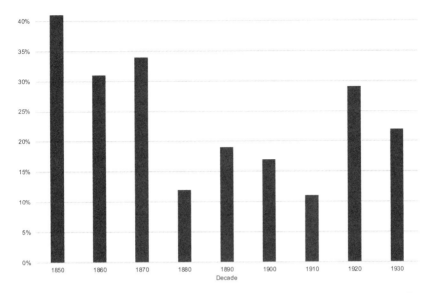

Figure 5-1: Rate of Invalidation of Federal Statutory Provisions in Constitutional Cases by Decade, 1850–1930   .

Court ruled in favor of Congress in dozens of cases that challenged important federal policies. The major legislative accomplishments of both Democratic and Republican Congresses were routinely hauled before the Court for scrutiny, and more often than not, the justices were willing to give their approval to what the legislators had done. Invalidations during this period tended to be most important when they involved major pieces of legislation, but there were quite a few instances in which the Court rendered a legally important decision while upholding a relatively minor piece of legislation. As legislators embarked on the project of building the national state, the justices cheered them on.

During the New Deal, constitutional scholar Edward Corwin looked back on these years and noted two competing visions of the Constitution. The Constitution could be "an instrument of popular power—sovereignty, if you will—for the achievement of progress." In that guise, the Constitution was a tool that leveraged power so that men might be "able to impart a desired shape to things and events." It looked to the future and "things needing to be done." An alternative vision of the Constitution looked to the past and sought to conserve "an already established order of things." That Constitution was a "symbol" of privilege rather than an "instrument" of progress. As a symbol, the Constitution was deployed "to protect and tranquilize private interest or advantage as against public power."[84] As a partisan in the intellectual, political, and legal battles of the early twentieth century, Corwin hoped to advance the Progressive vision of the Constitution as an instrument of popular power, but he thought the conservative forces of constitutional symbolism were often regnant. He feared that too often the lawyers and judges who held sway on the *Lochner* Court agreed with Thomas Cooley, the influential jurist from Michigan who emphasized that the very purpose of a written constitution is to impose "a limitation upon the powers of government" and preserve "the enjoyment of the rights and powers which [the citizenry] possessed before the constitution was made."[85]

Across these decades of the Gilded Age and Progressive Era, the federal government was pressured to take unprecedented actions to cope with a wide array of new social problems. Such innovations did not go unchallenged. Sometimes powerful interests were negatively affected by such policies, and they turned to the courts to vindicate their investment in the status quo. Sometimes isolated individuals and groups who stood on the very margins of society were negatively affected by such policies, and they turned to the courts for relief. On occasion, the Court deployed the Constitution to shield those claimants, but more often, it understood the Constitution to be a Progressive instrument that empowered Congress to respond creatively to new social problems and political demands.

In some cases, the Court rejected more radical challenges to laws it had previously constitutionally trimmed. Given what the Court had said in the *Employers' Liability Cases*, the El Paso & Northeastern Railway sought to avoid liability for the death of an employee working on a railroad operating in the New Mexico Territory. The justices insisted that the original statutory language was still valid in the federal territories, even if it could not be applied to railroads operating within states.[86] However, the justices later concluded that the federal government could address injuries suffered by railroad employees working on a bridge near Hoboken, New Jersey, so long as the railway was used by interstate carriers.[87] More fundamentally, the Court insisted that Congress had complete authority to impose regulations to enhance the safety of employees of carriers operating within interstate commerce.[88] Similarly, despite its ruling in *E. C. Knight*—that Congress could not regulate anticompetitive contracts in manufacturing that had only indirect effects on interstate commerce—the Court turned back more radical challenges to federal antitrust legislation. Shortly after *E. C. Knight*, the justices heard arguments that the congressional power to regulate commerce among the states was limited to countering protectionist state legislation and "does not include the general power to interfere with or prohibit private contracts between citizens." This limitation was perhaps reinforced by the Fifth Amendment guarantee of a liberty that included "a right to enter into certain classes of contract for the purpose of enabling the citizen to carry on his business." The justices were not persuaded and declared firmly that the commerce power was broad and included the authority to regulate or void private contracts (or, for that matter, the actions of state-chartered corporations).[89]

Although the Court insisted that Congress could not regulate economic activities that did not directly affect interstate commerce, it also emphasized that the congressional regulatory power was quite sweeping within its sphere of operation. As Congress moved to make more comprehensive use of its power, the Court worked to clear the channels of federal power. Under the umbrella of the interstate commerce power, for example, the Court found adequate authority for Congress to build bridges across navigable rivers and even seize private property and construct railroads within the boundaries of the states.[90] "Having the express power to make rules for the conduct of commerce among the states, the range of congressional discretion as to the regulation best adapted to remedy a practice found inefficient or hurtful is a wide one."[91] In exercising that power, Congress could regulate the liability of carriers for the goods they contracted to carry across state boundaries, regulate the fares charged by railroads, prohibit interstate railroads from carrying goods manufactured by their own companies, restrict the hours of railroad employees, and regulate employees of interstate carriers who were not themselves involved in interstate commerce.[92] The commerce clause provided an opening for Congress to exercise a general police power, for the Constitution did not guarantee "freedom of commerce among the states in all things."[93] As a result, Congress could allow state regulations related to alcohol to apply to goods imported into the state through interstate commerce, prohibit the interstate shipment of lottery tickets, ban the interstate transport of women for immoral purposes, and exclude from commerce drugs with misleading packaging.[94] The Court thought there was "no room for doubt as to the wholly unsubstantial and frivolous character of the constitutional question" of whether Congress could prohibit the importation of opium.[95]

The Court was willing to give Congress leeway in how it exercised its other enumerated powers as well. At the end of Reconstruction, the Court upheld the Comstock laws, observing that in excluding obscene materials from the mails, "the object of Congress has not been to interfere with the freedom of the press, or with any other rights of the people, but to refuse its facilities for the distribution of matter deemed injurious to the public morals."[96] From there, it was a simple matter to conclude in a case involving lottery materials that Congress's postal power included the discretion not "to assist in the dissemination of matters condemned by its judgment through the governmental agencies which it controls."[97] When exercising its spending power, Congress could require that federal contractors adhere to an eight-hour workday.[98] In managing the public lands, Congress had the authority to block neighboring property holders from enclosing the public land with fences.[99] In exercising its war powers, Congress could institute a military draft, punish seditious speech, and close brothels near military bases.[100]

As Congress embarked on new social crusades, the Court stood aside. The Republican Party denounced the polygamy practiced by the Mormons in the West as equally barbaric as the slavery practiced by the slavocracy in the South. When the postbellum Congress turned its attention to bringing the Church of Jesus Christ of Latter-day Saints to heel, the Court gave it a free hand.[101] When pressure built to restrict immigration from Asia, the Court largely endorsed the unprecedented and often draconian measures Congress adopted to exclude and expel immigrants and punish those who aided or employed them.[102] As Congress experimented with new approaches to integrating the Native American population into the mainstream of American society, the Court stayed its hand.[103]

The Court was willing to facilitate the early emergence of the administrative state. In these years, Congress began to experiment with new institutional structures to regulate the nationalizing economy and sought to place new policy-making powers in the hands of experts within the executive branch. These new regulatory bodies needed both discretion and power to be effective, and the Court was uniformly accommodating. Congress could, for example, require the compulsory production of corporate documents to advance regulatory actions, and it could enlist the courts' aid in regulatory investigations.[104] Like other courts across the country, the US Supreme Court gave Congress the green light to delegate substantial policy-making power to the executive branch.[105] The ruling did not come in a case involving one of the welter of new agencies and commissions being created during these decades; rather, it involved a provision of a tariff act that authorized the president to adjust import fees in response to the actions of the country's trading partners. Although Marshall Field & Co. argued that Congress had effectively delegated to the president the power to set tariff rates on imported goods, the Court asserted that "it is often desirable, if not essential," for Congress to be able to "invest the president with large discretion." The Court affirmed the principle that "congress cannot delegate legislative power to the president," but it would not be quick to conclude that the president was in fact engaged in "the making of law" rather than acting as a "mere agent of the law-making department."[106]

Conclusion

Perhaps the most striking feature of the Court's exercise of judicial review vis-à-vis Congress is how mundane it was. History remembers the highlights—the income tax cases, *E. C. Knight*, the child labor case—but this was only a small part of the Court's work and leaves a misleading impression of how judicial review was exercised. The "*Lochner* era" implies a concerted assault on government power by a determined, conservative judicial majority. Such a period of activism suggests the frenetic conflicts over the New Deal in the mid-1930s or the wholesale reimagining of the constitutional landscape of the Warren Court in the 1960s, but the Court at the turn of the twentieth century did not fit those images. Its actions were informed by a coherent constitutional vision, but few of its decisions were of great political moment, and the overall pattern does little to suggest an orchestrated campaign against the government.

The Court's record during this period reflects concrete judicial review in its classic sense. Unlike many twentieth-century constitutional systems in which the power of constitutional review is entrusted to a specialized body charged with answering abstract questions of constitutional meaning, the United States developed a system of decentralized, concrete judicial review in which every judge is authorized to take the Constitution into account when resolving the ordinary, individual disputes that come before the bench. Although the turn-of-the-century Court was sometimes mobilized by an organized litigation campaign to render a decision on a key matter of public policy, it often simply reached out to stay the hand of the state from acting against a particular individual. In doing so, the Court would set out a constitutional rule, but that rule was often relatively uncontroversial and of limited effect. In many instances, the Court's constitutional judgment was highly fact-specific.

The invalidations of federal statutes during this period were informed by a general constitutional vision, but it is hard to see them as part of a broader campaign against the government. Rather than building cumulatively, the Court dissipated its energy across a variety of doctrinally disconnected cases. While some particularly prominent decisions loom above the others, those decisions stand out precisely because they were so isolated. Even so, the Court effectively, though temporarily, obstructed some of the government's notable policy innovations, primarily the federal income tax and federal child labor regulation. More generally, the Court's decisions against the government were less reflections of a party platform than of a legal sensibility. Insulated from political pressures and immersed in legal tradition, the Court was less likely than Congress to look with approval on the suspension of traditional elements of criminal due process or backdoor efforts to raise revenue or extend federal police powers.

The Court rarely blocked a mobilized political majority on an important point of public policy. When it moved against such measures, it sometimes came in late and acted long after the majority had demobilized. Most obviously, this was the situation in the case of black civil rights, where the Court proved no more committed to Reconstruction-era statutes than was the rest of the federal government.

The Court sometimes acted only tangentially. It might act in a subject area of significant public debate, such as labor disputes or immigration, but only on legislative details that were marginal to those debates. When it was willing to act against legislative provisions embodying salient political principles, it did so with little risk of reprisal. The federal income tax, antitrust prohibitions, and child labor regulation were high-profile issues and powerful political symbols, but in these cases, the Court moved either in sympathy with the sitting administration (income tax and antitrust) or when the political costs to the administration were minimal (child labor). Grover Cleveland might have been forced to do business with the Populists in his party, but he and his justices strongly disagreed with many of their views. When the Republicans failed to hold the elected branches of the federal government in the face of a Progressive defection, their judicial appointees were unsympathetic to elements of the Democratic interregnum. The outputs of the legislature were too varied, and the points of agreement among partisans too few, to expect the Court to always fall in line. The Court's most politically salient decisions during this period reflected the constitutional commitments of successful presidential coalitions, sometimes to the dismay of their outlying wings.

Although the *Lochner* era was the cradle of the countermajoritarian difficulty, the countermajoritarian framework provides little leverage for evaluating the normative foundations of judicial review during this period. The Court interposed itself into complicated political environments, not stark majoritarian ones.

6

The Constitutional Revolution

The practice of judicial review was transformed over the course of the mid-twentieth century. Famously, the substance of constitutional law was upturned twice. The first constitutional revolution of the 1930s cast aside many of the features of the constitutional order developed by the Court after the Civil War. Inherited understandings of federalism, executive power, and property rights were abandoned to accommodate the more activist national state that emerged from the New Deal. The second civil rights and civil liberties revolution of the 1960s established new limitations on government power to be enforced by the courts. The Court began the process of articulating a new set of rights that continued to accommodate the core commitments of the New Deal.

Although much of the Court's concentration when laying down these new constitutional rules was on state and local governments, the scope of congressional authority did not escape its attention. The change can be seen in the composition of the constitutional issues heard by the Court in its review of federal statutes. Figure 6-1 divides these constitutional issues into three broad categories and tracks their prevalence over time. Structural issues include cases involving judicial power, separation of powers, and federalism. Early in the Court's history, such issues dominated its agenda, but their predominance has steadily slid over time. Although such issues rebounded a bit at the turn of the twenty-first century, they were largely pushed off the agenda in the mid-twentieth century, when structural issues gave way to the other two classes of cases. The sharp drop in structural cases in the 1870s and again in the 1940s was largely driven by shifts in the Court's interest in the boundary between the federal and state governments. Cases involving separation of powers and judicial power have been a fairly constant feature of the Court's agenda, but the proportion of federalism cases shrank during Reconstruction as various rights-related cases became more common. In the immediate post–New Deal period, the absolute number of federalism cases dropped dramatically from its height in the 1920s and 1930s, and as a consequence, they also shrank as a proportion of the docket.

Unlike structural issues, the other two categories of cases focus on the limits of the federal government's power relative to private actors. Economic issues include a range of constitutional questions addressing the regulation of private industry and private economic behavior by the central government, including taxation, the exercise of eminent domain, and contract rights. The third category, rights and equality, covers a range of noneconomic limits on government power, including matters of criminal and administrative procedure, civil rights and prohibited forms of discrimination, and various substantive rights, from religious liberty to free speech to sexual liberty.

These two types of constitutional cases rose in tandem over the course of the nineteenth century but sharply diverged after the New Deal, when economic cases almost dropped off the Court's docket entirely and cases involving individual rights surged. The constitutional revolution of the 1930s sharply reduced judicial monitoring of how Congress related to structural features of the Constitution and to its powers over economic affairs. The constitutional revolution of the 1960s, in contrast, sharply increased judicial monitoring of how congressional statutes affected personal liberty.

Decomposing rights-related claims also reveals some underlying differences. Pure procedural claims have consistently occupied a prominent portion of the Court's review of federal statutes, and until the Civil War, they accounted for all such claims. The postbellum period saw a brief burst of (noneconomic) substantive rights and equality claims, but both types of cases became much more prominent in the twentieth century (and drivers of the growth in this category in figure 6-1). Rights claims grew rapidly in the 1940s and 1950s to rival the prominence of pure procedural claims, with equality claims enjoying a relatively brief surge in the 1960s and 1970s before falling back to pre–Warren Court levels by the end of the twentieth century.

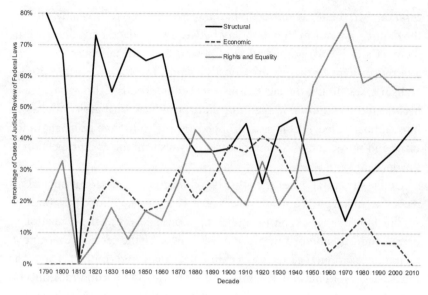

Figure 6-1: Constitutional Issues in Cases of Judicial Review of Congress, 1789–2018

A third revolution, less visible but also important, involved the institutional practice by which the Court accepted cases and exercised judicial review. That revolution was advocated by the justices but effectuated by Congress. Most important, the Judiciary Act of 1925 dramatically altered how cases reached the US Supreme Court. As Woodrow Wilson was leaving the White House, former president William Howard Taft was worried that the Court was being "swamped" by the rapidly growing federal caseload in the early twentieth century.[1] The number of ordinary federal cases was growing alongside the federal government itself, and the number of constitutional cases was growing apace. (See figure 1-1, which tracks the number of Court cases that reviewed federal statutes. Particularly notable is the dramatic increase in the number of cases in which the Court upheld federal statutory provisions against constitutional challenge.) Appointed in 1921 to the office he had most longed for—chief justice of the United States—Taft immediately set about persuading Congress to grant greater power and autonomy to the Court.[2] Congress allowed the justices to largely control their own docket by significantly reducing the circumstances in which the Court had to hear direct appeals from lower court rulings. Instead, the justices could decide which cases to take by granting a writ of certiorari (cert). Although judicial review cases continued to reach the

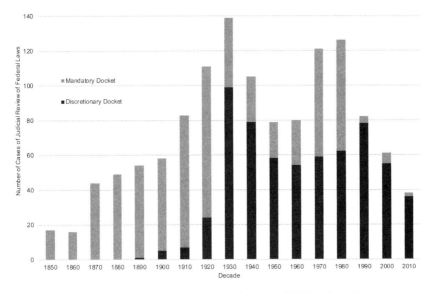

Figure 6-2: Discretionary and Mandatory Docket in Judicial Review Cases, 1850–2018

Court through means other than the cert petition, the justices had far more discretion over which challenges to federal statutes they would hear. They did not immediately throttle their docket, but they did take advantage of the opportunity to avoid cases of little interest and concentrate on constitutional questions of greater interest. Figure 6-2 documents the dramatic shift in the twentieth century from a largely mandatory docket of judicial review cases to a largely discretionary docket.

Taft was confident and aggressive in the 1920s in his efforts to shape the Court not only through institutional reforms but also through judicial selection. The chief justice advised President Warren Harding to look "for conservatives rather than Republicans" when selecting judges to nominate to the Supreme Court.[3] As president, Taft had followed his own advice. He had also been unusually lucky in having the opportunity to name six justices to the Court.[4] Harding and Calvin Coolidge had five vacancies to fill. By contrast, the intervening Democrat, Woodrow Wilson, made only three appointments to the Court during his eight years in office. Taft was convinced that a firm judicial hand was needed to check the radicals that infested both the Democratic and the Republican Parties. During his unsuccessful bid for reelection to the presidency in 1912, Taft assured his supporters, "I believe in popular Government, but I believe in popular government ordered by Constitution and by law." Representatives who are elected by a fraction of the voters can be trusted with "power over all the people" only if they are adequately "limited by constitutional restrictions" interpreted and enforced by "an independent judiciary."[5]

Taft's efforts helped set up future conflicts. Just as the US Supreme Court had reached a new plateau of activism after Reconstruction, it similarly found a new and higher equilibrium after World War I. In the Gilded Age and Progressive Era, the Court resolved half a dozen constitutional challenges to federal statutory provisions per year and, on average, ruled against Congress in just under one of them. Between 1920 and 1968 the Court, on average, heard more than ten such cases per year and issued judgments restricting congressional authority in nearly two and a half of them. Although the constitutional battles of President Franklin D. Roosevelt's first term grabbed the spotlight, the Court had been unusually active for more than a decade by the time FDR took the oath of office. In the 1920s the Court issued more than thirty opinions enforcing limits on the powers of Congress. Harding saw more laws struck down by the Court during his administration than had any previous president. The Court found itself at odds with Congress like it never had before.

The Taft Court may have attained new levels of activism in the 1920s, but the battles of the 1930s were clearly different from anything that had come before. Table 6-1 compares the Court's record of invalidating statutes across four distinct periods in the mid-twentieth century. The earlier *Lochner* Court (see chapter 5) is also included for comparison purposes. The table shows variations in some important aspects of how the Court exercised judicial review. Most basic was the sharp step-up in the total number of cases invalidating statutes from the *Lochner* period to the Taft Court. The Court then entered a brief period of intense conflict with Congress during FDR's first term. After the "constitutional revolution" of 1937, the Court retreated nearly to its pre-1920 level of activism, before resuming near Taft Court levels after Chief Justice Earl Warren assumed the bench.

Of course, the Court's rate of invalidating notable provisions of landmark legislation—the most important federal policies—was only a fraction of its overall rate of invalidation, but that fraction varied substantially over time.

Table 6-1: Cases per Annum Invalidating Federal Statutes, 1885–1968

	All Invalidations	Notable Provisions of "Landmark" Statutes	In Whole	In Part (as Applied)	Less than Nine Years Old	More than Nine Years Old
Lochner Court (1885–1919)	0.91	0.29	0.54	0.37	0.54	0.37
Taft Court (1920–1932)	3.15	0.38	0.92	2.23	1.77	1.38
New Deal Court (1933–1936)	5.00	1.75	3.25	1.75	3.25	1.75
Post–New Deal Court (1937–1954)	1.17	0.22	0.17	1.00	0.50	0.67
Warren Court (1955–1968)	2.57	1.07	0.93	1.54	1.07	1.50

The Taft Court actually dedicated less attention to those important cases and, as a result, issued those rulings at only a slightly higher rate than the *Lochner* Court did. The Taft Court was more activist than its predecessor in terms of sheer volume of invalidations, but the laws it nullified were relatively minor. Unsurprisingly, during the New Deal era, the Court was occupied with a high proportion of critical policies, but it is telling that the post–New Deal Court not only slowed the pace of invalidation but also disproportionately slowed the rate at which it struck down the most important congressional policies. As the Warren Court became more active in raw numbers, it also became more active in striking down important federal policies, nearly approaching the New Deal level. The Warren Court was more selective in how it wielded the judicial veto, but in cases involving important federal policies, the justices at midcentury were as active as any of their predecessors in blocking Congress. With only a short retreat from judicial activism after the bruising battle over Court packing, the Supreme Court in the Warren years was at least as comfortable and aggressive in exercising its power to review acts of Congress as the Taft Court had been prior to the New Deal.

Cases invalidating statutes can also be distinguished by how broadly sweeping the Court's judgment was. The New Deal stands out for the proportion of statutory provisions invalidated in their entirety. When the Court retreated after 1937, it pulled back from issuing such rulings; it restricted legislative text in part or as applied in a particular case, rather than voiding provisions in their entirety. Finally, the New Deal stands out for its unusual focus on recently adopted statutes (less than nine years old—the historic average of how long it takes provisions to be invalidated by the Court); however, a similar pattern is apparent if a shorter time frame is used. In summary, the years 1933–1936 were exceptional in terms of how the Court exercised the power of judicial review. The political reaction was exceptional as well.

For a brief moment, the Court chose to pursue a path of direct confrontation with Congress and the administration. It soon found that path unsustainable, and it was forced to retreat. But its retreat was not complete. Although the Court moved to accommodate the New Deal after 1937, it did not abandon judicial review. Instead, it found new ways to enforce limits on Congress in a manner that did not threaten core commitments of the governing coalition.

The Taft Court

Former president William Howard Taft took his place on the Court in the summer of 1921. He joined a Court shaped primarily by Republican presidents. Taft himself had appointed two of its members, who anchored a reliable conservative majority. A vocal Progressive wing of the Court had been only slightly bolstered by Woodrow Wilson's selection of labor lawyer Louis Brandeis for the bench.

It is no surprise that the Taft Court reviewed more Democratic statutes than its predecessors had during the Gilded Age and Progressive Era. Some policies adopted during the Wilson administration reached the Court before the Democrats were turned out of the White House in 1920, but more made their way through the litigation process after the government was back in Republican hands. The Democrats had enjoyed only six years of a unified government before losing Congress in 1918, but those were particularly productive years from a policy-making standpoint. The combination of the Democratic takeover after the 1912 elections and the outbreak of the First World War led to the passage of various legislative measures both great and small. Court challenges to their implementation were bound to follow, and the Taft Court was likely to be unsympathetic to many of those measures. As the Taft Court became unusually active in reviewing federal legislation, the proportion of Democratic measures that came under fire was unusually large. Across the more than three decades considered in chapter 5, the Court struck down federal statutes in only thirty-two cases. Only a quarter had been passed by a House of Representatives controlled by the Democratic Party. In the span of just over a decade, from 1920 to 1932, the Court struck down federal laws in forty-one cases, and nearly half of them involved laws passed by a Democratic House.[6] Throughout this period, the justices returned to constitutional issues raised by congressional actions taken during the Wilson administration. Such laws were not always highly partisan and did not always reflect core Democratic commitments, but they often involved the new pressures the federal government faced in the early twentieth century.

Only two of the Taft Court cases fit neatly into the expected Progressive narrative of the period, and as a consequence, they are both familiar from constitutional law casebooks. The *Child Labor Tax Case* dealt with Congress's response to the Court's earlier ruling in *Hammer v. Dagenhart*.[7] In the 1918

Dagenhart case, a narrow majority had struck down the Keating-Owen Act, which had banned from interstate commerce any goods made with child labor. Disappointed Progressives and New England manufacturing interests immediately sought a work-around. Even as *Dagenhart* was being argued before the Supreme Court, the Children's Bureau of the US Department of Labor pronounced 1918 the "Children's Year" and stumped for men to earn an adequate "family income" that enabled "mothers to care for their own children at home" and children to stay in school "until every other possible labor resource shall have been exhausted."[8] Children's Year events culminated in a White House conference, where it was resolved that sixteen should be the minimum age for "employment in any occupation" other than "agriculture and domestic service."[9] In February 1919 congressional allies of the child labor movement tacked onto the tail end of a general revenue bill a special 10 percent tax on net profits generated by businesses employing child labor.[10] Southern opponents of the measure admitted that the Supreme Court had seemingly given Congress carte blanche to exercise its taxation powers by upholding federal taxes on the sale of margarine, even though "the real object of the legislation was to put oleomargarine out of business in the interest of the dairymen of the country."[11] But, they insisted, the child labor tax was different, in that it tried to do indirectly what the Court had ruled Congress could not do directly because labor regulations were under the exclusive authority of the states. Massachusetts senator Henry Cabot Lodge admitted that the child labor tax was an "extreme method," even a "dangerous power to use," but his hand was forced by the abject failure of some states "to regulate it as it should be regulated."[12] Only one of the dissenters in *Dagenhart* was willing to support Congress when the child labor tax reached the Court in 1922, and Justice John Clarke did so without offering a written opinion. It was left to Chief Justice Taft to explain that here, Congress had stripped away even the fig leaf that might support a "presumption of validity." If Congress were allowed to simply use the magic word "tax" when adopting measures to regulate economic and social life, this would "break down all constitutional limitation of the powers of Congress and completely wipe out the sovereignty of the states."[13] As in *Dagenhart*, Congress was attempting to "coerce people of a state to act as Congress wishes them to act in respect of a matter completely the business of the state government under the federal Constitution," and the Court was obliged to intervene again.[14]

The next year, the Taft Court rejected another labor measure advocated by Progressives: the minimum wage. The Court had generally upheld a variety of labor regulations, including the state regulation of working hours for women, but the direct regulation of wages was a new issue for the Taft Court. The recently seated Justice Brandeis had been instrumental in promoting and defending many of those policies and was widely credited with persuading the Court to give state legislatures discretion in regulating how businesses dealt with female employees. In the early twentieth century, an international social reform movement took up the cause of a "living wage," but proponents recognized the legal and political obstacles posed by "that perverse individualism which prefers irrational liberty and industrial anarchy to a legal regime of order and justice."[15] Tactically, a minimum wage for women was thought to have a greater chance of success in both legislatures and the courts than a general minimum wage. If women could not be removed from the labor force entirely and persuaded to "accept woman's true functions, those of wife, mother, mistress of the home, and moulder of the moral and spiritual life of the race," they could at least be prevented from undercutting men's wages in the marketplace.[16] When it came to working hours, the *Lochner* Court had seemed to agree, admitting that "the physical wellbeing of woman becomes an object of public interest and care in order to preserve the strength and vigor of the race," and therefore the state had a unique interest in "special legislation restricting or qualifying the conditions under which she should be permitted to toil."[17] But the Court had long been inclined to think differently about the scope of the legislature's authority to regulate hours of service as opposed to wages.[18]

In 1918 Congress followed the Oregon model and set up a labor board for the District of Columbia that was empowered to establish a minimum wage for women and children. Congress was moved by the desire to protect the "fair and enlightened employer from underbidding competitors" and the need to maintain the "physical, mental, and emotional health" of the women who would eventually "bear and rear children for the coming generation."[19] Members of Congress were assured that the Court had, in fact, already upheld such laws "as a proper exercise of the police powers of the state, to preserve public health and welfare," but advocates glossed over the fact that an evenly divided Court had merely let stand, without offering an opinion, an Oregon judicial ruling upholding the law.[20] Justice Brandeis would have held the deciding vote in that case, but he did not participate because, before be-ing named to the Court, he had been the lawyer defending the Oregon law (future justice Felix Frankfurter took over from Brandeis). By the time the federal law reached the Court in 1923, however, the justices' ideology had shifted to the right. Brandeis continued to sit on the sidelines due to his personal entanglements with the minimum wage movement.[21] Taft assumed that *Lochner* had been effectively overruled, and as a result, legislatures were free to pass whatever policies they thought might improve workers' health, regardless of the broader effects on the community.[22] But he found himself in a three-person minority. Justice George Sutherland, who had been selected by Harding to replace a Wilson appointee, spoke for the majority in arguing that there was still life left in *Lochner*, despite some of the Court's subsequent decisions. The majority thought there was an important difference between laws designed to intervene "where work of long continued duration is det-rimental to health" and laws that struck at the "heart of the contract" and essentially engaged in "price fixing" and extracted an "arbitrary payment" from one private party to enrich another.[23] The law was evidently "the prod-uct of a naked, arbitrary exercise of power" to transfer wealth from a less-favored citizen to a more-favored one, and it was not hard to see that if this exercise of power was legitimated, a "swing of sentiment" could just as easily "strip the employee of his constitutional liberty of contract in the opposite direction."[24] Private interests must sometimes yield to the good of the com-munity, but the majority could not see a credible claim that the common good was at issue here.

Other cases invalidating Democratic policies in the 1920s evidenced the complex legacy of the Progressive movement rather than a straightforward battle between the forces of progress and the forces of reaction. In the early twentieth century, medical reformers busily sought to professionalize the manufacture and distribution of drugs and the training and credentialing of medical practitioners. The unregulated sale of narcotics ranging from mari-juana to opium was a key target. The Harrison Narcotic Act of 1914 marked the federal government's first major foray in the war on drugs. As with child labor, however, Congress was stymied by its lack of a general police power to regulate people's safety, health, and morals. Here too, Congress tried to use the tool that seemed most readily available: taxation. Thus, Congress re-quired that anyone producing, importing, distributing, or selling any derivatives of opium or coca leaves register with the collector of internal revenue; distribute drugs only with a written prescription, which must be preserved for federal inspection; and pay a special tax. Any person found to be in possession of any of the prohibited drugs whose name did not appear on the registry would be subject to fines and imprisonment.[25] Shortly thereafter, Dr. Charles Linder was convicted in Spokane, Oregon, of dispensing morphine and cocaine to a patient who was a known addict. The Court was obliged to point out that Congress had no constitutional authority to exercise the "direct control of medical practice in the states" and could not adopt such a regulatory scheme in the guise of a tax bill. Linder could be charged with a federal crime if he failed to pay the required tax, but he could not be charged with a federal crime for improperly practicing medicine or for distributing drugs to addicts; nor could his patients be charged with a federal crime for simply possessing narcotics. The Harrison Narcotic Act could be construed and administered only as a tax measure, and it was invalid and unenforceable to the extent that it operated "solely to the achievement of something plainly within the power reserved to the states."[26] Linder had registered and paid his tax; Congress had no constitutional authority to regulate how he conducted his medical practice.

The combination of World War I and Progressive reform finally gave nativists the upper hand in Woodrow Wilson's second term of office.[27] The political machines of the Gilded Age were adept at converting newly arrived immigrants into partisan citizens, so these politicians were resistant to efforts to close off immigration. The increasingly powerful labor unions of the turn of the century were generally opposed to admitting more workers into the country, but business interests were more welcoming. When he first ran for president in 1912, Wilson sought the votes of the foreign-born and pledged to keep America open to immigrants, and he vetoed the immigration bills championed by Theodore Roosevelt's longtime nativist ally Senator Henry Cabot Lodge. As war brewed in Europe, Roosevelt was among those castigating the "hyphenated American" who "calls himself an American citizen and who yet shows by his actions that he is primarily a citizen of a foreign land" and "plays a mischievous part in the life of our body politic."[28] Congress finally overrode Wilson's veto to pass the General Immigration Act of 1917, the first large-scale immigration reform measure since the Roosevelt administration. It extended earlier restrictions on immigration and added more, including aggressive new rules for deporting resident aliens. Among those targeted for deportation was a group of Chinese nationals being detained in San Francisco. Writing for a unanimous Court, Justice Brandeis was generally deferential to the will of Congress in deciding to deport those "unlawful[ly] remaining" in the United States. Two petitioners, however, claimed to be foreign-born sons of native-born American citizens, thus raising a constitutional objection to the congressional policy of summary deportation. The Court had previously held that newly arriving individuals who claimed to be American citizens were not entitled to a judicial hearing before being turned away at the border, but the individuals in question had been arrested in Arizona many months after entering the country.[29] The justices insisted that, under these circumstances, these individuals could not be deported by executive action; they were entitled to a judicial hearing to evaluate their claims of citizenship.[30]

Other Democratic statutes that ran afoul of the Taft Court were more concerned with the mechanics of American governance than with substantive policy. The Corrupt Practices Act, the first significant federal campaign finance statute, was initially passed by a Republican Congress and then amended by a Democratic one. The states were busily adopting similar laws of their own. A Republican candidate for US senator in Michigan ran afoul of the statute by exceeding the campaign spending limits in the primary election. Primary elections were an innovation of the Progressive Era, and the Court concluded that such elections came under the exclusive purview of the states, even if they involved candidates for federal office.[31] In two cases involving new administrative agencies, the Court both weakened and strengthened them. On the one hand, a unanimous Court objected to the new Federal Trade Commission's unchecked power to rummage through the books of any corporation that fell within its jurisdiction. The justices would prefer not to "attribute to Congress an intent to defy the Fourth Amendment."[32] On the other hand, Congress could not give "legislative or administrative jurisdiction" to the Supreme Court to review all aspects of the decisions of the District of Columbia's Public Utilities Commission.[33] Taft wrote for a divided Court in upholding President Wilson's authority to remove a postmaster without Senate approval, despite statutory protections adopted by a divided Congress at the tail end of Reconstruction. Taft offered an elaborate argument vindicating as constitutionally mandatory the First Congress's decision to entrust the president with the unilateral authority to remove lower executive officials.[34] Wilson appointee James McReynolds was equally emphatic in dissent, arguing that Congress had ample constitutional authority to check the "serious evils which followed the practice of dismissing civil officers as caprice or interest dictated."[35]

Both Democrats and Republicans ran into constitutional trouble with the Court over the administration of the tax code in nearly a dozen separate cases. Ratification of the Sixteenth Amendment in 1916 offered new opportunities for Congress to exercise its taxation authority, but the complexity of the new federal income tax, as well as other federal taxes being imposed by Congress, gave rise to a raft of lawsuits, including many that raised constitutional challenges to how the tax code was written, interpreted, and applied. Some objections were relatively familiar and straightforward, such as those involving the taxation of judicial salaries and goods bound for export.[36] Others were more esoteric, such as the timing of taxes on gifts and estates and adjustments for income on municipal bonds.[37] But in no case did the Court punch large holes in the congressional taxation scheme.

Republican-backed policies also ran into trouble with the Taft Court, but those cases likewise reflected tensions in the newly emerging federal administrative state, rather than fundamental ideological or partisan conflicts. The end of the First World War led to a sudden crash in global prices for agricultural products.[38] Although Americans were migrating to the cities in the early twentieth century, the crisis in the rural economy still directly affected nearly half the population. Moreover, farmers were organized and well represented in Congress, and the national legislature hustled to respond with a bushel of new laws designed to prop up agricultural prices and boost farm income. Among those measures was the Grain Futures Trading Act, which gave Calvin Coolidge's secretary of agriculture sweeping new powers to regulate commodity exchanges. Within a matter of months, the Court heard a case brought by members of the Chicago Board of Trade challenging a heavy tax on futures contracts that were not traded on a government-approved exchange. A unanimous Court concluded that Congress had gone too far, attempting to regulate commercial transactions that were entirely internal to and within the exclusive police powers of the state of Illinois.[39]

Congress quickly responded with detailed hearings to compile an adequate record demonstrating that the commodities exchanges were deeply intertwined with interstate commerce, and it passed a modified statute regulating them. Even as the Court was striking down the Grain Futures Trading Act, it was upholding another congressional effort to aid farmers: the Packers and Stockyard Act, which regulated livestock dealers. A nearly unanimous Court found that its "provisions are carefully drawn to apply only to those practices and obstructions which in the judgment of Congress are likely to affect interstate commerce prejudicially."[40] When the futures traders challenged the new regulatory statute, the justices endorsed Congress's effort to revise its first attempt, observing that the legislature had followed the Court's guidance from the previous case and focused its energies on contract manipulations that are a "constantly recurring burden and obstruction" to interstate commerce.[41]

Congress encountered procedural hurdles as much as jurisdictional hurdles as it augmented the national state. The Court found it necessary to remind Congress that it could not direct that railroad rates be set below cost. The "delegated regulatory authority" exercised by the Interstate Commerce Commission "operates in a field limited by constitutional rights."[42] Nor could Congress simply seize the assets of Russian corporations or insulate government contractors from patent infringement claims without making adequate provision for just compensation to the rightful property owners.[43] It could not enforce Prohibition by imposing "taxes" that effectively operated as criminal penalties without adequate procedural protections for assessing guilt;[44] nor could it authorize search warrants for contraband alcohol without adequate cause.[45]

When Congress tried to extend wartime rent controls in the District of Columbia well after World War I had ended, the Court balked. During the war itself, a narrow majority of the justices had accepted a congressional statement of a "publicly notorious and almost world-wide fact" and allowed it to meet a public need "in the way in which it has been met by most of the civilized countries of the world."[46] The Court was willing to defer to Congress in restricting conventional property rights in the midst of an emergency, but it was "not at liberty to shut its eyes to an obvious mistake, when the validity of the law depends upon the truth of what is declared."[47] When the emergency had passed, congressional emergency powers must diminish as well.

The Taft Court nibbled around the edges of some important congressional policies, but with few exceptions, it stayed out of the way of Congress as it pursued its primary objectives. Despite the innovative uses of federal power by Democrats and Republicans alike in the Progressive Era, the Taft Court raised only relatively minor objections. Although the Court thought Congress had gone too far in some of its efforts to enforce Prohibition, the justices turned back the most fundamental challenges to the federal ban on alcohol. In a single short opinion that provided only conclusions but no arguments, the Court swept aside a raft of constitutional challenges to Prohibition, including the adequacy of the congressional vote on proposing the Eighteenth Amendment, the sufficiency of congressional action to implement Prohibition, and the immediate conversion to contraband of existing inventories of alcoholic beverages.[48] The Court was similarly dismissive of those who raised objections to the validity of the Nineteenth Amendment and its subsequent enforcement.[49] Although it was unwilling to read the Harrison Narcotic Act as a police measure, the Court indicated that it would allow it to operate as a particularly punitive tax measure, especially when applied not to doctors in the course of their practice but to ordinary drug users and nonmedical dealers.[50] Three years after sheltering Dr. Linder from punishment under the statute, the justices informed a Seattle lawyer who smuggled morphine to his jailed clients that it "is too late to attempt to overthrow the whole act on *Child Labor Tax Case*."[51] The justices found it obvious that Congress could fix the prices of goods during wartime, since rights of property were "not absolute or universal" and could be regulated "whenever reasonably necessary to effect any of the great purposes for which the national government was created."[52] Or Congress could simply authorize the army to seize whatever it needed, whether snowplows or cigarettes.[53] The justices emphasized that Congress had an affirmative power to "foster, protect, and control the [interstate] commerce with appropriate regard to the welfare of those who are immediately concerned, as well as the public at large, and to promote its growth and insure its safety," which gave the national legislature a free hand in the "guardianship and control" of the railroads.[54] Famously, Justice Holmes used the occasion of upholding the federal protection of migratory birds to expound on his belief that the Constitution was an ever-evolving "organism."[55] As the nation emerged from the Roaring Twenties, the Court was actively monitoring how Congress exercised its constitutional powers, but it was generally quite accommodating to congressional ambitions.

The New Deal Court

After the stock market crash of 1929, it was not obvious that the Court would obstruct the congressional response to that event any more than it had interfered in the farm crisis a few years earlier. Franklin Roosevelt spent plenty of time on the campaign trail in 1932, denouncing not just the policies and personnel of the incumbent Republican administration but also its basic philosophy of government; however, he did not expend much effort criticizing the Court, its understanding of the Constitution, or how it had exercised the power of judicial review. He pledged that his administration would strive for something new—"social justice, through social action"—and would reject the "jungle law of the survival of the so-called fittest."[56] But he did not single out the justices as among those who would oppose the transition. He admitted that his reform efforts had sometimes run afoul of the courts, when they were "thinking in terms of the Seventeenth Century, as some courts do,"[57] and he sometimes hinted that judges were complicit in beclouding principles that should be "clear and simple."[58] But Roosevelt insisted that his program was only "as radical as the Constitution of the United States of America."[59]

Friends of the administration held out some hope that the courts would accept the New Deal. As Harold Laski observed during Roosevelt's first run for the presidency, the "great task of the next few years is the discovery of the formulas which will enable the Constitution to be adapted to the wants of the positive state."[60] Yale's Thurman Arnold dismissed critics who thought upholding the New Deal would require the Court "to invent a complete new set of legal terminology, to tear up familiar constitutional landmarks and to graft new doctrine on an ancient document." He insisted there was "no actual dilemma between logic and expediency" when it came to the New Deal, and the conservatives would be forced to invent "new doctrine and new terminology" if they rejected the legislation.[61] Early decisions suggested that the Court was prepared to "brush aside all the limiting excrescences that had grown up" around the Constitution.[62] The Court would, in the end, prove to be "pragmatic and open-minded" and ready to build a constitutional "bridge for peaceful transition to a collectivist order."[63] The justices would not confine themselves to the "petty juggling of small-minded precedents"; instead, they would "weigh considerations of policy transcending argumentative accusations of destruction of private business" and recognize that the federal government must have the power "to minister to weighty public needs."[64]

But skepticism about the fate of new policies when they found themselves before the Court was commonplace. Reviewing Edward Corwin's optimistic account of the "twilight of the Supreme Court," Harvard's Henry Hart was not prepared to take for granted the "success of the Roosevelt experiment," and he thought it naïve to think that the "Achilles heel of the Court is the recognized power of Congress to pack its membership."[65] As the Court began handing down its negative judgments on the New Deal, allies of the administration wondered "how many more such decisions touching the very foundation of national power in a modern industrial society can be absorbed without destroying the very Constitution the odd man on the Court thinks he is preserving."[66] The time was rapidly approaching when the country would have to realize that "instead of a Supreme Court we ought to have a Supreme Planning Council" staffed with appropriate "experts in social and economic management" and "ultimately responsible to the will of its citizens."[67]

Skepticism about the judicial reception of the New Deal proved to be well founded, and the Court launched an unprecedented wave of judicial invalidations of federal laws. The battle between the Court and the Roosevelt administration was intense but brief. The Court started deciding challenges to New Deal statutes as early as 1934, and it effectively abandoned the field of battle just three years later in 1937. Nonetheless, throughout Roosevelt's first term, the Court was extraordinarily active.

The Taft Court had been busier than its predecessors in striking down federal laws, but the early fight over the New Deal quickly eclipsed the activism of the 1920s. As table 6-1 illustrates, across a range of different measures, the Court's exercise of judicial review during Roosevelt's first term stands out. It was not merely striking down laws at a faster pace or in a greater number of cases; it was intervening in the legislative process in a qualitatively different way. The Court became a contemporaneous veto player that set itself up as a kind of third legislative chamber in a way that was wholly unfamiliar. Cases normally made their way to the justices at a glacial pace; only rarely did a constitutional challenge reach the Court in the same political season as passage of the statute. By contrast, challenges to the New Deal rushed up the judicial hierarchy in great number and in quick succession. The rapid legislative pace of the famed first hundred days of the Roosevelt administration was matched by the frenetic pace of the constitutional challenges to that legislation. The median time between the adoption of a statutory provision and its invalidation during the Taft Court was more than six years. By contrast, the median time from passage to judicial action during Roosevelt's first term was less than two years. The Court sprinkled in a handful of routine cases reviewing longer-lived statutory provisions, but much of its work during these three years was spent striking down laws that Congress had just passed. Moreover, the percentage of cases involving important federal policies was remarkably high. Nearly two-thirds involved landmark statutes, and nearly half involved the most important provisions of those statutes. The Court was not trimming around the edges of relatively unimportant pieces of legislation or ruling out tenuous applications of broadly worded provisions. It was regularly reviewing and then gutting the signature accomplishments of the New Deal Democrats before the president's first term was over. As one observer tallied the score, the Court in its entire history had struck down "only ten laws of first-rate significance," but in a span of months, the New Deal Congress had seen much of its handiwork "slaughter[ed] at the hands of the court."[68]

The steady drumbeat of invalidations was barely broken up by cases upholding laws. Although the Court was, in fact, resolving a large number of cases in which congressional power was vindicated, those cases were routine in terms of their legal and political implications. If anything, they were even less important than the Court's usual work product. These cases involved significantly older statutes compared with similar cases in the previous decade, and the statutes the Court upheld were heavily skewed toward less important measures. The justices were not leavening the bad news they were delivering to the New Dealers. Although congressional power scored some victories in the Court during FDR's first term, those victories rarely came in cases that mattered to the governing coalition. The Court had wandered into controversy before, but it had never seemed more obstructionist than it did from 1934 to 1936.

Matters were not helped by Roosevelt's bad luck when it came to the timing of judicial appointments. Whereas federal offices filled by election became available with clockwork regularity, the lifetime appointment of judges left vacancies to fate and to the discretion of incumbents. Across the Court's history, vacancies have occurred frequently but unpredictably. In his single

term as president, Taft was blessed with the opportunity to make six appointments to the Court. FDR, by contrast, shared the fate of Thomas Jefferson and James Monroe: no seats opened up on the Court during his first
term. He had no opportunity to shape the bench that would evaluate his
ambitious legislative program.[69]

The Court he inherited was not obviously hostile to the administration,
even though it was unlikely to be particularly friendly. Although Herbert
Hoover became a fierce critic of the New Deal and thought Roosevelt went
too far in regimenting society and the economy, he had risen to prominence
as a Progressive Republican. His choices for the Court did not bolster the
conservative hard-liners that were the legacy of Presidents Taft and Harding. Hoover appointed centrists Charles Evans Hughes and Owen Roberts
to replace the relatively conservative Chief Justice Taft and Justice Edward
Sanford; his final choice, famed Progressive Benjamin Cardozo, was likely
to be just as sympathetic to government initiatives as the justice he replaced,
Oliver Wendell Holmes. The result was a sharply divided Court, with the
"Four Horsemen" on the right (Pierce Butler, James McReynolds, George
Sutherland, and Willis Van Devanter), a solid Progressive contingent of
three justices on the left (Louis Brandeis, Benjamin Cardozo, and Harlan
Stone), and two swing justices between them (Charles Evans Hughes and
Owen Roberts).

It soon became apparent that the fate of the New Deal hinged on the votes
of the two centrists. The repeated split votes and strongly worded dissents
from the Court's more Progressive members put an unfamiliar spotlight on
the contingency of judicial outcomes. The Court's obstruction of the New
Deal was not merely the consequence of a restrictive Constitution and judicial review; more immediately, it was the result of the specific choices of
one or two individuals. A veto power was seemingly being wielded less by an
institution than by a person. These divisions reinforced the legal realist sentiment that legal outcomes are driven more by the personality of the judge
than by the logic of the doctrine. Constitutional law looked too much like
"the home-made hocus-pocus" of the old men who sat on the bench.[70] Senator George Norris grumbled, "These five to four Supreme Court decisions
on the constitutionality of congressional acts it seems to me are illogical and
should not occur in a country like ours."[71]

The Court's work during Roosevelt's presidency began fairly normally. As

Congress busied itself with drafting the first New Deal, the Court was hearing constitutional arguments on the National Prohibition Act of 1919 and the
Transportation Act of 1920 and making anodyne points, such as that Congress could not statutorily render unreasonable searches valid.[72] Nonetheless,
the peculiar circumstances of the Great Depression began to assert themselves. In reviewing state laws, the Court initially tread lightly in upholding
measures such as Minnesota's mortgage moratorium and New York's fixing
of milk prices.[73] Federal statutory provisions that ran afoul of the Court were
relatively minor. The justices all agreed that Congress could not cut the salaries of senior judges in the Independent Offices Appropriations Act of 1933 or
repudiate government obligations in the Economy Act of 1933.[74] There were
some constitutional limits to congressional belt-tightening.

But those were not the controversial features of the New Deal. As the New
Dealers were advancing momentous statutes such as the National Industrial
Recovery Act and the Agricultural Adjustment Act, conservatives were warning that the economic emergency did not justify the abandonment of traditional constitutional limits on government power. When cases involving
these measures began to reach the Court at the end of 1934, the stage was set
for a more serious confrontation with the administration. Working with an
enthusiastic Congress, the president did not have to rest on his own constitutional authority in making reforms. Instead, the president portrayed the
executive and the legislature as a two-horse team pulling the nation in the
same direction. The constitutional authority of Congress was at stake, even if
the president provided the leadership. With constitutional cases reaching the
Court, it was time for the justices to get in the harness as well. The American
people "expect the third horse to pull in unison with the other two."[75] But
the Court proved to be balky.

The National Industrial Recovery Act (NIRA) was a centerpiece of the
New Deal. A far-reaching but explicitly temporary effort to prop up prices
and regulate working conditions in manufacturing and commercial businesses, the first part of the statute built on the private-public partnerships
and associationalism Hoover had pioneered as secretary of commerce a
decade earlier and big business was aggressively seeking during the Great
Depression. Notably, the legislation authorized trade associations to create legally binding "codes of fair competition," provided such codes did not
"permit monopolies or monopolistic practices." An additional section of the

act authorized the president to prohibit from interstate commerce any oil that exceeded production quotas established by state regulatory authorities. Oil-rich states like Texas and Oklahoma tried to maintain an oil cartel to prop up prices, but it was hard to prevent rogue "hot oil" from entering the marketplace and undercutting the price targets. Roosevelt promptly directed Secretary of the Interior Harold Ickes to take whatever action necessary to stamp out hot oil.

The first significant challenge to the New Deal that reached the Court involved these hot-oil provisions. A small east Texas oil company, Panama Refining, argued that the federal government was simply using the criminal law to eliminate the competition of the big oil producers. The Interior Department decided to rush the case forward but found itself outmaneuvered.[76] In an eight-to-one decision, the Court found for the first time in its history that Congress had unconstitutionally delegated its lawmaking power to the president.[77] Examining the brief and hastily written section 9 of the NIRA, Chief Justice Hughes complained that Congress had established "no criterion to govern the President's course" and declared "no policy as to the transportation of the excess production." The act allowed the president to make policy and issue orders "as he may see fit" and to jail anyone who disobeyed him.[78] The president was thus left to exercise a legislative function, not an administrative one. Only Justice Cardozo was persuaded that the president was not merely exercising "a roving commission to inquire into evils" but was pursuing a goal that Congress clearly had in mind: facilitating industrial recovery by whatever means necessary.[79] The defeat was embarrassing, but it was limited to the idiosyncratic hot-oil regulations.

More consequential was a case argued just after the *Panama Refining* decision was handed down. Immediately after assuming office, Roosevelt moved to devalue the currency and remove gold from circulation, and Congress acted swiftly to endorse those efforts. Revaluing the currency was one thing, but revaluing debt was quite another. The Liberty Bonds issued by the federal government during World War I promised the bearer repayment in "gold of the present standard of value." The government owed some $100 billion in such obligations and was in no position to pay. In the summer of 1933 Congress declared that these gold bond obligations would be repaid only in current legal tender. By the start of the new year, creditors complained that the government had effectively repudiated half its national debt, and they filed

suit to recover the difference. Attorney General Homer Cummings personally argued the case, explaining to the justices that ruling against the government would unleash economic "chaos" and that suspension of the gold
clause should be seen as an essential measure in a national emergency. As the
justices deliberated, newspapers filled with stories about "hysterical" cabinet
officials who were planning to take immediate action against the Court if the
decision did not go the administration's way, and reporters speculated on
the odds that martial law would be declared. Privately, the Justice Department made plans to restructure the Court and demand a new ruling from
a new set of justices, even though it was coming around to the notion that
the government could simply ignore an adverse ruling and refuse to pay its
creditors.[80] The president prepared a radio address to be delivered in the
event of an adverse ruling. He intended to declare that the president had a
higher duty to protect the people and would not stand "idly by" while the
Court brought the nation to the brink of economic disaster; he would "carry
on the business of the country" on exactly the same financial terms as if the
Court had never issued a decision.[81]

The Court blinked. On the one hand, the chief justice asserted that Congress "has not been vested with authority to alter or destroy" its contrac-
tual obligations; therefore, the gold clause suspension was constitutionally
invalid. On the other hand, those obligations were only "binding upon the
conscience of the sovereign," for Congress "is under no duty to provide [its
creditors with] remedies through the courts"; therefore, the creditors had to
go home empty handed.[82] Departing from the prepared text from the four
dissenters, Justice James McReynolds sputtered, "the Constitution as many
of us have understood it has gone."[83] Driving the point home, FDR promptly
leaked his undelivered speech to confidant Arthur Krock, who published a
front-page report in the New York Times exclaiming that the power of judicial review could not be found in the Constitution anyway, and the president
might well have to lay the Court low "before the New Deal has been completed."[84]

Just a few weeks after deciding the Gold Clause Cases, the Court heard
arguments challenging the validity of the Railroad Retirement Act of 1934.
The Rail Pension Case dealt with a relatively minor piece of legislation, but it
raised basic questions about congressional power to enact the New Deal. The
railroads had long been one of the central forces in the creation of a national

marketplace, and the Court had been fairly deferential to a range of efforts by
Congress to promote and regulate the railroads as interstate carriers of commerce. But by the time of the New Deal, the once mighty railroads had fallen
on hard times, badgered by new modes of ground transportation even before
the onset of the Great Depression. The railroad industry's highly unionized
workforce was rapidly shrinking and graying. Railroad workers turned to
Senator Robert Wagner, who introduced a bill to require the railroads to pay
into a more generous pension plan that would both provide income to the
aged and encourage retirement, which would make room for the hiring of
younger workers. Wagner's bill was not to Roosevelt's liking, but he could
not easily oppose it.[85]

The railroads quickly filed suit, and in a sweeping five-to-four decision,
the Court struck down the law. Roberts cast the deciding vote and crafted the
opinion. Wagner's plan had several infirmities. The statute was retroactive,
requiring railroads to provide pensions to more than 100,000 former employees and to provide back pay for any former railroad workers (including
those who had worked for other, no-longer-existing companies) who might
be hired in the future. The majority thought this was self-evidently a redistri-
bution scheme—taking property from corporate shareholders and bestow-
ing it on unemployed railway workers—with little relationship to the stated
goal of enhancing the efficiency and safety of interstate transportation. It
likewise imposed new pension obligations on the railroads for current workers' past years of service; these large and "arbitrary" costs on private actors
had no obvious public benefit. As such, the Court found that this was "a
naked appropriation of private property" in violation of constitutional protections.[86] Moreover, to the extent the law simply provided a new benefit
to railroad employees, it bore only a tenuous relationship to the regulation
of interstate commerce. The Court had given Congress a wide berth in regulating interstate carriers, but those regulations must ultimately be tied to
the constitutional power of protecting the channels of interstate commerce
from obstruction. If Congress could legislate simply to entice an employee
of an interstate carrier to "do his work more cheerfully," the potential burden on an employer "tending to the satisfaction and comfort of his employees, seems endless." Congress's constitutional authority to clear obstructions
to interstate commerce could not extend so far as to require those engaging in interstate commerce to provide free medical care or housing for their

employees, free education for their employees' children, or anything else Congress might decide would "relieve the employee of mental strain and worry."[87] Chief Justice Hughes, writing for the dissenters, was not inclined to defend every detail of the pension act, but he thought the majority had gone too far by ruling the entire subject of railroad pensions out of Congress's sphere of influence. Congress was entitled to deference in its judgments about how particular railroad policies might relate to the efficiency, safety, and reliability of the nation's commercial traffic, so long as those policies were "closely and substantially related to the proper conduct of business enterprises."[88] If providing pensions was something railroads ordinarily did, then Congress could pass a law addressing that topic.

The decision in the *Rail Pensions Case* came down near the end of the Court's term in May 1935. Before the month was over, the Court announced three more cases restricting congressional power. The most consequential one involved the NIRA.[89] The *Hot Oil Case* had only obliquely addressed the core issues of the NIRA, and the government was actually on relatively firm ground in treating the oil market as part of interstate commerce before its case was derailed by the nondelegation issues. Making their way through the lower courts were numerous challenges to the codes of fair competition set up by the governmentally favored trade associations. The government had received an encouraging ruling from a Republican-appointed trial judge in its prosecution of a kosher poultry butcher in Brooklyn for flaunting industry codes and selling uninspected and potentially sick chickens, and the Schechter brothers were eager to challenge their conviction in a higher court. The government had assembled an extensive record detailing how the chickens slaughtered in Brooklyn had been raised and purchased in New Jersey and Pennsylvania before being shipped to New York, and it leaned heavily on the idea that saving the nation from impending "doom" justified any emergency measure Congress might want to take. Nevertheless, from his perch at Harvard, Felix Frankfurter cautioned the Justice Department that the case was filled with stumbling blocks.[90]

Frankfurter's reading of the Court turned out to be right. The "sick chicken" case was one of three decisions handed down against the administration on "Black Monday."[91] The justices were unanimous in striking down the NIRA's industrial codes provisions. Much to the president's dismay, even Justice Cardozo was forced to exclaim, "this is delegation running riot."[92] Similar to the provisions related to oil production, the justices objected that in drafting the statute, Congress had failed to perform "its essential legislative function" and instead had "attempted to transfer that function to others." Rather than making any hard policy choices itself and providing intelligible standards by which others could administer those policies, Congress was handing out "unfettered discretion" to trade groups and the president in a manner "unknown to our law" and "utterly inconsistent with the constitutional prerogatives and duties of Congress."[93] Moreover, regulating the hours, wages, prices, record keeping, and sanitation of the Brooklyn butchers was an impermissible federal intrusion into the regulatory domain of the state and local governments. The chickens were not in a continuous stream of interstate commerce; they "had come to a permanent rest within the state" and, in doing so, had passed beyond the control of Congress. The A. L. A. Schechter Poultry Corporation was not like the Chicago stockyards, which passed livestock along to their final destination out of state, or like the Maryland importer who received goods at the port of Baltimore and promptly shipped them out in their original packaging.[94] The Schechters were local butchers who happened to receive some of their inventory from out of state. If Congress could tell them how to run their shop, then there was little beyond its reach, and the Court was not yet persuaded that the Constitution provided for that. As the justices left the Court, Progressive hero Justice Brandeis pulled one of Roosevelt's aides aside and gave him a message for his boss: "We're not going to let this government centralize everything. It's come to an end."[95]

Roosevelt responded by taking his message to the people. On the one hand, many in and around the administration thought the Court's action was a blessing in disguise; it freed the administration from a controversial and struggling policy and dealt a blow to some of the more radical voices in the government. On the other hand, the Court's intransigence was clearly unpopular, and the White House could use that to reframe the debate in a way that benefited the president. Attorney General Homer Cummings confided to his diary that the losses in court were "a set-back for America" but "a God-send to the Administration."[96] The battle lines had been drawn. Cummings declared to FDR, "I tell you, Mr. President, they mean to destroy us. . . . We will have to find a way to get rid of the present membership of the Supreme Court."[97] With the justices in summer recess, the president summoned the press to the White House, where he held forth for an hour and a half on the failings of the Supreme Court and compared its performance to that of the *Dred Scott* Court. Regaling the reporters with supportive telegrams from the public, he insisted that the New Dealers were merely trying to exercise the powers that "every other Nation in the world" possessed, while the Court was determined to take the country back to the "horse-and-buggy age."[98] He declined to reveal, however, how the administration would deal with the obstructionist justices.

When the justices returned to work in the fall, they picked up where they had left off. They heard some minor cases of relatively limited importance and addressed some older statutes.[99] More consequentially, they also examined some New Deal statutes. The Court began modestly, issuing a unanimous ruling late in 1935 striking down a recent amendment to the Home Owners' Loan Act. The provision allowed a majority of the members of a savings and loan to covert the state corporation into a federal entity, which Justice Cardozo explained was a violation of the reserved power of the states.[100] Soon enough, the Court turned its attention to another key component of the New Deal: the Agricultural Adjustment Act (AAA). The core of the farm crisis was understood to be overproduction and low prices, so federal policy was aimed at shrinking agricultural output and raising market prices. To accomplish that objective, the AAA imposed a tax on processors, and the resulting revenue was supposed to be funneled back to farmers. The processors were expected to pass on the cost of the tax to consumers. The secretary of agriculture was tasked with setting a tax rate for each crop that would be adequate to pay farmers to reduce their acreage under cultivation and restore their income to pre–World War I levels. Conservatives were skeptical of the entire scheme, and they used a bankrupt cotton mill with a tax debt as the vehicle for a test case.[101] To no one's surprise, Justice Roberts wrote the opinion for a six-to-three majority striking down the act.[102] The Court found that, far from being a tax for the purpose of raising revenue for the general support of the government, the processing fee was simply "an expropriation of money from one group for the benefit of another." That might be acceptable if the tax were just an instrument of regulation, but Congress had no authority to regulate agricultural production.[103] The government had tried to persuade the justices that Congress's taxation authority should be understood as plenary and applicable to anything that might advance the "general welfare."

The majority was unpersuaded, concluding that the tax was self-evidently a "means to an unconstitutional end."[104] Roosevelt had assured farmers that New Deal programs reflected "democracy in the good old American sense of the word," as the federal government sought to "promote the general welfare, not by interfering unduly with individual liberties, but by bringing to the aid of the individual those powers of Government which are essential to assure the continuance of the inalienable rights which the Constitution is intended to guarantee."[105] Roberts responded that the framers of the Constitution never envisioned Congress as "a parliament of the whole people, subject to no restrictions save such as are self-imposed."[106] For the dissenters, Justice Stone reminded his brethren that, especially in the context of an economic emergency, the "Courts are not the only agency of government that must be assumed to have the capacity to govern," and they should not assume that the "legislature [is] lost to all sense of public responsibility." Congress should be trusted "to relieve a nationwide economic maladjustment by conditional gifts of money."[107]

After only a few months' pause, the Court struck a final blow at the end of its term in May 1936.[108] Like much of the early New Deal, the Bituminous Coal Conservation Act of 1935 (or the Guffey Act) imposed production quotas, fixed prices, and established wage rates, but in this case, the statute was tailored specifically to the coal industry. In a familiar six-to-three vote, the Court struck down core provisions of the act as suffering from the same kind of constitutional failings found in the NIRA. Justice Sutherland objected to Congress's apparent view that the act "could be sustained under some general federal power, thought to exist, apart from the specific grants of the Constitution." The Court thought it necessary to remind Congress that "beneficent aims, however great or well directed, can never serve in lieu of constitutional power." The opinion went on for what Sutherland admitted was "perhaps . . . unnecessary length" because the Court's disagreement with Congress about constitutional principles seemed so fundamental.[109] Like other statutes from the New Deal Congress reviewed by the Court, the coal legislation suffered from its effort to regulate an area of economic activity under the exclusive authority of the states, and it effectively delegated lawmaking power to the majority of workers and mine owners and empowered them to bind others to their preferred terms of business. The government had hoped it was on firmer ground in regulating the massive coal industry and building a case around coal designated for the interstate market, but the Court focused on the sweeping scope of the act, which covered even "captive coal" used at the mine site itself and not sold on the open market (Cardozo, in dissent, would have preferred to defer indefinitely a ruling on the constitutionality of those applications of the statute).[110]

The Post–New Deal Court

As the Court completed its work in the spring of 1936, the New Deal lay in tatters. Major components of President Roosevelt's legislative accomplishments had been struck down, and it was not clear whether there was a way to revive those policies in a version the justices might be willing to uphold. The administration's signature efforts to stabilize wages and prices had been declared beyond the power of Congress to legislate. If Roosevelt were to win a second term as president, he would have to regroup, but the question occupying Washington was whether the New Deal could operate within the constitutional confines the justices had described.

The administration's immediate reaction took observers by surprise. When reporters gathered in the White House at the close of the Court's session in 1936, they expected the president to tear into the justices as he had the year before with his "horse-and-buggy age" tirade. As one reporter recounted, "With the New Deal pretty comprehensively declared unconstitutional by the Supreme Court everybody was eager today to learn what the President proposed to do about it." The press flocked to the White House in "unprecedented numbers," assuming that the president would "fly off the handle and wallop the Supreme Court." Instead, the president deflected all discussion of the issue and claimed to have no plan on how to proceed. The constitutional questions were "too dangerous an issue to raise in the election," and it seemed the president would have no more to say on the matter "unless safely seated in office for another four years."[111]

The president's public silence on the judiciary in the run-up to the 1936 elections did not mean that courts were off the agenda. Activists on the left were vocal about the need for constitutional change. In the aftermath of the Guffey Act decision, New York labor lawyer and Socialist Party leader Louis Waldman called on the trade unions to recognize that their priority was to elect a Congress that would pass a constitutional amendment that stripped the Supreme Court of the power to strike down federal statutes. "Even more important than to organize for the re-election of President Roosevelt, it is necessary now to elect a Congress frankly committed to changes in the Constitution." It was time to appeal the Court's rulings "to the American people" for a final judgment.[112] New York City's Fiorello LaGuardia declared that "it was no use arguing with the Supreme Court." The time had come to "give to the representatives of the people the right to say what the law of the land should be."[113] The Socialist Party demanded an end to the "usurped power of the Supreme Court to declare social legislation unconstitutional."[114] For the Left, it was time to rewrite the constitutional rules and shift power from the courts to Congress.

For activists on the right, the Court had seemingly set the stage for a campaign that would tar the president as autocratic. As the "knockout season" ended, the conservative *Business Week* crowed that "all ways are closed," and the administration had failed in its "desperate effort to crack the Constitution."[115] The New Dealers had been exposed as constitutional villains. The only question was whether the Republican Party could find a "fighting candidate, who can make fullest use of the newly vitalized constitutional issue." The president seemed chastened by the critical reaction to his denunciations of the Court in 1935, and Republicans thought they could take their case to the people and show them that the Democrats could not be trusted to respect constitutional limits. They hoped the Court's "stern words" would still be "ringing in the ears of the electorate" by November, even though the president preferred not to discuss constitutional issues "when there are any voters within earshot."[116] The Republicans expressed confidence that the idea of "the New Deal written into an amendment" to the Constitution to overcome the Court's objection "shocks the conscience of the nation."[117]

While the president turned to "strong-arm methods to shut off questions" about the Court, a less direct campaign made it clear to the public what was at stake in the 1936 elections.[118] "Natural causes at no distant date may bring about a reconstitution of the court" that would allow the president to "resurrect New Deal measures" without any unnecessary constitutional controversies.[119] Presidential confidant Arthur Krock relayed the views of "Democratic steersmen," who believed the Court would "go down as arbitrary and dictatorial in the minds of the people." If Roosevelt were reelected, the "controlling appointments will be in his hands," and the administration believed "that the people will not be alarmed at the prospect of appointments to the Supreme Court by Mr. Roosevelt."[120] A few days later, Krock stated plainly that the Court's majority would "go more or less on trial in a presidential campaign for the first time in years." The justices would have to "accept the inevitable result in a democracy about to go to the polls," and one way or another, the "political argument" will be "over" once the votes are counted.[121] Both sides knew that, based on "the sad truth of mathematical chances," the winner of the 1936 presidential election would shape the Court for a generation. Some conservatives pondered whether a conservative justice could be persuaded to retire in the summer of 1936 so that the issue of a judicial vacancy would be front and center during the presidential campaign (it seemed to go without saying that Roosevelt could not with any propriety fill a Supreme Court seat before the election, despite the large Democratic majority in the Senate). It appeared that the president "has chosen to 'amend' the Constitution by the easy way rather than the hard way"—that is, by winning reelection, appointing new justices, and "'amending' the Constitution by judicial interpretation."[122] The task might not even require a large conceptual leap if, as some commentators posited, the early New Deal was best thought of as "emergency legislation" of somewhat dubious constitutionality and only short-term economic advantage. The Court had rejected only "flagrant abuses" in 1934–1936. "No doubt the Court will continue to place a liberal interpretation upon those powers which Congress actually possesses."[123] By the early summer of 1936, astute observers had already concluded that Roosevelt's reelection was "virtually certain," and Republicans were frustrated that the president declined "to be drawn into the trap" of open warfare with the Supreme Court. The president seemed content to observe the "actuarial statistics" and the "elderly men" on the Supreme Court and know that "most of his troubles would [soon] be over."[124]

Of course, Roosevelt did sail to victory in the fall of 1936. The Republican nomination of Alf Landon failed to undermine the president's popularity, and no credible challenge to the Democrats emerged from the left. Even before the little-known Kansas governor had secured the Republican Party nomination in the summer of 1936, journalists were reporting that "Republican leaders have all but admitted that the Presidential contest is hopeless."[125] By the end of the campaign, the only real question was the size of the defeat and the implications for contests in the House of Representatives. As it happened, the Democrats outperformed expectations. The president's victory over Landon was greater than his margin over Hoover four years earlier. The Democrats picked up seats in both the House and the Senate, consigning the Republicans to near oblivion in Congress, with a smaller minority than either party had seen since Reconstruction.

The president proved to be less patient than expected. Shortly after his second inauguration, Roosevelt announced his plan to "reorganize" the federal judiciary. The administration provided no advance notice of the announcement, and the White House had said little about the Court for nearly a year. On February 5, 1937, the president issued a special message to Congress, along with a proposed bill, asking the legislature to reorganize the judiciary "in order that it . . . may function in accord with modern necessities." After a lengthy buildup emphasizing that the "present congestion" of the judicial caseload and an epidemic of "aged or infirm judges" necessitated "the enlargement of the capacity of all the federal courts," the president let the language of the proposed bill reveal the real point: the president would be empowered in six months' time to nominate an additional US Supreme Court justice for each sitting justice over the age of seventy. The president coyly suggested that the courts needed "a constant infusion of new blood," lawyers who were willing to engage in "an examination of complicated and changing conditions" and look to the future rather than the past.[126]

The president's proposal was immediately dubbed a "Court-packing plan." The congressional Democratic leadership rushed to declare that the bill was "in no sense a violent innovation" and claimed it had nothing to do with the constitutionality of the New Deal. Republicans just as quickly proclaimed that the plan was "the beginning of the end of everything" and a transparent effort "to pack the Supreme Court to do [Roosevelt's] will, whether it is constitutional or not."[127] The predictable partisan split did not last. Republican critics soon self-consciously faded into the background, as Democratic critics stepped forward. Meanwhile, the president dropped his own pretense and used a "fireside chat" to rally the public to his cause. Gone was any concern about excessive judicial caseloads and lengthy waits for justice; now the president frankly denounced the Court's majority for usurping "the power to pass on the wisdom of these Acts of the Congress— and to approve or disapprove the public policy written into these laws." The "American people themselves" were demanding that the Court fall into line.

The Court needed "new blood," judges who would "bring to the Courts a present-day sense of the Constitution." The president was asking not for "spineless puppets who would disregard the law" but for "a reinvigorated, liberal-minded Judiciary" that could restore "a system of living law" and "undo what the Court has done."[128] The pitched battle in the Senate was the most closely fought of Roosevelt's presidency and lasted for weeks. It looked like the administration might have the upper hand, until Senate majority leader Joseph Robinson died of a heart attack on July 14, 1937. Wavering senators turned on the bill, and the Court-packing plan was abandoned just a few days later without a vote.[129] The size of the US Supreme Court remained fixed at nine justices, as it had been since the Reconstruction Republicans reconstituted the Court in 1869.

The justices themselves were not silent during the fight over the Court-packing plan. Chief Justice Charles Evans Hughes wrote a letter to the maverick Democratic senator from Montana, Burton Wheeler, rebutting the White House's claims that the federal judiciary was behind in its work.[130] Meanwhile, as the Court's fate was being decided in the elected branches, the justices were still deciding cases. As usual, the Court had opened the year by upholding federal statutory provisions in some relatively easy cases. As the president was settling into his second term, the Court issued unanimous decisions upholding congressional power to back the states in prohibiting commerce in goods made with convict labor, to amend bankruptcy statutes, to impose a retroactive tax, and to impose tougher penalties for violations of court orders involving the federal government.[131]

Far more consequential decisions were handed down after the Court-packing battle began. The administration's first significant victory came in a constitutional case involving a state law. At the end of March, the Court upheld Washington State's minimum wage law for women, with an opinion written by Chief Justice Hughes for a five-justice majority. Justice Owen Roberts joined the majority to overrule the Court's own precedent from 1923 and announce that liberty was subject to regulation, as long as it was "reasonable to its subject and is adopted in the interests of the community."[132] The same day, a similarly divided Court upheld a Virginia milk price–fixing law, and a unanimous Court upheld the federal Railway Labor Act, a modified Frazier-Lemke Farm Bankruptcy Act, and a dealer tax provision of the National Firearms Act.[133] The minimum wage decision in particular seemed to signal a more favorable attitude toward the New Deal, but each side in the Court-packing debate claimed that this turn of events supported its own position. As one Democrat cautioned, Roberts, like a circus acrobat, had swung on the trapeze, performed a somersault, and landed on the opposite platform, but there was "no telling when he will swing back again."[134]

Two weeks later, the Court's new Progressive majority demonstrated its persistence. In another five-to-four decision, the Court upheld the core provisions of the National Labor Relations Act of 1935, finding that Congress had the authority to regulate labor relations at a steel plant in Pennsylvania. Noting that the statute did not "purport to extend to the relationship between all industrial employees and employers," the majority concluded that steel production was an example of an intrastate activity that, "by reason of close and intimate relation to interstate commerce, may fall within federal control." Working hard to integrate the Court's past precedents constructively into his analysis, the chief justice emphasized that labor disputes affecting the production of steel threatened to burden the interstate commerce that Congress was empowered to promote and protect.[135] The dissenters thought it was obvious that such a "purely local industry" could not be brought under congressional control, given recent precedents, and they believed the majority's approach risked extending congressional power "into almost any field of human industry."[136] The justices similarly disagreed over whether the National Labor Relations Act could be applied to an editor in the New York office of the Associated Press, though here, the dissenters were more concerned that Congress was infringing on the free press by preventing a publisher from dismissing an editor.[137] The Court's decisions were immediately hailed as "revolutionary" and "materially modifying the American scheme of government," sweeping away all the "legal obstacles to the realization of most of the program of collectivist action and regimentation projected by the New Deal."[138] The *Wall Street Journal* concluded that the Court's sudden shift stripped away any justification for the "immoral judiciary bill," since there was no longer "even a color of plausibility that the high bench interprets the basic law without reference to changing economic or social conditions." Arthur Krock noted the administration's position in the *New York Times*, stating that although these favorable decisions were welcome, they still included language that unacceptably implied the existence of limits on the congressional power to regulate the economy.[139]

In May the Court upheld federal statutory provisions in four more cases. The most significant was *Steward Machine v. Davis*, in which a five-justice majority upheld the Social Security Act.[140] Congress had broad discretion to impose taxes on selected occupations and businesses and to offer financial inducements to the states to adopt favored policies. The dissenters worried that the majority was handing Congress a tool that could be used to subvert the independence and autonomy of the state governments. Even Republicans declared their support for the "more liberal state of mind on the part of the court regarding the flexibility of the Constitution."[141] As the term came to an end, a sympathetic columnist averred that the rulings had been a "foregone conclusion," foreshadowed by a majority of the Court "turning toward a more liberal interpretation of the Constitution" and by the "potency of facts over mere argument" in constitutional jurisprudence.[142]

The decisions seemed to be as important for the fate of the Court as for the fate of the New Deal. The president quipped that the country had now been thrown into "Roberts Land," and "only Justice Roberts knew where the court was going or what the Constitution was."[143] From the president's perspective, that was clearly insufficient. The administration thought it had the Court on the ropes, but officials feared that if they removed the pressure of the Court-packing plan, Roberts would swing back to join the Four Horsemen and "whittle away" their favored policies. Attorney General Homer Cummings announced to the nation that "the bunch still lacks a sufficient number of judges whose self-restraint is predictable." The decisions of 1937 would be an "empty victory" if the Court's conservatives were not forced into an unconditional surrender.[144] The Court could not be allowed to "come back" and "begin declaring everything unconstitutional again."[145] But others had more confidence that the Court's "changed attitude" was genuine and that the greater need was to lift the "threat of executive coercion" that risked weakening public confidence in the independent judiciary.[146]

The Court-packing plan received yet another blow when conservative justice Willis Van Devanter informed the president on May 18, days before the *Steward Machine* decision was handed down, that he would retire from the bench. (Democratic senator M. M. Logan took the opportunity to urge the other conservative justices to "follow his example, so we could end this present controversy.")[147] A month later, and days after the death of Senator Joe Robinson, conservative justice George Sutherland died of a heart attack. With two of the Four Horsemen gone, Roberts no longer had the swing vote, and the Court's center of gravity had moved firmly toward its Progressive wing. Moreover, it turned out that Roberts's swing to the left was durable, and he generally stuck with the new liberal majority until he retired from the bench in 1945.

An anonymous wag joked that a "switch in time saved nine." Passage of the Court-packing plan had never been a sure thing, but the actions of the justices in the spring of 1937 may well have been critical to its defeat. The unveiling of the Court-packing plan came too late to drive Roberts into the Progressive camp in the critical cases handed down in the spring, so the bruising battle in the Senate that drove wedges into the New Deal political coalition might have been unnecessary. The combination of the capitulation of Hughes and Roberts and the retirement of Van Devanter put an effective end to the Court's resistance to New Deal policies and removed some of the urgency to increase the size of the Court. Even if the Court did not make a "strategic retreat" to try to fend off the political threat to the judiciary, surely Roberts and Hughes could see that a judicial attempt to build an impenetrable wall to stop the New Deal would be futile.[148]

For the first time in nearly two decades, the Court ended its term in 1937 without striking down a single provision of a federal statute. It repeated the feat in 1938 and three more times in 1940–1942. In 1939 the Court broke the streak, only to the extent that it refused to construe the National Labor Relations Act as trenching in a constitutionally dubious way on the right of employers to dismiss employees for engaging in an illegal sit-down strike.[149] Moreover, the Court handed down a remarkable eighty-one decisions upholding federal statutory provisions against constitutional challenge in 1937–1942, and half those cases involved important statutes. Often, the decisions upholding statutes required the Court to reverse the rulings of lower courts. The Court had embarked on a project of reconstructing American constitutional law, and the lower courts needed some time to adapt to the new legal regime.

Roosevelt's bad luck in filling not a single vacancy on the Court during his first term had changed. The departure of Van Devanter and Sutherland from the bench in 1937 started a rapid process of remaking the Supreme Court. Roosevelt's unprecedented willingness, and ability, to break the convention against a third presidential term ensured that he would put his personal stamp on the Court like no other president since George Washington. By the time he entered his third presidential campaign in 1940, Roosevelt had placed five justices on the Court. Three of the conservative Four Horsemen had been replaced by Roosevelt's "liberal-minded" justices; in addition, two iconic Progressive justices (Benjamin Cardozo and Louis Brandeis) had been replaced by suitably younger men (Felix Frankfurter and William Douglas). Ensconced in his third term, Roosevelt replaced three more justices, including centrist Chief Justice Hughes and the last of the conservatives. Only Justice Roberts and Justice Harlan Fiske Stone (whom Roosevelt had elevated to chief justice in place of Hughes) outlasted Roosevelt, and they were both replaced by his successor, Harry Truman, not long after the end of World War II.

With the constitutional revolution of 1937, the Court turned its back on the constitutional doctrine it had built up over the course of the late nineteenth and early twentieth centuries. The reconstituted Roosevelt Court embarked on a project of consolidating a new constitutional order that continues today in some important respects. The contours of that new constitutional system, at least relative to Congress, were outlined primarily through the Court's upholding of federal statutes against legal challenge. The defining feature of the constitutional order constructed by the Roosevelt Court was expanded congressional power and greater judicial deference to that power.

The Court began its retreat in 1937, but over the next fifteen years, it elaborated on its new constitutional vision. The key opinions of 1937 written by Chief Justice Hughes abandoned only the Court's most recent precedents, while emphasizing the consistency between what the Court was doing now and what it had done prior to the New Deal. As the Roosevelt Court took shape, it went further and set the powers of Congress on a new foundation.

The Filled Milk Act of 1923 predated the New Deal but raised ongoing questions about the constitutionality of government regulation of economic affairs. The politically powerful dairy industry was often favored by state and federal legislators with laws putatively intended to protect the public health but with the undoubted effect of suppressing competition in the marketplace. The Court had generally vouched for the constitutionality of such legislation, but the Carolene Products Company objected to the federal prohibition on the interstate shipment of products made with skimmed milk and "any fat or oil other than milk fat." Justice Stone, writing in 1938, pointed to a substantial line of precedents affirming that "Congress is free to exclude from interstate commerce articles whose use in the states for which they are destined it may reasonably conceive . . . to be injurious to the public health, morals, or welfare," and legislatures were free to selectively exclude what they deemed to be an "inferior product" from the marketplace. Congress was entitled to substantial deference in making economic regulations. When the "question is at least debatable" whether a given product should "be left unregulated, or in some measure restricted, or wholly prohibited," the "decision was for Congress" to make, not a court. Justice Pierce Butler wrote only for himself in contending that a statute should fall when the prohibited products are "demonstrably . . . neither injurious to health nor calculated to deceive," but the majority thought Congress was entitled to the assumption that a dubious regulation "rests upon some rational basis within the knowledge and experience of the legislators."[150] Although little noticed at the time, Stone included a subsequently famous footnote qualifying this deferential assumption. The "operation of the presumption of constitutionality" might be appropriately narrowed if the legislation obviously ran afoul of a specific constitutional prohibition, restricted the political process, or embodied "prejudice against discrete and insular minorities." This "more searching judicial scrutiny" would have to wait for later, however.[151]

In other cases, the Roosevelt Court worked to remake the foundations of constitutional law to emphasize the broad scope of congressional authority. Whereas *Carolene Products* emphasized judicial deference to Congress's plausibly rational decisions affecting economic activities, other cases simply declared that Congress was constitutionally empowered to exercise sweeping discretion over private property and economic activities. For example, Congress was free to interfere "with the freedom of contract" of employers by prohibiting them from firing striking workers.[152] The Roosevelt Court reminded businesses that "inconvenience or even some dislocation of property rights, may be necessary in order to safeguard the right to collective bargaining," and Congress had amply empowered the National Labor Relations Board to determine when property rights might need to be dislocated.[153] Writing for a narrow majority in 1939, newly appointed Justice Hugo Black swept aside the Court's earlier criticism of the federal government's power to override gold clauses in debt contracts. When private parties contracted between themselves to repay debts in either gold dollar coins or an equivalent foreign currency, they could not "create vested rights which serve to restrict and limit an exercise of a constitutional power of Congress," and the Court held that the congressional resolution suspending transactions in gold likewise prevented demands for repayment through the foreign currency contingency.[154] Congress was free to control prices "for the protection and promotion of the welfare of the economy."[155] When governing the District of Columbia, Congress had constitutional authority to exercise the power of eminent domain for urban redevelopment by, for example, seizing the property of a profitable department store and turning it over to a land developer, for it was up to "the legislature, not the judiciary, [to be] the main guardian of the public needs to be served by social legislation," and any congressional determination that the appropriation of private property was in the public interest was "well-nigh conclusive."[156] In a rare exception, a sharply divided Court drew the line at Congress confiscating the property of "friendly aliens"; however, it did so only by adopting an implausible saving construction of the Trading with the Enemy Act, which the Court intoned should not be regarded as a "carefully matured enactment" but rather a "makeshift patchwork" that should not be read with "literalness."[157] The dissenters thought the majority's concerns were fanciful and chided their brethren that the judiciary's task was to "enforce, not frustrate, the legislative command."[158]

The Roosevelt Court was much busier turning back challenges to federal statutes that, it was argued, exceeded congressional powers in a federal system. From 1937 to 1954 it heard dozens of such cases. Of course, once the Roosevelt Court was at full strength, it issued its landmark decisions scrapping inherited interstate commerce clause doctrine and laying down a new and much more expansive rule. The *Jones & Laughlin Steel* decision in 1937, which pivoted on Justice Roberts and was written by Chief Justice Hughes, was carefully tailored to emphasize its consistency with Progressive-Era Supreme Court precedents.[159] When the Court handed down the *Darby Lumber* decision in 1941, Hughes struggled with it, complaining that the Fair Labor Standards Act of 1938 was a "highly unsatisfactory" statute that impermissibly "reaches into the field of production."[160] The job of writing the opinion was left to the much more enthusiastic Justice Stone, who explicitly "limited" the holding in the 1936 *Carter Coal* decision and ruled that Congress could prohibit goods produced under "substandard labor conditions" from entering the interstate marketplace, and to do so, it could choose "suppression of the production of the condemned goods" as a reasonable means of accomplishing that goal.[161] A year later, Hughes was gone, replaced by Attorney General Robert Jackson (and Stone assumed the center seat). When a farmer who raised only a small amount of wheat for consumption on his own farm challenged the application of the AAA's production quotas, Jackson explained to his law clerk that it was time for a "frank holding that the interstate commerce power has no limits except those which Congress sees fit to observe." The only law that would be unconstitutional on interstate commerce grounds after the New Deal was one "so absurd that it would be laughed out of Congress." In the future, congressional "excesses and irresponsibilities" must be "answer[ed] for at the polls," not at the courthouse.[162] Jackson tried to embody his laugh test in constitutional doctrine by holding that Congress could regulate any class of activities that exerted a "substantial economic effect on interstate commerce."[163] It is not clear that the Roosevelt Court needed such new doctrinal tools to uphold aggressive applications of Progressive statutes such as the Mann Act and the Pure Food and Drug Act or new statutes such as the Gamblers' Occupational Tax Act.[164] Similarly, the Court did not bother to cite its new cases when concluding that Congress could regulate a local newspaper because, in part, the paper published national news.[165] Likewise, in upholding the Housing and Rent Act of 1947, the Court noted, "If the war power can be used in days of peace to treat all the wounds which war inflicts on our society, it may not only swallow up all other powers of Congress but largely obliterate the Ninth and the Tenth Amendments as well." However, the Roosevelt Court was largely content to assume that Congress was "alert to its constitutional responsibilities."[166]

After the road bump the administration had encountered in setting industry codes, the Roosevelt Court soon reestablished and reemphasized the kind of judicial deference to the administrative state that had been familiar since the Gilded Age. When the Court heard another challenge to a provision of the Bituminous Coal Act after the 1937 revolution, Justice Douglas wrote for a nearly unanimous bench that the statute suffered from no constitutional defects, including its delegation of price fixing "in the public interest" to a commission. Fresh from his stint running the new Securities and Exchange Commission, Douglas opined that the "burdens of minutiae would be apt to clog the administration of the law" if Congress "were under the constitutional compulsion of filling in the details" of its policies, and to disallow such delegations of authority "would be to turn back the clock on at least a half century of administrative law." Congress could "bring to its aid the services of an administrative agency."[167] The Court paused only briefly to dismiss the National Broadcasting Company's concern that the Federal Communications Commission was exercising legislative power by granting radio station licenses when warranted by "the public interest."[168] When examining a curfew order for individuals of Japanese ancestry in a designated military zone on the West Coast, the Court thought it best to consider the case not from the perspective of the "congressional power to delegate" authority to executive officers but from the perspective of Congress and the executive "acting in cooperation" to empower military officers to assess national defense needs and take appropriate action.[169] Similarly, the Emergency Price Control Act of 1942 did not involve any unconstitutional delegations of legislative power because the Constitution is best understood as "a continuously operative charter of government [that] does not demand the impossible or the impracticable." Congress had engaged in the "essentials of the legislative function" and could leave the rest to an administrative officer with "ample latitude" to make decisions and take actions.[170] The president's authority to exclude aliens from the United States without a hearing did not involve an excessive delegation of the legislative power, in part because the "exclusion of aliens is a fundamental act of sovereignty" and, indeed, it is "inherent in the executive power to control the foreign affairs of the nation." Congress was merely assisting the president in "implementing" that inherently executive power.[171] When it came to removing aliens already in the United States, the Court required that Congress "only legislate so far as is reasonable and practicable," leaving "to executive officers the authority to accomplish its purpose."[172]

The Court found more opportunities to object where noneconomic rights were claimed. Although hardly an aggressive enforcer of civil liberties against congressional power, the Roosevelt Court was willing to narrow the scope of legislative power a bit. The Court was relatively direct in insisting that the due process clauses "set limits upon the power of Congress or that of a state legislature to make the proof of one fact or group of facts evidence of the existence of the ultimate fact on which guilt is predicated."[173] Although recognized in the context of judicial review of a federal statute, such a clear statement of the barriers imposed on legislative power by the due process clause had potentially greater relevance to judicial monitoring of the criminal justice systems of the states.[174] The Court was similarly direct when Congress tried to suspend the pay of a group of federal employees that it regarded as potential "subversives." In doing so, the justices concluded, Congress had effectively exercised a court-like judgment and run afoul of the little-noticed constitutional prohibition on bills of attainder.[175]

More often in the years after the Court-packing battle, the Court preferred a less direct approach. It leveraged its power of judicial review to narrow and limit the scope of problematic statutes. Often without a detailed explanation of the constitutional rule at stake, the justices simply asserted that there were constitutional concerns afoot, and federal statutes should not be construed to operate on the contestable fringes of congressional authority. Federal government officials were constrained and defendants were freed from their legal liabilities just the same.

Confronted with an effort to strip an individual of his citizenship on the grounds that his naturalization was fraudulently obtained because he was a member of the Communist Party and thus did not have allegiance to the Constitution of the United States, the Court balked. Coming just a handful of years after the Court-packing scare, the justices acknowledged their "high duty to carry out the will of Congress" but emphasized that they must also be guided "by the spirit of freedom and tolerance in which our nation was founded." The "heterogeneous people" of the United States were united by their desire to be "citizens in a free world in which men are privileged to think and act and speak according to their convictions, without fear of punishment or further exile so long as they keep the peace and obey the law." In the midst of World War II, "it is safe to assert that nowhere in the world today is the right of citizenship of greater worth to an individual than it is in this country."[176] Even so, the Court approached its task somewhat tentatively, asserting that it would not construe the provisions of the naturalization acts "to circumscribe liberty of political thought." The judicial majority was not willing to accept the government's restricted view of what it meant to have allegiance to the Constitution. The true core of the Constitution was simply "the guaranties of the Bill of Rights and especially that of freedom of thought contained in the First Amendment." Fortunately, the Court was unwilling to assume that a commitment to the Communist Party was necessarily inconsistent with a commitment to the Bill of Rights. Only by assuming that Congress implicitly agreed with that view could the statute be made consistent with "that freedom of thought[,] which is a fundamental feature of our political institutions." As a result, the petitioner could not be denaturalized.[177]

Again and again, the Roosevelt Court adopted this tactic to hem in congressional authority and delimit federal statutes. When federal authorities tried to deport Australian Harry Bridges for being a member of the Communist Party, the Court emphasized that "freedom of speech and of press is accorded aliens residing in this country," and the government had a duty to exercise "meticulous care" before depriving someone of the right to "stay and live and work in this land of freedom." By refusing to "believe that Congress intended to cast so wide a net as to reach" those who were not demonstrated to be violent revolutionaries, the Court was able to restrict the government's ability to deport aliens while claiming to avoid addressing directly "the larger constitutional questions" raised in the case.[178] Similarly, worried about an act of Congress "that touches the sensitive area of rights specifically guaranteed by the Constitution," the Court declined to allow the government "to detain an admittedly loyal citizen" of Japanese descent in a military zone.[179] Faced with a federal statute that apparently infringed on the right of labor unions to advocate on behalf of candidates for federal office, the Court insisted that Congress "did not want to pass any legislation that would threaten interferences with the privileges of speech or press or that would undertake to supersede the Constitution"; thus it refused to allow the government to restrict the electioneering activities of unions.[180] When asked to apply Reconstruction-era civil rights statutes against a state legislature's "Un-American Activities" committee, the Court preferred to presume that Congress did not "mean to overturn the tradition of legislative freedom achieved in England by Civil War and carefully preserved in the formation of State and National Governments here."[181] Likewise, the Reconstruction Congress could not have intended to regulate "a lawless political brawl, precipitated by a handful of white citizens against other white citizens," which the Court found did not fall within the federal authority established by the Fourteenth Amendment.[182] Nor could Congress have intended to include purely local manufacturers in its criminal statute requiring that all manufacturers of gambling devices register their business with the federal government and report on each device sold. Giving Congress the benefit of the constitutional doubt, the justices would not give effect to the "literal language of this Act," which would be appropriate only "if it were enacted for a unitary system of government." Such a statute could be applied only in circumstances that were actually within the constitutional authority of Congress.[183]

More often, of course, the Roosevelt Court simply upheld the exercise of federal authority against those who claimed protection under the constitutional guarantees of due process or individual liberty. Most infamously, with troops still in the field, the Court upheld the combined authority of the president and Congress to exclude those of Japanese ancestry from a war zone, even though the justices announced that "all legal restrictions which curtail the civil rights of a single racial group are immediately suspect" and subject "to the most rigid scrutiny."[184] The justices quickly dismissed the relevance of the Second Amendment to federal regulation of a sawed-off shotgun.[185] The Court thought it obvious that federal labor regulations that punished company officials for reading an antiunion speech to the company's employees addressed constitutionally unprotected "conduct," not constitutionally protected speech, even though in this case the conduct took the form of "pressure exerted vocally."[186] The federal government's decision to refuse a broadcast license to persons whose licensing was deemed not to be in the "public interest, convenience, or necessity" was not an abridgment of free speech, so long as the public-interest standard was not tantamount to choosing broadcasters based on their political views.[187] The federal government's effort to break up the Associated Press was wholly consistent with the First Amendment, since freedom of the press required the "widest possible dissemination of information from diverse and antagonistic sources"; therefore, the federal government could punish private media entities that sought "to restrain trade in news."[188] To federal government employees who objected to the Hatch Act's restriction on their political activities, the Court pointed out, "It is accepted constitutional doctrine that these fundamental human rights are not absolutes." It noted that the employees' political rights must be balanced against the congressional desire "to protect a democratic society against the supposed evil of political partisanship by classified employees of government."[189] As the Cold War was heating up, the Court was willing to give the federal government a relatively free hand to take action against the influence of Communists, whose freedom of speech was outweighed by the dangers they posed to American society.[190] When Congress sought to balance the public interest against individual rights, the Roosevelt Court was generally content to ratify Congress's conclusions about how those competing interests should best be managed.

The Warren Court

The constitutional revolution of 1937 marked a judicial retreat from challenging Congress on many of the traditional constitutional rules the Court had sought to enforce up to that point in its history. With the constitutional revolution of the Warren Court, it was once again willing to be an aggressive enforcer of constitutional rules against legislative power, but the rules were different now. Questions of constitutional structure and economic interests remained on the sidelines as the Court took a growing interest in noneconomic personal liberties. Where the Roosevelt Court had often urged deference to Congress in the resolution of competing societal interests, the Warren Court became more assertive in reviewing how those interests were balanced when noneconomic rights were affected. The heart of the civil rights and civil liberties revolution that took place in the 1950s and 1960s can be found in cases involving state and local government action, but the scope of congressional authority did not completely escape the Warren Court's scrutiny.

The Republican Party rode General Dwight Eisenhower's popularity to regain the White House for the first time in a quarter century. The Eisenhower administration had no interest in disturbing the New Deal settlement. His candidacy had been launched with an effort to reposition the party as "New Republicans" who could simply administer the New Deal state more efficiently and professionally than the Democrats had. They had no desire to reconstitute the Taft Court or reopen the constitutional debates of the 1920s and 1930s. In looking for Republican judges, Eisenhower and his attorney general, Herbert Brownell, were more likely to set their sights on those modeled after Charles Evans Hughes and Benjamin Cardozo rather than George Sutherland and Willis Van Devanter.

During his two terms of office, Eisenhower had the opportunity to name five justices. His preference was for "highly qualified," "middle of the road" candidates who could win bipartisan acclaim.[191] To the extent that he was willing to provoke controversy over his judicial nominees, he seemed most willing to lose the southern Democrats in the Senate. In fact, his selections tended to push the Supreme Court to the left, which was not unexpected by those assessing his choices at the time.[192] It was the professional credentials more than the constitutional sensibilities of Ike's Supreme Court appointments that distinguished them from those of his Democratic predecessor Harry Truman or successors John Kennedy and Lyndon Johnson. The construction of the Warren Court was very much a joint project of the New Republican Eisenhower and the New Frontier Kennedy.

By the 1950s, the United States was a different nation than it had been before the war. The postwar economic expansion freed a generation from the struggle for daily existence that had often been at the forefront of American political thought. The baby boomers who grew up in the postwar suburbs and enjoyed the fruits of what John Kenneth Galbraith dubbed the "affluent society" were far removed from their parents' experience in the Great Depression. The "consumers' republic" made room for the rise of "postmaterial values" that placed new demands on society and the political system.[193] The horrors of Nazism and the emergence of the Cold War with the Soviet Union reframed America's conception of itself, as well as its place in the world. By the end of the Truman administration, it was becoming commonplace to refer to the United States as the "leader of the free world." The designation not only specified the nation's new global role and set of alliances but also drew critical contrasts with its antagonists. The United States faced an ongoing security peril, to be sure, but it was ultimately fighting for freedom. We could not risk "defeating our own ends by encroaching upon the traditional rights of citizenship" or be seduced into emulating the "practices of foreign dictators and domestic demagogues."[194] In stumping for his own elevation to the White House, Vice President Richard Nixon urged audiences to remember that "the next President will not only be the leader of this country, but the leader of the free world," and in that role, the president stood not only as "the guardian of peace" but also as "the champion of freedom and liberty for all men throughout the world." In doing so, he echoed President Harry Truman's call to Americans to understand that "the United States has become the principal protector of the free world" and to join with "other free men the world over who believe as we do in liberty and justice and the dignity of man."[195] Swedish sociologist Gunnar Myrdal famously held a mirror to postwar America and declared that American nationalism was unusually ideological, grounded in an "American Creed" that "*ought* to rule" American life and that committed the nation to the "ideals of the essential dignity of the individual human being, of the fundamental equality of all men, and of certain inalienable rights to freedom, justice, and a fair opportunity."[196] Reconciling the demands of individual freedom and civic order took on a new urgency in midcentury America.

The Warren Court launched a constitutional departure, turning constitutional jurisprudence in a more liberal direction and more specifically cementing a concern for individual civil rights and liberties into the self-understanding of the judiciary. Conservatives in the Progressive Era had often warned that an "independent judiciary" was essential as "the bulwark of liberty, the protection of the weak against the strong, and the safeguard of the rights of the minority."[197] By midcentury, the political Left had joined them in praising the importance of an empowered judiciary. One of the architects of the Court-packing plan, Princeton's Edward Corwin, pivoted with the switch in time, warning against judicial "self-abnegation" and calling for the "enlargement of judicial review" so that the Court could "give voice to the conscience of the country in behalf of poor people against local prejudice and unfairness." Some freedoms, liberals now declared, were "indispensable conditions of a free society," and the courts themselves were the "palladium of freedom."[198]

Friends of the Warren Court praised it as heroic, and there is no doubt that the justices were willing to wade into political controversy. But the Warren Court is sometimes portrayed as if Robert Taft and Barry Goldwater had occupied the White House during those years, rather than Eisenhower, Kennedy, and Johnson. The Warren Court was constituted by political liberals, who dominated national electoral politics from the Great Depression until the Vietnam War and subsequently staffed the Court with their ideological allies and lent it support during political battles. When given the opportunity to appoint justices to the Court, Kennedy and Johnson looked to self-proclaimed "activists" and self-consciously sought to move the Court they had inherited from Roosevelt, Truman, and Eisenhower even further to the left.[199] As one observer concluded, the "best description of the period is that all three branches of government believed they were working harmoniously to tackle the nation's problems."[200] Corwin's proposal that the Court "give voice to the conscience of the country" was prophetic, as the Warren Court aggressively exercised the power of judicial review to disrupt long-standing public policy and constitutional arrangements in the states, particularly in the South, but largely left Congress and the federal government alone. The Warren Court was an extension of Congress, not an antagonist of it.

The Court's review of acts of Congress shifted in the Warren era compared with the Roosevelt Court. After the revolution of 1937, the justices dedicated themselves to upholding federal legislation, and the Court heard scores of constitutional cases that it decided in favor of congressional authority. In doing so, the Court remade constitutional law and removed many obstacles to the exertion of congressional power. The Warren Court had far less work to do on that front, and not surprisingly, it scaled back its efforts as it focused on monitoring the states.[201] It upheld federal statutes against constitutional challenges at half the rate of its predecessor. At the same time, the Warren Court became modestly more active in hemming in congressional power. As table 6-1 shows, the Warren Court decided more cases that were hostile to the constitutional powers of Congress, and it more often did so in cases involving important statutory provisions. Nonetheless, it continued to lean heavily on the Roosevelt Court's approach of limiting statutory authority rather than striking down legislative provisions in their entirety, and it continued to focus more of its critical attention on older statutes rather than striking down aspects of recently adopted federal policy.

The Warren Court's relatively sparse record of invalidations was no doubt aided by the fact that Congress was not heavily involved in the policy areas that occupied most of the Court's attention. In some areas, such as criminal justice, the Court imposed national sensibilities on the states and brought reform through the mechanism of constitutional law that had already been adopted by the federal government.[202] In other areas, the Court developed more robust conceptions of individual rights that cut into the states' police powers but had less relevance for the legislative authority of Congress. Landmark Warren Court decisions affecting religious liberty and legislative apportionment, for example, had few implications for Congress.

In the case of racial civil rights, the Warren Court's activism mostly redounded to the benefit of congressional authority. Immediately after the decision in *Brown v. Board of Education*, the Court took the natural, if textually awkward, step of striking down racially segregated schools in the District of Columbia. The Court papered over the legal differences between the two jurisdictions by asserting that the Fourteenth Amendment's equal protection clause was merely a more explicit statement of "the American ideal of fairness" contained in the Fifth Amendment's due process clause.[203] Having made its earth-shattering declaration in *Brown*, the Court largely retreated from the field and left the lower courts to fight the battle with Jim Crow. When the Court returned to the fray, it did so by backing Congress. First in evaluating the Civil Rights Act of 1964 and then in reviewing the Voting Rights Act of 1965, the Court endorsed more aggressive actions by Congress. Rather than reassessing the scope of its post-Reconstruction decisions on congressional authority under the Fourteenth Amendment, the Court leaned on the New Deal commerce clause precedents to clear the way for Congress to regulate private racial discrimination.[204] Justice Jackson's pronouncement in *Wickard* that Congress could reach any economic activity, no matter how "trivial by itself," made upholding the use of its power to regulate interstate commerce to prohibit racial discrimination in businesses a relatively straightforward judicial task.[205] Upholding the Voting Rights Act as an exercise of congressional authority under the Fifteenth Amendment required greater effort, but the Court emphasized Congress's work to justify and design a measure that would "banish the blight of racial discrimination in voting, which has infected the electoral process in parts of our country for nearly a century."[206] More creatively, the Court construed the Civil Rights Act of 1866 as barring "all racial discrimination, private as well as public, in the sale or rental of property," and it further upheld the statute, "thus construed," as "a valid exercise of the power of Congress to enforce the Thirteenth Amendment," a result that was in keeping with Congress's own recent effort in the Civil Rights Act of 1968.[207]

The civil liberties revolution at the federal level was particularly important in the context of America's new postwar engagement with the world, and its influence rippled through sets of closely related cases. One set reflected the uncertain constitutional landscape created by America's new superpower status in the awkward peace of the Cold War. To an unprecedented degree, the United States maintained a substantial military presence abroad, which created unusual legal dilemmas. In 1950 Congress adopted the Uniform Code of Military Justice (UCMJ) to govern the new standing army, and that code included a provision specifying that civilians employed by or accompanying the American military abroad fell within the jurisdiction of courts-martial. Such a power had traditionally been exercised in wartime, and Congress apparently assumed it could exercise the same power in peacetime. This arrangement had the benefit of offering an alternative to whatever local legal system might otherwise come into play if an American civilian committed a crime abroad, but it was unusual in subjecting an American civilian to military justice. Both Japan and England entered into executive agreements allowing the United States to take jurisdiction over cases involving American citizens on their soil. Not long thereafter, the wives of two servicemen stationed in Japan and England murdered their husbands as they slept, and they were both convicted in courts-martial. Relying on earlier decisions that Congress was empowered to set up "legislative courts" outside American territory, a divided Supreme Court held that Congress had the authority to subject the wives to military justice and try them without a jury.[208] The narrow majority was inclined to defer to Congress in determining how best to deal "with such a far flung situation as this" and with the delicate problem of international relations in the Cold War era.[209] Justice Felix Frankfurter included an odd note in the case reports, however, observing that the majority opinion by Justice Tom Clark had specifically declined to address whether the tribunals in these cases could be authorized under the legislature's constitutional power to make rules governing land and naval forces. Surprisingly, the Court agreed to reconsider the cases on that specific question the next term, and in doing so, it reversed its earlier ruling. With Clark now in dissent, the majority argued that the congressional power to establish rules for the military did not authorize it to extend the reach of military justice to civilians accompanying the military in times of peace. Members of the armed services were a narrow exception to the general constitutional requirement that American citizens charged with federal crimes must be tried in civilian courts with juries and appropriate procedural protections.[210] Two years earlier, the Court had held that soldiers discharged from military service could not be tried by courts-martial for crimes committed while in the military, despite another provision of the UCMJ.[211] Not long after the "case of the murdering wives," the Court similarly clarified that Congress did not have the constitutional authority to extend courts-martial to civilian employees or military dependents in either capital or noncapital cases.[212]

The Warren Court took somewhat longer to work through the implications of its reassessment of the scope of congressional power to strip Americans of their citizenship. The Immigration and Nationality Act of 1940, and its subsequent incarnations, laid out various circumstances that could lead to the loss of citizenship. Some of these provisions simply formalized the process of expatriation for those who wished to formally or informally renounce their American citizenship, but others allowed for the involuntary loss of citizenship, or denaturalization. In the case of Clemente Perez, a narrowly divided Court concluded that Congress possessed an implicit power "to enact for the effective regulation of foreign affairs," which included a power "to reduce to a minimum the frictions that are unavoidable in a world of sovereigns" and address the problems associated with "American citizens sojourning within their territories."[213] In the case of an American who stayed in a foreign country for long periods, who denied his American citizenship while the draft was in effect during World War II, and who voted in foreign elections, Justice Felix Frankfurter argued that Congress could recognize effective expatriation, although the Court specifically reserved the question of whether remaining abroad to avoid military service was constitutionally valid. In the case of an army deserter, Frankfurter lost Justice William Brennan, and thus his majority, and the Court announced that denaturalization as punishment for an offense violated the constitutional ban against cruel and unusual punishment.[214] Brennan could find no reasonable relationship between the act of stripping citizenship from a deserter and a legitimate enumerated power of the government, while Frankfurter thought the threat of denaturalization for desertion clearly served the congressional war power, regardless of whether one considered it an exceedingly harsh method of doing so. If the New Deal settlement had determined that the Court should defer to congressional judgment on the means it could use to advance constitutional ends, the dissenters thought the Court was returning to its pre–New Deal ways in second-guessing the policy tools Congress chose to get the job done.[215]

In a later case, the Court objected to Congress's disparate treatment of naturalized versus natural-born citizens when it came to expatriation. Only naturalized citizens lost their citizenship when living abroad for extended periods, which the Court said violated the nondiscrimination principle of the Fifth Amendment cited in *Bolling v. Sharpe*. By contrast, the dissenters emphasized that the statute did not simply punish naturalized citizens who lived abroad; it took notice of those who returned to their country of origin and remained there, which both Congress and foreign governments had long done.[216] Finally, the Court overturned its holding in *Perez* and announced that voluntarily voting in a foreign election could not be grounds for losing American citizenship, declaring broadly that the "very nature of our free government makes it completely incongruous to have a rule of law under which a group of citizens temporarily in office can deprive another group of citizens of their citizenship"; further, the text of the Fourteenth Amendment bestowed a perpetual grant of citizenship on those born or naturalized in the United States.[217]

Yet another bundle of cases charted the Warren Court's struggle with the limits of the national security state and domestic implications of the fight against international communism. On this subject, both the federal government and the states were active, and the Court's constitutional concerns stretched across cases arising from both jurisdictions. State loyalty oaths, un-American affairs investigations, and sedition prosecutions all generated constitutional disputes for the Court to resolve, and similar domestic security policies led the Court to examine the boundaries of congressional power and the scope of individual rights. Although the Senate repudiated Senator Joseph McCarthy at the end of 1954, and the second Red Scare had clearly peaked before Warren's appointment to the Court, domestic security concerns remained salient throughout the late 1950s.

These cases were much more politically controversial than those involving overseas military bases and denaturalization. The policies regarding Communists and domestic security had been deliberately adopted by Congress, and the Court's resistance to them was noted. The Court's timing was also unfortunate. Just as the segregationists were mobilizing in opposition to *Brown*, the Court gave its foes more ammunition. Its 1956 term was filled with domestic security cases in which a slim majority often favored the accused subversives. Many of these cases did not require the exercise of judicial review to enforce constitutional limits on Congress. In the infamous perjury case of labor leader Clinton Jencks (who had sworn under oath that he was not a Communist), for example, the Court insisted that criminal defendants must be able to view potentially exculpatory but classified government documents, leading Justice Tom Clark to rail in dissent that the "intelligence agencies of our Government engaged in law enforcement may as well close up shop" unless Congress acted to overturn the Court's decision.[218] Not long afterward, over the vocal but lonely dissent of Clark (Truman's former attorney general), the Court handed down four more antigovernment decisions on "Red Monday."[219]

Two of the Red Monday cases involved the constitutional powers of Congress. In *Yates v. United States*, the Court reviewed the sedition trial of fourteen accused Communists. Writing for the Court, Justice John Marshall Harlan II emphasized that Congress could not authorize prosecution of the mere advocacy of the forcible overthrow of the government as an "abstract doctrine"; only the actual organizing of an insurrection or the "advocacy of forcible action" was prosecutable.[220] In *Watkins v. United States*, the Court examined the authority of the House Un-American Activities Committee (HUAC). In an opinion by Chief Justice Earl Warren, the Court overturned the contempt of Congress conviction of labor organizer John Watkins, who had refused to answer questions about other potential members of the Communist Party. Warren chastised the legislature for authorizing "a new kind of congressional inquiry unknown in prior periods of American history" and intruding into the "private affairs of individuals." The Court was not prepared to draw a bright line protecting individual privacy against congressional encroachment, but it did object that Congress had provided neither the committee nor the witness with sufficient guidance as to the scope of its investigation.[221]

The next year, in a case involving an alleged Communist who had been denied a passport to travel abroad, Justice William O. Douglas wrote for a narrow majority and "employed the standard tactics of the Warren Court. First, he rattled the big stick of the Bill of Rights, warning that 'the right to travel' was protected by the due process clause. Then, after pointing to this constitutional protection, Douglas declared that it was unnecessary to decide such issues since the Secretary of State had relied on erroneous statutory interpretation. Congress had never authorized a denial of passports because of beliefs or associations."[222] Like other cases resolved in the 1940s and 1950s, the Court did not leave much doubt about the implications of its constitutional concerns. "We deal here with a constitutional right of the citizen, a right which we must assume Congress will be faithful to respect."[223] It was safe to assume that Congress had not granted the secretary of state the power to deny citizens the right to travel because Congress had no real authority to grant that power, and the dissenters called the majority on their subterfuge, pointing out that both the legislature and the executive branch had long assumed the authority to deny passports and would have done so in this case if not for the majority's newfound constitutional worries.

The political response to this string of decisions was immediate and vociferous. Although characteristically reticent in public, President Eisenhower's disappointment in his judicial selections seemed to hinge on the Communist decisions, not *Brown*. The National Association of Attorneys General adopted resolutions critical of the decisions, and with the chief justice in attendance, the American Bar Association lambasted the Court for subverting the government's ability to carry "out the first law of mankind—the right of self preservation." Debate on Court-curbing measures spiked in Congress, and there was loose talk of judicial impeachment. In the most significant legislative challenge to the Court since the Court-packing debate, the Senate nearly passed a bill sponsored by Republican William E. Jenner that would have stripped the appellate jurisdiction of the Supreme Court over a range of cases affecting domestic security. The good news for the justices, however, was that their national security decisions won plaudits from Senate liberals, who thought the Warren Court was on the right track in revitalizing individual rights, but they were a distinct minority.[224]

The Court got the message and stepped back. In the case of Lloyd Barenblatt, a psychology instructor who had been held in contempt for refusing to testify about his Communist associations to HUAC, a narrow majority walked away from its ruling in *Watkins*. The congressional interest in this area was as fundamental as it could be: the national "right of self-preservation," which overshadowed the First Amendment interests of the individual. "The constitutional legislative power of Congress in this instance is beyond question."[225] Justices Harlan and Frankfurter had apparently been tentative in agreeing to *Watkins* in the first place, and given the political reaction to that decision, they preferred to restrict rather than extend that precedent.[226] With Harlan emphasizing for the majority the need to balance societal and individual interests, Justice Black was left to develop his absolutist stance on First Amendment protections in dissent. With the new majority in place, the Court swept through a series of cases favoring government interests against the constitutional arguments of alleged Communists who lost public benefits, were investigated by legislative committees, were denied admission to the bar, and were forced to register their affiliations.[227]

The Court did not turn the corner on internal security until the liberal wing received reinforcements in 1962. In particular, the replacement of Felix Frankfurter, the Court's oracle of New Deal deference, with Arthur Goldberg, a self-proclaimed "activist judge," shattered the pro-government majority in internal security cases.[228] What were formerly dissents became majority opinions. Goldberg announced that the government could not abridge the Fifth Amendment's substantive, if implicit, liberty to travel by denying a passport to a Communist.[229] Douglas announced that the postal service could not intercept and destroy Communist propaganda in contravention of every individual's unfettered right to receive political information.[230] Warren announced that Congress could not bar Communists from leading labor unions, an effective bill of attainder.[231] Brennan announced that Congress could not require Communists to enter their party membership in a government registry, a form of self-incrimination.[232] Warren announced that Congress could not infringe on the freedom of association by barring Communists from employment in the defense industry, and Douglas similarly argued that they could not be barred from the merchant marine.[233]

Other federal cases addressed less contentious or less important policies but built on similar principles of free speech and due process. For example, building on the logic of the Communist Party registry, the justices rejected statutory provisions imposing separate criminal punishments on those who refused to register their unlawful activities, from gambling to the possession of firearms, as self-incrimination.[234] The Warren Court found at least some occasions when economic regulations might interfere with free speech. The majority read into the Railway Labor Act a limitation that prevented labor unions from expending the dues of dissenting members on political campaigns. Black thought the First Amendment would be gutted if Congress could coerce individual workers into groups and then authorize those groups to extract resources from dissenting workers for political purposes. Congress could neither directly nor indirectly "compel one man to expend his energy, his time or his money to advance the fortunes of candidates he would like to see defeated or to urge ideologies and causes he believes would be harmful to the country."[235] Frankfurter, by contrast, thought this "too fine-spun a claim for constitutional recognition." The framers protected only the right of individuals to express themselves, not their right to withdraw from collective activity with which they disagreed.[236] Black wrote for a unanimous Court in refusing to allow the Sherman Anti-Trust Act to reach associations seeking to influence politics and legislation. The Court should never "impute to Congress an intent to invade" the freedom of citizens, even when organized into corporations, to engage not in "business activity, but political activity." To do so would subvert the very basis of "representative government," which required people to have the ability "to make their wishes known to their representatives."[237]

Conclusion

Over the course of thirty years, the US Supreme Court was transformed from perhaps its most conservative incarnation into perhaps its most liberal one. The Court constructed and then led by William Howard Taft was as aggressive as any of its predecessors in enforcing constitutional limits on Congress. When Taft left the Court in 1930, he was replaced by a more centrist Republican in the form of Charles Evans Hughes, but the Court remained committed to its role as a guardian of constitutional verities and to a substantive constitutional vision that accepted the federal government's significant role in addressing social ills but one limited by state autonomy and private rights to property and personal freedom. The New Deal put unprecedented pressure on that constitutional vision. The Hughes Court staunchly resisted what it regarded as New Deal excesses, but it eventually cracked under the pressure and left the field to the ascendant New Dealers.

The result of the New Deal was a two-stage revolution in constitutional law. Most immediately, the revolution of 1937 abandoned many of the constitutional constraints the Court had defined and enforced since Reconstruction. The justices struggled to find a new role for the Court in this changed environment, but they were decisive in rejecting the continued relevance of hard structural constraints on congressional policy-making and the significance of traditional property rights as a barrier to economic regulation. As a result, the Court's most significant work from 1937 to the early 1950s was accomplished through its cases upholding the exercise of congressional authority. The second constitutional revolution of the Warren Court reemphasized civil rights and liberties and the role of the judiciary in protecting those freedoms. The Court once again turned its attention to striking down unconstitutional laws, but for the most part, that attention was not focused on federal statutes. Congress felt only the fringes of the Court's new emphasis on individual rights. Even so, the Court drew no clear lines between legislative authority at the federal and state levels. Congress faced its own constitutional limits and sometimes ran afoul of the Court's new rights jurisprudence.

During these years, the Court also faced the most intense political threats since Reconstruction. Both the Court-packing plan of the 1930s and the jurisdiction-stripping measures of the 1950s threatened to significantly weaken the independence and power of the Court, and they signaled the power of the political opposition to the Court's jurisprudence. Although it is possible that the Court could have weathered these storms without changing course, in both cases the Court chose to take a different direction, thus alleviating the political pressure building in Congress. The Court's willingness and ability to confront Congress had limits. The Court could be as active as it wanted in trimming around the edges of congressional policy commitments or working hand in hand with political leaders to advance their political agenda, but when the Court obstructed important federal policies that were central to the ascendant political coalition, the exercise of judicial review was less tolerated.

Throughout these changes, the Court solidified a more active role for itself in evaluating the constitutionality of federal laws than it had played at the beginning of the century. After a short-lived period of relative deference, the justices soon found their footing and rededicated themselves to the task of monitoring Congress for constitutional infractions. The active exercise of judicial review did not always mean that the Court threw itself into contemporary disputes and wielded the veto power of a third legislative chamber. In the first intense years of the Franklin Roosevelt administration, the Court became a force to be reckoned with as the New Dealers attempted to develop and implement their policy agenda. But more generally, the Court pecked away at older laws, less politically salient laws, and less central legislative provisions. The Court was active, but it was not often at the center of national political debates. Even its foray into domestic security came relatively late, as the force of the second Red Scare had already been spent. Nonetheless, the Court had demonstrated its potential utility to both sides of the political spectrum, and both liberals and conservatives found things to praise and to critique in the Court's performance. As the Court-packing proposal itself suggested, critics of the judiciary had shifted their political goals. They no longer wished to see the Court defanged and the power of judicial review shelved. Instead, they preferred to capture the Court and wield the power of judicial review for their own purposes. For the Court in the mid-twentieth century, that meant creating a "reinvigorated, liberal-minded judiciary" that would simultaneously empower Congress and develop new ideas about individual rights that were more consonant with a Progressive state.

7

Congress and the Conservative Court

Although the Warren Court was bolstered and backed by the ascendant liberal wings of the Republican and Democratic Parties, its work and its membership remained controversial. The John Birch Society, an extreme anti-Communist group, sprinkled the nation's highways with "Impeach Earl Warren" billboards in the years after *Brown* and Red Monday, and the chief justice recalled that they remained in place through most of his tenure on the Court.[1] As the 1960s progressed, the American Bar Association swung around to favor the Court. When, in the early 1960s, a group of state chief judges pushed for a constitutional amendment to give them the ability to overturn US Supreme Court precedents, a wide array of interests rallied in defense of the Warren Court, including state governors and legislatures.[2] Nationally, the Warren Court retained reasonable levels of support from the general public, but that support was hardly universal.[3] As the 1960s wore on, conservative members of Congress introduced a flood of bills to curb the judiciary, though such measures had little chance of passage.[4]

The Warren Court might have continued to add to its legacy if not for the sagging fortunes of the Democratic Party at the end of the 1960s. Once it became apparent to Chief Justice Earl Warren that a Democrat was unlikely to win the 1968 presidential race, he tried to ensure that his successor would be a like-minded jurist. He approached President Lyndon Johnson with a plan: Warren would retire upon the confirmation of his successor, and he recommended Justice Abe Fortas as the perfect choice for the job. Fortas was a Washington superlawyer, a Johnson confidant, and a recent addition to the Court's liberal wing. Johnson liked the plan. He quickly nominated Fortas for the center seat in June 1968, and the president nominated his longtime friend Homer Thornberry to succeed Fortas. With sixty-four Democratic senators, Johnson might have expected his former colleagues to act with alacrity and solidify a liberal majority on the Court for years to come.

But LBJ was not just an outgoing president. He was a severely weakened president who had been forced to withdraw from the race for reelection. The Democratic majority in the Senate was large, but it was not united, and many senators were less enamored with Fortas and Thornberry than Johnson was. Johnson misjudged the strength of his majority and made no effort to accommodate the concerns of potentially wavering senators. The political stratagem behind Warren's retirement was transparent, and conservative senators who were unhappy with the Warren Court, along with Republican politicians who envisioned the prospect of filling Warren's seat with their own nominee, cobbled together the votes to obstruct a speedy confirmation. Worse yet, the scrutiny surrounding the Fortas nomination revealed that the justice had engaged in ethically dubious financial dealings, and Fortas felt he had no choice but to resign from the Court. Instead of rejuvenating the center seat with a young liberal justice, the election-year maneuvering wound up handing two Supreme Court vacancies to the winner of the 1968 presidential election: Republican Richard Nixon.[5]

Richard Nixon began his presidency by replacing two liberal justices, setting the Court on a more conservative path. Between 1968 and 2017, Republican presidents selected thirteen new justices for the US Supreme Court, while Democratic presidents filled only four seats. Nixon alone replaced four justices before standing for reelection, leading many to hail (or jeer) the arrival of the "Nixon Court." Eisenhower had shown no interest in criticizing the direction of the Court and had chosen justices with an eye toward continuing rather than reversing its jurisprudential trajectory, and Nixon had given no indication that he would do otherwise in his losing campaign in 1960. Starting with Barry Goldwater's doomed 1964 presidential bid, however, Republican banner-carriers ran against the Court, whether the Warren Court of myth and memory or a stylized portrait of the more contemporary Court. The collapse of the Fortas nomination ushered in a new age of polarized, politically salient Supreme Court appointments featuring ideologically calculated nominations and bruising confirmation battles.

In that environment, presidents constructed a more conservative—if not necessarily a reliably conservative—Supreme Court. Although Republicans have had many opportunities to shape the Court since 1968, they have not had an entirely free hand. With his "law-and-order" campaign, Nixon was vocal in his disparagement of the Warren Court, but his actual interest in the Court was primarily rhetorical and electoral. His judicial selections were driven more by political convenience than by jurisprudential strategy. It was not until Ronald Reagan gained the White House in 1980 that the administration thought carefully about how to substantively affect the trajectory of constitutional law. Even so, that goal was constrained by the Republicans' inability to effectively control the Senate. Republicans have controlled the White House for 60 percent of the time since Johnson's departure, but they have held the Senate for less than 40 percent of that time. Moreover, the Senate majorities have been relatively small for both parties, forcing presidents to think carefully about how to navigate their nominees through a potentially hostile Senate chamber.

Republican activists have been able to steer the Court in a more conservative direction since Warren's retirement from the bench, but not as far as they would have liked. Divided government and close elections have been the rule rather than the exception for the past half century, and ideologically polarized parties have put a premium on battling over judicial vacancies.[6] Given those conditions, it is perhaps no surprise that activists on both sides of the ideological divide have often perceived that the Court has been captured by their opponents, and close observers of the Court have continually found themselves writing of the "counter-revolution that wasn't," of "a Court divided," and of a center that still holds.[7]

For a time, this more conservative Court gained a reputation as the "most activist in history."[8] In particular, the late Rehnquist Court—from the mid-1990s to the dawn of the twenty-first century—became notably more active in striking down federal laws. Often relying on a narrow majority of five conservative justices, the Court during this period focused on a remarkably coherent set of constitutional concerns. It repeatedly returned to the question of how far Congress was restricted by structural features of the Constitution, most notably federalism, and it often found that Congress was limited in ways that the Court had not emphasized since the first half of the twentieth century. Unsurprisingly, this line of decisions attracted attention from scholars and pundits alike.[9] For the Left, this was a "new activist Court."[10]

Charges of judicial activism from the right have been familiar for quite some time, and even the more conservative Court under Chief Justices Warren Burger, William Rehnquist, and John Roberts heard its share of such complaints. In the aftermath of the 1992 abortion rights decision in *Planned Parenthood of Southeastern Pennsylvania v. Casey*, authored by a trio of Reagan-Bush appointees, the social conservative journal *First Things* sparked a firestorm with a symposium on "The End of Democracy."[11] Contributors to the issue pondered whether a US government dominated by an unrestrained Court had lost legitimacy. For many on the right, "the Court's continuing injection of its power into so-called culture war issues" was the primary concern, and this had not abated with the appointment of more conservative justices.[12] Conservative politicians continued to rail against judicial activists, using bills introduced in Congress, party platforms, and congressional hearings to convey the message that the Supreme Court since Earl Warren's retirement was still a liberal activist Court.[13]

The resurgence of critiques of judicial activism from the left was a more recent development and therefore notable. The conservative Court of the Gilded Age and Progressive Era was routinely denounced as illegitimate by politicians and activists on the left, but those criticisms tended to fade away after 1937. New Dealers invented the term "judicial activism" to complain about the conservative judges that obstructed Progressive legislation.[14] Whereas conservative lawyers appealed to judicial independence and judicial review as the "only breakwater against the haste and the passions of the people" at the dawn of the twentieth century, by the mid-twentieth century, liberal lawyers were calling for the Court to aggressively defend individuals and minorities against mere "statistical democracy."[15] By the end of the twentieth century, complaints of "conservative judicial activism" had once again become commonplace.[16]

The Court in the late twentieth and early twenty-first centuries is distinctive, in that it has been criticized by both the Left and the Right. Both sides of the ideological divide are convinced the Court is allied with its adversaries. At the same time, both sides often find something to like in how judicial review has been exercised. How can this be so? Tom Keck's examination of the intellectual currents that shaped the Burger and Rehnquist Courts is a helpful starting point.[17] As he observed, Justice Felix Frankfurter emerged from early twentieth-century left-wing legal circles with the firm conviction that judicial review served primarily the class interests of the propertied elite. When President Franklin Roosevelt placed Frankfurter on the Court, he became the leading representative of the view that courts should generally be deferential to the policy choices of legislatures—a view developed by James Bradley Thayer and Oliver Wendell Holmes Jr., his predecessors at Harvard Law School. When Frankfurter departed the Court in 1962, there was no one to take up that mission and move it forward. His views were echoed to some degree by conservative jurists such as William Rehnquist and Robert Bork, who had matured after the New Deal but were wary of the Warren Court. Indeed, liberals in the 1980s lambasted Rehnquist and Bork for not being activist enough in striking down statutes.[18] But most of the conservatives appointed to the Court since 1969, as well as the liberals, have embraced the "rights-based constitutionalism" that was the hallmark of the Warren Court. Conservative and liberal justices might disagree about which laws should be struck down and why, but they both accept a robust role for the judiciary in monitoring and checking the other branches of government, and they reject the idea that legislatures should be corrected only or primarily by voters at the ballot box.

Appreciating the politics of judicial review since the Warren Court requires a recognition of this legacy. The liberals who dominated national politics after the Great Depression faced a choice about judicial review, and they ultimately decided to use it rather than to defang the Court. As Mark Tushnet has noted, an "activist government necessarily included an activist Court collaborating with the other branches of the national government to implement the regime's principles."[19] Conservatives might not like the direction the Warren Court took, but they had a long history of supporting judicial review. The more Populist notes sometimes struck by Richard Nixon and Ronald Reagan did not ultimately lead their political coalitions to abandon the idea of judicial review. Both the Republicans and the Democrats that struggled over judicial selection from the 1970s through the 2010s accepted as a matter of course that judicial review is a valid and valuable component of the American constitutional system. They quibbled over the details. The justices they appointed to the Court did not doubt their own importance in making America great, although they disagreed among themselves how best to do that.

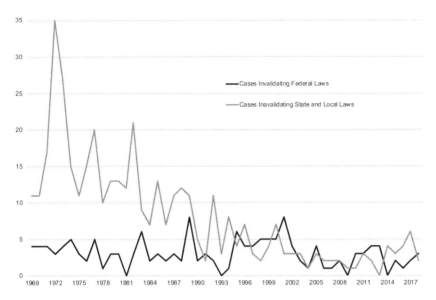

Figure 7-1: Number of Cases Invalidating State and Federal Statutes, 1969–2018

Although it is not the central focus here, it is worth noting that one way in which those disagreements manifested was a dramatic reduction in the number of US Supreme Court cases invalidating state and local legislation. The Warren Court was particularly active in striking down state and local policies, and through the 1970s, the Burger Court largely maintained that momentum. Sandra Day O'Connor's addition to the Court in 1981 put it on a different trajectory that became more pronounced over time. As figure 7-1 illustrates, the Court under the leadership of Rehnquist and Roberts became dramatically less active in exercising the power of judicial review, and that change was driven entirely by the Court's declining interest in reviewing state laws. The conservative justices have preferred to leave state policies in place; however, it is not evident that this restraint reflects a general commitment to judicial deference toward state policy decisions. The more liberal justices on the Court have continued to cast votes to invalidate state laws, but their ability to build a majority coalition to actually strike down state laws has been hindered.[20] Since the turn of the twenty-first century, the Supreme Court has struck down state laws at a historically low rate that has not been seen since before the Civil War.

Table 7-1: Cases per Annum Invalidating Federal Statutes, 1954–2018

	All Invalidations	Notable Provisions of "Landmark" Statutes	In Whole	In Part	Less than Nine Years Old	More than Nine Years Old
Warren Court	2.57	1.07	0.93	1.54	1.07	1.50
Burger Court	3.17	0.33	1.89	1.28	1.39	1.94
Rehnquist Court	3.63	0.68	1.47	2.16	1.74	1.89
Roberts Court	2.08	0.46	1.46	0.62	0.69	1.39

The Court's record in reviewing the constitutionality of federal legislation tells an entirely different story. The Court has struck down federal laws at a relatively steady pace that has generally exceeded the Warren Court's rate of federal invalidations. Even as the Court was easing up on the states, it was going harder on Congress. That effort peaked in the late Rehnquist Court in the 1990s, and thus far, the Roberts Court has drawn back to a pace of federal invalidations that only barely exceeds that of the Roosevelt Court after 1937. As table 7-1 illustrates, the Burger and Rehnquist Courts were more activist in striking down federal statutory provisions than any Court since the Taft and Hughes Courts. The Roberts Court, however, is perhaps the least active Court of the modern era in terms of nullifying statutes. To a remarkable degree, the justices of the Roberts Court have preferred to fill their docket with nonconstitutional cases and have left the development of constitutional law largely to the lower federal courts and the state courts. It remains to be seen whether Anthony Kennedy's departure from the Court results in a reinvigorated conservative majority that is more willing to strike down legislation or cements the Roberts Court's basic inclination to allow voters and politicians to do what they will.

The recent history of divided government and polarized political parties has left its mark on the Court. The US Supreme Court has become not only more conservative since the departure of Earl Warren but also more fractured. The internal fissures on the Court have been particularly evident in the context of judicial review. The justices are deeply divided among themselves about the best way to interpret and apply the Constitution, just as other political elites are divided on a host of policy issues.

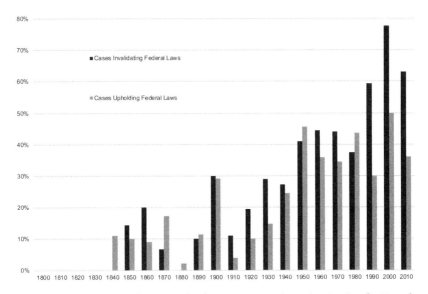

Figure 7-2: Percentage of Cases with Three or More Dissenting Justices by Decade, 1800–2018

This division on the Court is evident in the number of published dissents filed by the justices. Figure 7-2 tracks the number of cases in which three or more justices dissented from the majority judgment in a case. The cases are divided into those in which the majority voted to strike down or limit congressional power on constitutional grounds and those in which the majority voted to uphold congressional authority against a constitutional claim. One important qualification is that the Court was once guided by the notion that dissents should be rare. Justices who disagreed with the majority often expressed their dissenting views only in private and reserved published dissents for particularly serious occasions. That norm broke down in the early twentieth century, and justices are no longer reluctant to voice their disagreements; in fact, they often write individual opinions elaborating their views even when they largely agree with the majority's judgment.

Even within the modern context in which disagreements on the bench are publicized rather than hidden, the Court of the past three decades stands out. When it comes to striking down laws of Congress, that Court is not characterized by general agreement among the justices with some idiosyncratic dissenters. That Court is riven into distinct ideological wings, with a sizable number of justices persistently disagreeing with the judgment of the majority. If the Court in the early nineteenth century wanted to present a united front, especially on such momentous occasions when it nullified the work of the national legislature, the modern Court has presented a public portrait of deep, perhaps irreconcilable, division on fundamental issues of governance.

Disagreement among the justices has been noticeably different in cases invalidating versus upholding statutes. Significant dissent has been much less likely when the Court upholds congressional power (however, even in those cases, the Court in the first decade of the twenty-first century was remarkably divided). When the Court accedes to congressional authority, it often does so with relatively little dissent (at least compared with the Warren and Burger Courts). When the majority seeks to restrict congressional power, however, the justices are often divided, and the shift of only one or two votes might have salvaged the statute. Even the Court of the 1930s was not so narrowly divided when it struck down acts of Congress. There are still a sizable number of cases in which the justices are in general agreement that Congress has overstepped the bounds of the Constitution, but those cases are not nearly as common as they were even thirty years ago.

The contemporary Court is notable not only for being polarized but also for being volatile. In addition to having justices on both the right and the left, the Court has swing justices in the center who regularly join one wing or the other to form a majority coalition in constitutional cases. The existence of centrist swing justices is nothing new. Part of what distinguishes the contemporary Court from Courts in the twentieth century is that the number of centrist justices is small. The Taft and Burger Courts had centrist blocs, with several justices willing to hear arguments from both the left and right wings. The Rehnquist and Roberts Courts, by contrast, have been balanced on a knife's edge, with a single centrist justice listening to large blocs of justices occupying the two wings. (On occasion, the justices defy these groupings and shuffle their alignments, but most often, and across a wide range of constitutional cases, they tend to vote together in fairly predictable patterns.) Kennedy's departure might well reduce the Court's volatility, but it seems unlikely to reduce its polarization. The conservatives might find a narrow but stable majority, leading Justices Clarence Thomas and Samuel Alito to write fewer dissents and Justices Elena Kagan and Sonia Sotomayor to write more. The political Left often cheered decisions coming from the Rehnquist and Rob-

Table 7-2: Ideological Direction of Dissents in Cases Invalidating Federal Statutes, 1970–2018

	Dissents from the Right (%)	Dissents from the Left (%)
Burger Court	55	30
Rehnquist Court	54	54
Roberts Court	63	47

erts Courts. With Kennedy's departure, Democrats might find themselves more consistently unhappy with the Roberts Court.

Given the volatility of the contemporary Court, it cannot simply be classified as conservative, at least when it comes to evaluating the constitutionality of federal legislation. If the Court were simply polarized with a narrow but stable conservative majority, dissents would always come from the left wing, and votes to strike down federal statutes would always come from the right wing. Table 7-2 offers one perspective on the composition of coalitions to invalidate federal legislation. The table tracks whether one of the most conservative justices (on the right) or one of the most liberal justices (on the left) cast a dissenting vote in each case in which the majority voted to strike down a federal statute (that is, the dissenters would have preferred to uphold congressional power). Some cases involve a small number of dissents, so the coalition voting to strike down the statute is necessarily ideologically diverse. But it is informative to know whether those who object to striking down a law hail from the right or the left. In some cases, the dissenters might include justices from both ideological extremes; in others, the more extreme justices might find themselves in agreement and in the majority. Thus, the percentage of cases with dissents from the right and the left do not simply total 100 percent.

As table 7-2 illustrates, the Court since the Warren era cannot simply be characterized as conservative when it comes to striking down federal laws. Indeed, since 1969, the dissenting votes in cases invalidating federal statutes have been slightly more likely to come from the right wing of the Court than from the left wing. The frustrated advocates for congressional power have been at least as likely to come from the right as from the left, and by implication, the decision to narrow congressional authority has frequently included the most liberal members of the Court. In short, it has often been William Rehnquist and Antonin Scalia voting to uphold congressional power, and it has often been William Brennan and Ruth Bader Ginsburg voting to strike down federal laws. It is certainly true that swing justices such as Sandra Day O'Connor and Anthony Kennedy have been essential members of any coalition to strike down a law, and they were almost always represented in the invalidating majority. But they were swing justices precisely because they often joined the left wing of the Court to strike down a federal law over the objections of the right wing of the Court. The contemporary Court has struck down essentially all the laws that Kenney and O'Connor wanted to strike down, but in doing so, it has often struck down laws that either Scalia or Ginsburg would have upheld.

Of course, as figure 7-2 indicates, the Court has frequently upheld laws that a sizable number of justices would have preferred to strike down. Although the size of those dissenting coalitions has generally been smaller than the number of dissents in cases striking down laws, they still reflect a significant number of instances in which some justices would have preferred to further restrict Congress. Those dissents are indicative of where at least some of the pressure for greater judicial activism comes from on the Court.[21] If those dissenting justices could have found just a few more allies, they would have been able to strike down more and different laws. Since the 1950s, the dissenting votes in such cases have come primarily from the left wing of the Court. Thus, the wing of Douglas, Brennan, Stevens, and Sotomayor has been looking for a fifth vote to strike down more laws and not quite finding it. The conservative influence on the Court has been felt as much, or more, in the federal legislation that has survived constitutional scrutiny as in the provisions that have been struck down. If this pattern holds after Kennedy's departure from the bench, the Roberts Court will continue to strike down relatively few laws, and Sotomayor will frequently be writing dissents and complaining that the Court is too deferential to legislative policy choices. Democrats might be consistently unhappy with the Roberts Court, but their unhappiness might be driven by cases in which the conservatives are upholding legislative action rather than striking it down.[22]

The Burger Court

The Supreme Court after the departure of Chief Justice Earl Warren was often known as the Nixon Court, and the moniker is not inappropriate. The

Court was significantly reconstituted by Nixon's four appointees. Moreover, the Nixon Court reflected what Mark Tushnet has aptly called the "country club Republicanism" that prevailed before the Reagan revolution and the success of a self-conscious conservative legal movement in influencing a Republican White House.[23] It was a Court in which Kennedy-appointed Byron White and Eisenhower-appointed Potter Stewart held the balance of power, and Nixon-appointed William Rehnquist earned the nickname the "Lone Ranger" for his frequent solo dissents. Coalitions to strike down laws were generally built from the left. For a time in the 1970s, conservatives like Rehnquist were regularly dissenting when the Court struck down a federal law, while liberals like Brennan chafed at their inability to convince Stewart and White to strike down even more laws. Those numbers began to balance as Warren Burger was nearing the end of his tenure on the Court.

In the 1968 presidential election, former vice president and Republican candidate Richard Nixon and former Alabama governor and American Independent candidate George Wallace often competed in their denunciations of the Warren Court. Opinion polls showed that the public was worried about rising street crime, and the candidates responded by tying the Supreme Court to crime statistics and promising a federal fix. With Earl Warren's seat at stake, the election was in part a referendum on the future of the Warren Court, and the Court was not faring well. Although Wallace made a remarkable showing for an independent candidate, Nixon came to office with the promise to appoint justices who cared about crime victims more than criminals and who understood how to help the "peace forces" restore law and order.

Nixon's goals in making Supreme Court appointments were primarily political. He wanted to fulfill his campaign promises by appearing to be tough on crime, and he wanted to reward his hard-won voters in the white South. He followed Eisenhower's example rather than Kennedy's or Johnson's by picking candidates with judicial experience rather than political connections, hoping to work his way around a solid Democratic majority in the Senate. His first choice was easy, since Warren Burger was one of the most prominent Republican circuit court judges in the country and a vocal critic of the criminal justice decisions of the Warren Court. Subsequent choices proved more difficult. Nixon's effort to find an acceptable southerner for the Court ran aground not once but twice. Harry Blackmun had the advantage of being a personal friend of Burger's, reliable on criminal justice issues, and a safe nominee for the Senate, but he veered left over the course of his tenure. Lewis Powell was a well-credentialed southern Democrat, and William Rehnquist had been a loyal soldier for the administration as head of the Office of Legal Counsel. Nixon's ability to replace two liberals and two relative conservatives on the Warren Court with two moderates and two conservatives moved the Court to the right, but it did not set up the constitutional revolution that some expected. Gerald Ford was in no position to fight over a Supreme Court vacancy, but replacing the maverick liberal William O. Douglas with the establishment Republican John Paul Stevens likewise shrank the liberal wing of the Burger Court and bolstered its moderate center. When Ronald Reagan honored his campaign pledge to name a woman (O'Connor) to the Court, conservative activists were disappointed that they were likely replacing an Eisenhower Republican with something less than a Reagan Republican. Of the six justices appointed to the Burger Court by Republican presidents, only Rehnquist was an unquestionable hero to movement conservatives, and only he had the will and skill to cross swords with William Brennan, but all six shifted the Court's center of gravity in a more conservative direction.[24]

The substantive constitutional issues on Nixon's checklist mattered primarily for judicial review of the states. Congressional power was little affected by the Warren Court's decisions on criminal justice, busing, obscenity, or school prayer, so Nixon's appointments to the Court had only indirect implications for the judicial review of Congress. A greater judicial skepticism about civil rights and civil liberties claims in general might loosen legislative authority a bit at the national level as well as at the state and local levels, but this proved to be only partly true. Even as Nixon and his successors were pledging to appoint more "strict constructionists" who would follow the example of Felix Frankfurter, giving legislatures "great leeway to write [the] laws" and being "very conservative in overthrowing a law passed by the elected representatives of the people at the State or Federal level," the Burger Court they helped construct was finding more constitutional flaws in federal legislation than its predecessor had.[25]

Rather than reversing course when it came to the constitutional review of federal legislation, the Burger Court built on and surpassed its predecessor. Although the Warren Court had charted some new doctrinal paths regarding speech and due process, the Burger Court did not spend its time working through the implications of the Court's decisions from the 1960s. The Burger Court took off on its own, recognizing new rights claims that created their own implications. In doing so, the justices sometimes constrained significant policies, but rather than returning again and again to a limited policy domain—as the Warren Court had done with domestic security and subversives—the Burger Court touched on a diffuse set of political concerns and generated less political backlash.

While some of these doctrinal departures were conceptually innovative and symbolically important, their immediate political and policy consequences were often fairly modest. In one set of cases, the Court limited congressional authority to restrict the flow of government benefits to various disfavored groups. As Warren was preparing to leave the Court, he filed a dissent in a case with greater significance for the states than for the federal government. The District of Columbia, like many states, imposed a residency requirement on those seeking public assistance, and in an opinion authored by Justice Brennan, the Court found that the required waiting period (generally one year) impermissibly separated residents into two classes and invidiously discriminated against new arrivals while discouraging citizens from traveling freely from state to state.[26] Two years later, the Court unanimously leveraged that result to rule that Congress could not authorize the states to impose lengthy waiting periods before aliens lawfully residing in the country could receive public welfare benefits.[27] Not long thereafter, the Court summarily affirmed a lower court ruling that Congress could not distinguish between legitimate and illegitimate children for purposes of disbursing Social Security benefits. Drawing on the Court's decisions regarding state-level policies, the district court had held that this was simply "invidious discrimination, unrelated to the purpose of the law and to any legitimate legislative consideration governing the Social Security Act."[28] The Court soon lifted restrictions on unconventional households' access to food stamps, finding that Congress's statutory distinctions to reduce fraud and shape familial relationships were simply "irrational."[29] Justice Brennan was particularly dismissive of one provision's stated aim to prevent "hippie communes" from drawing on the food stamp program, asserting that it was not a "legitimate governmental interest" to discriminate against hippies.[30] Congress could not use public assistance as an instrument to shape societal relations.

In another set of cases related to government benefits, the Court plucked out various statutory provisions that distinguished between men and women for relatively minor purposes. Finding that legislative discrimination on the basis of sex was constitutionally suspect and required relatively strong justifications was a big step. Application of that principle to federal law as it existed in the 1970s, however, was hardly earth shattering. In cases involving the most consequential distinctions between the sexes, the Court flinched. With only two dissenters, the Court in 1981 upheld the congressional requirement that only men register for the military draft, given Congress's "broad and sweeping" power in the context of national security.[31] The justices disagreed among themselves but still upheld the differential military rules for men and women for up-or-out advancement.[32] In less consequential cases (often argued by Ginsburg), the Court was willing to strike down federal discrimination between the sexes, such as in cases involving differential rules on allowances for military spouses or gender-based distinctions in Social Security and welfare benefits (all of which generally favored women).[33]

The Warren Court's decision in *Bolling v. Sharpe* to locate an equal protection constraint on Congress in the due process clause of the Fifth Amendment opened the door to a great deal of litigation. As the Court's Fourteenth Amendment jurisprudence expanded in the context of state and local actors, interested parties began to probe the degree to which Congress ran afoul of those constitutional principles as well. Although there were some exceptions, the Burger Court was reluctant to find that the national legislature was guilty of engaging in "invidious discrimination." If Congress made distinctions among different groups of Americans, the majority of the justices were prone to find those distinctions reasonable rather than ill intentioned.[34] Coalitions to uphold federal statutory provisions against such equal-protection challenges were often constructed on the right, over the dissents of the most left-leaning justices.

The Burger Court's consideration of First Amendment claims against congressional authority was more consequential and pregnant with future possibilities. Some of these cases were of relatively minor effect and fairly uncontroversial, such as when the Court concluded that a statutory ban on public assemblies on Capitol grounds was overbroad or that the discretionary authority of a military base commander could not bar protesters from a public street.[35] Similarly, the justices thought that postal regulations obstructing the delivery of pornographic materials were constitutionally problematic, as was a ban on the unsolicited mailing of advertisements for contraceptives.[36] Justice Thurgood Marshall wrote for a unanimous Court that commercial speech conveying "truthful information relevant to important social issues," as in the case of such advertisements, was entitled to strong First Amendment protections.[37] The conservative justices were in greater disagreement when the majority held that Congress could not prohibit "editorializing" by stations receiving grants from the Corporation for Public Broadcasting.[38] The Court could not "easily set aside such a considered congressional judgment," but only an unrestrained "judicial inquiry" could protect the freedom of the press "as a check on legislative power."[39]

The Burger Court's most important imposition of free-speech limits on Congress fractured the Court. In *Buckley v. Valeo*, a majority of the justices found that the Nixon-era Federal Election Campaign Act (FECA) had gone too far in restricting the avenues of political activism.[40] The initial 1971 statute had broad support and established a system of campaign contribution transparency, a public financing option, and the creation of political action committees. In 1970 President Nixon had successfully vetoed a bill that would have limited the amount candidates for federal office could spend on television and radio advertisements. The president thought the goal of "controlling political campaign expenditures" was a laudable one, but he fretted that such a targeted approach would leave myriad forms of campaign spending unregulated and, consequently, create an uneven playing field that favored incumbents and the already famous to the detriment of little-known challengers, who needed a free hand to gain name recognition and influence voters.[41] When signing the broader 1971 bill, Nixon praised it as a more comprehensive effort to control campaign expenditures. The Watergate scandal and the Nixon campaign's rather creative use of reelection funds drove Congress to amend FECA in 1974 and create the Federal Election Commission (FEC) and stronger campaign contribution and spending limits.

When a variety of individuals and organizations, including a presidential candidate, a US senator, the Libertarian Party, and the American Civil Liberties Union, sued to block implementation of the law, the lower courts mostly upheld the statute. The justices proved to be more skeptical of how Congress had exercised its authority and questioned whether its statutory scheme "invidiously discriminates against nonincumbent candidates and minor parties."[42] Drawing on a range of opinions handed down by the New

Deal and Warren Courts, the Burger Court emphasized that FECA's regulation of "political expression" and the ability to organize for political action
and persuade citizens on public issues was at the very heart of the liberty protected by the First Amendment. Although, just a few years earlier, the Court
had upheld the congressional prohibition on the destruction of draft cards as
only incidentally restricting protesters' ability to make a symbolic statement
by burning them, the justices were not convinced that the "expenditure of
money" on political campaigns could be "equated with such conduct as destruction of a draft card."[43] The regulation of campaign money did not just
incidentally restrict speech while advancing some unrelated goal; it was expressly designed to suppress political communication. Money is intimately
connected to speech because "every means of communicating ideas in today's mass society requires the expenditure of money," and any restriction
on money "necessarily reduces the quantity of expression by restricting the
number of issues discussed, the depth of their exploration, and the size of the
audience reached." FECA's spending limits effectively "exclude all citizens
and groups except candidates, political parties, and the institutional press
from any significant use of the most effective modes of communication."
The campaign contribution limits, however, did not hamper anyone's ability
to communicate their message, so long as the limits did not prevent candidates "from amassing the resources necessary for effective advocacy."[44] Congress could regulate how money was funneled to politicians, but it could not
limit how anyone communicated with the public about matters of general
concern. Some of the justices would have gone further and struck down the
contribution limits as well, since, as Chief Justice Burger thought, such limits
were likely to "put an effective ceiling on the amount of political activity and
debate that the Government will permit to take place." Only Justice White
was willing to defer to the judgment of the "seasoned professionals" in Congress that the "communicative efforts" of candidates would not be "crippled
by the expenditure limits." It was more important to reassure the public that
federal elections were not "purely and simply a function of money" and that
federal offices were not "bought and sold."[45]

A decade later, the justices had drifted a bit on the issue, but not enough
to upset the Court's original ruling. As cases developed after *Buckley*, however, the justices began to diverge in their thinking about campaign spending. Liberal justices who generally favored unrestricted free speech proved

increasingly hostile to unrestricted spending on campaign speech, while conservative justices who were more accepting of material inequalities in other contexts were likewise comfortable with unequal spending on political speech.[46] The Presidential Campaign Election Act of 1971 provided a system of public support for presidential campaigns, and candidates accepting public funds were required to limit their campaign spending. One component of that overall scheme was a prohibition on campaign expenditures in support of a candidate by independent political committees. This was in keeping with the general goal of some campaign finance reformers to equalize the playing field for major political candidates by establishing both a floor for campaign spending (through public financing) and a ceiling (through caps on campaign expenditures). As Scot Powe noted, the imposition of spending caps "carried some startling consequences," such as criminalizing "the purchase of a single quarter-page advertisement for or against a candidate in a major newspaper."[47] When the Democratic Party complained to the FEC that the National Conservative Political Action Committee (NCPAC), led by the enterprising conservative activist Paul Weyrich, was planning to run ads in support of the reelection of President Ronald Reagan, the FEC sought to suppress any advertising by NCPAC. A majority of the Court extended the logic of *Buckley* to cover such expenditures by NCPAC, finding that individuals organized as committees possessed the same First Amendment freedoms as individuals acting on their own. Justices Brennan and Marshall, however, departed from the *Buckley* majority and joined White in dissent. As Marshall wrote separately, "I have come to believe that the limitations on independent expenditures challenged in [*Buckley*] and here are justified by the congressional interests in promoting 'the reality and appearance of equal access to the political arena.'"[48] The liberal justices were temporarily brought back into the fold when the FEC told the nonprofit corporation Massachusetts Citizens for Life that it could not editorialize in its newsletter that readers should vote "pro-life." In this context, Justice Brennan wrote for the Court that any worries about "the corrosive influence of concentrated corporate wealth" were inapt when dealing with a nonprofit created precisely to aggregate individual resources in order to more effectively advocate on behalf of favored political causes. Such a corporation was "formed to disseminate political ideas, not to amass capital," and Congress could not exclude such voices from the "political marketplace."[49]

A different component of the *Buckley* decision also pointed to the Burger Court's growing interest in issues of constitutional structure. To fairly regulate campaign spending (that is, fairly from the perspective of incumbent legislators), Congress devised an unusual institutional design. The FEC was charged with record keeping, investigation, rule-making, and enforcement of the new campaign finance laws. It consisted of six voting members evenly divided between Republicans and Democrats, with two appointed by the president pro tempore of the Senate, two by the Speaker of the House, and two by the president. All six commissioners had to be confirmed by a majority vote in each chamber of Congress. The Court balked. Congress had vested the commissioners with powers of federal officers, but it had not followed the procedure identified in the Constitution for appointing and confirming officers. The commission as constituted could not constitutionally perform an administrative function.[50] In amending the act, Congress retained the commission's powers and returned to a more traditional model of presidential appointment and Senate confirmation (but with a requirement that the members be equally divided between the two parties).

When drafting the amendments to the Federal Election Campaign Act, Congress included a new and potentially troublesome provision giving either chamber a legislative veto over FEC regulations. Although he signed the bill into law, President Gerald Ford warned that the legislative veto was unconstitutional, and he directed the attorney general "to challenge the constitutionality of this provision at the earliest possible opportunity."[51] So-called legislative vetoes that gave Congress, or its components, the authority to override executive rule-making had become increasingly common in the twentieth century, as Congress looked for tools to control the rapidly growing administrative state. While delegating substantial discretion to the executive branch, Congress hoped to retain some control over how that discretion was used by reserving the right to overturn executive decisions. As one congressman later remarked, "At the heart of this issue of congressional veto of administrative rules and regulations is the question: Who makes the laws in this country—the elected Representatives of the people or the unelected bureaucrats?"[52] Presidents objected that such veto mechanisms effectively allowed Congress to rewrite the underlying statute without going through the constitutional process of drafting a new law (and getting it past a possible presidential veto). If administrative agencies were simply implementing statutory requirements when they issued regulations, then the nullification of those subsidiary rules was, in effect, amending the statute itself. From a presidential perspective, Congress was either asserting an executive power to decide how to administer statutes, or it was asserting a legislative power to draft new legislation without adhering to the procedural requirements of passing a bill into law. Acting attorney general William P. Rogers had advised President Eisenhower, for example, that the legislative veto "tends to undermine the President's position as the responsible Chief Executive."[53]

The challenge to the legislative veto came before the Court several years later, and in a different context. The Immigration and Naturalization Act of 1952 authorized either chamber of Congress to nullify decisions by the attorney general to allow deportable aliens to remain in the country. Jagdish Rai Chadha, an alien who had overstayed his student visa, was found to be deportable by an immigration judge under established law, but the judge exercised the power delegated to him by the attorney general to suspend the deportation, on the grounds that it would cause extreme hardship. Congress received a report of the suspension, and after an extended delay, it reviewed a batch of similar cases. The House of Representatives, without a recorded vote, overturned the suspension order in a handful of cases, including Chadha's. Chadha appealed to the courts, and the Supreme Court eventually held that the legislative veto provision was unconstitutional (although the justices disagreed among themselves about the appropriate implications for Chadha). In an opinion by Chief Justice Burger, the Court adopted the long-standing presidential position that the legislative veto improperly sought to take an action with legal effect by means of a mere resolution that did not satisfy the lawmaking requirements laid out in the Constitution. It was the Court's duty to resist the "hydraulic pressure inherent within each of the separate Branches to exceed the outer limits of its power."[54] As a formal matter, the Chadha case had sweeping consequences for the many legislative veto provisions that had been embedded in federal statutes over the course of the twentieth century. As a practical matter, Congress has continued to write new provisions into law and has found other means to influence executive decision-making.[55]

Shortly before leaving the bench, Chief Justice Burger also authored the Court's opinion undoing a key provision of the Gramm-Rudman-Hollings Deficit Control Act of 1985. With many people both in and out of Congress complaining that federal politicians did not have the discipline to control growing deficits and balance the federal budget, and with pressure for a federal constitutional amendment mandating balanced budgets building, federal lawmakers looked for an innovative solution. The bipartisan Deficit Control Act set a multiyear timetable for reducing the deficit and empowered the comptroller general to impose automatic spending cuts if Congress failed to meet those statutory benchmarks. The comptroller general heads the General Accountability Office, a legislative agency that investigates how federal funds are spent. The comptroller general is nominated by the president (from a list of choices provided by the congressional leadership) and confirmed by the Senate, but he or she can be removed only for cause by a joint resolution of Congress. As Congress recognized when adopting the Deficit Control Act, entrusting the comptroller with the power to sequester federal funds posed a potential constitutional problem. The statute included a fallback provision in case the sequestration procedure were struck down, and as soon as the bill became law, Democratic representative Mike Synar filed suit to have it declared unconstitutional. The justices overwhelmingly rejected Congress's creative approach to the problem of persistent deficits. The founders had created a "vigorous Legislative Branch and a separate and wholly independent Executive Branch," and the Court thought it basic to that constitutional scheme that Congress cannot supervise the officers who execute the laws.[56] The structure of the comptroller's office rendered it inappropriate for him to have a hand in administering the laws. The statute was revised in light of the Court's action, shifting the sequestration power to the Office of Management and Budget and clearer presidential control, but with only modest effects on the deficit.

The Burger Court's concern with structural issues extended to problems of federalism as well. Most notably, at the outset of Burger's tenure, he found himself in dissent on a fractured Court that was reviewing the constitutionality of the Voting Rights Act Amendments of 1970. The law lowered the voting age to eighteen and banned literacy tests and state residency requirements in presidential elections. A liberal coalition of justices upheld most of these provisions and would have been content to uphold the law in its entirety. A bare majority of the justices was unwilling to authorize Congress to set the voting age in state and local elections. The Court thought that although Congress had long exercised the power to determine the qualifications of voters in federal elections under its constitutional authority to regulate the time, place, and manner of holding federal elections, that power did not extend to state and local elections, and the majority saw no evidence that the established voting age denied anyone the right to vote on the basis of race.[57] With the streets and college campuses filled with youthful protesters, Congress quickly sent a constitutional amendment to the states for ratification, lowering the voting age across the board. Within months of the Court's decision, it was overturned by the adoption of the Twenty-Sixth Amendment.

The Burger Court's other notable foray into enforcing federalism-based limits on congressional authority was only slightly more enduring. With the Republicans weakened by the Watergate scandal, labor unions made a concerted push for a minimum wage increase in 1973. Like earlier measures, the wage bill included provisions extending federal labor regulations to groups of workers left out of the original New Deal statute, including federal, state, and local government employees. The extension to government workers was a sidelight, but it was not without controversy. The administration, and Republicans in general, opposed the expansion. Secretary of Labor Peter Brennan advised Congress that the extension was "too great an interference with State prerogatives" and was likely to have a "disruptive impact on many State civil service systems"; moreover, "the additional costs could overburden many small governmental units."[58] The National League of Cities focused its attention on how federal overtime rules might disrupt municipal emergency services.[59] The bill's sponsors made some concessions for these workers, but in general, they contended that the government should "apply to itself the same standard it applies to private employees" and asserted that the financial effect of the new statutory requirements would be minimal. Congress was confident that it had the authority to regulate such employees under the Court's post–New Deal decisions, given that "the activities of government at all levels affect commerce."[60]

The National League of Cities immediately orchestrated a federal lawsuit to block implementation of the new labor rules. The lower courts felt constrained by an earlier Warren Court ruling involving a 1966 extension of the Fair Labor Standards Act to public hospital and schools. In that context, the Court had emphasized that the federal labor rules interfered only minimally with governmental functions and that Congress had full authority to regulate governments when they are "engaging in economic activities that are validly regulated by the Federal Government when engaged in by private persons." The Court would not "carve up the commerce clause to protect enterprises indistinguishable in their effect on commerce from private businesses, simply because those enterprises happen to be run by the states for the benefit of their citizens."[61] The judges noted that the Court's case dealt with state activities that "compete with private institutions" and not with "essential governmental functions" such as law enforcement, but they thought that distinction was best addressed by the Supreme Court.[62]

When the case reached the Court, Justice Rehnquist won a rare victory on the Burger Court. A narrow majority struck down the extension of federal labor regulations to state employees and overruled the earlier Warren Court decision. Writing for the Court, Rehnquist argued that the federal structure certainly did mean that there were carve-outs to Congress's Article I powers. In particular, there were limits on the "authority of Congress to regulate the activities of the States as States." The states had to be free from congressional interference "to structure integral operations in areas of traditional governmental functions," and the federal labor regulations would have to give way to that degree.[63] Rehnquist commanded only four votes, however. Justice Blackmun provided a fifth with a separate concurrence in which he insisted that the Court's opinion was best understood as laying out a "balancing approach" that weighed competing state and federal interests on a case-by-case basis. Justice Brennan, in dissent, accused Rehnquist of abandoning constitutional principles recognized by the Court since the tenure of Chief Justice John Marshall.[64] Less than a decade later, Blackmun had soured on *National League of Cities*. He switched his vote to join the liberal wing of the Court, overturned Rehnquist's "traditional governmental functions" exception to congressional power, and instructed the states to lobby Congress rather than litigate in the courts if they wanted to protect their interests against federal aggrandizement.[65] In dissent, Rehnquist contented himself with merely noting that state immunities never should have been understood as a balancing test and expressing confidence that his views would "in time again command the support of a majority of this Court."[66]

Despite its heightened activity in curtailing congressional authority under the Constitution, the Burger Court was even more active in upholding federal laws against constitutional challenge. These cases often required the conservative justices to override the desires of their more liberal colleagues and reflected the priorities of the Nixon Republicans. Whereas the liberal wing of the Court would have found the Hatch Act's prohibition on federal employees taking an "active part . . . [in] political campaigns" overly broad, the majority thought the rules were "sufficiently clear" to pass constitutional muster.[67] Similarly, the conservatives were content with a congressional power to prohibit the importation of obscene materials, while the liberals worried about "Federal Government censorship."[68] The conservatives accepted Congress's exclusion of two-time felons from federal drug treatment programs, thought the Uniform Code of Military Justice could prohibit "conduct unbecoming an officer and a gentleman" without being impermissibly vague, found that the Federal Communications Commission could constitutionally regulate the broadcast of a George Carlin monologue, and believed that the National Labor Relations Board could prohibit secondary picketing.[69] On occasion, however, the conservative justices were unable to pull together a majority to strike a statutory provision, such as the federal energy regulations that Justice O'Connor thought "conscript[ed] state utility commissions into the national bureaucratic army" or the federal age discrimination regulations that Chief Justice Burger thought would "usurp this fundamental state function" of selecting state employees to perform essential governmental functions.[70] To act on their constitutional sensibilities to protect the states from perceived congressional overreach, Rehnquist and O'Connor needed reinforcements that Presidents Nixon and Ford had not provided.

The Rehnquist Court

Presidents Ronald Reagan and George H. W. Bush provided those reinforcements. The resulting Court was not firmly under conservative control, but it was more frequently open to the arguments of the most conservative justices. Rehnquist's elevation to the bench had been something of a fluke, but he had emerged as an ideological stalwart on the Court. O'Connor was distrusted by movement conservatives and was considered unlikely to strike a blow against the right to abortion the Court had recognized just a few years before. She was, perhaps, the kind of justice President Nixon might have nominated on a good day, if she had won a seat on the Arizona Court of Appeals in 1969 rather than 1979. But if President Reagan were to fulfill his campaign pledge to appoint the first woman to the US Supreme Court, O'Connor was likely the best conservatives could hope for.

Rehnquist had played an important role in encouraging the growth of the conservative legal movement that flocked to the Reagan administration. Nixon had pledged to appoint strict constructionists to the Court, but the label had little content. Rehnquist gave some substance to the political label, emphasizing that judges should avoid making "an end run around popular government" by imposing from the bench "some other set of values for those which may be derived from the language and intent of the framers."[71] As an associate justice on the Burger Court, Rehnquist was frequently convinced that the majority was simply imposing its own values on the American public. He rarely joined his colleagues in striking down legislation, and a large percentage of his opinions were written in dissent.[72] Given that track record, it is no surprise that the attorneys leading the judicial selection process in the 1980s thought Rehnquist "was quite clearly the justice who most represented the judicial views of the Reagan administration."[73] He was, from their perspective, an "intellectual giant" and thus the perfect candidate for the center seat on the Court when Chief Justice Warren Burger retired in 1986.[74] Senator Edward Kennedy castigated Rehnquist as "outside the mainstream," but the Republican majority on the Senate Judiciary Committee countered that Rehnquist "is very much in the mainstream of the current Court." He was no longer the lone dissenter he had frequently been in the 1970s. As chief justice, he was nearly always in the majority.[75]

With Rehnquist leading from above, conservative lawyers were organizing from below. The Federalist Society was founded as a student group in a handful of elite law schools in 1982 to provide an alternative source of intellectual activity to that offered by the largely liberal faculty. It grew to become an essential network of conservative law students, attorneys, and legal academics that provided organization and intellectual capital for the conservative legal movement.[76] Two law professors and veterans of the Nixon and Ford administrations, Robert Bork and Antonin Scalia, were developing an elaborate theory of constitutional jurisprudence that emphasized judicial fidelity to the original meaning of the constitutional text. Longtime Reagan associate Edwin Meese moved from the White House to the post of attorney general in 1984 and became a high-profile advocate of the "new vision of the Constitution."[77]

The Reagan administration was unusually disciplined in its focus on policy rather than political goals when selecting judges. Like no administration since FDR's, it was committed to a set of constitutional values and understood that the staffing of the judiciary was a critical means of advancing them. Burger's departure from the Court made way not only for Rehnquist to assume the duties of chief justice but also for Antonin Scalia to take Rehnquist's seat. Robert Bork was the obvious next choice to fill a vacancy on the Supreme Court, and the announcement of Lewis Powell's retirement in 1987 created that opening. A conservative Democrat appointed by Nixon, Powell was a member of the centrist faction of the Burger Court, and a Bork confirmation would expand the ranks of the Court's right wing. Crucially, however, the Republicans had lost control of the Senate in the 1986 elections. The majority that had confirmed the nominations of Rehnquist and Scalia was gone, and Senator Kennedy found more traction when he took to the floor to denounce Bork as outside the mainstream. After an extended and unusually bitter battle, Bork was defeated in a near party-line vote. The White House eventually turned to Anthony Kennedy, a "respectable conservative" with no attraction to "eccentric and rigid theories of jurisprudence" of the type advanced by Scalia and Bork, and Kennedy was rewarded with a quick and uncontested confirmation.[78] President George H. W. Bush likewise had to manage a Senate controlled by the Democrats, but he had an even greater opportunity to shift the balance of power on the Court. Liberal stalwarts and Warren Court veterans William Brennan and Thurgood Marshall both left the bench during the Bush presidency. Determined to avoid a confirmation fight, the administration chose to gamble on "stealth justice" David Souter (who had served on the New Hampshire Supreme Court but had generated no paper trail of controversial rulings) and the more clearly conservative but little-known African American Clarence Thomas. President Bill Clinton had a friendly Senate, but he too preferred to avoid an extended confirmation fight as the administration focused on health care reform. Replacing centrists White and Blackmun with two reliable liberals, Ruth Bader Ginsburg and Stephen Breyer, Clinton completed the lineup of the Rehnquist Court that would serve together for the next decade.

The centrist justices of the Burger Court were all gone, and their seats were now occupied by justices who identified more strongly with the ideological wings of the Court. The broad majorities that had regularly formed under Chief Justice Burger were much harder to cobble together, and the more polarized Rehnquist Court often had to rely on narrow majorities. The appointments of Kennedy and Thomas proved to be particularly consequential. Kennedy, along with O'Connor, held a pivotal vote. He was willing to abandon his more conservative colleagues on issues both large and small and join coalitions built from the left.[79] But unlike Souter, who drifted rather firmly to the left, Kennedy still shared many of the commitments of the more conservative justices and could frequently be won over. As a consequence, Kennedy was the indispensable man on the Court and voted with the majority in more than 90 percent of the cases invalidating federal statutory provisions. Kennedy was not unusually activist in his sensibilities; nor was he more likely than the other justices to vote to strike down a law. It was simply very difficult to assemble a majority to strike a law without bringing Kennedy into the fold. The Court under Chief Justices Rehnquist and Roberts struck down federal laws as often as Kennedy wanted to, but no more often.[80]

Thomas, by contrast, embedded himself firmly in the right wing of the Court. His addition to the Court provided a crucial fifth vote for a host of conservative decisions that were not possible when his seat was occupied by Thurgood Marshall. Justice Brennan had long introduced his law clerks to "the most important rule in constitutional law": the ability to get five votes.[81] With Thomas on the Court, Rehnquist could finally count to five with some regularity. Moreover, Thomas has been characterized "as the best consumer of Federalist Society intellectual capital on the Supreme Court."[82] Thomas does not simply cast a reliable conservative vote. Although he has not often written the opinion for the Court, he has distinguished himself by writing separately to pursue unmoderated explorations of conservative constitutional principles. Thomas has been a less visible advocate of originalist theory than Scalia was, but he has been a fearless exponent of its application on the bench.[83] In his time on the Court, Thomas has been far less likely than Kennedy to vote with the majority striking down a federal law. Indeed, he has been only somewhat more likely to be in such a majority than Ginsburg. Both Thomas and Ginsburg are constrained in their choices of how to get to five votes, and as a result, they have been more frequently disappointed than Kennedy. But both Thomas *and* Ginsburg have found ample opportunities to join coalitions invalidating federal laws since they joined the Court.[84]

The Rehnquist Court's signature exercise of judicial review of federal statutes came in a set of cases examining the relationship between federal and state authority. Together, federalism cases accounted for nearly a quarter of Rehnquist Court decisions restricting the scope of federal statutes under the Constitution. They generated more dissents and narrower majorities than the remainder of Rehnquist Court cases striking down statutory provisions, and they frequently featured the same five justices building a coalition from the right wing of the Court: Rehnquist, Thomas, Scalia, O'Connor, and Kennedy. If those cases had been removed from the docket, the Rehnquist Court would have handed down invalidating cases at an annual rate much closer to that of the Warren Court, rather than at the highest rate since the battles over the New Deal. The Rehnquist Court's interest in federalism had not been significantly prefigured by the Burger Court, which largely ignored such issues, with the notable exception of Associate Justice Rehnquist's short-lived victory in *National League of Cities*. Nor has it been echoed in quite the same way by the Roberts Court, which has maintained the same basic commitment to federalism values but has applied them in only a handful of cases. Above all, these federalism cases gave the Rehnquist Court its fearsome reputation as an extraordinarily activist and conservative Court.

The environment for the Rehnquist Court's federalism revival was a particularly favorable one. Federalism constraints on Congress had been nearly banished from the constitutional system in the New Deal revolution. To effectively grapple with the economic forces of the early twentieth century, Congress had to be unshackled, and the states had to be displaced as the primary regulator of economic activity and the ultimate guarantor of social welfare. There was no going back, but the pressure to centralize had significantly lessened by the late twentieth century. Public trust in federal institutions had taken a beating, and emergent political problems no longer demanded national solutions with the urgency felt by the Progressives and New Dealers.[85] As a consequence, pro-decentralization judicial decisions were likely to be less costly to other political actors. The Court's effective range of politically acceptable action on federalism expanded as the drive for centralization on the part of other political actors lessened.

The normative environment with respect to federalism had also changed. Earlier in the century, the states had suffered from a perception of corruption, incompetence, and racism. By the end of the century, Congress was held in low regard and distrusted by the public and elites alike. As detailed by Mitchell Pickerill and Cornell Clayton, the Republican Party of the 1980s and 1990s embraced a commitment to ideas of "fixed federalism" that emphasized the hard boundaries on federal power, while the Democratic Party continued to advocate for a form of "flexible federalism" that focused on intergovernmental cooperation and pragmatic adjustment of federal-state relations.[86] Ronald Reagan made "fundamental federalism principles" a core part of the philosophical identity of his administration, the conservative movement, and the Republican Party.[87] Moreover, the courts were understood to play a particular role in articulating and enforcing those principles. Conservative politicians, lawyers, and scholars rejected the "political safeguards of federalism" celebrated by the New Dealers and their heirs and instead developed the "judicial safeguards of federalism."[88] Judicially enforced federalism as a system of limiting national governmental power became one of the animating ideals of the modern conservative legal movement.[89] State governments and conservative public law interest groups became interested in litigating such constitutional claims.[90]

The Rehnquist Court proved to be a willing vehicle for this new constitutional activism. The votes necessary to do so came through replacement rather than conversion. The Court's renewed interest in federalism is clearly part of the Reagan legacy. Of the five justices most often in the federalism majorities, three were Reagan appointees, and Rehnquist was elevated to chief justice by Reagan. The fifth justice, Thomas, was appointed by George H. W. Bush and clearly reflected the Reagan-era's legal conservatism. Federalism was not a priority of the Nixon administration, and to the extent that Nixon's appointment strategy was concerned with ideology, the theme of "law and order" took priority. By contrast, Reagan's appointment strategy was tightly focused on jurisprudential considerations, including "deference to states in their spheres" and "recognition that the federal government is one of enumerated powers."[91] Judicial appointments were an important strategy for making conservative commitments to decentralization credible and effective. Whereas elected politicians were frequently buffeted by political forces encouraging them to compromise their putative constitutional principles, judges had more freedom to dedicate themselves to those principles.

The Court's jurisprudence reflected these different presidential concerns. The Burger Court was more sympathetic to the "peace forces" and less sympathetic to criminal defendants, as Nixon would have hoped. With the exception of Rehnquist, however, the Nixon justices had no special sympathy for states and localities on federalism issues. Chief Justice Burger, who agreed with Rehnquist on many constitutional issues, was no more likely to agree with Rehnquist on federalism issues than was archliberal Justice Brennan. Reagan and Bush appointed conservative justices, but they were also much more conservative on federalism than their predecessors. With a single exception, each of the justices appointed by Reagan and Bush were far more likely to vote with Rehnquist on federalism issues than was the justice they replaced. Souter, however, was no more likely to agree with Rehnquist on these issues than was his predecessor, Brennan. Notably, even Kennedy and O'Connor, the swing justices on the Rehnquist Court and the primary limiting factors on the conservative wing, were firmly aligned with Rehnquist in this particular area of law.[92] As a consequence, once Thomas—a significant exponent of conservative federalism principles in his own right—joined the Court in 1991, Rehnquist was able to make good on his promise in his dissent in *Garcia* and once again speak for a majority in limiting Congress's ability to interfere with the states.

As has generally been the case across American history, the Court's coalition partners did not dictate the details of the constitutional principles they hoped to see implemented by the Court. The Reagan coalition included a commitment to federalism-based limits on congressional power and to a judiciary empowered to enforce those limits. The conservative justices exercised agency in choosing whether to pursue those goals, how best to do so, and how to translate those general principles into concrete constitutional doctrine. In this, they received suggestions from allies ranging from the US solicitor general to state attorneys general to intellectual entrepreneurs such as think tanks and conservative movement lawyers, but the justices themselves put together the new federalism offensive.

The Court pursued its federalism offensive across several lines of attack with only loosely related constitutional doctrines. It did not attempt to directly reinvigorate *National League of Cities* and carve out a Tenth Amendment exception to congressional authority under the commerce clause. The Court instead approached the problem from several different angles.

Perhaps most notably, for the first time since the New Deal, the Court found that Congress had run past the boundaries of its authority under the interstate commerce clause. Justice Jackson had told his clerk that a law would henceforth be valid under the commerce clause so long as it did not fail the laugh test, and the Court had held to that view since 1937.[93] As a practical matter, Congress proceeded as if the commerce clause gave it plenary authority to adopt nearly any statute regulating activity within the country.[94] In *National League of Cities*, the Court tried to carve out an exception for some state-run enterprises. In *United States v. Lopez* in 1995, Rehnquist took a different tack. He simply tried to give teeth to Jackson's doctrine of asking "whether a rational basis existed for concluding that a regulated activity sufficiently affected interstate commerce." The majority thought the congressional ban on the possession of firearms within a school zone was just an ordinary "criminal statute that by its terms has nothing to do with 'commerce' or any economic enterprise, however broadly one might define those terms."[95] Unless "limitations of congressional authority" were to be "solely a matter of legislative grace," the Court should not be willing to sign off on the congressional exercise of "a general police power of the sort retained by the States."[96] The policy impact of the Court's actions was fairly modest, however, and readily circumvented.[97] When a more substantial challenge was raised to the Controlled Substances Act of 1970, Kennedy and Scalia defected from the federalism coalition and demonstrated the limits of the new commerce clause jurisprudence.[98]

In a separate line of cases, the Court also dusted off the Tenth Amendment as a substantive limit on congressional authority. Justice O'Connor took the lead in a pair of cases decided in 1991 and 1992 that rested on the implications of the Tenth Amendment and the structural backdrop of a federal system of government and at least echoed Rehnquist's analysis in *National League of Cities*. When considering the applicability of the Age Discrimination in Employment Act (ADEA) to state judges, O'Connor began by noting that, as "every schoolchild learns, our Constitution establishes a system of dual sovereignty between the States and the Federal Government," which requires recognizing the "substantial sovereign authority" of the states.[99] For the ADEA, O'Connor leaned on the "plain statement rule" to read the statute to recognize that necessary exceptions were compatible with "our constitutional scheme." In examining the Low-Level Radioactive Waste Policy Act, O'Connor was more direct in invalidating the provision requiring that states "take title" to waste produced within their borders. The Court objected to the effort to "'commandeer' state governments into the service of federal regulatory purposes."[100] Scalia deployed the anticommandeering principle in the more high-profile but mostly symbolic *Printz* case, invalidating the requirement that local law enforcement officers conduct federal background checks before gun purchases.[101]

By far the most numerous cases, and perhaps the most arcane, involved state sovereign immunity. In one of its earliest constitutional decisions, the Jay Court ruled that states could be sued in federal court by unpaid creditors.[102] The Court was quickly overruled by passage of the Eleventh Amendment, stating that the federal judicial power did not extend to suits by citizens of other states or foreign states against one of the states. Left unresolved was whether the Eleventh Amendment simply recognized a broad background principle of state sovereign immunity or whether it carved out a very narrow exception from the federal judicial power granted in Article III of the Constitution. A century later, the Fuller Court explained that the Eleventh Amendment was best understood as a confirmation of the constitutional assumption of state sovereign immunity from suit, a textual marker for a set of extratextual principles.[103] Surprisingly, the Rehnquist Court reinvigorated and expanded this line of doctrine that had long had little relevance and had generally been held in some disrepute. In particular, the Court held that Congress could not easily abrogate state sovereign immunity and authorize nonconsensual suits against the states for money. Having raised this argument, the Court was then pressed to fill in the details in a series of cases elaborating in what circumstances and in what venues Congress could and could not authorize suits against the states.[104] Since Congress had frequently authorized such suits, the Court's decisions had implications for a range of statutes. The Court took away one small but nontrivial tool Congress had used to implement federal policy against reluctant state governments, forcing Congress to rely more heavily on other instruments to effectuate its policies.

The most consequential of the Rehnquist federalism cases might have been those that reexamined the scope of congressional authority under section 5 of the Fourteenth Amendment, which empowers Congress "to enforce, by appropriate legislation, the provisions" of the amendment. It was under this provision that the Reconstruction Congress had passed several civil rights acts, and in a series of notable cases, the Waite Court found that Congress had gone beyond enforcing the requirements of the Fourteenth Amendment, thereby infringing on the rightful authority of the states.[105] The

Rehnquist Court's cases were far less fraught. From a weak position, Congress challenged the Court by adopting the Religious Freedom Restoration Act of 1993 (RFRA), attempting to overturn the Court's reinterpretation of religious freedom in a 1990 case.[106] When a church in Texas sought to rely on the RFRA to defy a local building restriction, the Court held that Congress could not redefine through its own legislation the rights to which religious individuals were entitled against the states. Justice Kennedy intoned:

> If Congress could define its own powers by altering the Fourteenth Amendment's meaning, no longer would the Constitution be "superior paramount law, unchangeable by ordinary means." It would be "on a level with ordinary legislative acts, and, like other acts, . . . alterable when the legislature shall please to alter it." . . . Under this approach, it is difficult to conceive of a principle that would limit congressional power. . . . Shifting legislative majorities could change the Constitution.[107]

The Court was not inclined to allow Congress to use its enforcement power under the Fourteenth Amendment to reinterpret the substantive rights individuals possessed under that amendment. The justices were confident that the authority to determine what the Constitution means ultimately resides in the Court itself. This question of judicial supremacy in constitutional interpretation had particular implications for federalism, since it arose in the context of the scope of congressional authority to regulate the states, but in this instance, federalism principles were not the only constitutional issues of interest to the Court. Even here, Congress found work-arounds, and the Court itself soon identified limits as to how far it was willing to push on congressional authority under section 5.[108]

These federalism cases account for a remarkably large proportion of the liberal dissents in cases striking down provisions of congressional statutes. The left wing of the Rehnquist Court was fairly united in objecting to almost the entire line of doctrine being developed by the conservative majority. They found far fewer reasons to dissent from the remaining three-quarters of cases imposing constitutional constraints on Congress. Indeed, the right wing of the Court was more likely to be in dissent in nonfederalism cases, and many of those invalidating coalitions were built from the left. If federalism cases were removed from the docket, Ginsburg would have been in the majority striking down laws more often than Scalia or Thomas.

The federalism cases were distinctive not only in their appeal to the conservatives but also in their cohesiveness as a constitutional concern. The remainder of the Rehnquist Court's activity in constraining congressional authority was scattered across a wide range of policy and constitutional issue areas. Those cases were sometimes important or politically visible, but they did not necessarily build on one another to reflect a singular constitutional vision.

The Rehnquist Court decided more cases involving substantive rights claims or due process claims than federalism claims, and in each of those areas, the most conservative justices were more likely to be in dissent than were the most liberal justices.[109] Many of those cases involved free speech claims. Undoubtedly, the most emotional and publicly controversial case was the Court's invalidation of the Flag Protection Act of 1989. After the Court narrowly overturned the conviction of a protester who had burned an American flag at the 1984 Republican National Convention, the public pressure to pass a constitutional amendment outlawing flag-burning was intense. Within a few months, Congress had maneuvered to pass both the Flag Protection Act and resolutions condemning the Court's decision, providing political cover for vulnerable legislators to vote against a proposed constitutional amendment to the same effect. By the time the Court reaffirmed its earlier decision and struck down the federal flag-burning statute, public passions had cooled, and the threat of a constitutional amendment had largely passed.[110] Nonetheless, three of the conservative justices and Justice Stevens would have found that the national interest in protecting the symbolic value of the flag outweighed whatever burden was imposed on speakers hoping to use flag-burning to convey their message.[111]

Other speech cases were not surrounded by such a political firestorm. They were often handed down over the objections of conservative justices, but some drew support from the conservatives as well. In a handful of cases, the Court tempered congressional enthusiasm for regulating sexual communication. Congressional efforts to crack down on "dial-a-porn" services could not extend beyond prohibiting "obscene" messages and reach the merely "indecent" (although a trio of liberal justices would have gone further and struck down the obscenity component as well).[112] The Court took a similar view of later efforts to do the same with the internet.[113] A trio of conservative justices would have upheld Congress's urging of cable television operators to exclude indecent programming from public-access channels, but the majority of the Court again found that Congress was too restrictive when it came to sexual content.[114] Breyer joined three conservatives in arguing that Congress could impose limits on when and how cable operators could broadcast sexually explicit content, but the majority disagreed.[115] Justice Kennedy lost conservative votes in striking down a congressional ban on virtual child pornography, but he held them in striking down a ban on "youthful adult pornography."[116] Four of the conservative justices would have upheld congressional Republicans' restriction on the litigation efforts of the federally funded Legal Services Corporation, but Justice Kennedy thought the Court must be "vigilant when Congress imposes rules and conditions which in effect insulate its own laws from legitimate judicial challenge."[117] The Court was more united in other cases restricting speech, such as a federal restriction on the display of alcohol content on beer labels and a National Labor Relations Board order that a construction union stop distributing handbills encouraging shoppers to boycott a mall.[118]

The Rehnquist Court justices were generally not deeply divided in cases involving the separation of powers. Many such cases generated little controversy, such as the Court's ruling that the Federal Magistrates Act did not authorize magistrates to preside over the selection of federal juries, and its ruling that the Federal Advisory Committee Act did not apply to the Department of Justice's consultation with the American Bar Association on judicial nominees.[119] But all such cases were overshadowed by three high-profile constitutional challenges to creative congressional institution building. In only one did the Court object to what Congress had done. A fractured Court struck down the Line Item Veto Act in 1998. Providing the president with a line-item veto to cut unnecessary pork from large appropriation bills had been something of a hobbyhorse for fiscal conservatives since the early 1980s. Throughout his presidency, Reagan had lobbied for such a power, as well as a constitutional amendment requiring a balanced budget. When the Republicans surprisingly won control of both chambers of Congress in the midterm 1994 elections for the first time since the Eisenhower administration, they decided to act on some of the campaign promises packaged as the "Contract with America." One result was a statutory mechanism that authorized the president to delete specific budget items from an appropriations bill. Few thought that a mere statute could do the job, however. When President Clinton tried to make use of the line-item veto, a narrow majority of the Court objected, concluding that it suffered from a similar defect as the legislative veto mechanism struck down by the Burger Court.[120]

In two other cases, the Court upheld congressional innovations. Over the objection of Justice Scalia, the Court validated the 1978 statutory provisions establishing an independent counsel. Scalia argued from the core premise that all executive power was vested in the president alone, and insulating the independent counsel from the president violated that basic principle. Rehnquist took a less formalist approach and concluded that the creation of an independent counsel did not interfere with the essential constitutional duties of the president.[121] Less visible but quite consequential was the Court's decision the next year upholding the work of the Sentencing Commission. That panel, which included sitting federal judges, was empowered to draft binding sentencing guidelines for federal criminal cases. Scalia again wrote a lone dissent, complaining that the Sentencing Commission was "an agency created by Congress to exercise no governmental power other than the making of laws." In keeping with the Court's long history of deferring to congressional delegations of authority, the majority concluded that the "Constitution's structural protections do not prohibit Congress from delegating to an expert body located within the Judicial Branch the intricate task of formulating sentencing guidelines consistent with such significant statutory direction as is present here."[122]

The Rehnquist Court was unusually active in striking down or constraining the application of federal statutory provisions. It did not stand in the way of any significant policy goals being pursued by either the Democrats or the Republicans in the late twentieth and early twenty-first centuries, but it did issue several splashy opinions that sent a shot across the bow of Congress. After several decades of not having to give much consideration to federalism-based limits on national legislative authority, the conservative majority on the Court put such considerations back on the table, but it stopped short of hamstringing Congress's ability to achieve its core political and policy objectives. The Court was more inclined to set up "speed bumps" than "roadblocks" to congressional ambitions.[123] Outside of the federalism cases, the invalidation of federal statutory provisions was often accomplished with the participation, and sometimes the leadership, of the liberal justices. Those cases, however, lacked the overarching constitutional vision that so distinguished the federalism cases. They tended to continue and expand the varied civil libertarian commitments that had been regnant on the Court since the mid-twentieth century and often commanded the support of justices across the ideological divide. The Court pruned away congressional excesses but generally left Congress with the means to achieve much of its objective.

The Roberts Court

With the death of William Rehnquist and the retirement of Sandra Day O'Connor, the Court lost two of its most influential conservative voices since the New Deal. Their departures also created the first vacancies on the Court in a decade. The Court stood polarized between two wings, with only Anthony Kennedy likely to move between them. As it happened, those vacancies arose during the term of a newly elected Republican president working with a Republican Senate. President George W. Bush was rebuffed by his Senate allies when he tried to nominate Harriet Miers, a little-known lawyer but longtime acquaintance of the president, but he eventually placed John Roberts and Samuel Alito on the bench, two well-respected figures in the conservative legal movement. The surprising retirement of David Souter and the less surprising retirement of John Paul Stevens created vacancies on the left wing of the Court. Those openings came after the election of President Barack Obama, and he likewise benefited from a Senate that was in the hands of partisan allies, resulting in the placement of two well-established liberal lawyers on the bench: Sonia Sotomayor and Elena Kagan. The sudden death of Antonin Scalia near the tail end of Obama's presidency threatened to shift the balance on the Court after two decades of polarization. The Republicans had gained control of the Senate, however, and declined to act on his nomination of circuit judge Merrick Garland. Donald Trump's unexpected victory in the 2016 presidential election allowed Scalia's seat to be filled by another conservative jurist, Neil Gorsuch, temporarily preserving the Court's equilibrium.

In many ways, the Roberts Court was a continuation of the Rehnquist Court in terms of how it exercised judicial review of federal law.[124] In its first dozen years, the Roberts Court largely sustained the patterns of the late Rehnquist Court. It remained polarized and often relied on narrow majorities to strike down laws (although the majorities voting to uphold federal laws were often broader). Both liberal and conservative justices routinely voted to strike down legislative provisions. The conservative Antonin Scalia and the liberal Ruth Bader Ginsburg had an almost identical record of joining majorities to strike down laws, although Scalia was more likely to vote to limit the authority of Congress, while Ginsburg was more likely to vote to limit the authority of the state legislatures. The exercise of judicial review was a story not of conservative dominance but of shifting coalitions that drew from both ends of the ideological spectrum.

Cases involving federal statutes occupied a small share of the Court's docket. The Court's annual rate of invalidating federal statutory provisions dropped to levels not seen since the 1940s. Even with few cases to decide, the Roberts Court continued the historical pattern of resolving cases both large and small. Major decisions continued to be interspersed with decisions of less political and policy consequence. More unusually, the Roberts Court nearly removed from its docket cases in which the justices upheld federal statutes against constitutional challenge.[125] For the first time in its history, the Court entered a sustained period of striking down more federal laws than it upheld.

The Court's substantive vision of the Constitution also maintained the trajectory of the Rehnquist Court. The justices continued to be divided over themes the Court had been dealing with since the civil liberties revolution of the 1960s and the Reagan revolution of the 1980s. But the Roberts Court lacked the signature agenda item that had defined the Rehnquist Court. The conservative justices had not necessarily abandoned the decentralizing values driving the federalism offensive of the late 1990s and early 2000s, but they did not prioritize pioneering or extending constitutional doctrine in that area.

Neither the Left nor the Right was able to take firm command of the Court, but the right wing of the Court has achieved a wider range of victories in striking down federal laws under Chief Justice Roberts. The conservative and liberal justices have disagreed about which statutes ought to be struck down, but both wings of the Court have mustered narrow majorities to strike down laws. Under Rehnquist, those conservative majorities were largely congregated around federalism cases, while liberal majorities invalidated federal laws across a range of constitutional issues. Under Roberts, the conservatives have hung together to pursue a broader agenda, while the liberals have won more select victories.

The normal ideological patterns on the Court were scrambled in a series of consequential but complicated cases involving the right to juries in the late Rehnquist Court. In 2000 a narrow majority of strange bedfellows—Stevens, Ginsburg, and Souter on the left, and Scalia and Thomas on the right—held that New Jersey's hate-crime sentencing enhancement required a jury finding on the key facts affecting sentencing, and they extended that logic in a second case out of Washington State.[126] In 2005 the same justices concluded that the federal sentencing guidelines created by the US Sentencing Commission faced the same problem in a case involving admitted drug dealer Freddie Booker.[127] The justices on the Roberts Court have disagreed among themselves on how best to proceed in a post-*Booker* world. The Court relied on those precedents to conclude that judges could treat the sentencing guidelines only as advisory, rather than mandatory, when resentencing a defendant after the initial sentence had been set aside on appeal.[128] The justices disagreed along more traditional ideological lines when a liberal coalition held that the application of newly issued sentencing guidelines created an ex post facto problem for older offenses.[129] They were in general agreement when examining whether a sentencing enhancement based on a record of "violent felonies" was unconstitutionally vague.[130]

The justices were able to reach a fair amount of agreement in a range of cases, but often when the political stakes were relatively low. Late in the Clinton administration, Congress found it easy to prohibit the sale of depictions of animal cruelty. Congress asserted that animal cruelty videos were no better than obscenity or child pornography, and thus "no reasonable person would find any redeeming value" in such materials that might give rise to constitutional protections.[131] In a case involving videos of dogfights, eight of the justices cautioned Congress that they would not tolerate "a freewheeling authority to declare new categories of speech outside the scope of the First Amendment" (Alito would have preferred to include dogfighting videos in the same narrow category of unprotected expression as child pornography).[132] The justices were in full agreement that the 1946 Lanham Act could not deny trademark protection to matter that was "immoral, deceptive, or scandalous" or that "disparage[d]" persons or beliefs.[133] Except for Thomas and Scalia, the justices denied the government's ability to attach conditions to federal grants that inhibited the free speech of the recipients beyond the program funded by the grant, and only Thomas dissented from the conclusion that Congress could not distinguish between unwed citizen mothers and unwed citizen fathers in assessing the citizenship of foreign-born children.[134] More controversially, the three most conservative justices dissented from the Court's invalidation of the Stolen Valor Act. Passed rapidly through Congress, that feel-good piece of legislation cracked down on those who fraudulently claimed to have won military medals. As in the animal cruelty case, the majority reminded Congress of the inappropriateness of regulating the content of speech, except in the most extraordinary circumstances. Writing for the three dissenters, Justice Alito was impressed by the argument that such false claims had "no value in and of themselves," and suppressing them "does not chill any valuable speech."[135] Congress acted quickly to follow the road map laid down by the majority and resurrected the statute with a new clause punishing only those who made fraudulent claims with the intent to obtain something of value.[136]

A narrow liberal majority struck down federal legislation in two very significant cases in the first dozen years of the Roberts Court. The first involved the war on terror that had occupied the country since the attacks of September 11, 2001. In 2008 Justice Kennedy wrote on behalf of the liberal wing of the Court to severely limit the Military Commissions Act (MCA). The MCA had been passed by Congress in response to a series of earlier decisions by the Court regarding military detainees being held at Guantanamo Bay. In *Hamdi v. Rumsfeld*, the Court assessed the constitutionality of the George W. Bush administration's detention of foreign fighters captured during the war in Afghanistan and the broader war on terror.[137] Four of the justices thought the administration had been empowered to detain combatants by the 2001 Authorization of the Use of Military Force (AUMF), but they concluded that Congress could not authorize the detention of an American citizen captured on the battlefield without an appropriate process to evaluate why that individual was being held. Two additional justices preferred not to read the AUMF as authorizing such presidential action. Subsequent decisions expanded on that ruling and gave even noncitizen detainees access to the civilian courts.[138] The MCA sought to exclude civilian court oversight of the detainees in Cuba. The largely Republican-backed measure provided express statutory authority for military tribunals and suspended the detainees' habeas corpus appeals to civilian courts. A surprising variety of amici urged the Court to strike down the MCA, including Pennsylvania senator Arlen

Specter, who had voted for the act. In *Boumediene v. Bush*, a five-justice majority found the proceedings established by Congress and the administration to be inadequate; thus, the civilian courts must be allowed to intervene.[139] Although the Court's intervention provoked a lengthy legal struggle over the detainees, it did not secure their release, as some had hoped. One circuit court judge complained that "the whole process . . . becomes a charade prompted by the Supreme Court's defiant—if only theoretical—assertion of judicial supremacy."[140]

The second case involved the controversy over same-sex marriage that had roiled the country from the Clinton administration through the Obama administration. As Clinton entered the White House, the most visible national controversy over gay rights was whether and how homosexuals should serve in the military, which the president tried to finesse in 1993 by adopting a "don't ask, don't tell" policy. Meanwhile, the Hawaii Supreme Court pushed a new issue onto the national agenda when it held that the denial of marriage licenses to same-sex couples violated the state constitution's equality requirements. Soon state courts and legislatures were debating same-sex civil unions and marriage, and numerous states, including Hawaii, adopted laws specifically precluding same-sex marriage. In 1996 Clinton stated that although he "strenuously opposed discrimination of any kind," he had also "long opposed governmental recognition of same-gender marriage."[141] Not without reason, the president presented the issue as primarily an election-year ploy by Republicans "to divert the American people from the urgent need to confront our challenges together." He observed, "This is hardly a problem that is sweeping the country. No State has legalized gay marriage."[142] Two-thirds of the public opposed the recognition of same-sex marriages, making this a winning issue for the Republicans. The Republican Party platform endorsed a Defense of Marriage Act (DOMA) "to prevent states from being forced to recognize same-sex unions." The Democratic Party was silent on the issue. With substantial bipartisan support, DOMA passed Congress just weeks before the 1996 election. The president departed from his usual practice and made no remarks when he signed DOMA into law.

The politics of same-sex marriage shifted rapidly after the passage of DOMA. The act had two components: it asserted that no state was required to recognize same-sex marriages certified in another state, and it defined "marriage" under federal law as meaning "only a legal union between one man and one woman."[143] Within a few years, several states had adopted civil union statutes as an alternative legal mechanism to recognize same-sex couples. In 2002 conservatives began to push for a federal constitutional amendment to bar same-sex marriage, which was soon incorporated into the Republican Party platform. The next year the US Supreme Court struck down state laws criminalizing sexual acts between persons of the same sex. For the majority, Justice Kennedy noted that this ruling did not speak to the question of whether "the government must give formal recognition to any relationship that homosexual persons seek to enter." Justice O'Connor wrote a concurring opinion asserting that such criminal laws should be distinguished from laws that "promote the institution of marriage." Justice Scalia argued for three dissenters that the case undermined the legal basis for laws prohibiting same-sex marriage.[144] Later that year the Massachusetts Supreme Court declared that limiting marriage to heterosexual couples violated the state constitution, making Massachusetts the first state to recognize same-sex marriages.[145] The number of states specifically barring same-sex marriage grew rapidly in the 1990s and peaked in 2010, when more than forty states had such a policy. By 2013, however, nearly a third of the states had adopted laws allowing same-sex marriage, including most of the reliably Democratic states. Barack Obama endorsed civil unions but not same-sex marriage in his first presidential campaign in 2008; the Democratic Party platform called for the repeal of DOMA and denounced "all attempts to use this issue to divide us." In 2011 Attorney General Eric Holder announced that the president had concluded that DOMA was unconstitutional and had instructed the Department of Justice to cease defending it in court.[146] In that year, for the first time, a majority of Americans indicated that they supported legalizing same-sex marriages. As Obama ran for reelection in 2012, the Democratic platform more directly declared, "We support marriage equality and support the movement to secure equal treatment under law for same-sex couples." The Republican platform continued to endorse "the traditional concept of marriage." A large majority of Republican voters agreed with that position, but a growing majority of Democrats and independents favored the new Democratic position.

In 2013 the Court heard a challenge to the component of DOMA that adopted the traditional definition of marriage for purposes of federal law. Because the Department of Justice would not defend the constitutionality of the statute, the House of Representatives hired Paul Clement, the solicitor general during the Bush administration, to argue the case before the Court. The Department of Justice filed a brief urging the Court to strike down the law. Justice Kennedy, writing for a five-person majority, declared that that section of DOMA violated the equality principle implicit in the Fifth Amendment's due process clause. The four conservative justices produced a total of three dissenting opinions. For the majority, Kennedy linked federalism and equality principles, arguing that Congress had departed from the norm by intervening in an area of "state power and authority" and had done so solely "to impose restrictions and disabilities" on a class of individuals on which some states had chosen to confer "dignity and status of immense import." "DOMA seeks to injure the very class New York [in this case] seeks to protect."[147] In dissent, Roberts argued that Kennedy was too quick to assume "that the Act's principal purpose was to codify malice, and that it furthered *no* legitimate government interest." But he worked even harder to demonstrate that the logic of Kennedy's argument should not necessarily lead to the conclusion that the states that chose not to recognize same-sex marriage were in violation of constitutional requirements. Characteristically, Scalia was more biting in his dissent, concluding that Kennedy had provided "a lecture on how superior the majority's moral judgment in favor of same-sex marriage is to the Congress's hateful moral judgment against it. I promise you this: The only thing that will 'confine' the Court's holding is its sense of what it can get away with."[148] The president promptly applauded the Court for striking down "discrimination enshrined in law."[149] In the aftermath of *Windsor*, the remaining states rapidly moved toward recognizing same-sex marriage (primarily by court decision). The Court's 2015 ruling in *Obergefell* that state laws asserting the traditional definition of marriage were also unconstitutional was somewhat anticlimactic.[150] By then, only thirteen states still refused to recognize same-sex marriage, and just over a third of Americans still believed that same-sex marriages should not be recognized, although Republican voters remained overwhelmingly against such marriages.

The conservative justices on the Roberts Court were more successful in drawing the pivotal Justice Kennedy to their side in a range of other cases. Some of those conservative victories were for relatively small stakes. In assessing the unusual procedure for appointing and removing members of the Public Company Accounting Oversight Board contained in the Sarbanes-

Oxley Act, a narrow conservative majority objected to how doubly insulated those executive officers were from the possibility of presidential removal.[151] Some cases were of mixed effect. In one of the Court's most high-profile cases, the conservatives lost Roberts while holding on to Kennedy—an unusual turn of events. Conservative activists were convinced that the Affordable Care Act (ACA), or "Obamacare," exceeded congressional authority, whereas liberals were convinced there could be no serious controversy on that point. When a conservative journalist asked Speaker of the House Nancy Pelosi about Congress's constitutional authority to adopt an individual health mandate, she infamously responded in astonishment, "Are you serious? Are you serious?" Conservatives found it telling that the Democratic congressional leader was so dismissive of a constitutional argument they had been building up.[152] Liberals, in contrast, thought the Speaker was obviously "right to be dismissive of the fringe right-wing theory behind this question, which has no basis in the Constitution itself."[153] After a bitter debate and a filibuster attempt in the Senate, the ACA was adopted by a party-line vote and signed into law in 2010. When the states and conservative legal groups immediately filed constitutional challenges to Obamacare, the law proved to be just as polarizing in the courts as it had been in Congress.

The Affordable Care Act faced two distinct constitutional challenges, one of which received far more public attention than the other. The more prominent issue involved the individual mandate, which required individuals to purchase health insurance from a private provider. Like other federal economic regulations, the ACA relied on the congressional authority to regulate "economic activity [that] substantially affects interstate commerce."[154] The unusual feature of the ACA was that it arguably forced individuals who were not otherwise engaged in an economic activity into the marketplace. For libertarian-minded conservatives, the individual health mandate implied that Congress could require Americans to do anything Congress thought might be good for them, such as buying (if not necessarily eating) broccoli.[155] Legal defenders of the mandate countered that everyone would eventually enter the health care market, unlike the broccoli market, and even those who were not actively preparing for those purchases were already engaged in the "activity" of self-insurance. The four more liberal justices were persuaded by this argument. The five more conservative justices were not; they thought the mandate provision stretched the Court's interstate commerce precedents too far. Roberts broke from his conservative colleagues, however, to save the provision. He accepted the government's fallback position that the mandate was best understood as an exercise of Congress's taxing authority, rather than an exercise of its authority to regulate interstate commerce. The penalty for failing to comply with the mandate was a small tax collected by the Internal Revenue Service and deposited in the public treasury. Roberts contended that this penalty for noncompliance could simply be understood as an avoidable tax, and the congressional power to tax was adequate to cover what Congress had done in the ACA.[156]

The less prominent issue involved the congressional mandate to the states. Congress required the states to expand the coverage offered through Medicaid, the program operated jointly by the states and the federal government to provide health care to low-income individuals. Congress did not attempt to commandeer state policy-makers and force them to expand coverage; instead, it used its spending power to induce the states to adopt the more generous policy. In particular, Congress conditioned its Medicaid grants to the states on the states' adjustment of individual eligibility requirements. Roberts argued that, in the ACA, Congress had moved from financial inducements to encourage voluntary participation by partnering states to financial coercion of noncompliant states. Congress was free to give new funds only to states that implemented the more generous eligibility requirements, but it could not penalize noncompliant states by withdrawing Medicaid funds that financed the old program. The four more conservative justices agreed with this argument invalidating the Medicaid expansion, while the four more liberal justices dissented. The opinion gave new teeth to the relatively accommodating constitutional doctrine regarding the spending power laid down by Chief Justice Rehnquist when upholding the requirement that states raise the legal drinking age to obtain federal highway funds.[157] It also made it easier for some Republican-controlled states to continue to hold out and refuse to participate in the Obamacare expansion of Medicaid, which ultimately gave those states less of a stake in preserving Obamacare when Republicans in Congress pursued its repeal.[158] The mixed decision both frustrated liberals, who found the conservative position indefensible, and angered conservatives, who were provoked to wonder whether "Roberts [is] as bad as Souter."[159]

In two consequential cases, the five conservatives hung together to strike down important federal statutory provisions over the objections of the four liberals. One involved a provision of the venerable Voting Rights Act of 1965 (VRA). The VRA included several different provisions designed to enforce the Fifteenth Amendment to the Constitution and prevent state and local governments from abridging the right to vote based on race. The fourth and fifth sections of the statute imposed a "preclearance" rule that required some states to receive approval from the Department of Justice before altering any electoral rules. The requirement was imposed on those states that had used prohibited "tests or devices" to abridge the right to vote prior to 1964 and had low voter registration or turnout in the 1964 presidential election.[160] The Warren Court was dismissive of South Carolina's immediate challenge to these provisions, arguing that Congress had ample authority to protect voting rights in this "inventive manner" in order to combat "nearly a century of systematic resistance to the Fifteenth Amendment" and "to limit its attention to the geographic areas where immediate action seemed necessary." The Court thought the "doctrine of the equality of States" was best confined "to the terms upon which States are admitted to the Union, and not to the remedies for local evils which have subsequently appeared."[161]

The conservatives on the Roberts Court had become skeptical of the Voting Rights Act's coverage formula. The contested sections of the VRA had regularly been amended and extended by Congress with bipartisan support, most recently in 2006.[162] Congress created a "bailout" procedure that allowed states and localities to escape the preclearance requirement if they could demonstrate that they had been free from discriminatory actions for an extended period. When a recently created public utility district in Texas sought to bail out from the preclearance requirement or, alternatively, to have the requirement declared unconstitutional as applied to jurisdictions such as itself, the Court emphasized that "the Act imposes current burdens and must be justified by current needs," and it questioned whether Congress had established an adequate justification for extending a coverage formula rooted in misbehavior from the increasingly distant past. Justice Thomas would have preferred to resolve the constitutional claim, but the other eight justices held that the bailout provision should be interpreted more liberally, so as to provide a meaningful avenue for political units to escape the strictures of the preclearance requirement.[163]

In 2013 the Court faced the constitutional question squarely in a case involving Shelby County, Alabama, and a five-justice majority concluded that the coverage formula no longer met constitutional muster. Roberts characterized this section of the VRA as "extraordinary measures to address an extraordinary problem" and "a drastic departure from basic principles of federalism," particularly "from the principle that all States enjoy equal sovereignty."[164] From the majority's perspective, "the conditions that originally justified these measures no longer characterize voting in the covered jurisdictions." They acknowledged that "voting discrimination still exists; no one doubts that." However, the majority was not persuaded that Congress had demonstrated that "disparate treatment of the States" was still warranted, or at least warranted in the same way as it was at the dawn of the civil rights era.[165] Borrowing heavily from the language of the Texas public utility case, which "eight members of the Court [had] subscribed to," Roberts contended that the "exceptional conditions" the Court had relied on in upholding the VRA in 1966 no longer applied.[166] Thomas, writing separately, noted that he would have gone even further than the majority and dispensed with preclearance itself, not just the coverage formula that treated the states differently.[167] Speaking for the four dissenters, Ginsburg thought the case ultimately boiled down to the question of whether Congress or the Court should decide when the provisions of the VRA were no longer justifiable, and she argued that Congress should have primacy.[168] On this, the liberal dissenters on the Roberts Court echoed the views of the dissenters on the Rehnquist Court, who had been more inclined than the conservatives to defer to congressional judgment on how to interpret and enforce the terms of the Reconstruction Amendments against the states. The *Shelby County* case did not disturb the federal government's ability to intervene on a case-by-case basis when it thought localities were engaged in racially discriminatory electoral practices, but it shifted the burden of proof for some localities that had been subjected to closer supervision by the Department of Justice. President Obama immediately called on Congress "to pass legislation to ensure that every American has equal access to the polls," but with Republicans in control of the House of Representatives and Democrats in control of the Senate, there was little prospect of Congress reaching bipartisan agreement on how to update and revive the coverage formula, and competing proposals stalled in committee.[169]

The final set of cases in which the conservatives on the Roberts Court overrode the liberals' objections to enforce constitutional limits on congressional authority involved campaign finance. The Burger Court's original campaign finance case, brought by independent senator James Buckley (a future federal judge and brother of *National Review* founder William F. Buckley), had attracted justices from across the ideological spectrum to reject congressionally imposed limits on the amount of money that could be spent to persuade voters to elect a candidate for federal office.[170] A parade of primarily conservative groups and activists such as the National Conservative Political Action Committee, the Massachusetts Citizens for Life, and the Colorado Republican Federal Campaign Committee objected to the Watergate-era campaign finance rules, which interfered with their efforts to communicate with potential voters. In response, the justices' thinking about restrictions on campaign spending began to polarize, with the conservatives generally favoring a more aggressive approach to evaluating these statutory provisions and the liberals generally favoring a more deferential approach.[171]

The statutory scheme was reset with the adoption of the Bipartisan Campaign Reform Act of 2002, also known as the McCain-Feingold Act. The growth of relatively unregulated donations to the political parties, so-called soft money, put increasing pressure on the original legal framework that sharply limited donations to individual candidates. The Democrats were particularly eager to restrict soft money, which they thought worked to their disadvantage, while the Republicans made the opposite calculation and resisted such efforts. Across the 1990s, no agreement could be reached to move legislation forward. Voters favored campaign finance reform, but it was not a priority for them, and Americans disagreed about what kind of reform was desirable.[172] Republican John McCain championed the cause of campaign finance reform in his losing presidential primary bid in 2000. The eventual Republican nominee, George W. Bush, distanced himself from such proposals, but Democratic nominee Al Gore embraced them. After the contested presidential election resulted in Bush's elevation to the White House, momentum built for a reform bill, and a contingent of Republican legislators peeled off to join the fairly united Democrats to pass a comprehensive statute. President Bush announced his support for a bill restricting soft-money donations by corporations and labor unions but protecting "the rights of citizen groups to engage in issue advocacy."[173] As the Senate overrode a threatened filibuster to pass the bill, Republican Mitchell McConnell warned his colleagues, "This is a stunningly stupid thing to do." It would create a "new world" with severely weakened political parties and "a battle of billionaires over the political discourse," with the major media outlets serving as "the biggest corporate soft money operation in America."[174] When the bill reached the president, he signed it into law but issued a signing statement that outlined its many constitutional deficiencies, and he noted, "I expect that the courts will resolve these legitimate legal questions as appropriate under the law."[175]

McConnell was among those who immediately filed suit to have parts of the McCain-Feingold Act declared unconstitutional, taking advantage of a fast-track provision to facilitate a quick judicial decision. The late Rehnquist Court mostly demurred. O'Connor joined the four justices from the liberal wing to uphold the statute against most of the challenges. The majority thought the restriction on soft-money contributions for party-building activities involved "only marginal restrictions upon the contributor's ability to engage in free communication," and any negative effects on minor parties were tolerable as part of a broader effort to apply the same rules to everyone; restrictions on party operatives' ability to solicit funds for other organizations was justifiable to prevent efforts to circumvent the central financing rules, among other provisions. The Court did strike down a provision prohibiting campaign contributions by minors, and it held that several other challenges were not yet properly before the Court.[176] Thomas wrote a particularly scathing dissent in which he criticized the majority for upholding "what can only be described as the most significant abridgment of the freedoms of speech and association since the Civil War." He would have reopened *Buckley* itself as unduly restricting political contributions.[177] The other conservatives did not go so far, but Kennedy objected to the statute's provisions that "force speakers to abandon their own preference for speaking through parties and organizations" and "provide safe harbor to the mainstream press" and "corporate media alone" to have the unfettered right to engage in political speech.[178] Scalia found the law "offensive," for "we are governed by Congress, and this legislation prohibits the criticism of Members of Congress by those entities most capable of giving such criticism loud voice," including parties and corporations.[179]

O'Connor's departure from the bench proved to be consequential for some of the issues left unresolved in the 2003 *McConnell* decision. Her replacement, Samuel Alito, shared the other conservative justices' basic view of the scope of congressional authority to restrict spending on electioneering. McCain-Feingold prohibited the expenditure of corporate funds on political ads within sixty days of a federal election. *McConnell* had upheld a ban on "express advocacy" ads, and as a primary election approached, the nonprofit corporation Wisconsin Right to Life wanted to continue running its "issue ads," which encouraged citizens to call their senators and urge them to oppose a filibuster on judicial nominees. It sought a judicial ruling to prevent the Federal Election Commission from barring those commercials as "sham issue ads" that were really designed to influence an election. When the case reached the Court on its merits, a narrow majority struck down the restriction on corporate ads near an election as it applied to a nonprofit's issue ads. The three holdover conservative justices reaffirmed that, in their opinion, *McConnell* had been wrongly decided on the question of corporate political speech. Roberts and Alito merely held that *McConnell* did not control this type of situation and should not be extended to cover it.[180] Writing for the liberal dissenters, Souter emphasized that the "indispensable ingredient of a political candidacy is money for advertising." The conservatives thought this fact was fatal to congressional efforts to squelch the expenditure of money on campaign advertising (though they continued to accept that Congress could limit funds donated to a candidate). The liberals now argued that the primacy of money to effective campaigning raised issues beyond the perception of the possible corruption of candidates who accepted funds from deep-pocketed donors. It created voter "cynicism" about democratic politics and a general worry about "concentrations of money in politics [that] has reached an unprecedented enormity."[181] Congress had the constitutional authority to constrain corporate speech not only to protect against corruption but also to limit the political influence of "immense aggregations of wealth."[182]

The next year the same narrow majority struck down the so-called Millionaire's Amendment in McCain-Feingold. The provision had not been adjudicated in *McConnell*, but it created a distinctive regulatory scheme when a candidate spent more than $350,000 of personal funds on a political campaign. *Buckley* had held that Congress could not cap a candidate's ability to self-finance a campaign. The Millionaire's Amendment sought to work around that constraint by changing the rules: when one candidate crossed the self-financing threshold, the other candidate was authorized to raise campaign funds under more generous donation limits and to coordinate campaign spending with party operatives. Democratic businessman Jack Davis was accused of exceeding this limit in his attempt to unseat an incumbent Republican congressman, and Alito wrote the opinion for the Court, concluding that Davis had a First Amendment right to spend as much of his personal wealth as he desired in support of his own candidacy without being singled out for a disadvantageous regulatory scheme. Congress could not impose asymmetrical campaign finance limits to burden one candidate in the race or to "level electoral opportunities" so as "to reduce the natural advantage of wealthy individuals" in a campaign, as the government argued.[183] Stevens, in dissent, argued that Congress had the authority to level the playing field in electoral campaigns, so long as it did not prevent a candidate from getting his or her message out.

Most notoriously, in *Citizens United*, the conservative majority overruled a portion of *McConnell* and struck down the prohibition on spending corporate funds on campaign advertisements near an election. Unlike the issue ads at stake in *Wisconsin Right to Life*, the nonprofit corporation Citizens United sought to release a documentary critical of Hillary Clinton as she began her 2008 campaign for the Democratic presidential nomination. In *Wisconsin Right to Life*, Kennedy had authored a three-justice concurrence arguing that *McConnell* was wrong on this point and that corporate political speech should be fully protected by the First Amendment. In *Citizens United*, he was able to command five votes behind that opinion. The corporate speech ban would impose criminal sanctions on the Sierra Club, the National Rifle Association, or the American Civil Liberties Union if any of them ran ads near Election Day urging Americans to vote in a particular way. To Kennedy, these were "classic examples of censorship." The purpose of the provision was to "silence entities whose voices the Government deems to be suspect," and Kennedy thought this ran afoul of the First Amendment, which was intended to protect both the speaker who wanted to criticize government officials and the listener who wanted to hear such messages.[184] The dissenters countered that the First Amendment allowed Congress to distinguish between corporate and noncorporate speech and to impose special disabilities on the former, so long as those disabilities did not hinge on the substantive content of particular corporate speech. Further, Congress could restrict speech not only to avoid "*quid pro quo* corruption" but also to prevent speakers from "distort[ing] public debate in ways that undermine rather than advance the interests of listeners."[185] The same majority subsequently struck down the aggregate donation limit in the Bipartisan Campaign Reform Act as well. The aggregate limit capped how much an individual could donate in total to all candidates and campaigns during a two-year period. The majority found that the aggregate limit on donors could not be justified under the same anticorruption rationale used to uphold limits on donations to individual candidates or campaigns; instead, the aggregate limit had the primary effect of limiting how much political speech an individual could engage in, as if the government had told a newspaper "how many candidates it may endorse."[186]

Conclusion

Chief Justice Earl Warren's announcement of his retirement from the Supreme Court and Richard Nixon's election as president in 1968 brought an end to the liberal dominance on the Court since 1937. During that thirty-year window, the Supreme Court revolutionized constitutional law and repositioned itself as an activist institution on behalf of the civil libertarian values favored by the New Deal coalition in the middle of the twentieth century. Nixon's explicit message focused on changing the course of constitutional law, particularly in the area of criminal justice, and rejecting the liberal judicial activism that had characterized the Court in the 1960s.

Many expected the Nixon Court to embark on a conservative counterrevolution that would uproot the accomplishments and commitments of the Warren Court. The counterrevolution never arrived. The conservatives never gained firm control over the Supreme Court, despite years of Republican presidential appointments, and the Warren Court's civil libertarian commitments had deep roots in the political and legal culture. The Supreme Court took a more conservative turn, but it found itself adjusting, extending, and building on the Warren legacy rather than demolishing it.

The Court also found itself affected by a new set of constitutional challenges and a conservative legal movement with a new set of ideas about constitutional law as the twentieth century ended and the twenty-first began. The Court had neither the appetite nor the opportunity to relitigate the battles of the 1960s, let alone the battles of the 1930s. Congress continued to generate new policies to address new issues; as it did so, it considered what had come before but also moved off in new directions. Rather than dusting off a set of constitutional doctrines that had been exiled in the Progressive and New Deal eras, the conservative justices were grappling with the state as they found it, and they struggled to translate into new constitutional doctrine the ideas and values brought to the fore by the Reagan revolution that reconfigured the Republican Party.

The combination of persistently divided government, closely contested national elections, ideologically opposed political parties, and happenstance since the 1980s produced a Court that was polarized in unprecedented ways in American history. Increasingly distant left and right wings could rarely agree on when to strike down laws; as a result, narrow majorities often overrode a sizable group of bitter dissenters. Because neither wing could fully consolidate its hold on the Court, decisions evaluating the constitutionality of federal statutes could be built with coalitions constructed from either end of the political spectrum. In the process, the Rehnquist and Roberts Courts alternately horrified and delighted political activists and leaders on both the left and the right.

Conclusion

Americans sometimes tell themselves a story about the Supreme Court. In this story the justices stand removed from politics, like priests working in a marble temple. Constitutional law imposes fixed limits on the arena of political choice, and the elected members of Congress operate within boundaries marked out and defended by unelected justices who lean against the prevailing democratic winds. This story is sometimes told in a fearful tone, with the people and their representatives subjugated to the will of distant philosopher-kings. It is sometimes told in a more hopeful tone, with the benighted masses and feckless politicians defanged by wise jurists. But in both versions the justices occupy an Archimedean point outside the world of politics and from there can reshape the course of events.

For better or worse, we should doubt that the Court is as independent of politics as that story suggests. The individuals who become justices are socialized into a political world they share with their contemporaries. The justices are elevated to the bench through a political appointments process that filters out those who are likely to be dramatically at odds with the political leaders who assemble victorious electoral coalitions. The justices live in the world and are buffeted by the same maelstroms of opinion and emotion that affect those around them. Their work sometimes involves matters of arcane knowledge and obscure significance, but it often involves matters of fundamental values and partisan contestation. The justices are not disinterested observers of the political world; they are powerful actors within it.

To be sure, the justices are somewhat insulated from daily politics. They are not readily held accountable for their decisions, and they cannot be easily replaced if their actions become wearisome. They do not have to look ahead to a day of reckoning if they wish to keep their seats. They do not have to look behind to see if they are being outmaneuvered by scheming rivals. They need not seek out votes or campaign contributions or good publicity.

That insulation differentiates the judiciary from other institutions of democratic governance, and it promises advantages and disadvantages for the effective functioning of the constitutional system. But that insulation has limits. If the Court were to stray too far from the mainstream or become too great of an obstacle to an important political program, elected officials have tools at their disposal to bring the Court to heel. Presidents and legislators and political activists have sometimes rattled the saber at the judiciary to remind the justices that they are vulnerable, but saber-rattling, let alone the unsheathing of political weapons, has rarely been necessary to keep the Court in line. The ordinary operation of the American political system is sufficient to keep the justices in the orbit of party leaders.

Robert Dahl provocatively posited that the Court is mostly a congressional lapdog.[1] The power of judicial review gave the justices the ability to cast a vote on federal legislation, though they could weigh in only after the members of Congress had cast their votes to enact a bill into law and the president had cast a vote on whether to veto it. The justices could be presumed to have federal policy preferences, just as other members of the governing class did, and they could be expected to share the basic policy preferences of their partisan coalition partners. With a bit of luck and the passage of time, victorious political parties could expect to stock the bench with their ideological and political allies. Having done so, those party leaders could expect the justices to give their stamp of approval when the laws of their coalition partners were brought before the Court for constitutional review. If those party leaders had the misfortune of losing their electoral majorities, they might expect the justices to do them the favor of vetoing their opponent's legislative efforts until the justices lost their majorities as well. If "the judge be a mere machine" with the party at the controls, then judicial nullifications of federal statutes should be rare and self-evidently partisan.[2]

There might be reason to believe that the US Supreme Court would be more aggressive in reviewing and invalidating the actions of the states.[3] The states might more easily be out of sync with the constitutional views and political preferences represented in the federal judiciary. The states have fewer tools with which to influence the Court, and national political leaders have more reason to want the Court to adopt an activist posture relative to the state governments. Judicial activism against the states is perfectly consistent with framing the "Court as a national policy-maker."

The history of the judicial review of federal statutes meets Dahl on his chosen ground. It is in this context that Dahl has argued that the Court has been most consistently politically aligned with elected officials and has proved most deferential. If the justices were to act as coalition partners and the Court were to act as part of a political system, this should find its purest expression in the Court's review of federal legislation, and that history of review should reveal a pacific Court.

Dahl was no doubt correct to emphasize the Court's place within the political regime. The Court has not stood apart from the forces that move American politics generally. The justices swim in the same political waters as other federal government officials. The Court acts within bounds set by other political actors, and it acts on goals shared by its political allies.

Dahl was less persuasive on *how* exactly the Court fits into the workings of the larger political system. Dahl anticipated that durable, unified political majorities would take effective control of the Supreme Court, and the justices' policy commitments would not distinguish them in any particular way from their co-partisans in the elected branches of the federal government. These were not unreasonable assumptions for a behavioral political scientist writing in the aftermath of the New Deal, and they generated some clear expectations about the exercise of judicial review. But they were oversimplified and ultimately misleading.

In exercising the power of judicial review of federal statutes across American history, the Court has operated from a political perspective and in alliance with coalition partners elsewhere in the government. The Court has not generally operated as an antidemocratic force obstructing the plans and policies of legislative majorities. It has, on occasion, vetoed important federal policies, but it has more often operated within dominant political coalitions than against them. It has exploited fissures within democratic majorities rather than setting itself against those majorities. It has advanced primarily the values and policies that have won electoral support rather than those that have met electoral defeat.

The justices are best understood as political partners. They are not minions who simply do the bidding of party leaders. They are allies of coalition leaders, not their agents. As such, they exercise some modicum of independence and discretion. They are able to articulate their own understandings of constitutional values and commitments. Those commitments may well be shared by others, and they may be advanced through party platforms and legislative debates, but the justices give them shape and effectiveness. The justices set their own priorities and, in many cases, have their own distinctive set of concerns.

Theoretical Implications

There are two related strands of theoretical and empirical research on the relation between the courts and elected officials that are of particular relevance to this study of the judicial review of federal statutes. Those literatures are concerned with the behavior and status of courts generally and are not exclusively focused on judicial review, but the exercise of judicial review is of particular significance to them. The development of constitutional law and the enforcement of constitutional constraints on legislatures are among the most important duties courts can perform, and they are especially politically sensitive.

One strand of research traces back to Robert Dahl and examines the extent to which the US Supreme Court works in opposition to the preferences, interests, and desires of the political branches. Dahl anticipated that a politically appointed judiciary would have little interest in nullifying the policies put in place by those who appointed them. The courts would be captured by the politicians and would be unwilling to act to defend the politically powerless. Dahl thought the history of the judicial review of federal statutes would be particularly informative in evaluating the truth of this hypothesis.

This book adds to the literature that has grown out of this initial insight. Dahl underestimated the extent to which a politically appointed Court would strike down laws of Congress. He thought political influence on the Court would express itself through judicial passivity when reviewing congressional lawmaking. As Mark Graber and others have shown, political leaders are not implacably opposed to the exercise of judicial review. A judicial veto can sometimes serve the interests of leaders of fractious coalitions. A politically aligned Court need not necessarily be passive. The political system can also influence the substance of constitutional law and the principles the Court seeks to enforce against other government officials.

A second strand of research examines the political foundations of judicial independence and the conditional nature of that independence. Although the American courts benefit from a variety of formal features designed to secure their independence from political influence, they remain relatively fragile and politically weak. If political leaders were determined to neuter the courts, they have a variety of tools at their disposal to do so. If the judicial invalidation of statutes threatens core interests of government officials, why would they tolerate an independent judiciary capable of wielding that weapon against them? One answer might be that courts are more powerful and have more political resources than is apparent at first glance. Perhaps politicians do not curb the courts because they cannot do so successfully, and judges are unrestrained in their ability to strike down important public policies. But perhaps courts survive by working within boundaries set by other political actors, playing within the zone of discretion tolerated by the politicians the courts seek to check.

The judicial review of federal statutes considered here reinforces the conditional quality of judicial independence. The Court has operated as a partner and an ally of political leaders. In practice, this role has often been consistent with significant judicial activity in patrolling the boundaries of legislative authority. The Court has been willing and able to exercise independent judgment in defining and enforcing constitutional limits on congressional power. From their earliest cases—when they refused to follow federal statutes requiring them to perform duties inconsistent with the terms of Article III of the Constitution—to their most recent cases—when they imposed limits on Congress's ability to twist the arms of state and local government officials—the justices of the US Supreme Court have been able to identify issues and principles of particular importance to them and insist that legislators respect them.

The Court's willingness and ability to push Congress have not been limitless. The Court has operated mostly at the margins of the political landscape.

Table C-1: Distribution of Cases by Outcome and Partisan Divergence, 1789–2018

	Invalidating (%)	Upholding (%)
Divergent	13	34
Convergent	13	40

It has trimmed legislation, but it has rarely gutted important public policies. It has seldom set itself against determined political majorities. When the Court has attacked important public policies, it generally did so in concert with political leaders who had their own doubts about such policies. The Court has been successful when it intervened in internecine struggles, when it took sides with powerful allies to advance a common agenda. The Court has refrained from charging out on its own to resist the massed political will of the broader society. Those who expected the Court to stand as a bulwark against democracy have generally been disappointed. It struck down a federal income tax wedged into the US code by a well-placed contingent of Populists, but it beat a retreat when a bipartisan coalition in Congress demonstrated an interest in retaining the anti-Communist internal security measures adopted at the outset of the Cold War. It weathered a brief political firestorm when it defended the right of protesters to burn the American flag, but it sank into quiescence when a broad coalition of national political leaders adopted draconian measures to return fugitives to slavery.

One straightforward way of analyzing these issues is to observe how the Court resolved constitutional challenges to federal statutes adopted by its political allies. This echoes Dahl's partisan perspective on how the Court fits into the broader policy-making system. Dahl told us to expect the Court to almost always uphold the laws passed by a politically convergent legislature and to reserve its veto for laws adopted by politically divergent legislatures. A Republican Court should be more likely to uphold laws passed by a Republican Congress and invalidate laws passed by a Democratic Congress.

Table C-1 poses a bit of a challenge for traditional Dahlians. It shows the distribution of cases across two key variables: whether the case resulted in the invalidation of a statutory provision, and whether the policy in question was adopted by a House of Representatives controlled by the same party as the majority of the justices reviewing it. There are, of course, many ways to measure and evaluate the partisan relationship between the Court and the federal statutes it reviews, but the partisan composition of the House that passed the policy in question and the partisan identities of the presidents who appointed a majority of the justices are both intuitive and representative.[4] As table c-1 indicates, the relationship between partisan opposition and judicial vetoes is not a strong one. Across its history, the Court has struck down the statutes of partisan allies and partisan foes at about the same rate. Politically divergent laws fare as well as in the Court as politically convergent laws.

The distribution of cases in table c-1 ought to suggest that a simple Dahlian narrative is not very compelling and that the actual relationship between the Court and Congress is complicated. There have been periods when the Court really seemed to find the laws of its partisan opponents repugnant and the laws of its partisan allies commendable, but that does not reflect how the Court has generally exercised the power of judicial review. In practice, the justices have often objected to the legislation adopted by their coalition partners. The ideological congruity between the justices and the parties from which they emerged is less than complete, which is no surprise, given the fractious nature of the coalitions that make up American political parties. The Court's partisan allies can be ideologically feckless, which is to be expected from politicians who care more about reelection than principle. The justices systematically care more about constitutional values and technical details than do the elected representatives charged with writing statutes. The justices are not lapdogs, and they have often bitten the hand of the party that placed them on the bench.

The justices have proved themselves to be the allies of political coalition leaders, but they are not their servants. Presidents have elevated like-minded lawyers to the Court, and over the course of their tenures, those justices tend to construe the Constitution in a manner consistent with the sensitivities of their time and their party. Lincoln Republicans on the Court shared the pro-Union, free-labor ideology of Lincoln Republicans off the Court. Progressive justices were recognizably part of the broader Progressive movement. New Deal justices embraced the positive state nationalism heralded by Franklin Roosevelt. Legal movement conservatives on the Court shared the constitutional sensibilities of legal movement conservatives in Ed Meese's Department of Justice. The battle of ideas in the political arena has consequences for the shape of constitutional law, which is articulated by justices who are often interested observers, if not actual veterans, of those battles.

Table C-2: Distribution of Cases by Outcome and Policy Importance, 1789–2018

	Invalidating (%)	Upholding (%)
More important	5	16
Less important	22	57

Howard Gillman has distinguished between the "low politics" of "partisan favoritism" and the "high politics" of "ideological policymaking."[5] The Court is shaped by and contributes to high politics in this sense; it has always been and will always be a political institution. Constitutional values are the subjects of political debates and electoral campaigns as well as lawyers' briefs. Our effective constitutional commitments are determined by popular mobilization and political victory, not just by legal argumentation. The history of the judicial review of federal statutes is very much consistent with the Court's engaging in this form of high politics. The justices absorb, develop, and articulate a set of constitutional principles that are contested and contestable, and the design of the American constitutional system helps keep those principles tethered to the realities of ordinary politics. It is far more rare, and more disconcerting, for the justices to engage in low politics and put their thumbs on the scale to benefit the electoral fortunes of their partisans. Many political science accounts of judicial and American politics, including Dahl's, tend to collapse the distinction between these two levels of politics, which might lead us to expect the Court to serve as a footman to ever-changing partisan interests. The justices are rarely called to act in such a nakedly partisan manner, and they have little incentive or desire to do so. A Democrat on the bench is not the same as a Democrat in Congress, but that is not to say that there is no relation between the two.

If the Court is a semiautonomous agent within the political system with the power to frustrate the political plans of both its friends and its foes, then how does it sustain that power over time? Table C-2 provides a glimpse of the answer. It shows the distribution of cases involving the judicial review of federal statutory provisions across two dimensions: whether the Court struck down the provision for exceeding the scope of congressional authority, and whether the provision was important. As before, the proxy of political importance used here is whether the statutory provision was listed as a piece of landmark legislation in the Congressional Research Service study. This is a fairly high bar, and relatively few statutory provisions that come before the Court can cross it. But the table captures two important points about the political history of the judicial review of federal statutes. First, only in a tiny fraction of cases has the Court invalidated a key provision of an important statute. Most of the policies struck down by the Court have been relatively unimportant. This is not to say that those policies were trivial or had no constituencies with an interest in their passage or survival, but it emphasizes that the Court has rarely gotten in the way of Congress's most fundamental legislative commitments. Those moments when the Court struck down the federal income tax or the National Industrial Recovery Act or the preclearance requirement of the Voting Rights Act were particularly noteworthy, consequential, and memorable in part because they were so exceptional. Second, the bulk of the Court's work has involved statutory provisions of relatively little importance. It is not merely that the Court has spent much of its time *deferring* to important federal policies but that it has spent most of its time *evaluating* less important ones. When the Court strikes down a statutory provision, the policy in question is generally not central to American politics and the political calculations of coalition leaders. But it is also true that when the Court upholds a statutory provision against constitutional challenge, that policy is unlikely to be of great significance. Members of Congress spend much of their time in the weeds, drafting legislation that might marginally benefit some of their constituents rather than engaging in historic debates over watershed pieces of public policy. The justices are in much the same situation, and they often hear arguments over legislative arcana of little consequence rather than tilting their lances at fundamental threats to the constitutional order.

The simple fact is that judicial review, as it has historically been practiced, is a fairly low-stakes game. Political leaders can afford to tolerate an independent judiciary armed with the power to invalidate statutes because the justices generally do little political damage. If the Court were to change its behavior and dramatically shift its caseload to important legislation, and particularly if it acted to invalidate such statutes, that would no doubt test the limits of judicial independence. When the Court was thought to be operating in such a way, it invited controversy and even existential threats to its stature and institutional integrity. When Reconstruction Republicans thought the Court might try to obstruct their efforts to secure the peace and reform the South, they were blunt in waving the justices off. When the Court objected to the Populist platform of the Gilded Age, the Populists made it clear that if they won a political majority, they would permanently hobble the Court. When the Court set itself against the New Deal, Roosevelt went to war against the Court and forced it to surrender. The Court must pick its battles, and it has thrived by picking winnable battles. It has aligned itself with, rather than against, national political leaders and unified political majorities, and it has been rewarded with a degree of autonomy to pursue its own constitutional priorities. It has exploited fissures within national political coalitions and, in doing so, has left its mark without inviting the wrath of vengeful politicians.

Historical Implications

This excavation of the political history of the judicial review of federal statutes has various implications for our understanding of the historical record itself. Some of those implications relate to the history of judicial review and the development of American constitutional law as a whole. Some of them speak primarily to our understanding of particular periods in American history.

First and most fundamentally, the judicial review of federal laws has been far more extensive than is generally appreciated. Our historical memory and immediate attention are drawn to the handful of high-profile cases that command national headlines. The Court sometimes intrudes into the national spotlight and issues decisions of substantial political importance, but behind those notable cases are scores of less remarkable decisions. It is primarily through that ordinary work of judicial review that the Court has defined and enforced the constitutional scope of congressional powers. Through these low-profile and routine cases, the Court has established itself as a constitutional actor on the national stage with the authority to delimit the reach of the legislature and shield groups and individuals from the effects of duly adopted legislation.

Even so, the pace of judicial activity pales in comparison to the pace of legislative activity. Even during its periods of greatest activism, the Court has ruled on the constitutionality of only a tiny fraction of enacted legislative provisions. Of course, this is as it should be, if Congress is operating within its constitutional bounds. The Court is far from a "third legislative chamber" that must give its imprimatur before a bill becomes law. Proposed legislation dies every day in the committees and chambers of Congress. The president turns aside even more with his veto pen. Relatively few laws die in a courtroom. Even in the busiest years, the number of cases involving the constitutionality of a federal law can be counted on two hands. The number of cases striking down or limiting federal statutory commands only rarely exceeds a handful each year. Judicial review of federal laws has become a routine feature of the American constitutional system, but it is still true that judicial intervention in any policy dispute is exceptional. Congress goes about its legislative business with limited consideration of what the Court might do. The federal courts occupy only a small space in the history of American politics and policy-making.

The exceptional cases of judicial nullification of federal laws have absorbed most of our attention. These attention-grabbing cases are exceptional not only because they are politically salient (whereas most of the Court's work is politically obscure) but also because they actually strike down a provision of the federal code (whereas most of the Court's decisions uphold the authority of Congress). When the Court reviews the constitutionality of federal policy, it generally concludes that the policy is constitutionally valid. Judicial review only occasionally result in a veto; it far more often bestows a stamp of approval. If the Court is acting as a constitutional umpire calling balls and strikes, its tendency has been to grant the pitcher a very lenient strike zone. The Court has only rarely felt obliged to inform Congress that it has gone outside constitutional bounds. Across the Court's history as a whole, congressional authority has prevailed about three-quarters of the time. Even in its most activist phases, when it has been most assertive in striking down laws, the Court still ruled in favor of Congress more often than not.

The constitutional founders hardly anticipated how much power the judiciary would exercise in the American republic. The experiment with limited popular government under written constitutions was too new for them to have a firm grasp on the role the courts might eventually play. The anti-Federalist writer Brutus pointed to the federal judicial power as a reason for voting down the proposed US Constitution in 1798. Brutus recognized that the practice of judicial review was a logical implication of the American constitutional scheme. If "the legislature must be controlled by the constitution, and not the constitution by them," then the legislature would have no "right

to set aside any judgment pronounced upon the construction of the constitution." For anti-Federalists concerned about the unchecked powers of the
new federal government, the possibility of a judicial check on the national
legislature might have been welcomed. But Brutus was not reassured, for he
thought the "judicial power will operate to effect, in the most certain, but
yet silent and imperceptible manner, what is evidently the tendency of the
constitution." The "judicial power of the United States, will lean strongly in
favor of the general government" and will, over time, "give such an explanation to the constitution, as will favor an extension of its jurisdiction." The
many "general and indefinite terms" laying out the powers of the federal
government in the Constitution "are either equivocal, ambiguous, or require
long definitions to unfold the extent of their meaning," thus inviting judicial
resolution of their meaning. The new federal courts would work assiduously
to encourage "every extension of the power of the general legislature."[6] The
federal courts would be in no position to mandate that Congress take actions
it had thus far refrained from taking, but "it is easy to see, that in their adjudications they may establish certain principles, which being received by the
legislature, will enlarge the sphere of their power beyond all bounds."[7] The
Supreme Court could be expected to serve as a cheering section for Congress
and to work with it to expand, rather than shrink, the power of the national
legislature. When Alexander Hamilton took up his pen to respond to Brutus,
he tried to reassure the anti-Federalists that although the new federal courts
were capable of standing up to the "ill humors" of the elected legislature,
they were "the least dangerous branch" and too weak to threaten liberties on
their own.[8] But Hamilton could offer less reassurance about how the courts
might interpret the powers of the federal government.

Brutus was largely right about the Court. Litigants have asked for declarations of whether certain exercises of congressional power are consistent
with the requirements of the Constitution, and the Court has regularly pronounced on what those requirements are. More often than not, the Court
has propounded principles that expand rather than restrict the authority of
the national legislature. The sympathies of members of the federal judiciary
have tended to lie with Congress, and courts have used their authority to
build up the national state and bolster the ability of Congress to pursue national interests. Although the Court has occasionally ruled against Congress,
it has rarely set itself against Congress and systematically sought to resist the

initiatives favored by legislative majorities. Across its history, as Congress has embarked on new state-building initiatives to expand the federal government's scope and alter the relationship between the government and the citizenry, the Court has mostly blessed those new initiatives and helped quash dissenters who stubbornly clung to the old ways.

Across the more than two centuries the Court has sat in judgment of the work of Congress, both the form of judicial review and the substance of constitutional disputes have shifted and changed. As the Gilded Age transitioned into the Progressive Era, scholars, lawyers, and activists debated whether and how American courts should exercise the power of judicial review. Historical narrative played a part in that debate. Conservatives argued that the courts had always played an important role in keeping legislatures' democratic impulses in check. Progressives argued that the courts had rarely attempted to obstruct the will of the people, and on the few occasions when they did, it was illegitimate. Scholars in those decades did pioneering work uncovering the history of judicial review, but quite a bit remained obscure, and our histories remained incomplete.

The nature of judicial review itself has changed in the Court's two centuries of existence. The justices took to exercising the authority to review the constitutionality of federal laws without much hesitation. As the state courts were doing, the federal courts quickly accepted that the written Constitution was a law that controlled the actions of government officials and took priority over mere statutes. When the commands of Congress came into conflict with the commands of the Constitution, the justices considered it their duty to apply the latter to the cases at hand and curtail the former as necessary. They did not generally position themselves, however, as special guardians of the Constitution. They had a duty to perform, and they did it. On occasion, political activists tried to draw the courts into broader political disputes and leverage the judicial authority to interpret the Constitution as a weapon for overturning disfavored public policies. Such occasions were relatively uncommon early in the Court's history, but they became more common as the decades wore on. And the Court's rulings became more ambitious. Ordinary litigation raising incidental constitutional questions continued to account for a sizable fraction of the Court's workload, but an increasingly prominent part of the docket was occupied by parties asking the justices to exercise a veto power over federal legislation. By the end of the nineteenth century, both judicial advocates and judicial critics viewed the Court and the power of judicial review as potential obstructions to democratic policy-making. It was not merely the case that the justices should apply the law—all the law—faithfully and correctly in the cases that came before them. The justices were increasingly positioned as an important part of the constitutional system of checks and balances, and a modern debate emerged over when and how that constitutional check should be applied. The elaboration of constitutional law ceased to be an incidental by-product of the judicial resolution of ordinary legal disputes. Constitutional interpretation became an end in itself and an important function of the Court. When the Supreme Court was finally given discretionary control over most of its docket in the early twentieth century, it largely ceased to play its traditional role as an appellate court of last resort and embraced its more modern role as a producer of law.

The history of the judicial review of federal laws revealed here is at odds with some traditional accounts of the Court and its activity. The Court was far more active in evaluating the constitutionality of federal laws and curtailing their application during the first decades of the republic than has generally been appreciated. The most politically contested cases of the early repub-lic—cases in which the justices elaborated on their role in the constitutional system—have been remembered and either denounced or celebrated in part because they seem the most modern and familiar. The far more routine cases in which the Court heard constitutional arguments and sheltered parties from congressional overreach were of limited political significance and did not spark public controversy; as a result, they have languished, mostly un-read. The justices did not trumpet their superior constitutional authority and avoided disparaging Congress for its constitutional infidelity, but they assumed their right and duty to interpret the Constitution and repel statu-tory directives that ran afoul of that fundamental law. In doing so, they built up the Court's own stature, laid down markers on the constitutional limits to congressional power, and familiarized Americans with the understanding that statutes that violated the terms of the Constitution had no legal force.

The history of the Court's review of federal laws in the last decades of the nineteenth century and early decades of the twentieth century does not fit neatly with the Progressive narrative of a Court bent on obstructing Pro-gressive policies and shielding corporate greed. To be sure, the Court was a relatively conservative institution throughout those years, with justices appointed primarily by conservative presidents and drawn from a conservative class of lawyers who were skeptical of radical change. But the Court nonetheless operated within the political mainstream and accepted the constitutionality of most of the reforms adopted by Congress. The Court chipped away at the margins of federal policies, but whether the victims of political majorities were interstate railroads or Chinese immigrants, the Court was unwilling to stand starkly against Congress. The Court sometimes told Congress it had gone too far or pursued its goals in the wrong way, but it rarely told Congress that its political objectives were constitutionally impossible.

Some of the Court's behavior across these years is familiar, but it becomes clearer when properly situated against the background of the Court's broader history. The Court's effort to block the New Deal during Franklin Roosevelt's first term stands out all the more starkly when contrasted with the many years it accommodated the growth of the administrative state. For a few short years, the Court was unusually aggressive in going to war with a united political majority, and the political fallout was nearly disastrous for the judiciary. The contemporary Court has been unusually polarized in terms of how it resolves constitutional controversies surrounding congressional power. The number of dissents notably jumped in the postwar period as the Vinson and Warren Court justices disagreed among themselves over imposing restrictions on Congress. In the late years of the Rehnquist Court, the justices disagreed even more, but the pattern of dissent crystallized in new ways. The contemporary Court has been deeply divided in the cases invalidating federal laws but notably less so when upholding laws. Those stark divisions are particularly persistent, pitting the same conservative and liberal justices against each other in case after case. Interestingly, and unlike many other periods in the Court's past, the dissenters in these contemporary cases have not been locked into a permanent minority position. The justices have rotated in and out of the majority position, generally depending on the vagaries of Justices Sandra Day O'Connor and Anthony Kennedy. With Kennedy's departure from the Court, we may well be entering a period of more conventional judicial behavior in which the dissenting justices always find themselves on the losing side of divided cases. Such a situation has proved to be politically sustainable only when the losing justices are allied with a political coalition that is similarly a persistent loser in national electoral politics. The Court is in a much more difficult political position when its dissenters are allied with a coalition that enjoys sustained political power elsewhere in the government.

Normative Implications

Normative theories about whether and how the courts should exercise the power of judicial review are, by their nature, critical and reformist. They inevitably question how the Court has behaved in the past while offering guidance on how the Court should behave in the future. Normative theories are disinclined to simply take the Court as it is. They are driven by the desire to make the Court better.

Even so, normative theorizing about judicial review is fanciful and idle if it does not grapple with the institutions and political dilemmas that actually exist in the American constitutional system. Such theories strive to describe a recognizable political world and offer plausible prescriptions to be implemented. Although they necessarily abstract from some of the details and complexities of our lived experience, and although they are unavoidably somewhat idealistic, in that they imagine political actors (including justices) can be shamed or cajoled into behaving in desirable ways, they seek to be meaningful in our less than ideal world. The actual political history of American judicial review should therefore be informative for our efforts to construct normative theories about judicial review.

The so-called countermajoritarian difficulty has framed a great deal of the normative debate surrounding judicial review. Beginning with the Populists of the late nineteenth century, the judiciary's power to strike down laws as unconstitutional has been criticized as antidemocratic.[9] Alexander Bickel gave the critique its canonical form when arguing that "judicial review is a deviant institution in the American democracy"; it is "undemocratic" and allows judges to exercise "control, not in behalf of the prevailing majority, but against it."[10] If judicial review is a "deviant institution" in our democratic system, then it might require special justification, and over the past several decades, a great deal of academic work has focused on providing such justification and establishing the principles by which a judicial veto could legitimately be deployed.

As many have noted, however, the countermajoritarian difficulty is a problematic framing for examining how American courts have in fact exercised the power of judicial review.[11] Bickel asserted that, "without the mystic overtones," what "actually happens" when the Court exercises the power of judicial review is that the judiciary "thwarts the will of the representatives of the actual people of the here and now," and this is obviously true in a formal sense.[12] When the Court strikes down a statutory provision as unconstitutional, it has obstructed the expressed will of a popularly elected legislative majority. To say that this is "antidemocratic" and "countermajoritarian" in anything more than a formal sense, however, we would need to know to what degree the electoral majorities are actually invested in the policies being blocked by the Court and to what degree a judicial opinion actually hampers those majorities' ability to realize their policy goals. The mere existence of a statutory provision on the books does not tell us very much about its political significance, and the mere existence of a judicial decision enforcing constitutional constraints on Congress does not tell us very much about how confining those constraints actually are.

The countermajoritarian difficulty trades on the prominence of the Hughes Court's battle with Roosevelt over the New Deal, but as we have seen, this episode is not particularly representative of how the Court has exercised the power of judicial review across its history. The Court has rarely struck down major policies that were at the heart of the legislative agenda of an ascendant electoral majority. The Court has far more often nibbled at the edges of congressional policy-making or laid down stumbling blocks to congressional policy-making, directing legislators to pursue their policy objectives by different means. It has carved away some possible applications of a statutory provision, and it has nullified older ordinances of little interest to "the actual people of the here and now." It has excised minor features of complex statutes, struck down statutes of limited political salience, and knocked off legislation possessing symbolic value but little policy importance.

These are exercises of political power to be sure. The Court has regularly modified federal policy in ways both large and small, and it has frequently done so in a manner that cannot be easily altered by Congress. If these judicial interventions into congressional policy-making are normatively problematic, however, it is not clear that the countermajoritarian difficulty is the most useful description of the problem. There may well be some decisions by the Court that fit that description and can be properly analyzed in terms of whether the judiciary should be able to obstruct the concerted will of the people. Those decisions are important and normatively challenging, but they represent the extreme tail of cases of judicial review. It might be objectionable for the Court to prevent a committed majority of the people from pursuing their preferred social policies, but the objections raised might be less apt in cases involving legislative logrolling, special-interest rent seeking, legislative ineptitude, policy-maker oversight, or political grandstanding. Recognizing the varied circumstances in which the Court has exercised the power of judicial review can deflate our normative concerns about the practice, allowing us to grapple with the more diverse set of normative puzzles spawned by the judicial enterprise.

The Court's historical track record in exercising the power of judicial review can also be compared to the standard set by our ideal theory of judicial review. How well has the Court measured up to our favored normative metric of how such an awesome political power ought to be exercised? If the Court has rarely measured up to the posited ideal, we should at least recognize that our normative theories require a substantial departure from our lived experience and might even require the Court to behave in ways that are politically implausible and historically surprising. We might want to know how realistic it is to close the perceived gap between theory and practice.

Of course, there is no single agreed-upon normative theory of how the Court ought to exercise the power of judicial review. Moreover, the theories that have found adherents among contemporary academics generally do not match the historical self-understanding and commitments of the justices themselves. It would be an interesting challenge to see, for example, whether a compelling Dworkinian theory of constructive interpretation of the Constitution or a well-developed theory of originalist constitutional interpretation could provide adequate authority for most of the cases in which the Court has struck down a provision of a federal statute. I will not take up that herculean challenge here, but I have my doubts about whether the corpus of constitutional law developed by the Court over the past two centuries can fit within the confines of such theoretical models. From the perspective of our preferred normative theory, we might have to conclude that the Court has frequently misused the power of judicial review.

Perhaps such theories are too demanding. They are substantively rich in delineating what the content of constitutional law should be, and they generally make controversial normative claims that have not yet won widespread support on or off the Court. Perhaps it would be less demanding to ask whether the Court has at least managed to accomplish the task it set for itself in *Carolene Products*: protecting "the politically powerless" and aiding the smooth functioning of the political process.[13] We might ask, as Scot Powe did a few years ago, "Does Footnote Four Describe?"[14] Powe's answer to that question is harsh. The Court's work could perhaps (and in part) fit within the contours of footnote four of the *Carolene Products* case for a few years in the mid-twentieth century, but the Court's broader record hardly aligns with that theory. Moreover, he suggests, a more compelling descriptive theory of the Court's actions during that brief period is simply that the justices followed the lead of their political partners in the federal government. When the "Northern elites" who wrote the Civil Rights Act of 1964 dominated national politics, the Court smiled upon the same "politically powerless" groups favored by those elites. When national political leaders had different interests and commitments, the Court was generally on the same page.[15] Looking across a wider expanse of time and focusing specifically on racial minorities, Leslie Goldstein reaches much the same conclusion. "Has the Court over the long haul been more supportive of the Constitutional rights of unpopular racial minorities than the other branches?"[16] It is possible to answer in the affirmative if we focus on federal judicial interventions in state and local affairs, where the Court often acted as the other two branches backed off. Although the Court had the capacity and initiative to bring recalcitrant states to heel, its substantive values and commitments were shaped by the same forces that shaped the values and commitments of other national institutions. Minorities who are actively disfavored by national government officials have found little succor from federal judges, but benign neglect in Congress or the White House might translate into favorable rulings in the Supreme Court. The Court has "helped to some degree, some of the time."[17]

We might take yet another minimalist approach to the Court's authority to exercise judicial review. The Court might provide a "sober, second thought," enforcing the "deliberate, permanent, settled desire" of the American people when the legislature has fallen victim to the "immediate passion and desire of the passing hour."[18] Such arguments have often been used to bolster the power of the independent judiciary. Alexander Hamilton contended that the Court could help counteract the temporary "ill humors" that might seize the legislature or even the people themselves, and Alexander Bickel thought the countermajoritarian difficulty could be solved if the Court tempered the legislature's tendency to give in to the "expedient and agreeable" by taking the "long view" and articulating principles that would "gain general consent" from the people.[19] Regardless of how the idea is operationalized, judicial review as a sober second thought should produce results consonant with long-run understandings of constitutional commitments. Judicial invalidations from such a Court might be controversial in the moment, as the justices run up against the transitory passions of the electorate, but in hindsight, they should stand as uncontroversial affirmations of consensus values.

If the Court has served primarily as a sober second thought for ill-considered acts of Congress, then it ought to be possible to identify many cases in which the Court was unquestionably correct in its judgment. Has the Court been able to correctly anticipate when history would condemn a repugnant law? On first impression, this seems unlikely. Many of the Court's invalidations are famous precisely because we think the justices made the *wrong* call. But if we take the school desegregation cases as the modern lodestar of correct judicial invalidation, perhaps we might find that although the Court frequently erred in the distant past, it eventually embraced the correct view of its institutional mission and assembled a better track record.

Is this a plausible account of how the Supreme Court has used its power to strike down federal statutes? To consider this, it might be useful to divide the Court's invalidations into cases decided before and after the *Bolling* decision striking down racial segregation in schools in the District of Columbia. We might further distinguish among cases based on the importance of the policy in question. We might likewise distinguish among cases based on how the justices chose to confine the objectionable statutory provision. Finally, we might distinguish cases based on the type of constitutional issue raised.

Not every statutory provision invalidated by the Court is intrinsically important. The most politically salient cases are the ones that generate the most attention at the time of the Court's action and from later observers. But most statutory provisions are not important from either a policy or a political perspective, and as a result, their obstruction by the Court poses less of a challenge to the democratic will (such as it is). Routine instances of judicial review in low-profile cases are politically different from exceptional instances of judicial review in high-profile cases. But if low-profile cases of judicial invalidation do not challenge democratic values, they must also count for less in the historical ledger weighing the significance and value of the power of judicial review. For present purposes, we might distinguish among important provisions of landmark statutes, marginal provisions of landmark statutes, and provisions of less important statutes. If the Court were to strike down a central provision of an important statute, it would make a large policy and political splash. If the Court were to strike down a provision of an unimportant statute, it would barely make a ripple in the stream of contemporary policy-making and politics.

In deciding cases, the Court does not treat every constitutional objection in the same way. The Court sometimes strikes down a statute in whole, and it sometimes strikes down only part of a statute or a specific application of it. Those differences partly reflect a judicial choice about how expansive to make an opinion. Deciding "one case at a time" might allow the justices to commit themselves less fully, leaving room for future deliberation.[20] To some degree, those differences in treatment reflect variations in the legal posture by which cases reach the Supreme Court and how close a given application is to the core of the policy established by a statute. And to some degree, those differences reflect variations in statutory language and draftsmanship. Short, precisely written statutes may force decisions that invalidate the statute in whole. Long, complex, broadly worded statutes may allow the justices to invalidate some interpretations and applications and to circumscribe the constitutional authority of Congress without necessarily vetoing all possible applications of the statute.

Finally, the exercise of judicial review involves constitutional issues as well as statutory provisions. Congress might run afoul of a variety of constitutional objections arising from different constitutional provisions, rules, and principles. We can abstract from the details of these myriad constitutional rules and construct three broad categories of constitutional objections: civil rights and liberties, economic, and structural. The Court's own agenda and understanding of the constitutional rules have changed over time, altering the mix of constitutional issues involved in the judicial invalidation of statutes.

The Supreme Court cases invalidating provisions of federal law decided between 1789 and 1953 are organized along these three dimensions in table c-3. As the table indicates, in the bulk of these cases, the Court struck down statutory provisions only in part and as applied. Moreover, half the cases

Table C-3: Cases Invalidating Statutes by Importance and Issue, 1789–1953

		Struck in Whole			Struck as Applied	
Important provision		Rights	2		Rights	6
of landmark statute	17	Economic	5	18	Economic	3
		Structural	10		Structural	9
Marginal provision of		Rights	3		Rights	11
landmark statute	12	Economic	5	31	Economic	13
		Structural	4		Structural	7
Provision of less		Rights	8		Rights	13
important statute	30	Economic	6	47	Economic	20
		Structural	16		Structural	14

Note: Rights include due process, substantive rights, and equality; structural issues include separation of powers and federalism.

involved relatively unimportant statutes, and less than a quarter involved relatively important legislative provisions. This suggests a Court working on the margins of American politics rather than within its central core.

If any of the Court's invalidations were to gain our retrospective approval, they would likely involve relatively unimportant federal policies. The Court's decisions striking down important federal policies are especially unlikely to win unanimous support now. Judicial nullifications of major policies—the ban on slavery in the territories, wartime legal tender, Reconstruction-era civil rights statutes, the federal income tax, the prohibition on child labor, central components of the New Deal—were controversial at the time they were decided and have failed to gain much additional support in subsequent generations. If anything, such decisions are likely to look even worse in hindsight than they did at the time. From the perspective of the present, the Court was far more likely to get it wrong when striking down important federal policies, making the power of judicial review more of a liability than an asset.

The constitutional issues that dominated the Court's docket also tend to work against a favorable historical reassessment of the Court's handiwork in its first century and a half. The Court's docket was crowded with cases claiming that Congress had violated structural features of the Constitution (primarily federalism) or exceeded limitations on its power to intervene in economic affairs. From a post–New Deal perspective, most of the Court's efforts to enforce structural or economic limits on congressional power have a bad odor. The Court spent the bulk of its time enforcing constitutional rules that have since been repudiated. Rather than defending widely accepted constitutional values against temporary political departures, the Court was more often advancing contested political values that lost support over time.

The corner of the Court's historical docket that was most likely to invoke enduring constitutional principles involved matters of legal procedure. Such cases were unlikely to involve challenges to important statutory provisions, however. Perhaps the sole exception was *Ng Fung Ho v. White*, which challenged a core provision of the General Immigration Act of 1917.[21] Congress authorized the deportation of aliens by executive order, but Gin Sang Get claimed to be the child of a US citizen and was therefore entitled under the Fifth Amendment to a judicial hearing before being deported. Writing for a unanimous Court, Justice Brandeis agreed. Similarly, in *Wong Wing v. United States*, the Court addressed a more marginal provision of an earlier statute that authorized the sentencing of Chinese aliens found on American soil to imprisonment and hard labor after only a summary hearing.[22] The justices thought the imposition of such criminal punishment required a jury trial. Those decisions marked rare instances in which the Court obstructed important policy decisions in the name of constitutional principles that remain vibrant today.

Other procedural cases nibbled at the margins of congressional statutes. When Congress declared that inhabitants of the newly acquired Alaska Territory were not entitled to traditional jury trials, the Court objected in *Rasmussen v. United States*.[23] When Congress determined that the expediency of collecting taxes necessitated the imposition of time limits on trials to dispute tax assessments, the Court insisted in *United States v. Phelps* that the legislature could not interfere with judges' ability to grant continuances that they considered necessary to ensure a fair trial.[24] Upon revising the internal duties on tobacco, Congress announced that only those who had already paid taxes under the old rate were exempt. When a Virginia tobacco trader was fined for paying only the old duty rate on products that had already been stamped when the new law went into effect, he objected. The Court agreed that Congress had, in effect, adopted an ex post facto law that punished those who were in compliance with the relevant laws at the time of the new statute's enactment.[25]

In such marginal cases, the Court also advanced protections for property and economic activities that might still seem appealing. In several cases, the Court balanced broader procedural concerns with specifically economic interests. At the end of the nineteenth century, for example, the Court insisted that Congress could not determine what constituted just compensation when the federal government seized private property. Congress could determine when private property was needed for a public purpose, but only a court could ascertain what the constitutionally required level of compensation should be.[26] When the Marshall Court was asked to apply a federal statute that purported to resolve a disputed boundary between territory controlled by Virginia and the US government (in favor of land titles acquired from the federal government), the Court observed that Congress could not constitutionally "adjudicate in the form of legislation," and as a consequence, Congress's action was impermissible.[27]

In myriad tax cases, the Court was called on to determine whether Congress had accidentally (or perhaps not so accidentally) stumbled across a constitutional line. The principles at stake in those cases are no more politically salient today than they were at the time, but the Court's efforts to preserve them remain unobjectionable. The War Revenue Act of 1898, for example, generated a lengthy stream of constitutional litigation. In *Fairbank v. United States*, the Court pointed out that a stamp tax on a foreign bill of lading is "in substance and effect equivalent to a tax on the articles included in the bill of lading, and therefore a tax or duty on exports, and in conflict with the constitutional prohibition."[28] The Court applied the same prohibition to bar taxes on charters to foreign ports, taxes on marine insurance on cargo for export, and taxes on sales that were simply steps in the export process.[29] Similarly, the Court held that Congress could not impose a gift tax on gifts that had already been fully consummated or an estate tax on land that had already been transferred.[30]

Although the Court's decisions on structural issues generally went against the grain of post–New Deal constitutional jurisprudence, there are some potential exceptions. The congressional struggle to identify how best to handle the transition from territorial to federal courts upon the achievement of statehood has no modern significance. Even to those who regularly made

Table C-4: Cases Invalidating Statutes by Importance and Issue, 1954–2018

		Struck in Whole			Struck as Applied	
Important provision of landmark statute	15	Rights	11	15	Rights	11
		Economic	0		Economic	0
		Structural	4		Structural	4
Marginal provision of landmark statute	35	Rights	26	38	Rights	26
		Economic	2		Economic	2
		Structural	7		Structural	10
Provision of less important statute	45	Rights	30	42	Rights	29
		Economic	3		Economic	3
		Structural	12		Structural	10

Note: Rights include due process, substantive rights, and equality; structural issues include separation of powers and federalism.

decisions related to statehood, such issues were of minimal political significance. Perhaps as a consequence, the Court's determination that Congress could not authorize the US Supreme Court to continue to hear cases on appeal from the Florida territorial court after Florida had become a state caused little more than embarrassment in the legislature.[31] The problem of the judicial transition from territorial to state and federal courts was largely a matter of neglect. However, the congressional effort to specify that Oklahoma's capital could not be moved by the government or the people of the state for several years after statehood cannot be chalked up to mere neglect. The Court's conclusion that this statutory provision violated the "constitutional equality of the States" is as persuasive now as it was then (although some today might be eager to limit that principle so that Congress can treat states differently in at least some circumstances).[32]

Table C-4 repeats the categories found in table C-3 but shifts the time frame to the period after the *Bolling* decision. As a comparison of the two tables shows, the Court's exercise of judicial review has shifted significantly since the mid-twentieth century. The Court invalidated federal laws in roughly the same number of cases decided in the past six decades as it did in the prior sixteen, and it has become much more likely to strike down statutory provisions in their entirety rather than in part or as applied. The Court has also become less likely to strike down provisions of unimportant statutes; such cases once accounted for half of all invalidations, but they constitute just over one-third of the cases decided since midcentury. This does not necessarily mean that the Court has focused on more important policies, however. For the most part, the Court has shifted its attention to less important provisions of landmark statutes, but there has been little change in how often it strikes down core provisions of important statutes.

More striking than the shift in the importance of the policies nullified by the Court is the shift in the constitutional issues at stake. Whereas the Court's work prior to *Bolling* was almost equally divided among civil rights and liberties, economic issues, and structural issues (though leaning toward the last), the Court since midcentury has directed the bulk of its attention to the first class of issues. Economic issues have nearly disappeared from the Court's more recent agenda, and federalism cases have been cut in half, while the number of civil rights and civil liberties cases has more than doubled. The shift away from economic and federalism issues and toward civil rights and liberties has been even more dramatic in the set of cases involving landmark statutes; since the mid-twentieth century, when the Court invalidates statutory provisions on federalism or economic grounds, those statutes are likely to be unimportant ones.

This shift in the Court's constitutional agenda might be a good sign for a minimalist theory of judicial review. To the extent that judicial review based on economic issues and federalism is unlikely to win much favor from modern commentators, the Court might be avoiding some controversy by side-stepping such issues. Unfortunately for a minimalist theory, however, the types of civil rights and civil liberties issues that have absorbed the Court's attention in recent decades are themselves likely to be controversial, perhaps particularly when marshaled in the context of federal statutes.

Whether involving due process, substantive liberties, or civil rights, the Court's invalidations of federal policies in such cases are frequently controversial. Probably leading the list of controversial rulings would be the line of campaign finance cases that began with *Buckley v. Valeo*.[33] Although *United States v. Windsor* might eventually win consensus approval as public opinion continues to shift in support of same-sex marriage, we are not yet at that point.[34] The Court's invalidation of congressional funding restrictions on the Legal Services Corporation is probably just as controversial today as it was in 2001 when it was decided.[35] It seems likely that the Court's procedural objection to the use of dependent child income tax deductions to determine eligibility for food stamps would continue to attract dissent.[36] The Court's objection to warrantless OSHA inspections is likely still controversial, and the Court's invalidation of a federal program to send public school teachers to parochial schools to provide remedial education services has been formally overruled.[37] *Boumediene*'s objection to the Military Commissions Act of 2006 has been accommodated but hardly embraced.[38] Then, of course, there are the controversies surrounding the Court's modern federalism and separation of powers decisions, from *INS v. Chadha* to *Clinton v. New York City* to *Shelby County v. Holder.*[39]

But perhaps there are still modern cases that, in hindsight, would win widespread support. In *Reno v. American Civil Liberties Union*, a unanimous Court struck down a provision of the Communications Decency Act.[40] Although President Bill Clinton publicly bewailed the Court's action, administration officials privately recognized that the act was unconstitutional.[41] The same might be said for the invalidation of the Flag Protection Act of 1989, although it is not clear that mass opinion would readily align with elite opinion on the scope of constitutional protections for flag burners.[42] Similarly, the Court's unanimous decision to carve out a ministerial exception in the Americans with Disabilities Act is probably coherent with contemporary norms and might be regarded by Congress as a friendly amendment to the statute (although public and elite opinion about the desirability of religious exemptions from generally applicable rules has become sharply polarized in the years since Congress embraced that principle to great acclaim in the Religious Freedom Restoration Act of 1993).[43] Early gender equity cases such as *Califano v. Goldfarb* and some equality cases such as *Jimenez v. Weinberger* were once controversial, but now they would undoubtedly win unanimous support.[44] Timothy Leary's unanimous victory against the 1937 Marihuana Tax Act likely stands the test of time.[45] Despite the dissent of Justice Alito, the Court's decision to strike down Congress's initial effort to regulate depictions of animal cruelty might command general acceptance, as would the unanimous decisions objecting to efforts to censor the federal mails and extending First Amendment protections to protesters using public streets running through an open military base.[46] The once controversial case of *Trop v. Dulles*, determining that Congress could not use the revocation of US citizenship as a criminal punishment, is probably now beyond controversy, although it is hard to say whether the general public would uniformly line up behind that principle if the issue regained political salience (and the denaturalization of American citizens does seem to be reemerging as a political issue).[47]

Whether from the political Right or the political Left, the Court's decisions invalidating federal policies routinely generate controversy. Even in hindsight, those decisions often seem misguided to large sectors of the political elite and the mass public. Rather than providing a sober second thought, the Court is more likely to act as yet another partisan participant in the policy-making process, wielding a veto power to strike down policies that many would have preferred to leave in place, and doing so in the name of constitutional values that many would reject. For much of its history, the Court regularly acted on constitutional principles that are now regarded as defunct. But even in the modern period, the Court routinely strikes down laws that, in its opinion, conflict with principles that are deeply controversial.

Even so, the Court has sometimes acted in ways that would, at least in hindsight, win plaudits rather than denunciations. This is perhaps most true in cases involving largely procedural protections, whether narrowly within the scope of due process or more broadly involving free speech. Such values have proved to be enduring, but they have come under pressure from precisely the kind of passionate politics that causes democratic theorists to worry. American-style judicial review might also be particularly useful in enforcing those principles, since they often arise in the context of specific applications of broadly worded statutes. The Court has often stepped in to carve out exceptions to policies that were perhaps more broad-reaching than even the legislators themselves intended. Being down in the trenches of legal applications allows judges to see specific examples of where policy and principle might come into conflict. Political insulation allows federal judges to protect the rights of unpopular minorities and dissenters who might otherwise be singled out for bad treatment, even when Americans fail to respect the abstract principles they claim to value.

The historical record also suggests a possible addendum to the minimalist theory of judicial review. The sober second thought scenario emphasizes the possibility that a relatively insulated and detached judiciary can rise above tumultuous democratic passions and preserve enduring principles. But these instances of horizontal judicial review by the US Supreme Court only occasionally evince either democratic turbulence or judicial steadfastness. The record does suggest, however, how judicial review might be useful without having to appeal to thick and controversial normative theories. Often what the justices bring to the table of American politics is less Bickelian principle than technical expertise about complicated but relatively uncontroversial constitutional rules. While we might imagine that the legislative branch could develop a comparable expertise and thus avoid constitutional errors, legislators might reasonably prefer to delegate that task to the courts and rely on friendly judges to correct their mistakes.[48] At the same time, legislators have repeatedly shown that other imperatives—such as extracting revenue or winning reelection—often take priority, making constitutional errors a systematic feature of American governance. A judiciary that leans in favor of liberty just as much as the legislature leans in favor of national security, public morality, or material enrichment might play a useful countervailing role without necessarily being broadly countermajoritarian.

On the whole, a minimalist theory of judicial review would have a difficult time accounting for most of the Court's actual work in exercising the power of horizontal judicial review. The Court, on occasion, intervenes in the political process in ways that win widespread support. Far more often, however, the Court's actions are controversial, not only at the time of the decision but in hindsight as well. To justify the historical record of how the Court has used the power of judicial review, we would have to turn to a thicker—and more controversial—set of normative arguments. We would need to justify a Court that was countermajoritarian in a deeper sense—a Court that not merely formally obstructs the expressed legislative will but also blocks the substantive realization of democratic policy preferences as such and advances constitutional values that the people themselves do not actually (or at least universally) hold.

The antidemocratic character of these exercises of judicial review is complicated, however, by the Court's close relationship with elected political leaders. The Court often defies Congress in the name of values to which party leaders are putatively committed. Those decisions might well be persistently controversial, either in the sense that the general public does not overwhelmingly endorse them or in the sense that legislators are incapable of constructing a majority willing to cast the same vote themselves. The Court's insulation and independence allow the justices to do things that the elected members of Congress might be unwilling and unable to do, even if they are not implacably opposed. The Court has rarely stood for universally embraced and historically enduring political principles, in part because there are few such principles—or at least few such principles that must be deployed to invalidate an action of Congress. Congress rarely violates universally embraced and historically enduring principles. Congress does, however, routinely violate principles that are more contested and less enduring but nonetheless command substantial political support within a given historical era. When the Court intervenes to vindicate those principles against an errant national legislature, it is often doing the political work that political leaders want it to do. It is acting as a player within democratic politics, not simply as a constitutional guardian standing outside of democratic politics.

Appendix
Identifying Cases of Judicial Review

Identifying the cases in which the US Supreme Court has restricted the scope of a statute, or invalidated it entirely, on the grounds that the federal law is unconstitutional is surprisingly difficult. When scholars first began to seriously debate the origins and use of the power of judicial review—and young constitutional scholar Edward Corwin first gave it a name—there was no canonical list of cases in which the Court had struck down laws. Estimates ranged from zero to dozens. The US Supreme Court itself did not maintain such a list or clearly identify cases as exercises of judicial review when they were decided, although one Court reporter eventually drafted an influential list of such cases. Finally, at the request of Congress, Edward Corwin assembled a list of cases in which the Court had "struck down, in whole or in part," federal statutes. That list from the mid-twentieth century has been maintained by the Congressional Research Service (CRS).[1]

But that list is incomplete and is subject to more uncertainty than might be assumed. Cases were added to *and deleted from* early versions of Corwin's list, as the scope of the task was refined. Most notably, some (but not all) cases in which the Court had struck down a statutory provision as applied to a particular factual situation were removed from the initial list.[2] As a consequence, there has been no systematic accounting of cases in which the Court has refused to apply federal law on constitutional grounds.[3] Some cases in which the Court invalidated statutory provisions in their entirety were overlooked (especially in the early decades, when neither the justices nor the reporter were always clear about what they were doing, and the political stakes were often low).[4] Even more significantly for present purposes, Corwin did not even attempt to identify cases in which statutory provisions had been upheld against constitutional challenge—and neither did anyone else.

The complications of creating a better list are multiple. The syllabus prepared by the Court reporter is not always an accurate guide (especially in the nineteenth century). Judicial opinions are not always clear about what the Court intended to do and what the effects of a decision might be. The conceptualization of the very object under examination—judicial review—is not as well established as one might expect. To what extent do cases striking down the application of a law count as judicial review? When exactly has the Court upheld a statute against challenge? What separates statutory interpretation from judicial review? What are the implications of various "avoidance" doctrines? The approach taken for this study seemed to be an improvement over existing inventories of cases of judicial review, but there is little doubt that there is room for reasonable disagreement on the margins, and other lists might be either more or less inclusive, depending on the goal of the analysis.

The goal here is to identify cases in which the US Supreme Court *deliberately defined and enforced* constitutional limits on the legislative authority of Congress. This immediately omits many exercises of judicial review. It ignores federal constitutional review of the state governments. It sets aside the many cases in which the Supreme Court reviewed the constitutionality of judicial or executive actions that did not rely on or implicate congressional legislative authority. (For example, much of constitutional criminal procedure—a very large set of cases—is aimed at judicial and executive actors, and its application does not define or impinge on legislative authority.[5]) The small number of cases involving congressional actions but not legislative authority (e.g., the congressional power of contempt or impeachment) are also ignored.[6] Of course, this also excludes exercises of judicial review by lower courts that are not eventually resolved by the US Supreme Court.[7]

To address these problems, the data set reported here was constructed from the ground up. The full text of every US Supreme Court opinion, with accompanying notes, is available electronically from a variety of services such as Lexis-Nexis. Word search terms were identified that would cast an

extremely wide net over the relevant cases but would at least make an initial cut at excluding irrelevant cases that did not raise constitutional issues
about federal statutes. Keywords were identified that would call up at least
every case on the list of invalidated cases maintained by the Congressional
Research Service, as well as cases of judicial invalidation of federal statutes
identified by subsequent scholars.[8] A full-text search of all cases decided by
the US Supreme Court resulted in a list of roughly 10,000 cases, which were
then read to determine whether the legislative power of Congress under the
Constitution had been reviewed by the Court. Additional cases subsequently
cited by the Supreme Court as establishing relevant constitutional principles
or cited in the existing literature were also read.

This data set is concerned with cases in which the justices explicitly considered a constitutional challenge to the scope of federal legislative authority and rendered a substantive judgment as to whether the case fell within
or without that authority. Although, in principle, every case creates the opportunity to exercise the power of judicial review, the Court relatively rarely
defines and enforces the constitutional limits on the national legislature's
power. The data set *excludes* cases in which the Court simply applied federal
law without explicit constitutional deliberation, as well as the more difficult
cases in which the Court noted the existence of a constitutional challenge but
did not address it, explicitly declined to answer it, or refused to articulate a
binding constitutional rule because the case was disposed of on jurisdictional
or other unrelated grounds.[9] Also *excluded* are cases in which the Court made
trivial references to Congress's constitutional authority to pass the law being
applied or dismissed a constitutional challenge without elaboration as fully
resolved in an earlier case (cases in which the Court invalidated or limited
legislative authority but with very little explanation or justification of its actions are included).[10]

Cases are *included*, even when the Court's opinion airily dismissed a constitutional challenge as easily resolved with minimal analysis, if it is evident
that the constitutional issue was in fact raised and contested by the parties or
that the Court later relied on that case for the constitutional proposition at
issue. Cases that contained a single-sentence reference to a precedent settling
the constitutional claim are *excluded*, but cases are *included* if the justices felt
obliged to explain, expound upon, or further develop existing precedents,
even when they asserted that the issue was not new.[11]

Cases are *included* as limiting congressional authority under the Constitution (invalidating or narrowing a statute) whenever a constitutional proposition limiting the power of the national legislature was cited to disallow the application of a statute to the case at hand, even when that involved a creative "interpretation" of the statute's meaning rather than an explicit nullification of the statute. "Saving constructions" that have the effect of placing hard constraints on congressional power and severing the application in question from the scope of the legislation in order to salvage the broader statute's constitutionality are recognized as exercises of the Court's power of judicial review to limit Congress.[12] Notably, such saving constructions do not, in fact, avoid the constitutional question or avoid imposing limits on legislative authority. In contrast to Justice Brandeis's suggestion in *Ashwander v. Tennessee Valley Authority*, the Court in these cases "typically interpreted the Constitution in ways that settled potential statutory questions," rather than "interpreted [the] statutes in ways that enabled [the] Justices to avoid potential constitutional questions."[13] Moreover, these cases do not necessarily "save" the statute from wholesale nullification because both the litigants and the justices are, in the first instance, concerned with the application of the statute before the Court in a given case. There is no necessary challenge to the statutory provision as a whole or as it might be applied in other situations, and the Court does not necessarily vouchsafe the validity of the law as it might be applied in all future cases. It does not interpret the law so as to "uphold" it against a constitutional challenge in such cases. It rules out the effort to apply the law in the particular case as being beyond the constitutional authority of Congress, even as it indicates the possibility that the same statutory provision might have other applications that are constitutionally valid. The scope of the statute is narrowed on constitutional grounds in such cases, and congressional authority is circumscribed by judicial interpretation of the Constitution. Cases are *excluded*, however, when the Court explicitly left the constitutional question open or left Congress with the power to overturn the Court's constitutionally driven interpretive assumptions, such as with constitutionally motivated "clear statement" rules.[14]

This process yielded a total of 1,308 cases in the data set, approximately 13 percent of the cases returned from the initial electronic search (as of the conclusion of the Court's October 2017 term). Of these, 345 invalidated or limited statutory provisions, and 963 upheld federal legislation against constitutional challenge.

The full list of cases is archived as the "Judicial Review of Congress" data set at www.princeton.edu/~kewhitt. The archived materials include both a text list of cases evaluating the constitutionality of federal statutes comparable to the CRS list and a data set of cases and associated political and legal variables.

NOTES

PREFACE

1 Keith E. Whittington, *Constitutional Construction* (Cambridge, MA: Harvard University Press, 1999).

2 Keith E. Whittington, *Political Foundations of Judicial Supremacy* (Princeton, NJ: Princeton University Press, 2007).

3 Thomas M. Keck, *The Most Activist Supreme Court in History* (Chicago: University of Chicago Press, 2004).

4 Robert A. Dahl, "Decision-Making in a Democracy: The Supreme Court as a National Policy-Maker," *Journal of Public Law* 6 (1957): 279. On regime theory, see Thomas M. Keck, "Party Politics or Judicial Independence? The Regime Politics Literature Hits the Law Schools," *Law and Social Inquiry* 32 (2007): 511; Mark A. Graber, "Constructing Judicial Review," *Annual Review of Political Science* 8 (2005): 425; Julie Novkov, "Understanding Law as a Democratic Institution through U.S. Constitutional Development," *Law and Social Inquiry* 40 (2015): 811.

5 Edward S. Corwin, *The Constitution of the United States of America: Analysis and Interpretation* (Washington, DC: Government Printing Office, 1953).

6 Mark A. Graber, "Naked Land Transfers and American Constitutional Development," *Vanderbilt Law Review* 53 (2000): 71.

7 Howard Gillman, Mark A. Graber, and Keith E. Whittington, *American Constitutionalism*, 2 vols. (New York: Oxford University Press, 2013).

CHAPTER 1. THE POLITICS OF JUDICIAL REVIEW

1 Barack Obama, "Statement on the United States Supreme Court Ruling on the Defense of Marriage Act, June 26, 2013," in *Public Papers of the President of the United States* (Washington, DC: Government Printing Office, 2014).

2 Chris McGreal, "Obama Warns 'Unelected' Supreme Court Not to Strike down Healthcare Law," *Guardian*, April 2, 2012.

3 Charlie Savage and Sheryl Gay Stolberg, "Obama Says Liberal Courts May Have Overreached," *New York Times*, April 30, 2010, A15.

4 George W. Bush, "Statement on the United States Supreme Court Ruling on Individual Gun Rights, June 26, 2008," in *Public Papers of the President*.

5 George W. Bush, "Statement on the Decision of the Massachusetts Supreme Judicial Court on Same-Sex Marriage, February 4, 2004," in *Public Papers of the President*. For present purposes, I bracket the debate over *how* judges ought to interpret and apply the Constitution. It should be noted, however, that President

Bush tended to use the phrase "judicial restraint" less to denote deference to legislative decisions than to mean "faithfully interpret[ing] the Constitution, and not us[ing] the courts to invent laws or dictate social policy." Conversely, "judicial activists" are not simply judges who overturn the expressed will of the elected legislature but those who do not "strictly interpret the law" and instead "legislate from the bench," regardless of whether that results in upholding or striking down legislation. George W. Bush, "Remarks to the Cincinnati Chapter of the Federalist Society in Cincinnati, Ohio, October 6, 2008," in *Public Papers of the President*; "Remarks at the Max M. Fisher National Republican Leadership Award Dinner in Livonia, Michigan, June 25, 2008," ibid. Such a political posture is more in keeping with recent conservative constitutional theory; see, e.g., Keith E. Whittington, "The New Originalism," *Georgetown Journal of Law and Politics* 2 (2004): 599.

6 Savage and Stolberg, "Obama Says Liberal Courts May Have Overreached"; Michael D. Shear, "G.O.P. Turns to the Courts to Aid Agenda," *New York Times*, January 4, 2015, A1.

7 Jamin Raskin, "Idiots, Maniacs, and the Problem with Judicial Activism," *Huffington Post*, January 23, 2013, http://www.huffingtonpost.com/jamie-raskin/idiots-maniacs-and-the-pr_b_4124613.html; Brian S. Brown, "National Organization for Marriage (NOM) Issues Statement Following US Supreme Court Decision on Marriage," *Christian News Wire*, June 26, 2015.

8 *Cong. Rec.*, 111th Cong., 1st sess. (August 5, 2009), 8851.

9 *Cong. Rec.*, 109th Cong., 1st sess. (September 21, 2005), 10251. Notably, when discussing Bush's nomination of Roberts, Leahy characterized the "essential function of the judiciary" as providing "a check on Presidential power." Ibid.

10 *Cong. Rec.*, 109th Cong., 1st sess. (November 16, 2006), 26350.

11 Thomas M. Keck, *The Most Activist Supreme Court in History* (Chicago: University of Chicago Press, 2004).

12 Brian Resnick, "Anthony Kennedy: The U.S. 'Is Not a Functioning Democracy,'" *National Journal*, October 4, 2013.

13 Adam Liptak, "Court Is 'One of the Most Activist,' Ginsburg Says, Vowing to Stay," *New York Times*, August 25, 2013, A1.

14 Antonin Scalia, "Mullahs of the West: Judges as Moral Arbiters" (unpublished manuscript, August 24, 2009), 14, http://www.rpo.gov.pl/pliki/12537879280.pdf.

15 Keith E. Whittington, "The Least Activist Supreme Court in History? The Roberts Court and the Exercise of Judicial Review," *Notre Dame Law Review* 89 (2014): 2219.

16 See Keith E. Whittington, "Legislative Sanctions and the Strategic Environment of Judicial Review," *I-Con: The International Journal of Constitutional Law* 1 (2003): 446.

17 Alexander Hamilton, James Madison, and John Jay, *The Federalist Papers*, ed. Clinton Rossiter (New York: American Library, 1961), No. 78.

18 See John Ferejohn, "Independent Judges, Dependent Judiciary: Explaining Judicial Independence," *Southern California Law Review* 72 (1999): 353.

19 See Bradley C. Canon, "Defining the Dimensions of Judicial Activism," *Judicature* 66 (1983): 237; Keenan Kmiec, "The Origins and Current Meaning of Judicial Activism," *California Law Review* 92 (2004): 1441.

20 See, e.g., Gregory A. Caldeira and Donald J. McCrone, "Of Time and Judicial Activism: A Study of the U.S. Supreme Court, 1800–1973," in *Supreme Court Activism and Restraint*, ed. Stephen C. Halpern and Charles M. Lamb (Lanham, MD: Lexington Books, 1982); Keck, *Most Activist Supreme Court in History*; Lori A. Ringhand, "Judicial Activism: An Empirical Examination of Voting Behavior on the Rehnquist Natural Court," *Constitutional Commentary* 24 (2007): 43; Stephanie Lindquist and Frank B. Cross, *Measuring Judicial Activism* (New York: Oxford University Press, 2009).

21 See William G. Ross, *A Muted Fury* (Princeton, NJ: Princeton University Press, 1994); Barry Friedman, "The History of the Countermajoritarian Difficulty, Part Three: The Lessons of *Lochner*," *New York University Law Review* 76 (2001): 1383.

22 James B. Weaver, *A Call to Action* (Des Moines, IA: n.p., 1892), 67, 70, 73.

23 James Bradley Thayer, "The Origin and Scope of the American Doctrine of Constitutional Law," *Harvard Law Review* 7 (1893): 130, 135.

24 Henry Steele Commager, "Judicial Review and Democracy," *Virginia Quarterly Review* 19 (1943): 417. See also Barry Friedman, "The History of the Countermajoritarian Difficulty, Part Four: Law's Politics," *University of Pennsylvania Law Review* 148 (2000): 971.

25 Learned Hand, *The Bill of Rights* (Cambridge, MA: Harvard University Press, 1958), 74.

26 Alexander M. Bickel, *The Least Dangerous Branch* (Indianapolis: Bobbs-Merrill, 1962), 16, 17. See also Laura Kalman, *The Strange Career of Legal Liberalism* (New Haven, CT: Yale University Press, 1996); Barry Friedman, "The Birth of an Academic Obsession: The History of the Countermajoritarian Difficulty, Part Five," *Yale Law Journal* 112 (2002): 153.

27 Jeremy Waldron, *Law and Disagreement* (New York: Oxford University Press, 1999). Waldron has subsequently softened his stance; see, e.g., Jeremy Waldron, "The Core of the Case against Judicial Review," *Yale Law Journal* 115 (2006): 1346.

28 Gerald N. Rosenberg, *The Hollow Hope*, 2nd ed. (Chicago: University of Chicago Press, 2008); Matthew E. K. Hall, *The Nature of Supreme Court Power* (New York: Cambridge University Press, 2011); Martin J. Sweet, *Merely Judgment* (Charlottesville: University of Virginia Press, 2010).

29 See, e.g., Robert M. Howard and Jeffrey A. Segal, "A Preference for Deference? The Supreme Court and Judicial Review," *Political Research Quarterly* 57 (2004): 131; Thomas M. Keck, "Party, Policy, or Duty: Why Does the Supreme Court Invalidate Federal Statutes?" *American Political Science Review* 101 (2007): 321;

Stefanie A. Lindquist and Rori Spill Solberg, "Judicial Review by the Burger and Rehnquist Courts," *Political Research Quarterly* 60 (2007): 71.

30 Georg Vanberg, "Legislative-Judicial Relations: A Game-Theoretic Approach to Constitutional Review," *American Journal of Political Science* 45 (2001): 346; Laura Langer, *Judicial Review in State Supreme Courts* (Albany: State University of New York, 2002); Tom S. Clark, *The Limits on Judicial Independence* (New York: Cambridge University Press, 2011); Jeffrey A. Segal, Chad Westerland, and Stefanie A. Lindquist, "Congress, the Supreme Court, and Judicial Review: Testing a Constitutional Separation of Powers Model," *American Journal of Political Science* 55 (2011): 89; Anna Harvey, *A Mere Machine* (New Haven, CT: Yale University Press, 2013).

31 Robert A. Dahl, "Decision-Making in a Democracy: The Supreme Court as a National Policy-Maker," *Journal of Public Law* 6 (1957): 283, 291.

32 Ibid., 281, 280.

33 Ibid., 284.

34 Ibid., 285. See also Robert G. McCloskey, revised by Sanford Levinson, *The American Supreme Court*, 6th ed. (Chicago: University of Chicago Press, 2016); Howard Gillman, "Robert G. McCloskey, Historical Institutionalism, and the Arts of Judicial Governance," in *The Pioneers of Judicial Behavior*, ed. Nancy L. Maveety (Ann Arbor: University of Michigan Press, 2003); Cornell W. Clayton, "The Supreme Court and Political Jurisprudence: New and Old Institutionalisms," in *Supreme Court Decision-Making*, ed. Cornell W. Clayton and Howard Gillman (Chicago: University of Chicago Press, 1999).

35 See, e.g., Richard Funston, "The Supreme Court and Critical Elections," *American Political Science Review* 69 (1976): 795; Jonathan D. Casper, "The Supreme Court and National Policy Making," *American Political Science Review* 70 (1976): 50; Roger B. Handberg and Harold F. Hill Jr., "Judicial Activism and Restraint on the United States Supreme Court: A Political-Behavioral Analysis," *California Western Law Review* 20 (1984): 173.

36 Dahl, "Decision-Making in a Democracy," 291.

37 Michael J. Klarman, *From Jim Crow to Civil Rights* (New York: Oxford University Press, 2004); Barry Friedman, *The Will of the People* (New York: Farrar, Straus & Giroux, 2009); Jeffrey Rosen, *The Most Democratic Branch* (New York: Oxford University Press, 2006); Reva B. Siegel, "Constitutional Culture, Social Movement Conflict, and Constitutional Change: The Case of the de Facto ERA," *California Law Review* 94 (2006): 1323.

38 Mark Ramseyer, "The Puzzling Independence of Courts: A Comparative Approach," *Journal of Legal Studies* 23 (1994): 721; Tom Ginsburg, *Judicial Review in New Democracies* (New York: Cambridge University Press, 2003); Matthew Stephenson, "When the Devil Turns . . . : Political Foundations of Independent Judicial Review," *Journal of Legal Studies* 32 (2003): 59; Georg Vanberg, "Establishing and Maintaining Judicial Independence," in *The Oxford Handbook of*

Law and Politics, ed. Keith E. Whittington, R. Daniel Kelemen, and Gregory A. Caldeira (New York: Oxford University Press, 2008).

39 Quoted in Charles Warren, *The Supreme Court in United States History* (Boston: Little, Brown, 1922), 1:86.

40 Mark A. Graber, "The Nonmajoritarian Difficulty: Legislative Deference to the Judiciary," *Studies in American Political Development* 7 (1993): 35; Dahl, "Decision-Making in a Democracy," 286. See also Lucas A. Powe Jr., *The Supreme Court and the American Elite, 1789–2008* (Cambridge, MA: Harvard University Press, 2009); Howard Gillman, "How Political Parties Use the Courts to Advance Their Agendas: Federal Courts in the United States, 1875–1891," *American Political Science Review* 96 (2002): 511; Jack M. Balkin and Sanford Levinson, "Understanding the Constitutional Revolution," *Virginia Law Review* 87 (2001): 1045.

41 Keith E. Whittington, *Political Foundations of Judicial Supremacy* (Princeton, NJ: Princeton University Press, 2007); Mark A. Graber, "The Nonmajoritarian Difficulty: Legislative Deference to the Judiciary," *Studies in American Political Development* 7 (1993): 35.

42 The theory reached its canonical form in Walter Dean Burnham, *Critical Elections and the Mainsprings of American Politics* (New York: W. W. Norton, 1970). For a broad critique, see David R. Mayhew, *Electoral Realignments* (New Haven, CT: Yale University Press, 2002).

43 Dahl, "Decision-Making in a Democracy," 284.

44 Cornell W. Clayton and J. Mitchell Pickerill, "The Politics of Criminal Justice: How the New Right Regime Shaped the Rehnquist Court's Criminal Justice Jurisprudence," *Georgetown Law Journal* 94 (2006): 1385; Kevin J. McMahon, *Nixon's Court* (Chicago: University of Chicago Press, 2011).

45 See, e.g., Kevin J. McMahon, *Reconsidering Roosevelt on Race* (Chicago: University of Chicago Press, 2010); Mark Tushnet, "The Burger Court in Historical Perspective: The Triumph of Country-Club Republicanism," in *The Burger Court*, ed. Bernard Schwartz (New York: Oxford University Press, 1988).

46 Hamilton, Madison, and Jay, *Federalist Papers*, No. 48.

47 Lochner v. New York, 198 U.S. 45 (1905).

48 Brown v. Board of Education of Topeka, 347 U.S. 483 (1954).

49 Roe v. Wade, 410 U.S. 113 (1973).

50 Eakin v. Raub, 12 Serg. & Rawle 330, 356 (1825).

51 Thayer, "Origin and Scope of American Doctrine of Constitutional Law," 154, 155.

52 Oliver Wendell Holmes, "Law and the Court," in *Collected Legal Papers*, ed. Harold J. Laski (New York: Harcourt, Brace & Howe, 1920), 195–196.

53 Henry Steele Commager, *Majority Rule and Minority Rights* (New York: Oxford University Press, 1943), 27.

54 Dred Scott v. Sandford, 60 U.S. 393 (1857).

55 Pollock v. Farmers' Loan & Trust Co., 157 U.S. 429 (1895); Pollock v. Farmers' Loan & Trust Co., 158 U.S. 601 (1895).

56 Commager, *Majority Rule and Minority Rights*, 41, 55, 56.

57 See John B. Gates, *The Supreme Court and Partisan Realignment* (Boulder, CO: Westview Press, 1992); Jonathan P. Kastellec, "Judicial Federalism and Representation," *Journal of Law and Courts* 6 (2018): 51.

58 Mark Tushnet, *Weak Courts, Strong Rights* (Princeton, NJ: Princeton University Press, 2009); Alec Stone Sweet, *Governing with Judges* (New York: Oxford University Press, 2000).

59 For a consideration of how compelling such denials might be, see Matthew S. Brogdon, "Political Jurisprudence and the Role of the Supreme Court: Framing the Judicial Power in the Federal Convention of 1787," *American Political Thought* 6 (2017): 171; Eric J. Segall, *Supreme Myths* (New York: Praeger, 2012).

60 See, e.g., Edward S. Corwin, "The Establishment of Judicial Review," *Michigan Law Review* 9 (1910): 102; Charles Grove Haines, *The American Doctrine of Judicial Supremacy* (New York: Macmillan, 1914), 16n2.

61 For explorations of this conceit, see Gary Lawson and Guy Seidman, *A Great Power of Attorney* (Lawrence: University Press of Kansas, 2017); Phillip Hamburger, *Law and Judicial Duty* (Cambridge, MA: Harvard University Press, 2008); William Baude and Stephen E. Sachs, "The Law of Interpretation," *Harvard Law Review* 130 (2017): 1079.

62 For one take on the various "subjects" of constitutional limitations, see Nicholas Quinn Rosenkranz, "The Subject of the Constitution," *Stanford Law Review* 62 (2010): 1209.

63 Brutus, No. 11, in Howard Gillman, Mark A. Graber, and Keith E. Whittington, *American Constitutionalism*, 2nd ed. (New York: Oxford University Press, 2017), 1:57.

64 In general, I refer to statutes and statutory provisions interchangeably, but in most cases, a particular provision of a larger statute is at issue. Of course, in some circumstances, the statute as a whole might fall, along with the constitutionally invalid provision.

65 United States v. Salerno, 481 U.S. 739, 745 (1987).

66 Richard H. Fallon Jr., "As-Applied and Facial Challenges and Third-Party Standing," *Harvard Law Review* 113 (2000): 1325–1326.

67 I use the terms "invalidate," "strike down," and "constitutionally narrow the scope" interchangeably to refer to both types of invalidation cases.

68 See, e.g., Jeffrey A. Segal and Harold J. Spaeth, *The Supreme Court and the Attitudinal Model Revisited* (New York: Cambridge University Press, 2002); Christopher Zorn, "Institutions and Independence in Models of Judicial Review," in *Institutional Games and the U.S. Supreme Court*, ed. James R. Rogers, Roy B. Flemming, and Jon R. Bond (Charlottesville: University of Virginia Press, 2006).

69 See also Keith E. Whittington, "'Interpose Your Friendly Hand': Political Supports for the Exercise of Judicial Review by the United States Supreme Court," *American Political Science Review* 99 (2005): 589–593.

70 See Whittington, *Political Foundations of Judicial Supremacy*, 105–120.

71 On varying responses to judicial review, see J. Mitchell Pickerill, *Constitutional Deliberation in Congress* (Durham, NC: Duke University Press, 2004).

72 Dahl, "Decision-Making in a Democracy," 284.

73 On parties and constitutional disputes, see Kevin J. McMahon, *Nixon's Court* (Chicago: University of Chicago Press, 2011); H. W. Perry Jr. and L. A. Powe Jr., "The Political Battle for the Constitution," *Constitutional Commentary* 21 (2004): 641; J. Mitchell Pickerill and Cornell W. Clayton, "The Rehnquist Court and the Political Dynamics of Federalism," *Perspectives on Politics* 2 (2004): 233; Andrew E. Busch, *The Constitution on the Campaign Trail* (Lanham, MD: Rowman & Littlefield, 2007).

74 See James Rogers, "Information and Judicial Review: A Signaling Model of Legislative and Judicial Interaction," *American Journal of Political Science* 45 (2001): 84.

75 See Thomas M. Keck, "Party, Policy, or Duty: Why Does the Supreme Court Invalidate Federal Statutes?" *American Political Science Review* 101 (2007): 321.

76 See Keith E. Whittington and Amanda Rinderle, "Making a Mountain out of a Molehill? *Marbury* and the Construction of the Constitutional Canon," *Hastings Constitutional Law Quarterly* 39 (2012): 823; Keith E. Whittington and Daniel Frost, "A Man for All Seasons: Historical Memory and John Marshall," *Polity* 49 (2017): 575.

77 Legislative Reference Service, *The Constitution of the United States: Analysis and Interpretation*, S. Doc. No. 82-170, 82nd Cong., 2nd sess. (1952), 1241. The current version can be found at www.congress.gov/constitution-annotated/.

78 Legislative Reference Service, *The Constitution of the United States: Analysis and Interpretation*, S. Doc. No. 88-39, 88th Cong., 1st sess. (rev. ed., 1964), 1401.

79 Mark A. Graber, "Naked Land Transfers and American Constitutional Development," *Vanderbilt Law Review* 53 (2000): 73; Mark A. Graber, "New Fiction: *Dred Scott* and the Language of Judicial Authority," *Chicago-Kent Law Review* 82 (2007): 177.

80 The only substantial effort to do so was Linda Camp Keith, *The U.S. Supreme Court and Judicial Review of Congress* (New York: Peter Lang, 2008). In an impressive feat of data collection, Keith extended back in time the specific coding rule used by Harold Spaeth in constructing the Supreme Court database for the second half of the twentieth century (a version of that database can now be found at www.supremecourtdatabase.org). Significantly, Keith restricted her search to the case syllabus provided by the Court reporter. I cast a wider net by searching the entire case record for clues that might help identify potential instances of judicial review. The two search procedures result in some

notable differences, and those differences are not randomly distributed across American history. The catalog of cases reported here is 44 percent larger than that reported by Keith, with nearly half the additional cases involving the invalidation of statutes. I found slightly more than twice as many cases in the nineteenth century than Keith did. Perhaps more surprising, I found nearly 50 percent more cases in the years since the New Deal. As a consequence, Keith concludes that the Court has invalidated statutes in 17 percent of the cases in which it rendered a decision. I find the invalidation rate to be higher, at 26 percent. Part of the difference is attributable to my casting a wider net in the initial search for potential cases of judicial review, but part of the difference is likely attributable to how narrowly judicial review is defined. The Spaeth data set closely mirrors the count by the Congressional Research Service (CRS) in its overlapping years, focusing on laws struck down in their entirety. By contrast, when Nicholas Zeppos attempted to identify all the cases in which the Supreme Court invoked "constitutional norms to limit legislative power in the period 1938 to 1992," he developed a distinctly larger set of cases, in part because he included the kind of "as applied" challenges that the CRS (partly) excised from Corwin's list. Zeppos's concern with cases of statutory interpretation that were "influenced" by "constitutional norms" is broader than my concern with cases in which the Court imposed hard constraints on what Congress is legislatively allowed to do. However, our approaches are more comparable in capturing the Court's treatment of particular subsets of potential applications of statutory provisions. Nicholas S. Zeppos, "Deference to Political Decisionmakers and the Preferred Scope of Judicial Review," *Northwestern University Law Review* 88 (1993): 296.

81 *Annals of Congress*, 2nd Cong., 1st sess., vol. 3 (April 13, 1792): 557.

82 Even constitutional law casebooks are far more likely to include cases that declare laws unconstitutional than cases that uphold them, even though both types elaborate the constitutional rules that govern American politics.

83 Recognizing the significance of cases upholding laws against constitutional challenge is one of the virtues of the label "judicial review," which emphasizes the courts' work in *reviewing* constitutional claims. The earlier nomenclature that focused on the particular power to declare laws unconstitutional necessarily obscured the inverse: the power to declare laws constitutionally valid.

84 United States v. Wonson, 28 F. Cas. 745, 750 (C.C.D. Mass. 1812) (No. 16,750). Senator (and federal constitutional convention delegate) Gouverneur Morris of New York went further in suggesting that judges would "never presume to believe, much less to declare, that you meant to violate the Constitution" and would simply misread even clear statutory commands so as to bring them into line with constitutional requirements. See Graber, "New Fiction," 185.

85 Ashwander v. Tennessee Valley Authority, 297 U.S. 288, 345 (1936) (Brandeis, J., concurring).

86 Thayer, "Origin and Scope of American Doctrine of Constitutional Law," 130.

87 Joel Prentiss Bishop, *Commentaries on the Criminal Law* (Boston: Little, Brown, 1856), 1:142.

88 It should be noted that the unit of analysis in the figure is a case striking or upholding a statute, not the number of statutes struck or upheld. The legal implications of a given case might well extend to numerous statutes.

89 See Justin Crowe, *Building the Judiciary* (Princeton, NJ: Princeton University Press, 2012).

90 On the historical shift in the Court's docket in general, see Richard L. Pacelle Jr., *The Transformation of the Supreme Court's Agenda* (Boulder, CO: Westview Press, 1991); Sandra L. Wood, Linda Camp Keith, Drew Noble Lanier, and Ayo Ogundele, "The Supreme Court, 1888–1940: An Empirical Overview," *Social Science History* 22 (1998): 212–213.

91 On average, the Roberts Court has decided one-third fewer cases striking down federal laws, but four-fifths fewer cases upholding federal statutes. For a consideration of these dynamics, see Benjamin Johnson and Keith E. Whittington, "Why Does the Supreme Court Uphold So Many Laws?" *University of Illinois Law Review* 2018 (2018): 103.

92 The periodization varies slightly for federal and state invalidations. For the invalidation of federal laws, the periods are 1789–1876, 1877–1919, and 1920–2018. For the invalidation of state laws, the periods are 1789–1866, 1867–1912, and 1913–2018. The periodization was determined through a piecewise linear function, estimating regression lines with the smallest slope.

93 The count of invalidated state statutes is drawn from the list maintained by the Congressional Research Service (updated by the author).

94 As the total number of judicial review cases increased in the twentieth century, the swings between restraint and activism became more pronounced (and with their larger baseline, the swings in cases invalidating state laws were even larger). A similar figure cast in percentile terms would show larger swings in the nineteenth century and relatively consistent swings across the twentieth century.

95 See Whittington, "Least Activist Supreme Court in History?" 2219.

96 Arguably, not even the early Court adopted such a generally deferential posture. In its early decades, the Court invalidated federal laws at a fairly high rate. The most dramatic difference from later Courts was the size of its docket, not its willingness to strike down laws.

97 Obergefell v. Hodges, 135 S. Ct. 2071 (2015).

98 Reed v. Town of Gilbert, Arizona, 135 S. Ct. 2218 (2015).

99 It is worth noting in this context that measures of judicial invalidation of legislative actions provide little insight into how legislatures might anticipate judicial review. It is possible that the prospect of judicial invalidation has led Congress to adopt fewer or different statutes than it otherwise might have, and to that degree, judicial review might have been more consequential than the record of resolved cases indicates.

100 See Zorn, "Institutions and Independence in Models of Judicial Review."

101 The figure is illustrative of only the congressional side of the judicial review equation. There is a lag between when Congress passes a law and when it might reasonably be evaluated by the Supreme Court. Moreover, the entire corpus of federal code—not just recently passed laws—is subject to judicial review at any time. While such refinements might be notable, figure 1-3 is adequate for these purposes.

102 The interval has been fairly stable across American history, with the exception of substantial variation in the early republic, when the number of judicial review cases was small. Overall, the average time between Congress's latest revision of a statutory provision and its review by the Court is nearly fifteen years (although the median is just over eight years). The median time to a decision striking down a provision is more than nine years; decisions striking down a provision in its entirety are handed down in a relatively short six years, while cases striking down provisions as applied take more than eleven years. The median time to a decision upholding a statute is just under eight years. Taking into account the time to decide cases upholding statutes also puts into context Dahl's finding that relatively few laws are struck down soon after adoption. The fact is that constitutional litigation tends to move slowly, whatever the end result.

103 The overall probability of invalidation of a statutory provision decreases as the statute ages (across a longer time horizon than that represented in figure 1-4), but the probability of invalidation of the *application* of a statutory provision increases for the first few decades of a statute's life. Nearly 20 percent of decisions upholding legislation are rendered more than a quarter century after passage of the statutory provision; however, nearly a quarter of decisions invalidating applications of a statute also occur in that time frame. See Tom S. Clark and Keith E. Whittington, "Ideology, Partisanship and Judicial Review of Acts of Congress, 1789–2006" (working paper, 2011).

104 Stephen W. Stathis, *Landmark Legislation, 1774–2012*, 2nd ed. (Washington, DC: CQ Press, 2014).

105 It is also generally true that some statutes undergo multiple rounds of judicial review by the US Supreme Court, regardless of whether they are "landmarks." Statutes reappear before the Court, sometimes within fairly short intervals, as the justices explore different potential applications and litigants make different types of challenges. The Bipartisan Campaign Reform Act of 2002 provides a recent example, as the Court has repeatedly examined its different provisions in cases stretching over more than a decade. With the campaign finance law, litigants have been especially successful in asking the Court to invalidate its components. By contrast, the Court repeatedly revisited aspects of the Volstead Act of 1919, which established Prohibition, but generally upheld the government against those constitutional challenges.

106 Califano v. Goldfarb, 430 U.S. 199 (1977).

107 Cases involving important provisions are likely to be resolved relatively quickly, however. Cases heard more than two years after passage of a statute are less likely to involve important provisions of landmark statutes.

108 McCulloch v. Maryland, 17 U.S. 316, 400 (1819).

109 Marbury v. Madison, 5 U.S. 137, 176 (1803).

CHAPTER 2. THE ROAD TO JUDICIAL REVIEW

1 Marbury v. Madison, 5 U.S. 137 (1803).

2 Marshall's opinion was much more controversial on other topics, such as the judiciary's authority to oversee the actions of executive officials and the point at which commissions of office became valid and empowered the putative office-holder. It was on these disputed points that his contemporaries found *Marbury* to be a notable opinion. Keith E. Whittington and Amanda Rinderele, "Making a Mountain out of a Molehill? *Marbury* and the Construction of the Constitutional Canon," *Hastings Constitutional Law Quarterly* 39 (2012): 823. See also Michael J. Klarman, "How Great Were the 'Great' Marshall Court Decisions?" *Virginia Law Review* 87 (2001): 1111; Robert Lowry Clinton, Marbury v. Madison *and Judicial Review* (Lawrence: University Press of Kansas, 1989).

3 See Philip Hamburger, "A Tale of Two Paradigms: Judicial Review and Judicial Duty," *George Washington Law Review* 78 (2010): 1162.

4 As reported by John Adams, *The Works of John Adams*, ed. Charles Francis Adams (Boston: Little & Brown, 1850), 2:525.

5 Horace Gray, "Appendix," in *Reports of Cases*, ed. Josiah Quincy (Boston: Little, Brown, 1865), 441.

6 Bonham's Case, 8 Co. Rep. 107, 114a (1610).

7 See S. E. Thorne, "Dr. Bonham's Case," *Law Quarterly Review* 54 (1938): 543; Theodore F. T. Plucknett, "Bonham's Case and Judicial Review," *Harvard Law Review* 40 (1938): 30; Charles M. Gray, "Bonham's Case Reviewed," *Proceedings of the American Philosophical Society* 116 (1972): 35; Douglas E. Edlin, *Judges and Unjust Laws* (Ann Arbor: University of Michigan Press, 2008).

8 Philip A. Hamburger, "Revolution and Judicial Review: Chief Justice Holt's Opinion in *City of London v. Wood*," *Columbia Law Review* 94 (1994): 2091.

9 William Blackstone, *Blackstone's Commentaries*, ed. St. George Tucker (Philadelphia: Birch & Small, 1803), 2:162.

10 Ibid., 1:91. Blackstone thought judges should interpret statutes to avoid such results, so long as they could do so without "defeat[ing] the intent of the legislature, when couched in such evident and express words, as [to] leave no doubt whether it was the intent of the legislature or no." Ibid.

11 On Adams and Otis, see Philip Hamburger, *Law and Judicial Duty* (Cambridge, MA: Harvard University Press, 2008), 275–276; James M. Farrell, "The Writs of

Assistance and Public Memory: John Adams and the Legacy of James Otis," *New England Quarterly* 79 (2006): 533.

12 James Otis, *The Rights of the British Colonies Asserted and Proved*, 3rd ed. (London: J. Williams, 1766), 109.

13 Quoted in Hamburger, *Law and Judicial Duty*, 276.

14 Edmund Pendleton, *The Letters and Papers of Edmund Pendleton, 1734–1803*, ed. David John Mays (Charlottesville: University Press of Virginia, 1967), 1:23. See also Hamburger, *Law and Judicial Duty*, 276–280.

15 Blackstone, *Blackstone's Commentaries*, 2:151, 161.

16. See Forrest McDonald, *Novus Ordo Seclorum* (Lawrence: University Press of Kansas, 1985). It should be noted that Locke's ideas about natural law were just as critical as his ideas about popular sovereignty for the development of American constitutionalism. See also Edward S. Corwin, *The "Higher Law" Background of American Constitutional Law* (Indianapolis: Liberty Fund, 2008).

17 Blackstone, *Blackstone's Commentaries*, 1:vii, 2:160n21.

18 Ibid., 1:52n9.

19 See Donald S. Lutz, *The Origins of American Constitutionalism* (Baton Rouge: Louisiana State University Press, 1988).

20 See Jack P. Greene, *Peripheries and Center* (Athens: University of Georgia Press, 1987); John Phillip Reid, *Constitutional History of the American Revolution*, abridged ed. (Madison: University of Wisconsin Press, 1995); Andrew C. McLaughlin, *The Foundations of American Constitutionalism* (New York: New York University Press, 1932); Barbara A. Black, "The Constitution of the Empire: The Case for the Colonists," *University of Pennsylvania Law Review* 124 (1976): 1203.

21 Blackstone, *Blackstone's Commentaries*, 1:110.

22 Daniel Dulaney, *Consideration of the Propriety of Imposing Taxes in the British Colonies for the Purposes of Raising Revenue*, 2nd ed. (London: J. Almon, 1766), 46.

23 Francis Bowen, ed., *Documents of the Constitution of England and America* (Cambridge, MA: John Bartlett, 1854), 57, 58, 69.

24 Quoted in Mary Sarah Bilder, *The Transatlantic Constitution* (Cambridge, MA: Harvard University Press, 2004), 2.

25 Ibid., 10. See also Elmer Beecher Russell, *The Review of American Colonial Legislation by the King in Council* (New York: Columbia University Press, 1915).

26 Mary Sarah Bilder, "The Corporate Origins of Judicial Review," *Yale Law Journal* 116 (2006): 502.

27 Quoted in Hamburger, *Law and Judicial Duty*, 267.

28 Bilder, *Transatlantic Constitution*, 10.

29 Hamburger, *Law and Judicial Duty*, 462.

30 Charles Grove Haines, *The American Doctrine of Judicial Supremacy* (New York: Macmillan, 1914), 82.

31 See James M. Varnum, *The Case, Trevett against Weeden* (Providence, RI: John Carter, 1787); William Michael Treanor, "Judicial Review before *Marbury*," *Stanford Law Review* 58 (2005): 476–478; Scott Douglas Gerber, *A Distinct Judicial Power* (New York: Oxford University Press, 2011), 168–169; Hamburger, *Law and Judicial Duty*, 435–449.

32 On Bayard v. Singleton, 1 N.C. 5 (1787), see Treanor, "Judicial Review before *Marbury*," 478–480; Gerber, *Distinct Judicial Power*, 205–206, 341–342; Hamburger, *Law and Judicial Duty*, 449–460.

33 James Iredell, *The Life and Correspondence of James Iredell*, ed. Griffith J. McRee (New York: D. Appleton, 1858), 2:145.

34 Quoted in William Michael Treanor, "The *Case of the Prisoners* and the Origins of Judicial Review," *University of Pennsylvania Law Review* 143 (1994): 501. The case was reported in Commonwealth v. Caton, 8 Va. 5 (1782).

35 Quoted in Treanor, "*Case of the Prisoners*," 512.

36 Ibid., 513.

37 The other two amici were John Francis Mercer, who would serve as a delegate from Maryland at the Philadelphia Convention, and William Nelson, who would become a judge and law professor.

38 Quoted in Treanor, "*Case of the Prisoners*," 523.

39 Ibid., 525.

40 Here, the private notes of the justices diverge from how the case was eventually reported. See Ibid., 529–533.

41 Commonwealth v. Caton, 8 Va. 8 (1782).

42 Quoted in Treanor, "*Case of the Prisoners*," 530.

43 Jean Edward Smith, *John Marshall* (New York: Henry Holt, 1996), 95.

44 Case of the Judges, 8 Va. 142 (1788). The legislature did not respond kindly, and the judges eventually resigned from office in protest.

45 Kamper v. Hawkins, 3 Va. 20 (1793).

46 Ibid., 24.

47 Ibid., 30–31.

48 Ibid., 31.

49 Ibid., 38, 39.

50 Thomas Jefferson, "Notes on Virginia, Query XIII," in *The Writings of Thomas Jefferson*, ed. H. A. Washington (New York: Riker, Thorne, 1854), 8:868.

51 *Kamper v. Hawkins*, 37.

52 Jefferson, "Notes on Virginia," 859–860.

53 See Treanor, "Judicial Review before *Marbury*"; Gerber, *Distinct Judicial Power*; Hamburger, *Law and Judicial Duty*.

54 Respublica v. Duquet, 2 Yeates 493, 498 (1799).

55 Ham v. M'Claws, 1 S.C.L. 93, 98 (Ct. Com. Pl. 1789).

56 Kentucky Constitution of 1799, Art. XII, sec. 28.

57 Treanor, "Judicial Review before *Marbury*," 503–504.

58 Ibid., 510.

59 Joseph P. Cotton, ed., *The Constitutional Decisions of John Marshall* (New York: G. P. Putnam's Sons, 1905), 1:xii–xiii.

60 Louis B. Boudin, "Government by Judiciary," *Political Science Quarterly* 26 (1911): 249.

61 William Winslow Crosskey, *Politics and the Constitution* (Chicago: University of Chicago Press, 1953), 2:1007.

62 Edward S. Corwin, "The Supreme Court and Unconstitutional Acts of Congress," *Michigan Law Review* 4 (1906): 624, 626, 627.

63 William M. Meigs, *The Relation of the Judiciary to the Constitution* (Philadelphia: William J. Campbell, 1919), 11.

64 Charles A. Beard, *The Supreme Court and the Constitution* (New York: Macmillan, 1912). Corwin thought the historical record was more complicated than Beard admitted. Edward S. Corwin, book review, *American Political Science Review* 7 (1913): 330.

65 Henry M. Hart, "Professor Crosskey and Judicial Review," *Harvard Law Review* 67 (1934): 1456, 1457, 1486.

66 Alexander M. Bickel, *The Least Dangerous Branch* (Indianapolis: Bobbs-Merrill, 1962), 15. More interesting than the historical question of where the idea of judicial review came from, Bickel thought, was the normative question of how it could best be justified now.

67 The question of the founders' intent on this question has particular resonance for constitutional originalists, although many of those who have engaged in the debate over time (including Beard and Corwin) are distinctly not originalists. Yale's Harold D. Laswell, for example, dismissed Crosskey's effort as the product of "an inadequate theory of law" and "superfluous" from the "perspective of a comprehensive, value oriented jurisprudence" of the kind that modern lawyers ought to follow. Harold D. Laswell, book review, *George Washington Law Review* 22 (1954): 385, 386.

68 Records of the debates at the Philadelphia Convention are somewhat sketchy and not completely reliable. Several delegates kept their own notes on the debates, which were later assembled and published. The most complete record was kept by James Madison. All the notes of the convention debates suffer from later editing and revision. See Mary Sarah Bilder, *Madison's Hand* (Cambridge, MA: Harvard University Press, 2015); James H. Hutson, "The Creation of the Constitution: The Integrity of the Documentary Record," *Texas Law Review* 65 (1986): 1.

69 Max Farrand, ed., *The Records of the Federal Constitution of 1787* (New Haven, CT: Yale University Press, 1911), 1:28.

70 Several modern commentators interpret Paterson's reference to a "check" as meaning judicial review. See Raoul Berger, *Congress v. the Supreme Court* (Cambridge, MA: Harvard University Press, 1969), 50; Saikrishna B. Prakash and John

C. Yoo, "The Origins of Judicial Review," *University of Chicago Law Review* 70 (2003): 940. Traditional Montesquieu-style theories of the separation of powers regarded the mere existence of an independent judiciary entrusted with the power to interpret and apply the law to individual cases as an important check on legislative and executive power.

71 Farrand, *Records*, 1:97.

72 Ibid., 1:109.

73 Ibid., 2:76.

74 Ibid., 2:73, 391.

75 Ibid., 2:74, 78.

76 See Prakash and Yoo, "Origins of Judicial Review," 943–947; Berger, *Congress v. the Supreme Court*, 50–81; Haines, *American Doctrine of Judicial Supremacy*, 143–149; Beard, *Supreme Court and the Constitution*, 15–67; Edward S. Corwin, "The Establishment of Judicial Review I," *Michigan Law Review* 9 (1910): 117–124; Randy Barnett, "The Original Meaning of the Judicial Power," *Supreme Court Economic Review* 12 (2004): 121–124.

77 Farrand, *Records*, 2:430.

78 Ibid., 2:93.

79 Ibid., 2:376.

80 Ibid., 1:21.

81 Ibid., 2:28.

82 Ibid., 2:29.

83 There were a few dissenters from the general consensus, but their remarks are ambiguous. John Mercer of Maryland supported the proposal for a council of revision and "disapproved of the Doctrine that the Judges as expositors of the Constitution should have the authority to declare a law void." John Dickinson of Delaware agreed that "no such power [to set aside the law] ought to exist." Ibid., 2:298–299. It is not clear that they disagreed with the proposition that judges would in fact have and use such a power, given the constitutional text that was being adopted. In the ratification debates, Dickinson went on to cite judicial review of federal laws as a positive feature of the proposed constitution. Berger, *Congress v. the Supreme Court*, 64.

84 For references to judicial review of Congress in the ratification debates, see Beard, *Supreme Court and the Constitution*, 68–73; Haines, *American Doctrine of Judicial Supremacy*, 149–153; Prakash and Yoo, "Origins of Judicial Review," 956–975; Berger, *Congress v. the Supreme Court*, 120–143.

85 Iredell, *Life and Correspondence*, 2:170.

86 Jonathan Elliot, ed., *The Debates in the Several State Conventions on the Adoption of the Federal Constitution* (Washington, DC: Jonathan Elliott, 1836), 3:553.

87 Ibid., 2:446.

88 Ibid., 2:196.

89 Alexander Hamilton, James Madison, and John Jay, *The Federalist Papers*, ed.

Clinton Rossiter (New York: American Library, 1961), No. 78; Brutus, No. 11, in Howard Gillman, Mark A. Graber, and Keith E. Whittington, *American Constitutionalism*, 2nd ed. (New York: Oxford University Press, 2017), 1:57.

90 Thomas Jefferson to James Madison, March 15, 1789, in *The Writings of Thomas Jefferson*, ed. H. A. Washington (Washington, DC: Taylor & Maury, 1853), 3:3.

91 See Mark A. Graber, "Establishing Judicial Review: *Marbury* and the Judicial Act of 1789," *Tulsa Law Review* 38 (2003): 609.

92 See Hunter v. Fairfax's Devisee, 18 Va. 1 (1814).

93 1 *Stat.* 73, 85–86 (1789).

94 *Annals of Congress*, 1st Cong., 1st sess., vol. 1 (August 31, 1789): 861. Gerry's argument was even more pointed because this claim was made in the context of observing that Congress could not deny a lower federal court any part of the jurisdiction and "judicial power" the Constitution vested in such courts. Once established by Congress, an Article III court necessarily possessed all the power vested in it by that article, and any statutory provision that attempted to restrict that power would be unconstitutional. The system of restriction "would be a nullity." Ibid.

95 Representative Elias Boudinot even celebrated the prospect that his legislation would be struck down by the Court. He found it reassuring that, "if from inattention, want of precision, or any other defect, I should do wrong, there is a power in the government, which can constitutionally prevent the operation of a wrong measure from affecting my constituents. . . . It is the glory of the constitution, that there is a remedy for the failures even of the legislature itself." Given the backstop of judicial review, he urged his colleagues to vote to establish the Bank of the United States, despite any doubts they might have about their power to do so. *Annals of Congress*, 1st Cong., 3rd sess., vol. 2 (February 4, 1791): 1978. It was precisely such a dereliction of legislative duty that James Bradley Thayer feared an activist Court would encourage, freeing legislators from the ultimate responsibility for their actions. See James Bradley Thayer, "The Origin and Scope of the American Doctrine of Constitutional Law," *Harvard Law Review* 7 (1893): 155–156. See also Mark Tushnet, *Taking the Constitution away from the Courts* (Princeton, NJ: Princeton University Press, 1999), 57–62.

96 James Wilson, *The Works of the Honorable James Wilson, L.L.D.*, ed. Bird Wilson (Philadelphia: Bronson & Chauncey, 1804), 1:460, 461, 462.

97 See Treanor, "Judicial Review before *Marbury*," 518–533.

98 Vanhorne's Lessee v. Dorrance, 2 U.S. 304 (1795).

99 Ibid., 308.

100 See Whittington and Rinderele, "Making a Mountain out of a Molehill?" 844–848.

101 Quoted in Bilder, "Corporate Origins," 544.

102 Varnum, *The Case, Trevett against Weeden*, 27.

CHAPTER 3. EXERCISING JUDICIAL REVIEW
BEFORE THE CIVIL WAR

1 Marbury v. Madison, 5 U.S. 137 (1803). On the significance of *Marbury*, see William H. Rehnquist, *The Supreme Court* (New York: Morrow, 1987), 99–100; G. Edward White, *The Marshall Court and Cultural Change, 1815–1835* (New York: Macmillan, 1991), 7; Jean Edward Smith, *John Marshall* (New York: H. Holt, 1996), 2.

2 Dred Scott v. Sandford, 60 U.S. 393 (1857). The "self-inflicted wound" characterization is that of Chief Justice Charles Evans Hughes. Charles Evans Hughes, *The Supreme Court of the United States* (New York: Columbia University Press, 1928), 50.

3 See Mark A. Graber, "Constructing Judicial Review," *Annual Review of Political Science* 8 (2005): 425.

4 Compare Larry D. Kramer, *The People Themselves* (New York: Oxford University Press, 2004); Robert Lowry Clinton, Marbury v. Madison *and Judicial Review* (Lawrence: University Press of Kansas, 1989).

5 For an important analysis of late Jacksonian attitudes toward judicial activism, see Mark A. Graber, "The Jacksonian Origins of Chase Court Activism," *Journal of Supreme Court History* 25 (2000): 17.

6 See Mark A. Graber, "Establishing Judicial Review? *Schooner Peggy* and the Early Marshall Court," *Political Research Quarterly* 51 (1998): 221; Mark A. Graber, "Federalist or Friends of Adams: The Marshall Court and Party Politics," *Studies in American Political Development* 12 (1998): 229; Mark A. Graber, "The Passive-Aggressive Virtues: *Cohens v. Virginia* and the Problematic Establishment of Judicial Power," *Constitutional Commentary* 12 (1995): 67.

7 U.S. v. The William, 28 F. Cas. 614 (D. Mass., 1808).

8 Evans v. Weiss, 8 F. Cas. 888 (C.C. Pa., 1809).

9 United States v. Bainbridge, 24 F. Cas. 946 (C.C. Mass., 1816).

10 In re Susan, 23 F. Cas. 444 (C.C. Ind., 1818).

11 Miller v. McQuerry, 17 F. Cas. 335 (C.C. Oh., 1853); United States v. Hanway, 26 F. Cas. 105 (C.C. Pa., 1851); Jones v. Van Zandt, 13 F. Cas. 1047 (C.C. Oh., 1843); Ex parte Simmons, 22 F. Cas. 151 (C.C. Pa., 1823).

12 In re Klein, 14 F. Cas. 716 (C.C. Mo., 1843); In re Irwine, 13 F. Cas. 125 (C.C. Pa., 1842); Michell v. Great Words Milling & Manuf'g. Co., 17 F. Cas. 496 (C.C. Me., 1843).

13 See William Michael Treanor, "Judicial Review before *Marbury*," *Stanford Law Review* 58 (2005): 455; Scott Douglas Gerber, *A Distinct Judicial Power* (New York: Oxford University Press, 2011).

14 See William E. Nelson, "Changing Conceptions of Judicial Review: The Evolution of Constitutional Theory in the States, 1790–1860," *University of Pennsylvania Law Review* 120 (1972): 1166; Jed Handelsman Shugerman, "Economic Crisis

and the Rise of Judicial Elections and Judicial Review," *Harvard Law Review* 123 (2010): 1061.

15 See Matthew P. Harrington, "Judicial Review before John Marshall," *George Washington Law Review* 72 (2003): 51; Mark A. Graber, "Establishing Judicial Review: *Marbury* and the Judicial Act of 1789," *Tulsa Law Review* 38 (2003): 609.

16 Keith E. Whittington, *Political Foundations of Judicial Supremacy* (Princeton, NJ: Princeton University Press, 2007), 105–114.

17 United States v. Yale Todd (1794), reported in United States v. Ferreira, 54 U.S. 40, 53 (1852).

18 For an overview of the Invalid Pensions Acts cases, see Maeva Marcus, ed., *The Documentary History of the Supreme Court of the United States* (New York: Columbia University Press, 1998), 6:33–45; Charles Warren, *The Supreme Court in United States History*, rev. ed. (Boston: Little, Brown, 1926), 1:69–90.

19 The justices of the Supreme Court met collectively to carry out the original and appellate jurisdictions of the Court. They also sat individually with the various circuits, exercising the trial and appellate jurisdictions of those courts.

20 Hayburn's Case, 2 U.S. 409, 411 (1792).

21 Ibid., 410.

22 *Gazette of the United States*, May 9, 1792, quoted in Warren, *Supreme Court*, 1:76; *National Gazette*, April 12, 1792, quoted in ibid., 1:70n1, 80n1. Iredell had written to the president before any cases presented themselves, but he questioned the validity of acting as a commissioner in an either official or private capacity. *Hayburn's Case*, 413–414.

23 *Hayburn's Case*, 409. Hayburn himself petitioned Congress for relief, "the Court having refused to take cognizance of his case." *Annals of Congress*, 2nd Cong., 1st sess., vol. 2 (April 13, 1792): 556.

24 "Proceedings of the United States House of Representatives, January 9, 1793," in Marcus, *Documentary History of the Supreme Court*, 6:376.

25 "Report of the Attorney General of the United States to the Secretary of War, February 17, 1794," in Marcus, *Documentary History of the Supreme Court*, 6:381.

26 United States v. Ferreira, 54 U.S. 40, 53 (1852).

27 "Report of a Committee of the United States House of Representatives, March 5, 1794," in Marcus, *Documentary History of the Supreme Court*, 6:383. Marcus finds this to be evidence that the Court ruled on statutory grounds in *Yale Todd*, but it hardly seems decisive. Ibid., 6:43–45. The legislators who were about to grant relief to war veterans in 1794 had every reason to suggest that the delay and inconvenience suffered by these men were due to the judges who had failed to act as commissioners, rather than the legislators themselves for passing an unconstitutional law. Moreover, the committee report's substantive point was that the petitioner had already satisfied all the material conditions for being entered on the pension rolls, even though his certificate was invalid on technical grounds that had nothing to do with the merits of his claim. Thus, it would be

appropriate for Congress, acting prospectively, to overlook the formalities and act on the merits.

28 *American Daily Advertiser*, April 16, 1792, quoted in Warren, *Supreme Court*, 1:72.

29 *National Gazette*, April 16, 1792, quoted in ibid., 1:73.

30 *National Gazette*, May 9, 1792, quoted in ibid., 1:76.

31 Fisher Ames, *Works of Fisher Ames*, ed. Seth Ames, 2nd ed. (Boston: Little, Brown, 1854), 1:117.

32 *Ferreira*, 40, 53.

33 131 U.S. App. ccxxxv (1888).

34 Samuel Freeman Miller, *Lectures on the Constitution of the United States* (New York: Banks & Brothers, 1891), 351–355; William Marshall Bullitt, *The Supreme Court of the United States and Unconstitutional Legislation* (Louisville, KY: n.p., 1924), 7; Benjamin Abbott and Austin Abbott, *A Treatise upon the United States Courts, and Their Practice* (New York: Diossy, 1869), 1:191–192; Hampton L. Carson, *The Supreme Court of the United States* (Philadelphia: John V. Huber, 1891), 627; Wilfred J. Ritz, "*United States v. Yale Todd* (U.S. 1794)," *Washington and Lee Law Review* 15 (1958): 221; Charles Fairman, *History of the Supreme Court of the United States*, vol. 6, *Reconstruction and Reunion, 1864–88* (New York: Macmillan, 1971), 52.

35 James Bradley Thayer, *Cases on Constitutional Law* (Cambridge, MA: Charles W. Sever, 1894), 1:105n1.

36 Max Farrand, "The First Hayburn Case, 1792," *American History Review* 13 (1908): 283; Brinton Coxe, *An Essay on Judicial Power and Unconstitutional Legislation* (Philadelphia: Kay & Brother, 1893), 13–14; Charles Grove Haines, *The American Doctrine of Judicial Supremacy* (New York: Macmillan, 1914), 159–160; David Hunter Miller, "Some Early Cases in the Supreme Court of the United States," *Virginia Law Review* 8 (1921): 112–115; Marcus, *Documentary History of the Supreme Court*, 6:43–45.

37 "Proceedings of the Supreme Court, February 15, 1794," in Marcus, *Documentary History of the Supreme Court*, 6:380; "William Bradford, Jr., to Henry Knox, June 2, 1794," ibid., 6:384.

38 Treanor, "Judicial Review before *Marbury*," 537n423.

39 Penhallow v. Doane's Administrators, 3 U.S. 54 (1795).

40 Ibid., 80.

41 Ibid., 92.

42 Ibid., 111–112.

43 Ibid., 117.

44 Ibid., 80.

45 See, generally, Henry J. Bourguignon, *The First Federal Court* (Philadelphia: American Philosophical Society, 1977). See also Thomas Sergeant, *Constitutional Law*, 2nd ed. (Philadelphia: Abraham Small, 1830), 7–8 ("the legality of

all captures on the high seas . . . might be implicated with foreign nations in the results of its administration, Congress had for this purpose a right of maintaining a control by appeal").

46 For a similar but more extended case, see Gary D. Rowe, "Constitutionalism in the Streets," *California Law Review* 78 (2005): 401.

47 "No. 65: Remonstrance of New Hampshire against the Exercise of Certain Powers by the Judiciary of the United States," *American State Papers*, vol. 1, *Miscellaneous* (Washington, DC: Duff Green, 1834), 123.

48 Nathan Dane, *A General Abridgment and Digest of American Law* (Boston: Cummings, Hilliard, 1829), vol. 9, appendix 1.

49 Joseph Story, *Commentaries on the Constitution of the United States*, 2nd ed. (Boston: Hilliard, Gray, 1851), 1:138–154; James Kent, *Commentaries on American Law*, 3rd ed. (New York: E. B. Clayton, James Van Norden, 1836), 1:212.

50 Hylton v. United States, 3 U.S. 171 (1796).

51 *Annals of Congress*, 3rd Cong., 1st sess. (May 29, 1794), 4:730; James Madison to Thomas Jefferson, June 1, 1794, in *The Writings of James Madison*, ed. Gaillard Hunt (New York: G. P. Putnam's Sons, 1906), 6:217.

52 1 *Stat.* 373 (June 5, 1794).

53 Daniel Hylton stipulated to a tax bill of $2,000 in order to "ascertain a constitutional point," but his understanding with the government was that if he lost the lawsuit, he would pay only the amount he had actually been assessed: $16. The larger amount was necessary to meet the jurisdictional requirements of the Supreme Court. The federal government also found a lawyer for Hylton when his original counsel, Jeffersonian firebrand John Taylor, resigned once it became clear that taking the case to the Supreme Court would likely result in the setting of an unfavorable precedent. Warren, *Supreme Court*, 1:147n1; Robert P. Frankel Jr., "Before *Marbury*: *Hylton v. United States* and the Origins of Judicial Review," *Journal of Supreme Court History* 28 (2003): 1.

54 *Hylton* 171, 173, 178, 181.

55 *Writings of Madison*, 8:405, 6:353.

56 1 *Stat.* 369 (May 22, 1794).

57 1 *Stat.* 176 (August 4, 1790); 1 *Stat.* 370 (May 22, 1794).

58 United States v. La Vengeance, 3 U.S. 297, 300, 299 (1796).

59 Ibid., 301.

60 Chase generally had little patience with the requirement for jury trials. See Keith E. Whittington, *Constitutional Construction* (Cambridge, MA: Harvard University Press, 1999), 52–57.

61 United States v. The Schooner Betsey and Charlotte, 8 U.S. 443, 452 (1807). Despite this explicit constitutional argument, Thomas Sergeant used these cases in his influential treatise on constitutional law to illustrate the logic of the congressional policy choice in a different statute. Sergeant, *Constitutional Law*, 205. By contrast, in his famous treatise, James Kent framed the cases in terms of

constitutional law, observing, "It is not in the power of congress to enlarge that jurisdiction [admiralty] beyond what was understood and intended by it when the constitution was adopted, because it would be depriving the suitor of the right of trial by jury, which is secured to him by the constitution." Kent was skeptical of the Court's finding that this *was* within the power of Congress. "It may be a question, whether they [Congress] had any right to declare them to be cases of admiralty jurisdiction, if they were not so by the law of the land when the constitution was made. The Constitution secures to the citizen trial by jury." But Kent thought the Court could have saved Congress and itself from this error by interpreting the "rather ambiguous" Judiciary Act of 1789 differently and simply insisting that Congress had never authorized the courts to exercise admiralty jurisdiction in such cases. Kent, *Commentaries on American Law*, 1:371, 375. John Marshall later acknowledged the constitutional dimension of these cases, while distinguishing them from another case in which "the only question" was "not what was the constitutional authority of Congress, but how far it had been exercised; not what was the extent of the admiralty and maritime jurisdiction granted in the constitution, but how far it had been conferred by Congress upon any particular Court of the Union." United States v. Wiltberger, 18 U.S. 76, 109 (1820).

62 This is a theme that Justice Joseph Story emphasized in the cases arising out of *La Vengeance*. Story, *Commentaries on the Constitution*, 3:531.

63 See Douglas Lamar Jones, "'The Caprice of Juries': The Enforcement of the Jeffersonian Embargo in Massachusetts," *American Journal of Legal History* 24 (1980): 315–319. In 1808 Federalist-appointed district court judge John Davis upheld the power of Congress to impose a general embargo. United States v. The William, 28 F. Cas. 614 (D. Mass. 1808).

64 1 *Stat.* 78 (1789) (emphasis added).

65 "The Judicial Power shall extend . . . to Controversies . . . between a State, or the Citizens thereof, and foreign States, Citizens or Subjects." US Constitution, Art. III, sec. 2.

66 Mossman v. Higginson, 4 U.S. 12 (1800).

67 Hodgson and Thompson v. Bowerbank and Others, 9 U.S. 303 (1809).

68 Jackson v. Twentyman, 27 U.S. 136 (1829).

69 Francis J. Troubat and William M. Haly, *The Practice in Civil Actions and Proceedings in the Supreme Court of Pennsylvania* (Philadelphia: R. H. Small, 1837), 1:91. See also Sergeant, *Constitutional Law*, 115 ("these general words must be restricted by the constitution . . . and the statute cannot extend the jurisdiction beyond the limits of the constitution"); Alfred Conkling, *A Treatise on the Organization, Jurisdiction and Practice of the Courts of the United States* (Albany, NY: Wm. & A. Gould, 1831), 64 ("it is declared in unqualified terms by the judicial act that the circuit courts shall have original cognizance of all civil suits where an *alien* is a *party*; yet . . . it is held that the jurisdiction of these courts is limited

by the constitution to the cases therein specified; and that it does not extend to suits *between aliens*"); John Bouvier, *Institutes of American Law* (Philadelphia: Childes & Peterson, 1858), 3:107 ("these general words must be restricted by the provisions of the constitution . . . the statute cannot extend jurisdiction beyond the limits of the constitution"); Benjamin Vaughan Abbott, *A Treatise upon the United States Courts* (New York: Diossy, 1871), 2:54 ("For the enactment giving jurisdiction where an alien is a party, must be construed in connection with and conformity to the Constitution of the United States").

70 Conkling, *Treatise*, 66.

71 John Norton Pomeroy, *An Introduction to the Constitutional Law of the United States* (New York: Holt & Houghton, 1868), 517.

72 Troubat and Haly, *Practice in Civil Actions*, 1:91; Sergeant, *Constitutional Law*, 115; Abbott, *Treatise*, 2:54. These commentators included former justice Benjamin Curtis. Benjamin Robbins Curtis, *Jurisdiction, Practice, and Federal Jurisprudence of the Courts of the United States* (Boston: Little, Brown, 1880), 111–112. Notably, Kent states the following rule: "if it appeared on record that one party was an alien, it must likewise appear affirmatively that the other party was a citizen." But he does not explain the rationale for why the Court "confined" the statutory grant of jurisdiction. Kent, *Commentaries on American Law*, 1:344. By the end of the nineteenth century, by which time the 1789 statutory provision had been displaced, former attorney general Augustus Garland asserted in his treatise on federal courts that the Judiciary Act of 1789 is "*also* the language of the Constitution on the same subject," and neither allowed cases in which both parties were aliens. A. H. Garland and Robert Ralston, *A Treatise on the Constitution and Jurisdiction of the United States Courts* (Philadelphia: T. & J. W. Johnson, 1898), 1:177 (emphasis added). Dennis Mahoney points to Kent to support the claim that early observers did not view *Hodgson* as a constitutional decision, but he overlooks others who clearly did. Dennis J. Mahoney, "A Historical Note on *Hodgson v. Bowerbank*," *University of Chicago Law Review* 49 (1982): 737.

73 Thomas F. Gordon, *A Digest of the Laws of the United States* (Philadelphia: Thomas Gordon, 1827), 1.

74 Prentiss v. Brennan, 19 F. Cas. 1278, 1279 (1851 C.C.N.D. N.Y.). See also Florence Sewing Machine Company v. Grover and Baker Sewing Machine Company, 110 Mass. 70, 80–81 (1872): "we think such a construction would make it conflict with the Constitution of the United States, and therefore must presume that such was not the intention with which the act was framed; or if it was so, then the intention must be held to be ineffectual. . . . In applying the statute, its general terms are made to conform to narrower limits of the judicial powers as established by the constitutional provisions."

75 Hinckley v. Byrne, 12 F. Cas. 194, 195–196 (1867 C.C.D. Calif.).

76 Piquignot v. Pennsylvania Railroad Company, 57 U.S. 104, 106 (1854). See also Cissel v. McDonald, 5 F. Cas. 717, 718 (1879 C.C.S.D. N.Y.).

77 The Court did find a constitutionally acceptable exertion of jurisdiction in a case involving two foreigners in Mason v. Blaireau, 6 U.S. 240 (1804) (admiralty jurisdiction could be exercised in a case in which both parties were aliens and consented to the suit).

78 Edmund Randolph to James Madison, June 30, 1789, in *The Papers of James Madison*, ed. Charles Hobson and Robert Rutland (Charlottesville: University Press of Virginia, 1979), 12:274. Randolph also anticipated the result: "Will the courts be bound by any definition of authority, which the Constitution does not in their opinion warrant?" Ibid.

79 On the compromised nature of the Judiciary Act of 1789, see Maeva Marcus and Natalie Wexler, "The Judiciary Act of 1789: Political Compromise or Constitutional Interpretation?" in *Origins of the Federal Judiciary*, ed. Maeva Marcus (New York: Oxford University Press, 1992); Justin Crowe, *Building the Judiciary* (Princeton, NJ: Princeton University Press, 2012).

80 18 *Stat.* 470 (1875).

81 Vanhorne's Lessee v. Dorrance, 28 F. Cas. 1012 (1795); Kamper v. Hawkins, 3 Va. 20 (1788).

82 On Federalists, the Sedition Act, and the judiciary, see Whittington, *Political Foundations*, 233–248.

83 The "Jeffersonian crisis" referred to in the heading of this section is the characterization of Richard E. Ellis, *The Jeffersonian Crisis* (New York: Oxford University Press, 1971).

84 United States v. Callender, 25 F. Cas. 239, 256, 254 (C.C. Va., 1800).

85 William Branch Giles quoted in Warren, *Supreme Court*, 1:193; Thomas Jefferson, *The Writings of Thomas Jefferson*, ed. H. A. Washington (Washington, DC: Taylor & Maury, 1854), 4:424–425.

86 Hodgson and Thompson v. Bowerbank and Others, 9 U.S. 303 (1809); Jackson v. Twentyman, 27 U.S. 136 (1829).

87 For background, see Ellis, *Jeffersonian Crisis*; Bruce Ackerman, *The Failure of the Founding Fathers* (Cambridge, MA: Harvard University Press, 2005).

88 Stuart v. Laird, 5 U.S. 299, 303 (1803).

89 Ibid., 309.

90 Justice of the peace was not one of the offices created by the infamous Judiciary Act of 1801; it was the result of another 1801 statute expanding the local government in the newly created District of Columbia. 2 *Stat.* 103 (1801).

91 Thomas Jefferson to William Findley, March 24, 1801, in *The Works of Thomas Jefferson*, ed. Paul Leicester Ford (New York: G. P. Putnam's Sons, 1905), 9:225.

92 Levi Lincoln was the acting secretary of state at the outset of the Jefferson administration. He soon moved to the position of attorney general, and James Madison took over as secretary of state. It is not clear that Marbury's commission ever came into Madison's possession.

93 Marbury v. Madison, 5 U.S. 137, 176 (1803).

94 Ibid.

95 Among the voluminous literature analyzing *Marbury*, see Edward S. Corwin, "*Marbury v. Madison* and the Doctrine of Judicial Review," *Michigan Law Review* 12 (1914): 538; William van Alstyne, "A Critical Guide to *Marbury v. Madison*," *Duke Law Journal* 18 (1969): 1; Susan Low Bloch and Maeva Marcus, "John Marshall's Selective Use of History in *Marbury v. Madison*," *Wisconsin Law Review* 1986 (1986): 301; James M. O'Fallon, "*Marbury*," *Stanford Law Review* 44 (1992): 219; Dean Alfange Jr., "*Marbury v. Madison* and Original Understandings of Judicial Review: In Defense of Traditional Wisdom," *Supreme Court Review 1993* (1993): 329; Mark A. Graber, "The Problematic Establishment of Judicial Review," in *The Supreme Court in American Politics*, ed. Howard Gillman and Cornell Clayton (Lawrence: University Press of Kansas, 1999); William E. Nelson, *Marbury v. Madison* (Lawrence: University Press of Kansas, 2000).

96 *Marbury*, 177.

97 Jackson v. Twentyman, 27 U.S. 136 (1829).

98 1 *Stat.* 80 (1789)

99 36 *Stat.* 1156 (1911).

100 David P. Currie, *The Constitution in the Supreme Court: The First Hundred Years* (Chicago: University of Chicago Press, 1985), 70, 69.

101 For an interesting perspective on why cases become canonical, see Jack M. Balkin and Sanford Levinson, "The Canons of Constitutional Law," *Harvard Law Review* 111 (1998): 963. For revisionist literature that has recently questioned the significance of *Marbury*, see Michael J. Klarman, "How Great Were the 'Great' Marshall Court Decisions," *Virginia Law Review* 87 (2001): 1111; Davison M. Douglas, "The Rhetorical Use of *Marbury v. Madison*: The Emergence of a 'Great' Case," *Wake Forest Law Review* 38 (2003): 375; Keith E. Whittington and Amanda Rinderle, "Making a Mountain out of a Molehill? *Marbury* and the Construction of the Constitutional Canon," *Hastings Constitutional Law Quarterly* 39 (2012): 823; Graber, "Passive-Aggressive Virtues"; Nelson, *Marbury v. Madison*; Clinton, Marbury v. Madison *and Judicial Review*; Kramer, *People Themselves*; Treanor, "Judicial Review before *Marbury*."

102 See Warren, *Supreme Court*, 1:243–257 (describing Jeffersonian newspapers' reaction to *Marbury*).

103 Ex parte Bollman, 8 U.S. 75, 101 (1807).

104 On the Jeffersonian split, see Noble E. Cunningham Jr., "Who Were the Quids?" *Mississippi Valley Historical Review* 50 (1963): 262; David A. Carson, "That Ground Called Quiddism: John Randolph's War with the Jefferson Administration," *Journal of American Studies* 20 (1986): 71; Donald A. MacPhee, "The Yazoo Controversy: The Beginning of the 'Quid' Revolt," *Georgia Historical Quarterly* 49 (1965): 23; Norman K. Risjord, *The Old Republicans* (New York: Columbia University Press, 1965).

105 United States v. Fisher et al., 6 U.S. 358, 384 (1805).

106 Ibid., 396.

107 Ibid., 379.

108 Ibid., 396.

109 Parsons v. Bedford, 28 U.S. 433, 445, 447 (1830).

110 Ibid., 450, 452, 454.

111 Ibid., 448, 449. As one prominent commentator summarized, "Congress cannot constitutionally confer upon the Supreme Court authority to grant a new trial by a re-examination of the facts once tried by a jury, except to redress errors of law." George Ticknor Curtis, *Commentaries on the Jurisdiction, Practice, and Peculiar Jurisprudence of the Courts of the United States* (Philadelphia: T. & J. W. Johnson, 1854), 1:182. The statute extending federal jurisdiction over Louisiana had done so incautiously and, to that extent, was defective.

112 1 *Stat.* 677 (1799).

113 Ex parte United States in the matter of the United States v. Phelps, et al., 33 U.S. 700, 703 (1834).

114 Ibid., 702. Digests and treatises citing the 1799 law subsequently took note of the requirement that, where necessary to gather evidence to mount a real defense, "a continuance must be given," despite the statute. Robert Desty, *A Manual of Practice*, 9th ed. (San Francisco: Bancroft-Whitney, 1899), 2:1191. See also Conkling, *Treatise*, 215n; Abbott, *Treatise*, 2:140.

115 Sampeyreac and Stewart v. United States, 32 U.S. 222, 238–239 (1833).

116 Cary and Cary v. Curtis, 44 U.S. 236, 245–246 (1845). Congress responded with a new statute explicitly giving taxpayers the right to sue customs collectors. Jerry Mashaw, "Administration and 'The Democracy': Administrative Law from Jackson to Lincoln, 1829–1861," *Yale Law Journal* 117 (2008): 1568, 1678.

117 Sheldon and Sheldon v. Sill, 49 U.S. 441 (1850).

118 Dynes v. Hoover, 61 U.S. 65, 82 (1858).

119 Garcia v. Lee, 37 U.S. 511 (1838).

120 Haydel v. Dufresne, 58 U.S. 23, 29–30 (1855).

121 United States v. Ritchie, 58 U.S. 525, 533–534 (1855). *Ritchie* cut against the grain of the Taney Court's decisions by requiring a system of de novo review of administrative actions, whereas the Taney Court tended to give the executive branch greater autonomy from judicial oversight. Mashaw, "Administration and 'The Democracy,'" 131–133.

122 10 *Stat.* 112 (1852).

123 Pennsylvania v. Wheeling and Belmont Bridge Company, 54 U.S. 518 (1851).

124 Pennsylvania v. Wheeling and Belmont Bridge Company, 59 U.S. 421, 431–432 (1856).

125 Den ex dem. Murray and Kayser v. Hoboken Land and Improvement Company, 59 U.S. 272, 280–281 (1856).

126 Waring and Dalman v. Clarke, 46 U.S. 441, 459 (1847).

127 Ibid., 457.

128 Ibid., 463.

129 New Jersey Steam Navigation Company v. Merchants' Bank of Boston, 47 U.S. 344, 386 (1848). In giving federal courts admiralty jurisdiction over the Great Lakes, Congress limited its authority to ships moving between different states and territories. In *Allen v. Newberry*, 62 U.S. 244, 247 (1859), the Court reemphasized its view that such a "limitation of the jurisdiction" was merely declaratory of the constitutional requirement, which was binding "independently of any act of Congress."

130 Propeller Genesee Chief v. Fitzhugh, et al., 53 U.S. 443, 453, 454 (1852).

131 Ibid., 455, 457.

132 The People's Ferry Company of Boston v. Beers and Warner, 61 U.S. 393, 400 (1858).

133 Ibid., 401.

134 Ibid., 401, 402.

135 Simon Greenleaf, *A Treatise on the Law of Evidence*, 6th ed. (Boston: Little, Brown, 1860), 3:424; W. D. Dabney, *Outlines of Federal Jurisdiction and Law Procedure* (Charlottesville, VA: G. W. Olivier, 1897), 20.

136 John C. Calhoun, "Address on the Relation which the States and General Government Bear to Each Other," in *The Works of John C. Calhoun*, ed. Richard K. Cralle (New York: D. Appleton, 1855), 6:71.

137 Hunter v. Martin, 18 Va. 1, 40 (1815).

138 Martin v. Hunter's Lessee, 14 U.S. 304, 338, 340 (1816).

139 Cohens v. Virginia, 19 U.S. 264, 377, 388 (1821).

140 Ableman v. Booth, 62 U.S. 506 (1859).

141 On the politics of repeal of section 25, see Mark A. Graber, "James Buchanan as Savior? Judicial Power, Political Fragmentation, and the Failed 1831 Repeal of Section 25," *Oregon Law Review* 88 (2009): 95.

142 Osborn v. Bank of the United States, 22 U.S. 738, 818, 822–823 (1824).

143 McCulloch v. Maryland, 17 U.S. 316 (1819).

144 For background, see Mark Killenbeck, *M'Culloch v. Maryland* (Lawrence: University Press of Kansas, 2006); Richard E. Ellis, *Aggressive Nationalism* (New York: Oxford University Press, 2007).

145 Steven A. Engel, "Note: The *McCulloch* Theory of the Fourteenth Amendment: *City of Boerne v. Flores* and the Original Understanding of Section 5," *Yale Law Journal* 109 (1999): 118. On the limits of congressional authority laid out in *McCulloch*, see A. I. L. Campbell, "'It Is a Constitution We Are Expounding': Chief Justice Marshall and the 'Necessary and Proper' Clause," *Journal of Legal History* 12 (1991): 190; Howard Gillman, "The Struggle over Marshall and the Politics of Constitutional History," *Political Research Quarterly* 47 (1994): 877.

146 *McCulloch*, 401.

147 On this theme, see Keith E. Whittington, "The Road Not Taken: *Dred Scott,* Judicial Authority, and Political Questions," *Journal of Politics* 63 (2001): 365.

148 James Madison, "Veto Message, January 30, 1815," in *A Compilation of the Messages and Papers of the Presidents,* ed. James D. Richardson (Washington, DC: Government Printing Office, 1897), 2:540.

149 See Graber, "Federalist or Friends of Adams."

150 Whittington, "Road Not Taken" ("stricken off" from Spencer Roane).

151 James Madison, *The Writings of James Madison,* ed. Gaillard Hunt (New York: G. P. Putnam's Sons, 1910), 9:59.

152 Whittington, "Road Not Taken."

153 Graber, "Jacksonian Origins."

154 On the hostility of the Taney Court justices to *McCulloch,* see Graber, "Jacksonian Origins."

155 United States v. Marigold, 50 U.S. 560, 566, 567, 568 (1850).

156 See Mark A. Graber, "The Jacksonian Makings of the Taney Court" (unpublished manuscript).

157 See Whittington, "Road Not Taken"; Graber, "Jacksonian Origins"; Gerald N. Magliocca, *Andrew Jackson and the Constitution* (Lawrence: University Press of Kansas, 2007).

158 Edward J. Balleisen, *Navigating Failure* (Chapel Hill: University of North Carolina Press, 2001), 109, 128.

159 Nelson v. Carland, 42 U.S. 265, 277 (1843).

160 Ibid., 280.

161 Ex parte the City Bank of New Orleans in the matter of Christy, 44 U.S. 292, 323 (1844).

162 Gibbons v. Ogden, 22 U.S. 1, 187, 197 (1824).

163 United States v. Coombs, 37 U.S. 72 (1838).

164 Worcester v. Georgia, 31 U.S. 515, 558–559 (1832).

165 United States v. Gratiot, 39 U.S. 526, 537–538 (1840).

166 Searight v. Stokes and Stockton, 44 U.S. 151, 180 (1845).

167 Ibid., 166.

168 Pollard v. Hagan, 44 U.S. 212 (1845).

169 Thomas M. Cooley, *A Treatise on Constitutional Limitations* (Boston: Little, Brown, 1868), 526.

170 Mayor of New Orleans v. United States, 35 U.S. 662, 737 (1836).

171 "Recent Decisions—Editorial Note," *Western Jurist* 1 (1867): 167. See also Louis Houck, *A Treatise on the Law of Navigable Rivers* (Boston: Little, Brown, 1868), 81; Permoli v. The First Municipality of New Orleans, 44 U.S. 589 (1845).

172 Withers v. Buckley, et al., 61 U.S. 84, 92–93 (1858).

173 See Roger Foster, *Commentaries on the Constitution of the United States* (Boston: Boston Book Company, 1895), 1:331; John M. Gould, *A Treatise on the Law of Waters* (Chicago: Callaghan, 1900), 95.

174   Gibbons v. Ogden, 22 U.S. 1 (1824).

175   Veazie v. Moor, 55 U.S. 568, 573–574 (1853).

176   *McCulloch*, 407.

177   Alexander Hamilton, James Madison, and John Jay, *The Federalist Papers*, ed. Clinton Rossiter (New York: New American Library, 1961), No. 37.

178   See Dr. Bonham's Case, 8 Co. 114a, 118a (C.P. 1610).

179   United States v. Cantril, 8 U.S. 167 (1807).

180   The Court later chose to take the interpretive approach with a different fraud statute that similarly left out the word "purport." United States v. Howell, 78 U.S. 432 (1870).

181   In his antebellum legal treatise, for example, Joel Prentiss Bishop cites *Cantril* as an example of a repugnancy doctrine illustrating his argument that there are "other limits to the legislative power, besides those which are expressly laid down in the constitution of the United States." Joel Prentiss Bishop, *Commentaries on the Criminal Law* (Boston: Little, Brown, 1856), 1:53, 56. *Cantril* differs significantly from other cases he cites, however. See, e.g., Joel Prentiss Bishop, *Commentaries on the Law of Statutory Crimes*, 2nd ed. (Boston: Little, Brown, 1883), 42n3; Albertson v. State, 9 Neb. 429 (1879) ("the well-known rule applies, that where there is an irreconcilable conflict between different sections in parts of the same statute the last words stand, and those in conflict therewith are, so far as there is a conflict, repealed"). The report on *Cantril* is slight, and it was also taken to support the proposition that courts cannot proceed on defective indictments. See, e.g., Joseph Chitty, *A Practical Treatise on the Criminal Law*, 3rd ed. (Philadelphia: Isaac Riley, 1836), 1:173.

182   Thus, the Pennsylvania Supreme Court cited *Cantril* as authority for the proposition that such impractical statutory provisions are "unconstitutional" and "nugatory and void." Joseph Story extended its logic to include cases in which the "words in the act are too vague." Hall v. Bank of the United States, 6 Whart. 585 (Pa. 1840); United States v. La Coste, 2 Mason 129 (C.C.D. Ma., 1820). See also Opinion by the Justices, 249 Ala. 88, 91 (Ala. 1947) (a statute is void when it "is so incomplete, so conflicting or so vague and indefinite, that it cannot be executed and the court is unable by the application of the law and accepted rules of construction to determine what the legislature intended"). The Ohio Supreme Court described its own fraud statute as "not very skillfully drawn" but "understood and enforced by all our courts," distinguishing it from the "legislative blunder" voided by the Court in *Cantril*. Mackey v. State, 3 Ohio St. 362, 365 (1854). See also Hand v. Stapleton, 135 Ala. 156 (Ala. 1903) ("no ground for striking down or nullifying [the statute] . . . where the intention of the Legislature and its real purposes can be effectuated").

183   2 *Stat.* 423 (February 24, 1807).

184   Fletcher v. Peck, 10 U.S. 87 (1810). See also Mark A. Graber, "Naked Land

Transfers and American Constitutional Development," *Vanderbilt Law Review* 53 (2000): 73.

185 An Act to Extend the Time for Locating Virginia Military Land Warrants, 3 *Stat.* 424 (1818).

186 Reynolds v. M'Arthur, 27 U.S. 417, 435 (1829).

187 The federalism dimension would be central to future cases. See Pollard v. Hagan, 44 U.S. 212 (1845); New Orleans v. United States, 35 U.S. 662 (1836).

188 William G. Myer, *Vested Rights* (St. Louis, MO: Gilbert Book Company, 1891), 18.

189 United States v. Percheman, 32 U.S. 51, 87 (1833). W. W. Willoughby later observed that passages like the one in *Percheman* were "strong language, but there is no suggestion that it does not lie within the legal power of the new government (subject, of course, to the limitations of its own constitutional laws) to act as it might seem fit with regard to the private as well as the public rights of the inhabitants of annexed territories." W. W. Willoughby, *The Fundamental Concepts of Public Law* (New York: Macmillan, 1924), 333. It was the limitation of constitutional law that Marshall was determined to impose.

190 An Act for Ascertaining Claims and Titles to Land within the Territory of Florida, 3 *Stat.* 717 (1822).

191 An Act to Provide for the Final Settlement of Land Claims in Florida, 4 *Stat.* 405 (1830); An Act Supplementary to the Several Acts Providing for the Settlement and Confirmation of Private Land Claims in Florida, 4 *Stat.* 286 (1828).

192 Payson Jackson Treat, *The National Land System, 1785–1820* (New York: E. B. Treat, 1910), 228.

193 Harry L. Coles Jr., "Applicability of the Public Land System to Louisiana," *Mississippi Valley Historical Review* 43 (1956): 51–53.

194 *Percheman*, 51, 63, 88, 89, 90, 91, 92, 90.

195 A quarter century after the Louisiana Purchase, in a case arriving by appeal from the territorial courts in Florida, the Court had announced that the "government possesses the power of acquiring territory." American Insurance Company, et al. v. Canter, 26 U.S. 511, 542 (1828).

196 Foster and Elam v. Neilson, 27 U.S. 253, 304, 307 (1829) (emphasis added).

197 Ibid., 314, 315, 316.

198 *Percheman*, 88, 89 (emphasis added).

199 As chief justice, Roger Taney endorsed this reconciliation of the two cases. Garcia v. Lee, 37 U.S. 511, 519–522 (1838).

200 Foster v. Neilson, 27 U.S. 253 (1829).

201 Pollard's Lessee v. Files, 43 U.S. 591 (1844).

202 Catron also wrote the Court's opinion in the last constitutional case arising from the Spanish cession. Both French and Spanish authorities had granted land with "no definite boundaries" in the Louisiana Territory before it was taken over

by the United States. Surveys had to be completed before landholders could take possession of such grants, and at the time of the Louisiana Purchase, some "unlocated claims" were still awaiting legal surveys to distinguish them from the public domain. The courts could do nothing "with these incipient claims," so claimants had to rely on congressional action. In 1807 Congress established land commissioners to order the necessary surveys and adjudicate these claims. The statute provided that with regard to such claims, the commissioners' decisions would be final, but one claimant objected that Congress could not shield this determination from judicial review. The Court demurred. In the case of "vague grants[,] . . . title attached to no land," and there were no independent facts for "a court of justice [to] ascertain." Congress had complete discretion to dispose of such cases, and there was no constitutional infirmity in the procedures set up by the 1807 act. West v. Cochran, 58 U.S. 403, 413, 416 (1855).

203 Lytle, et al. v. Arkansas, et al., 50 U.S. 314, 325–326, 669, 333–334, 335 (1850).

204 Aurora v. United States, 11 U.S. 382, 386 (1813).

205 Ibid., 388.

206 United States v. Smith, 18 U.S. 153, 156, 158 (1820).

207 Ibid., 159.

208 Wayman v. Southard, 23 U.S. 1, 43 (1825).

209 Bank of the United States v. Halstead, 23 U.S. 51, 61 (1825).

210 Loughborough v. Blake, 18 U.S. 317, 318, 324–325 (1820).

211 Benner, et al. v. Porter, 50 U.S. 235 (1850).

212 McNulty v. Batty, et al., 51 U.S. 72 (1851). *McNulty* is complicated by the fact that the 1848 extension of the 1847 appellate jurisdiction act made no explicit reference to cases of this type, apparently based on the assumption that no additional action "was necessary to preserve or give effect to the jurisdiction of the court over it." The Court's opinion makes it clear that the result would be the same whether jurisdiction failed because the implied jurisdiction created by the statute was inadequate or because Congress lacked the authority to provide jurisdiction in the case either implicitly or explicitly. The statute was not fixable under the Constitution.

213 Abbott and Abbott, *Treatise*, 1:279.

214 Slavery was more of an issue in the Court's nonconstitutional cases, where it was frequently called on to address the application of federal statutes related to slavery and the disposition of slave property. See, e.g., Keith E. Whittington, "The Supreme Court and Slavery," in *The Political Thought of the Civil War*, ed. Alan Levine, Thomas W. Merrill, and James R. Stoner, Jr. (Lawrence: University Press of Kansas, 2018); William M. Wiecek, "Slavery and Abolition before the United States Supreme Court, 1820–1860," *Journal of American History* 65 (1978): 34.

215 See Crowe, *Building the Judiciary*, 84–131.

216 Quoted in Charles Warren, *The Supreme Court in United States History* (Boston: Little, Brown, 1922), 3:21.

217 Prigg v. Pennsylvania, 41 U.S. 539, 622, 618–619 (1842). On *Prigg*, see Paul Finkelman, "Story Telling on the Supreme Court: *Prigg v. Pennsylvania* and Justice Joseph Story's Judicial Nationalism," *Supreme Court Review 1994* (1994): 247.

218 Jones v. Van Zandt, 46 U.S. 215, 230 (1847).

219 Ableman v. Booth, 62 U.S. 506, 526 (1859).

220 Dred Scott v. Sandford, 60 U.S. 393, 441, 448 (1857) (emphasis added).

221 Ibid., 452.

222 Senator John Clayton, in *Cong. Globe*, 30th Cong., 1st sess. (July 19, 1848): 950; Justice John Catron quoted in James Buchanan, *The Works of James Buchanan* (Philadelphia: J. B. Lippincott, 1910), 10:106. On the evolution of the Court's approach to the *Dred Scott* case, see Earl Maltz, Dred Scott *and the Politics of Slavery* (Lawrence: University Press of Kansas, 2007); Don E. Fehrenbacher, *The* Dred Scott *Case* (New York: Oxford University Press, 1978).

223 See Whittington, *Political Foundations*, 180–181.

224 See Mark A. Graber, "The Nonmajoritarian Difficulty: Legislative Deference to the Judiciary," *Studies in American Political Development 7* (Spring 1993): 46–50; Wallace Mendelson, "Dred Scott's Case—Reconsidered," *Minnesota Law Review* 38 (1953): 16; Whittington, *Political Foundations*, 246–256.

225 *Cong. Globe*, 31st Cong., 1st sess. (June 7, 1850): 1155.

226 *Works of James Buchanan*, 10:106.

227 Whittington, *Political Foundations*, 251–254.

228 Graber, "Nonmajoritarian Difficulty," 282–287; Mendelson, "Dred Scott's Case—Reconsidered," 24; Barry Friedman, "The History of the Countermajoritarian Difficulty, Part One: The Road to Judicial Supremacy," *New York University Law Review 73* (1998): 415–416.

229 1 *Stat.* 302 (1793).

230 Ex parte in the Matter of the Commonwealth of Kentucky v. Dennison, 65 U.S. 66 (1861).

231 See, e.g., Prigg v. Pennsylvania, 41 U.S. 539, 622 (1842); James Kent, *Commentaries on American Law*, 4th ed. (New York: O. Halsted, 1840), 2:32nc ("I do not know of any power under the authority of the United States by which he could be coerced to perform the duty. Perhaps the act of congress may be considered as prescribing a duty, the performance of which it cannot enforce.").

232 See, e.g., 1 *Stat.* 65 (1789) ("it shall be the duty of the Secretary of the Treasury to digest and prepare plans for the improvement and management of the revenue"); 1 *Stat.* 63 (1789) ("it shall be the duty of such collector or surveyor to grant a permit to land or unload such cargo"); 1 *Stat.* 254 (1792) ("it shall be the duty of the consuls and vice consuls of the United States, to give receipts for all fees which they shall receive"); 1 *Stat.* 234 (1792) ("it shall be the duty of the Postmaster General, to give public notice in one or more newspapers").

233 See Paul Finkelman, "The Kidnapping of John Davis and the Adoption of the Fugitive Slave Law of 1793," *Journal of Southern History* 56 (1990): 397.

234 David Rorer, *American Inter-State Law* (Chicago: Callaghan, 1879), 220 ("a *moral*" duty); Samuel T. Spear, *The Law of Extradition* (Albany, NY: Weed, Parsons, 1879), 291 ("no question as to the validity of the law for this purpose" of stating when governors should act on their own constitutional duty to extradite fugitives).

CHAPTER 4. REVIEW OF CONGRESS DURING THE CIVIL WAR AND
RECONSTRUCTION

1 "Suspension of the Privilege of the Writ of Habeas Corpus, July 5, 1861," in *Opinions of the Attorneys General* (Washington, DC: Government Printing Office, 1868), 10:85, 77. See, generally, Keith E. Whittington, *Political Foundations of Judicial Supremacy* (Princeton, NJ: Princeton University Press, 2007), 34–35, 68–70; Barry Friedman, "The History of the Countermajoritarian Difficulty, Part One: The Road to Judicial Supremacy," *New York University Law Review* 73 (1998): 413–430.

2 *Trial of Andrew Johnson* (Washington, DC: Government Printing Office, 1868), 2:228, 91.

3 See Keith E. Whittington and Amanda Rinderle, "Making a Mountain out of a Molehill? *Marbury* and the Construction of the Constitutional Canon," *Hastings Constitutional Law Quarterly* 39 (2012): 852–853; Stanley I. Kutler, *Judicial Power and Reconstruction Politics* (Chicago: University of Chicago Press, 1968).

4 *Cong. Globe*, 37th Cong., 2nd sess. (1861), 26, 27. See also Howard Gillman, Mark A. Graber, and Keith E. Whittington, *American Constitutionalism*, 2nd ed. (New York: Oxford University Press, 2017), 1:248–253.

5 See Mark A. Graber, "The Jacksonian Origins of Chase Court Activism," *Journal of Supreme Court History* 25 (2000): 17.

6 Ex parte Merryman, 17 F. Cas. 144 (1861).

7 Philip G. Auchampaugh, "A Great Justice on State and Federal Power Being the Thoughts of Chief Justice Taney on the Federal Conscription Act," *Tyler's Quarterly Historical and Genealogical Magazine* 18 (1936): 72.

8 See, e.g., The Prize Cases, 67 U.S. 635 (1863).

9 Edward G. Spaulding, *History of the Legal Tender Paper Money* (Buffalo, NY: Express Printing Company, 1869), 15.

10 Ibid., 27.

11 *Cong. Globe*, 37th Cong., 2nd sess., (1862), 523.

12 Hepburn v. Griswold, 75 U.S. 603, 625 (1869).

13 McCulloch v. Maryland, 17 U.S. 316, 421 (1819).

14 Legal Tender Cases, 79 U.S. 457, 529, 536, 549 (1870).

15 See Texas v. White, 74 U.S. 700 (1869). Compare James G. Randall, *Constitutional Problems under Lincoln* (Urbana: University of Illinois Press, 1951).

16 12 *Stat.* 502 (1862); 13 *Stat.* 424 (1865).

17 See U.S. v. Klein, 80 U.S. 128 (1871).

18 12 *Stat.* 423 (1862).

19 Bennett v. Hunter, 76 U.S. 326, 335, 336, 337 (1869).

20 Tacey v. Irwin, 85 U.S. 549, 551 (1873). Lower courts got the message, "from the tenor and spirit" of the Court's language, that Congress "could not constitutionally prohibit payment of the tax by an agent." Lee v. Kaufman, 15 F. Cas. 204 (1879).

21 Stewart v. Kahn, 78 U.S. 493, 506–507 (1870).

22 Miller v. United States, 78 U.S. 268, 307 (1870). See also Kirk v. Lynd, 106 U.S. 315 (1882).

23 Hamilton v. Dillin, 88 U.S. 73, 97 (1873).

24 "Democratic Policy," *Old Guard* 1 (1863): 259.

25 Mississippi v. Johnson, 71 U.S. 475, 501 (1866).

26 Ex parte McCardle, 74 U.S. 506 (1868). See also Mark A. Graber, "Legal, Strategic, or Legal Strategy: Deciding to Decide during the Civil War and Reconstruction," in *The Supreme Court and American Political Development*, ed. Ronald Kahn and Ken I. Kersch (Lawrence: University Press of Kansas, 2006).

27 John A. Leland, *A Voice from South Carolina* (Charleston, SC: Walker, Evans & Cogswell, 1879), 166.

28 United States v. Reese, 92 U.S. 214, 218, 219 (1875).

29 United States v. Cruikshank, 92 U.S. 542, 553 (1875). See also United States v. Harris, 106 U.S. 629 (1883); The Civil Rights Cases, 109 U.S. 3 (1883).

30 United States v. Reese, 92 U.S. 214, 221 (1875). See also Pamela Brandwein, *Rethinking the Judicial Settlement of Reconstruction* (New York: Cambridge University Press, 2011).

31 Ku Klux Klan Cases, 16 U.S. 140 (1870).

32 Ex parte Yarbrough, 110 U.S. 651, 657, 668 (1884).

33 Ex parte Virginia, 100 U.S. 338, 345, 347 (1879).

34 Ex parte Siebold, 100 U.S. 371, 394 (1879). See also Ex parte Clarke, 100 U.S. 399 (1879).

35 Mayor v. Cooper, 73 U.S. 247, 253 (1867).

36 Tennessee v. Davis, 100 U.S. 257, 263 (1878). See also Mitchell v. Clark, 110 U.S. 633 (1884).

37 Railway Company v. Whitton's Administrator, 80 U.S. 270, 289–290 (1871). See also Insurance Company v. Dunn, 86 U.S. 214 (1874); Gaines v. Fuentes, 92 U.S. 214 (1876).

38 Hylton v. United States, 3 U.S. 171 (1796); Loughborough v. Blake, 18 U.S. 317 (1820).

39 McCulloch v. Maryland, 17 U.S. 316 (1819); Weston v. Charleston, 27 U.S. 449 (1829); Dobbins v. Commissioners of Erie County, 41 U.S. 435 (1842).

40 Collector v. Day, 78 U.S. 113 (1870).

41 United States v. Railroad Company, 84 U.S. 322 (1872). Congress could, however,

tax notes issued by state banks, even when the goal was to drive such notes out of circulation. Veazie Bank v. Fenno, 75 U.S. 533 (1869); Merchants' National Bank v. United States, 101 U.S. 1 (1879).

42 The Court distinguished estate tax on land, which it held was not a direct tax, as well as penalties on unpaid direct taxes. Scholey v. Rew, 90 U.S. 331 (1874); De Treville v. Smalls, 98 U.S. 517 (1878).

43 Springer v. United States, 102 U.S. 586 (1880). See also Pacific Insurance Co. v. Soule, 74 U.S. 433 (1868).

44 Hadden v. Collector, 72 U.S. 107, 113 (1866).

45 Stockdale v. Atlantic Insurance Co., 87 U.S. 323 (1873).

46 United States v. Singer, 82 U.S. 111 (1872).

47 Pace v. Burgess, 92 U.S. 372 (1875).

48 Willard v. Presbury, 81 U.S. 676 (1871); Mattingly v. District of Columbia, 97 U.S. 687 (1878).

49 United States v. Dewitt, 76 U.S. 41, 45 (1869).

50 In re Trade-Mark Cases, 100 U.S. 82, 93 (1879).

51 Ibid., 96–97. In a separate case, the Court also rebuffed efforts to leverage the congressional power to make bankruptcy law to criminalize frauds that were independent of a bankruptcy filing. Against such acts, "the State can alone legislate." United States v. Fox, 95 U.S. 670, 672 (1877).

52 21 *Stat.* 502 (1881).

53 United States v. Holliday, 70 U.S. 407 (1865); United States v. Forty-Three Gallons of Whiskey, 93 U.S. 188 (1876).

54 Pensacola Telegraph Company v. Western Union Telegraph Company, 96 U.S. 1, 9 (1877).

55 South Carolina v. Georgia, 93 U.S. 4 (1876).

56 In re Clinton Bridge, 77 U.S. 454 (1870); Bridge Company v. United States, 105 U.S. 470 (1881); Miller v. Mayor of the City of New York, 109 U.S. 385 (1883).

57 The Daniel Ball, 77 U.S. 557 (1870).

58 White's Bank v. Smith, 74 U.S. 646 (1868).

59 Lord v. Steamship Company, 102 U.S. 541 (1880).

60 Sinking-Fund Cases, 99 U.S. 700 (1878).

61 Ex parte Jackson, 96 U.S. 727 (1877).

62 Burrow-Giles Lithographic Co. v. Sarony, 111 U.S. 53 (1884).

63 Reichart v. Felps, 73 U.S. 160 (1868); Johnson v. Towsley, 80 U.S. 72 (1871); Beecher v. Wetherby, 95 U.S. 517 (1877).

64 Gordon v. United States, 69 U.S. 561 (1865); The Alicia, 74 U.S. 571 (1869); Justices v. Murray, 76 U.S. 274 (1870).

65 United States v. Simmons, 96 U.S. 360 (1878).

66 United States v. Great Falls Manufacturing Co., 112 U.S. 645 (1884).

67 Ex parte Curtis, 106 U.S. 371 (1882).

68 Reynolds v. United States, 98 U.S. 145 (1878); Murphy v. Ramsey, 114 U.S. 15 (1885).

69 Freeborn to Smith, 69 U.S. 160 (1864).

70 Kohl v. United States, 91 U.S. 367 (1875).

71 Close v. Glenwood Cemetery, 107 U.S. 466 (1883).

72 Wood v. United States, 107 U.S. 414 (1883).

CHAPTER 5. CONGRESS AND THE *LOCHNER* COURT

1 New York v. Lochner, 198 U.S. 45 (1905).

2 See Howard Gillman, *The Constitution Besieged* (Durham, NC: Duke University Press, 1993).

3 See James Bradley Thayer, "The Origin and Scope of the American Doctrine of Constitutional Law," *Harvard Law Review* 7 (1893): 129; William E. Nelson, *The Roots of American Bureaucracy, 1830–1900* (Cambridge, MA: Harvard University Press, 1982); Robert Cover, "The Origins of Judicial Activism in the Protection of Minorities," *Yale Law Review* 91 (1982): 1287.

4 Thomas Kilby Smith, "The Rise of Federal Judicial Supremacy in the United States, Part I," *American Law Register* 46 (1898): 521.

5 Arnold M. Paul, *Conservative Crisis and the Rule of Law* (Ithaca, NY: Cornell University Press, 1960); William F. Swindler, *Court and Constitution in the Twentieth Century* (Indianapolis: Bobbs-Merrill, 1969).

6 Charles Warren, "The Progressiveness of the United States Supreme Court," *Columbia Law Review* 13 (1913): 295.

7 Robert G. McCloskey, *The American Supreme Court* (Chicago: University of Chicago Press, 1960), 151. See also Michael J. Phillips, *The Lochner Court: Myth and Reality* (Westport, CT: Praeger, 2001); Melvin I. Urofsky, "Myth and Reality: The Supreme Court and Protective Legislation in the Progressive Era," *Yearbook of the Supreme Court Historical Society* (1983): 53.

8 Warren, "Progressiveness," 310.

9 Robert A. Dahl, "Decision-Making in a Democracy: The Supreme Court as a National Policy-Maker," *Journal of Public Law* 7 (1957): 285–286.

10 Stephen W. Stathis, *Landmark Legislation 1774–2012*, 2nd ed. (Washington, DC: CQ Press, 2014).

11 The disparity would be even more notable if we pulled back the lens a bit and considered cases that came faster or slower than the Court's historical median time to decision in invalidation cases, which is roughly nine years. Seven of the nine cases involving statutory provisions adopted by a Democratic House arrived before this threshold, but only twelve of the twenty-three cases involving Republican statutes were similarly fast-moving.

12 Employers' Liability Cases, 207 U.S. 463 (1907).

13 Henry F. Pringle, *The Life and Times of William Howard Taft* (New York: Farrar & Rinehart, 1939), 1:139–143; *The Letters of Theodore Roosevelt*, ed. Elting E. Morison (Cambridge, MA: Harvard University Press, 1952), 6:1298.

14 Quoted in George E. Mowry, *The Era of Theodore Roosevelt and the Birth of Modern America, 1900–1912* (New York: Harper & Brothers, 1958), 142.

15 *Letters of Theodore Roosevelt*, 6:889.

16 Ibid., 903–904.

17 *Employers' Liability Cases*, 490, 497.

18 Ibid., 505, 537.

19 Theodore Roosevelt, "Eighth Annual Message," in *A Compilation of the Messages and Papers of the Presidents*, ed. James D. Richardson (New York: Bureau of National Literature, 1900), 15:7215–7216, 7217.

20 William Letwin, *Law and Economic Policy in America* (Chicago: University of Chicago Press, 1965), 85.

21 Democratic Party Platform (June 5, 1888), in *The National Conventions and Platforms of All Parties, 1789–1901*, ed. Thomas Hudson McKee (Baltimore: Friedenwald, 1901), 235.

22 *Cong. Rec.* 19 (1888), 6041. See also Letwin, *Law and Economic Policy*, 87–88.

23 Letwin, *Law and Economic Policy*, 92–94.

24 *Cong. Rec.* 21 (1890), 2460, 3148, 1768, 3147. See also Donald D. Morgan, *Congress and the Constitution* (Cambridge, MA: Harvard University Press, 1966), 148–149; Mark A. Graber, "The Nonmajoritarian Difficulty: Legislative Deference to the Judiciary," *Studies in American Political Development* 7 (1993): 50–53.

25 Grover Cleveland, "Inaugural Address," in *Compilation of the Messages and Papers of the Presidents*, 11:5823.

26 Carl Brent Swisher, *American Constitutional Development* (Boston: Houghton Mifflin, 1943), 428, 430.

27 United States v. E. C. Knight, 156 U.S. 1 (1895).

28 Letwin, *Law and Economic Policy*, 122.

29 Grover Cleveland, "Annual Message," in *Compilation of the Messages and Papers of the Presidents*, 9:745.

30 Letwin, *Law and Economic Policy*, 134, 139. One of those prosecutions did run afoul of the rule laid down in *E. C. Knight*. The Court concluded that a livestock exchange in Kansas was merely an "aid of commerce" but "not of an interstate commercial nature." Hopkins v. United States, 171 U.S. 578, 592 (1898).

31 United States v. Harris, 106 U.S. 629 (1883).

32 Baldwin v. Franks, 120 U.S. 678 (1887).

33 James v. Bowman, 190 U.S. 127 (1903).

34 Hodges v. United States, 203 U.S. 1, 20 (1906).

35 Butts v. Merchants & Miners Transp. Co., 230 U.S. 126 (1913).

36 See Civil Rights Cases, 109 U.S. 3, 19 (1883).

37 See Keith E. Whittington, *Constitutional Construction* (Cambridge, MA: Harvard University Press, 1999), 93–106.

38 Richard E. Welch Jr., *The Presidencies of Grover Cleveland* (Lawrence: University Press of Kansas, 1988), 129–130.

39 Ibid., 132.
40 Grover Cleveland to William L. Wilson, in *Letters of Grover Cleveland*, ed. Allan Nevins (Boston: Houghton Mifflin, 1933), 357.
41 On the centrality of New York to national Democratic politics and policy-making in the Gilded Age, see Scott C. James, *Presidents, Parties, and the State* (New York: Cambridge University Press, 2000), 42–56.
42 *Cong. Rec.* 26 (1894), 6637.
43 "Clevelandism Again," *New York Times*, November 21, 1896, 4.
44 Pollock v. Farmers' Loan and Trust, 157 U.S. 429 (1895); Pollock v. Farmers' Loan and Trust, 158 U.S. 601 (1895).
45 *Pollock I*, 583.
46 Donald Grier Stephenson Jr., *Campaigns and the Court* (New York: Columbia University Press, 1999), 107–128.
47 Grover Cleveland to David B. Hill, in *Letters of Grover Cleveland*, 415.
48 Woodrow Wilson, *Constitutional Government in the United States* (New York: Columbia University Press, 1908), 179, 177–178, 187. As president, William Howard Taft felt similar pressures and endorsed the creation of a federal children's bureau bill in his reelection year, even as he privately griped at the "disposition to unload everything on the federal government that the states ought to look after." See Pringle, *Life and Times of Taft*, 2:622.
49 Arthur S. Link, *Woodrow Wilson and the Progressive Era, 1910–1917* (New York: Harper & Brothers, 1954), 226–227; Stephen B. Wood, *Constitutional Politics in the Progressive Era* (Chicago: University of Chicago Press, 1968), 65–67.
50 Hammer v. Dagenhart, 247 U.S. 251 (1918).
51 Wood, *Constitutional Politics*, 156.
52 See William Graebner, "Federalism in the Progressive Era: A Structural Interpretation of Reform," *Journal of American History* 64 (1977): 353–354.
53 See Wilson v. New, 243 U.S. 332 (1917); Wood, *Constitutional Politics*, 77–78; Keith E. Whittington, "Taking What They Give Us: Explaining the Court's Federalism Offensive," *Duke Law Journal* 51 (2001): 510–517.
54 There was only one additional case that involved a law passed by a unified Democratic government. The 1894 Joint Resolution Authorizing the Secretary of the Interior to Approve a Certain Lease Made in Polk County, Minnesota, which had been made by Mon-Si-Moh to Ray Jones, was invalidated in *Jones v. Meehan*, 175 U.S. 1 (1899). An additional case involved a statute passed by a Democratic Congress during a Whig presidency. The Court concluded that the Donation Land Claim Act of 1850 could not be construed to deny newly formed states control over submerged lands; Shively v. Bowlby, 152 U.S. 1 (1894). Neither law could be regarded as a national or party priority. A handful of other cases involved laws adopted by a divided Congress.
55 See Daniel J. Tichenor, *Dividing Lines* (Princeton, NJ: Princeton University Press, 2002), 124–128.

56 34 *Stat.* 898, 899–900 (1907).

57 Keller v. United States, 213 U.S. 138, 148 (1909).

58 Ibid., 149–151. See also Rogers M. Smith, *Civic Ideals* (Cambridge, MA: Harvard University Press, 1997), 443–445.

59 War Revenue Act of June 13, 1898, 30 *Stat.* 448, 459 (1898).

60 Fairbank v. United States, 181 U.S. 283, 289 (1901).

61 Ibid., 311–312.

62 See, e.g., Thames & Mersey Marine Ins. Co. v. United States, 237 U.S. 19 (1915); United States v. Hvoslef, 237 U.S. 1 (1915); Butts v. Merchants & Miners Transp. Assoc., 230 U.S. 126 (1913); Choat v. Trapp, 224 U.S. 665 (1912); Muskrat v. United States, 219 U.S. 346 (1911); United States v. Evans, 213 U.S. 297 (1909); Rassmussen v. United States, 197 U.S. 516 (1905); Jones v. Meehan, 175 U.S. 1 (1899); Wong Wing v. United States, 163 U.S. 228 (1896); Monongahela Navigation v. United States, 148 U.S. 312 (1893). A norm favoring public unanimity by the Court may have reduced the number of published dissents in these cases. See Robert Post, "The Supreme Court Opinion as Institutional Practice: Dissent, Legal Scholarship, and Decisionmaking in the Taft Court," *Minnesota Law Review* 85 (2001): 1267.

63 Before passing the Removal Act changing the state capital, the Oklahoma legislature facilitated judicial resolution of the constitutional issue by passing a statute giving the Oklahoma Supreme Court original jurisdiction to hear objections to the legality of the removal of the state capital from Guthrie. Coyle v. Smith, 221 U.S. 559, 563 (1911).

64 Muskrat v. United States, 219 U.S. 346 (1911).

65 Monongahela Navigation v. United States, 148 U.S. 312 (1893).

66 Jones v. Meehan, 175 U.S. 1 (1899). The retrospective application of a bankruptcy provision similarly ran afoul of vested property rights. Holt v. Henley, 232 U.S. 637 (1914).

67 Choat v. Trapp, 224 U.S. 665 (1912).

68 Wong Wing v. United States, 163 U.S. 228 (1896). See also Lem Moon Sing v. United States, 158 U.S. 538 (1894); Fong Yue Ting v. United States, 149 U.S. 698 (1893). The Court also clarified that Chinese born in the United States were natural-born citizens and thus could not be excluded as aliens by Congress. United States v. Wong Kim Ark, 169 U.S. 649 (1898).

69 Rasmussen v. United States, 197 U.S. 516, 518 (1904). The Court distinguished the situation in Alaska from the situation of holdings acquired by the Spanish-American War, including Hawaii (Hawaii v. Mankichi, 190 U.S. 197 [1903]), Puerto Rico (Downes v. Bidwell, 182 U.S. 244 [1901]), and the Philippines (Dorr v. United States, 195 U.S. 138 [1904]). The Court likewise objected to a congressional statute that gave limited immunity to grand jury witnesses because it failed to fully meet the requirements of the Fifth Amendment. Counselman v. Hitchcock, 142 U.S. 657 (1892).

70 Adair v. United States, 208 U.S. 161 (1908).

71 *Adair* included an extended discussion of whether Congress could reach unionization of railroads under the interstate commerce clause, with the majority concluding that it could not. The commerce clause analysis tended to soften the effect of the liberty-of-contract claim, especially as the Court's conclusions in this case seemed idiosyncratic. Thus, Charles Warren found the decision surprising and thought it would be overruled "with fuller enlightenment of the Court" on the factual relationship between labor disputes on railroads and the smooth flow of interstate commerce. See Charles Warren, *The Supreme Court in United States History* (Boston: Little, Brown, 1926), 2:175; Barry Cushman, *Rethinking the New Deal Court* (New York: Oxford University Press, 1998), 109–112.

72 Coppage v. Kansas, 236 U.S. 1 (1915); Hitchman Coal & Coke v. Mitchell, 245 U.S. 229 (1917).

73 George I. Lovell, *Legislative Deferrals* (New York: Cambridge University Press, 2003), 71.

74 Ibid., 78–80. Although Olney simply incorporated this provision from the commission's proposal, it appears that by then, he had concluded that although "an ordinary employer was and ought to be entirely free in his choice of his employees," a properly organized union could prevent the economic disruption encouraged by more radical labor leaders such as Eugene Debs. See Henry James, *Richard Olney and His Public Service* (Boston: Houghton Mifflin, 1923), 62–69.

75 Lovell, *Legislative Deferrals*, 83–89. Olney himself published a brief law-review article observing that a judicial reaction against growing national intervention in economic affairs was to be expected, but that the Court in *Adair* underestimated the fact that individual liberty was "necessarily liberty regulated by law" and, more importantly, that efforts by employers to dismiss unionized employees would only lead to violent strikes and economic disruption. See Richard Olney, "Discrimination against Union Labor—Legal?" *American Law Review* 42 (1908): 164–166.

76 See Richards v. Washington Terminal Co., 233 U.S. 546 (1914).

77 In re Heff, 197 U.S. 488 (1905).

78 United States v. Evans, 213 U.S. 297 (1909).

79 Callan v. Wilson, 127 U.S. 540, 549 (1898). The Court also restricted how Congress could allocate street improvement fees in the district. Martin v. District of Columbia, 205 U.S. 135 (1907).

80 United States v. Hvoslef, 237 U.S. 1 (1915); Thames & Mersey Marine Ins. Co. v. United States, 237 U.S. 19 (1915).

81 Kirby v. United States, 174 U.S. 47 (1899).

82 Boyd v. United States, 116 U.S. 616, 630 (1888).

83 Howard Gillman, "How Political Parties Can Use the Courts to Advance Their Agendas: Federal Courts in the United States, 1875–1891," *American Political Science Review* 96 (2002): 511.

84 Edward S. Corwin, "The Constitution as Instrument and as Symbol," *American Political Science Review* 30 (1936): 1072 (emphasis omitted).

85 Ibid., 1071, quoting Thomas M. Cooley, *Constitutional Limitations*, 2nd ed. (Boston: Little, Brown, 1871).

86 El Paso & Northeastern Railway Company v. Gutierrez, 215 U.S. 87 (1909).

87 Pedersen v. Delaware, Lackawanna & Western Railroad Co., 225 U.S. 146 (1913).

88 Mondou v. New York, New Haven & Hartford Railroad Co., 223 U.S. 1 (1912).

89 Addyston Pipe & Steel Co. v. United States, 178 U.S. 211 (1899); Northern Securities Company v. United States, 193 U.S. 197 (1904). See also Standard Oil Company of New Jersey v. United States, 221 U.S. 1 (1911).

90 California v. Central Pacific Railroad Co., 127 U.S. 1 (1888).

91 Atlantic Coast Line Railroad Co. v. Riverside Mills, 219 U.S. 186, 202–203 (1911).

92 Ibid., 186; Louisville & Nashville Railroad Co. v. Mottley, 219 U.S. 467 (1911); United States ex rel. Attorney General v. Delaware & Hudson Co., 213 U.S. 366 (1909); Baltimore & Ohio Railroad Co. v. Interstate Commerce Commission, 221 U.S. 612 (1911); Texas & Pacific Railway Co. v. Rigsby, 241 U.S. 33 (1916).

93 In re Rahrer, 140 U.S. 545, 561 (1891).

94 Ibid., 545; Champion v. Ames, 188 U.S. 321 (1903); Hoke and Economides v. United States, 227 U.S. 308 (1913); Seven Cases v. United States, 239 U.S. 510 (1916).

95 Brolan v. United States, 236 U.S. 216 (1915).

96 Ex parte Jackson, 96 U.S. 727, 736 (1877).

97 Ex parte Rapier, 143 U.S. 110, 135 (1892).

98 Ellis v. United States, 206 U.S. 246 (1907).

99 Camfield v. United States, 167 U.S. 518 (1897).

100 Arver v. United States, 245 U.S. 366 (1918); Schenck v. United States, 249 U.S. 47 (1919); Frohwerk v. United States, 249 U.S. 204 (1919); McKinley v. United States, 249 U.S. 397 (1919).

101 Reynolds v. United States, 98 U.S. 145 (1879); Murphy v. Ramsey, 114 U.S. 15 (1885); Late Corporation of the Church of Jesus Christ of Latter-Day Saints v. United States, 136 U.S. 1 (1890).

102 See, e.g., Nishimura Ekiu v. United States, 142 U.S. 651 (1892); Fong Yue Ting v. United States, 149 U.S. 698 (1893); Lees v. United States, 150 U.S. 476 (1893); Yamataya v. Fisher, 189 U.S. 86 (1903); United States v. Ju Toy, 198 U.S. 253 (1905); United States v. Sing Tuck, 194 U.S. 161 (1904).

103 United States v. Kagama, 118 U.S. 375 (1886); Cherokee Nation v. Hitchcock, 187 U.S. 294 (1902); Lone Wolf v. Hitchcock, 187 U.S. 553 (1903).

104 Interstate Commerce Commission v. Baird, 194 U.S. 25 (1904); Interstate Commerce Clause v. Brimson, 154 U.S. 447 (1894).

105 See Keith E. Whittington and Jason Iuliano, "The Myth of the Nondelegation Doctrine," *University of Pennsylvania Law Review* 165 (2017): 379.

106 Field v. Clark, 143 U.S. 649, 691, 693 (1892). See also In re Kollock, 166 U.S. 526 (1897).

CHAPTER 6. THE CONSTITUTIONAL REVOLUTION

1 William Howard Taft, "Three Needed Steps of Progress," *American Bar Association Journal* 8 (1922): 34.

2 See Justin Crowe, *Building the Judiciary* (Princeton, NJ: Princeton University Press, 2012), 203–212.

3 Quoted in Walter F. Murphy, "In His Own Image: Mr. Chief Justice Taft and Supreme Court Appointments," *Supreme Court Review 1961* (1961): 171.

4 Taft was perhaps less fortunate in the longevity of his judicial selections. Only one of his nominees (Willis Van Devanter) remained on the Court for an above-average period of time, and three of Taft's justices were replaced in the next presidential administration (by Woodrow Wilson).

5 "All Taft Wants Is a Square Deal," *New York Times*, March 20, 1912, 4.

6 Notably, more than twice as many Republican statutes as Democratic statutes were landmark statutes, although only a handful of cases involved notable provisions of such statutes.

7 Hammer v. Dagenhart, 247 U.S. 251 (1918).

8 US Department of Labor, Children's Bureau, *Children's Year Working Program* (Washington, DC: Government Printing Office, 1918), 8, 9.

9 US Department of Labor, Children's Bureau, *Minimum Standards for Child Welfare* (Washington, DC: Government Printing Office, 1920), 4.

10 40 *Stat.* 1138 (1919).

11 *Cong. Rec.*, 65th Cong., 3rd sess. (December 18, 1918), 609. See McCray v. United States, 195 U.S. 27 (1904).

12 *Cong. Rec.*, 65th Cong., 3rd sess. (December 18, 1918), 611.

13 Bailey v. Drexel Furniture Co., 259 U.S. 20, 38 (1922).

14 Ibid., 39.

15 John A. Ryan, *A Living Wage* (New York: Grosset & Dunlap, 1906), 313.

16 Ibid., 137.

17 Muller v. Oregon, 208 U.S. 412, 421, 420 (1908).

18 See Bunting v. Oregon, 243 U.S. 426 (1917).

19 *Minimum-Wage Board for the District of Columbia*, H. Rept. No. 571, 65th Cong., 2nd sess. (1918), 2, 3.

20 Ibid., 5; Stettler v. O'Hara, 243 U.S. 629 (1916).

21 Brad Snyder, *The House of Truth* (New York: Oxford University Press, 2017), 350. In particular, Brandeis's daughter worked at the minimum wage board, although his connections to the case ran deeper than that.

22 Adkins v. Children's Hospital of the District of Columbia, 261 U.S. 525, 563 (1923).

23 Ibid., 554, 558.

24 Ibid., 561.

25 38 *Stat.* 785 (1914).

26 Linder v. United States, 268 U.S. 5, 18, 17 (1925).

27 See Daniel J. Tichenor, *Dividing Lines* (Princeton, NJ: Princeton University Press, 2002).

28 Theodore Roosevelt, *Fear God and Take Your Own Part* (New York: George H. Doran, 1916), 362.

29 United States v. Ju Toy, 198 U.S. 253 (1905).

30 Ng Fung Ho v. White, 258 U.S. 276, 284–285 (1922).

31 Newberry v. United States, 256 U.S. 232 (1921). Congress was free to prohibit the solicitation of political contributions from federal employees for use in primary campaigns. United States v. Wurzbach, 280 U.S. 396 (1930).

32 Federal Trade Commission v. American Tobacco Company, 264 U.S. 298, 307 (1924).

33 Keller v. Potomac Electric Co., 261 U.S. 428, 444 (1923).

34 Myers v. United States, 272 U.S. 52 (1926).

35 Ibid., 179.

36 Evans v. Gore, 253 U.S. 245 (1920); Miles v. Graham, 268 U.S. 501 (1925); A. G. Spalding & Bros. v. Edwards, 262 U.S. 66 (1923).

37 Blodgett v. Holden, 275 U.S. 142 (1927); Untermyer v. Anderson, 276 U.S. 440 (1928); National Life Insurance Co. v. United States, 277 U.S. 508 (1928). This is not to say that such decisions were beyond public controversy. The *New Republic* fulminated on the Court's putting "the Constitution at the disposal of [tax] evaders." "The Supreme Court and a Balanced Budget," *New Republic*, April 27, 1932, 287.

38 Giovanni Federico, "Not Guilty? Agriculture in the 1920s and the Great Depression," *Journal of Economic History* 65 (2005): 939; James H. Shideler, *Farm Crisis 1919–1923* (Berkeley: University of California Press, 1957); Bill Winders, *The Politics of the Food Supply* (New Haven, CT: Yale University Press, 2009).

39 Hill v. Wallace, 259 U.S. 44 (1922). See also Trusler v. Crooks, 269 U.S. 475 (1926).

40 Stafford v. Wallace, 258 U.S. 495, 529 (1922).

41 Board of Trade of the City of Chicago v. Olsen, 262 U.S. 1, 32 (1923). The Court made a similar journey in considering a long-running dispute arising out of a 1914 coal miner strike in Arkansas. In 1922 the Court concluded that since mining was not interstate commerce, the provisions of the Sherman Anti-Trust Act could not be applied to the union's "local and sporadic" obstruction of mining operations. United Mine Workers of America v. Coronado Coal Co., 259 U.S. 344, 409 (1922). After another trial and appeal, however, the Court became convinced that the evidence demonstrated that the union in this case had intended "to stop the production of nonunion coal and prevent its shipment to markets of other states than Arkansas," making the union more like the colluding

livestock dealers and grain futures speculators in Chicago. Coronado Coal Co. v. United Mine Workers of America, 268 U.S. 295, 310 (1925).

42 Atchison, Topeka & Santa Fe Railway v. United States, 284 U.S. 248, 262 (1932). See also Ann Arbor Railroad Co. v. United States, 281 U.S. 658 (1930); Chicago, Rock Island & Pacific Railway Co. v. United States, 284 U.S. 80 (1931).

43 Russian Volunteer Fleet v. United States, 282 U.S. 471 (1931); Richmond Screw Anchor Co. v. United States, 275 U.S. 331 (1928).

44 Lipke v. Lederer, 259 U.S. 557 (1922).

45 Grau v. United States, 287 U.S. 124 (1932); Sgro v. United States, 287 U.S. 206 (1932).

46 Block v. Hirsch, 256 U.S. 136, 154–155 (1921).

47 Chasleton Corp. v. Sinclair, 264 U.S. 543, 547 (1924).

48 State of Rhode Island v. Palmer (National Prohibition Cases), 253 U.S. 350 (1920).

49 Leser v. Garnett, 258 U.S. 130 (1922).

50 Casey v. United States, 276 U.S. 413 (1928). See also United States v. Doremus, 249 U.S. 86 (1919); Nigro v. United States, 276 U.S. 332 (1928); Alston v. United States, 274 U.S. 289 (1927).

51 *Casey*, 420. Some of the justices continued to struggle with the "eagerness to use federal law as a police measure to combat the opium habit—a purpose for which Congress has no power to legislate." Ibid., 428.

52 Highland v. Russell Car & Snowplow Co., 279 U.S. 253, 261 (1929).

53 Liggett & Myers Tobacco Co. v. United States, 274 U.S. 215 (1927). Such seizures were treated as an exercise of eminent domain, entitling the owner (eventually) to just compensation.

54 Dayton-Goose Creek Railway Co. v. United States, 263 U.S. 456, 478 (1924).

55 Missouri v. Holland, 252 U.S. 416, 433 (1920).

56 Franklin D. Roosevelt, "Campaign Address at Detroit, Michigan, October 2, 1932," in *Public Papers and Addresses of Franklin D. Roosevelt*, ed. Samuel I. Rosenman (New York: Random House, 1938), 1:771.

57 Ibid., 1:774.

58 Franklin D. Roosevelt, "Campaign Address in Portland, Oregon, September 21, 1932," ibid., 1:732.

59 Ibid., 1:742.

60 Harold J. Laski, "A Statesman of the Law," *New Republic*, August 24, 1932, 50.

61 Thurman Arnold, "The New Deal Is Constitutional," *New Republic*, November 15, 1933, 8.

62 "The Supreme Court Eats Crow," *New Republic*, March 27, 1934, 147.

63 "The Supreme Court in Reverse," *New Republic*, November 21, 1934, 36.

64 "Advice of Counsel," *New Republic*, December 19, 1934, 154.

65 Henry M. Hart Jr., "The Supreme Court Carries On," *New Republic*, April 3, 1935, 221, 222.

66 "A Dred Scott Decision," *New Republic*, May 22, 1935, 34.

67 "Social Control vs. the Constitution," *New Republic*, June 12, 1935, 118.

68 Howard Lee McBain, "The Issue: Court or Congress?" *New York Times*, January 19, 1936, 22.

69 If Chief Justice Hughes is to be believed, Congress might have inadvertently contributed to FDR's bad luck in this regard. Just weeks before the 1932 election, Congress, in a cost-saving move, slashed the retirement salaries of federal employees. Hughes believed that two of the Four Horsemen had been about to retire but resolved to stay on, given their new financial situation. If they had retired, Roosevelt would have filled those seats, and the New Deal would have had a solid majority on the Court early in his presidency. They did retire immediately after Congress increased the benefits again in 1937. William F. Swindler, *Court and Constitution in the 20th Century* (Indianapolis: Bobbs-Merrill, 1970), 2:5; Artemus Ward, *Deciding to Leave* (Albany, NY: SUNY Press, 2003), 136–137.

70 Fred Rodell, "Justice vs Justices," *New Republic*, December 23, 1936, 251.

71 Quoted in William E. Leuchtenburg, *The Supreme Court Reborn* (New York: Oxford University Press, 1995), 88.

72 Interstate Commerce Commission v. Oregon-Washington Railroad & Navigation Co., 288 U.S. 14 (1933); Nathanson v. United States, 290 U.S. 41 (1933); United States v. Chambers, 291 U.S. 217 (1934).

73 Home Building & Loan Assn. v. Blaisdell, 290 U.S. 398 (1934); Nebbia v. New York, 291 U.S. (1934).

74 Booth v. United States, 291 U.S. 339 (1934); Lynch v. United States, 292 U.S. 571 (1934).

75 Franklin D. Roosevelt, "Fireside Chat, March 9, 1937," in *Public Papers of Roosevelt*, 6:124.

76 See Peter H. Irons, *The New Deal Lawyers* (Princeton, NJ: Princeton University Press, 1982), 65–74.

77 On the accommodating quality of the nondelegation doctrine, see Keith E. Whittington and Jason Iuliano, "The Myth of the Nondelegation Doctrine," *University of Pennsylvania Law Review* 165 (2017): 379.

78 Panama Refining Co. v. Ryan, 293 U.S. 388, 415 (1935).

79 Ibid, 435.

80 David Glick, "Conditional Strategic Retreat: The Court's Concession in the 1935 Gold Clause Cases," *Journal of Politics* 71 (2009): 806; Keith E. Whittington, *Political Foundations of Judicial Supremacy* (Princeton, NJ: Princeton University Press, 2007), 36–38.

81 Howard Gillman, Mark A. Graber, and Keith E. Whittington, *American Constitutionalism*, 2nd ed. (New York: Oxford University Press, 2017), 1:417.

82 Perry v. United States, 254 U.S. 330, 354 (1935).

83 Glick, "Conditional Strategic Retreat," 812.

84 Whittington, *Political Foundations*, 38.

85 See Leuchtenburg, *Supreme Court Reborn*, 29–33.

86 Railroad Retirement Board v. Alton, 295 U.S. 330, 350 (1935).

87 Ibid., 368.

88 Ibid., 380.

89 One case involved a minor issue of legal proceedings; Stewart v. Keyes, 295 U.S. (1935). The other involved a more broadly consequential bailout of bankrupt farmers; Louisville Joint Stock Land Bank v. Radford, 295 U.S. 555 (1935).

90 Irons, *New Deal Lawyers*, 310n18 (National Recovery Administration Litigation Division chief A. G. McKnight on "doom" and the "rule of self-preservation"), 94 (Frankfurter's advice to Solicitor General Stanley Reed).

91 The other two cases announced that day were Louisville Joint Stock Land Bank v. Radford, 295 U.S. 555 (1935) (striking down the Frazier-Lemke Farm Bankruptcy Act), and Humphrey's Executor v. United States, 295 U.S. 602 (1935) (upholding the Federal Trade Commission Act's limitation on the president's authority to remove independent commissioners). All three were without dissent.

92 A. L. A. Schechter Poultry Corp. v. United States, 295 U.S. 495, 553 (1935). On Roosevelt's reaction, see Eugene C. Gerhardt, *America's Advocate* (Indianapolis: Bobbs-Merrill, 1958), 99.

93 *Schechter*, 530, 537.

94 Swift & Co. v. United States, 196 U.S. 375 (1905); Brown v. Maryland, 25 U.S. 419 (1827).

95 Arthur M. Schlesinger Jr., *The Age of Roosevelt* (Boston: Houghton Mifflin, 1960), 3:280.

96 Quoted in Kevin J. McMahon, *Reconsidering Roosevelt on Race* (Chicago: University of Chicago Press, 2004), 237n118.

97 Schlesinger, *Age of Roosevelt*, 3:288–289.

98 Franklin D. Roosevelt, "Press Conference, May 31, 1935," in *Public Papers of Roosevelt*, 6:218, 209.

99 United States v. Constantine, 296 U.S. 287 (1935); Becker Steel Co. v. Cummings, 296 U.S. 74 (1935); Helvering v. Helmholz, 296 U.S. 93 (1935).

100 Hopkins Savings & Loan Association v. Cleary, 296 U.S. 315 (1935).

101 For background, see Irons, *New Deal Lawyers*, 181–185.

102 As the prospects for sustaining the program dimmed, the processors turned against it and rushed into the district courts seeking injunctions to block the government from collecting the tax, even as they continued to charge consumers the higher prices. Alger Hiss was tasked with ushering the case through the appeals process, but he found it difficult to "avoid the appearance of arbitrary, ruthless government interference in an area where the government had never attempted to intervene before." Irons, *New Deal Lawyers*, 187.

103 United States v. Butler, 297 U.S. 1, 61 (1936).

104 Ibid., 68.

105 Franklin D. Roosevelt, "Address on Agriculture, Fremont, Nebraska, September 28, 1935," in *Public Papers of Roosevelt*, 4:379.

106 *Butler*, 78. The Court did not think a subsequent amendment to the statute fixed the fundamental problem: the "exaction . . . lacks the quality of a true tax"; it was instead a "regulation of agricultural production, a matter not within the powers of Congress." Rickert Rice Mills v. Fontenot, 297 U.S. 111, 113 (1936).

107 *Butler*, 87, 88.

108 The Court delivered more bad news to Congress in two additional end-of-term decisions, but neither had the same salience as the New Deal case. See Baltimore & Ohio Railroad Co. v. United States, 298 U.S. 349 (1936) (Congress cannot authorize the Interstate Commerce Commission to impose confiscatory rates); Ashton v. Cameron County Water Improvement District No. 1, 298 U.S. 513 (1936) (Congress cannot readjust municipal debts).

109 Carter v. Carter Coal Co., 298 U.S. 238, 289–290, 291, 296 (1936).

110 Ibid., 325.

111 Arthur Sears Henning, "President Will Dodge Issue of Supreme Court," *Chicago Tribune*, May 20, 1936, 1.

112 "Court Curb Urged by Socialist Chief," *New York Times*, May 19, 1936, 17.

113 Emma Bugbee, "Constitution Change Urged by LaGuardia," *New York Times*, May 26, 1936, 1A.

114 "Socialists Demand Constitution Shift," *Boston Globe*, May 27, 1936, 7.

115 "Court Ends Its Knockout Season," *Business Week*, June 6, 1936, 36; "All Ways Are Closed," *Business Week*, May 23, 1936, 48.

116 "Guffey Ruling Arms G.O.P. for Campaign," *Christian Science Monitor*, May 19, 1936, 1.

117 "Republican Heads Attack New Deal," *New York Times*, May 21, 1936, 17.

118 Franklyn Waltman, "Politics and People: President Uses 'Strong-Arm' Method on Question Concerning Guffey Ruling Reactions," *Washington Post*, May 20, 1936, 2.

119 Arthur Sears Henning, "President Will Dodge Issue of Supreme Court," *Chicago Tribune*, May 20, 1936, 1.

120 Arthur Krock, "In Washington: Democrats See Guffey Ruling as Aid in the Campaign," *New York Times*, May 20, 1936, 20.

121 Arthur Krock, "In Washington: Supreme Court Knows It Is on Trial in Election," *New York Times*, May 27, 1936, 22.

122 Edwin D. Canham, "The Wide Horizon: 'Amending' the Supreme Court," *Christian Science Monitor*, May 25, 1936, 18.

123 "Time to Face Realities," *Washington Post*, May 21, 1936, 8.

124 "Future Policy of Mr. Roosevelt: After the Election Constitution and Supreme Court," *Manchester Guardian*, June 6, 1936, 11.

125 "The American Elections: Mr. Roosevelt Safe Return Expected Opponents' Blunders," *Manchester Guardian*, June 9, 1936, 9.

126 Franklin D. Roosevelt, "Message to Congress on the Reorganization of the Judicial Branch of the Government, February 5, 1937," in *Public Papers of Roosevelt*, 6:35.

127 "Joy and Anger in Congress over Message of President," *Boston Globe*, February 6, 1937, 4.

128 Franklin D. Roosevelt, "Fireside Chat, March 9, 1937," in *Public Papers of Roosevelt*, 6:122.

129 The battle in the Senate is detailed in Leuchtenburg, *Supreme Court Reborn*, 132–154. See also Barry Cushman, "Court-Packing and Compromise," *Constitutional Commentary* 29 (2013): 1.

130 Leuchtenburg, *Supreme Court Reborn*, 140.

131 Kentucky Whip & Collar Co. v. Illinois Central Railroad Co., 299 U.S. 334 (1937); Kuehner v. Irving Trust Co., 299 U.S. 445 (1937); United States v. Hudson, 299 U.S. 498 (1937); Hill v. United States, 300 U.S. 105 (1937).

132 West Coast Hotel v. Parrish, 300 U.S. 379, 391 (1937), overruling Adkins v. Children's Hospital, 261 U.S. 525 (1923).

133 Highland Farms Dairy, Inc. v. Agnew, 300 U.S. 608 (1937); Virginia Railway Co. v. System Federation No. 40, 300 U.S. 515 (1937); Wright v. Vinton Branch of Mountain Trust Bank of Roanoke, 300 U.S. 440 (1937); Sonzinsky v. United States, 300 U.S. 506 (1937).

134 Leuchtenburg, *Supreme Court Reborn*, 143.

135 National Labor Relations Board v. Jones & Laughlin Steel Corp., 301 U.S. 1, 31, 37 (1937).

136 Ibid., 78, 94.

137 Associated Press v. National Labor Relations Board, 301 U.S. 103 (1937). The majority found the free-press issue insignificant, given that the employee was fired because of his unionizing efforts, not the content of his editorial work.

138 Arthur Sears Henning, "Opens Way for Another NRA," *Chicago Tribune*, April 13, 1937, 1.

139 "The Federal Power Broadens," *Wall Street Journal*, April 13, 1937, 4; Arthur Krock, "In the Nation: Why in Court Fight Cry Is Still 'Forward,'" *New York Times*, April 16, 1937, 22.

140 Steward Machine Co. v. Davis, 301 U.S. 548 (1937). See also Helvering v. Davis, 301 U.S. 672 (1937); Cincinnati Soap Co. v. United States, 301 U.S. 308 (1937); Anniston Manufacturing Co. v. Davis, 301 U.S. 337 (1937).

141 "Both Sides in Court Battle Claim Gains as Result of Security Decisions," *Boston Globe*, May 25, 1937, 11.

142 Franklyn Waltman, "Politics and People: Supreme Court Approval of Security Program Was Foregone Conclusion Several Weeks Ago," *Washington Post*, May 25, 1937, 2.

143 Albert L. Warner, "President—Despite Wagner Act Decisions, Orders No Compromise in Plan to Remake the Court," *New York Herald Tribune*, April 14, 1937, 1.

144 Sidney Olson, "Bench Still Lacks Judges of Self-Restraint, Cummings Declares in Plea for Reform Plan," *Washington Post*, April 20, 1937, 1.

145 Rep. Maury Maverick, quoted in "Congressmen Tell Views," *Los Angeles Times*, May 25, 1937, 1.

146 "Under a Cloud," *Washington Post*, May 26, 1937, 8.

147 "Each Side Says Resignation Is Aid to Its Cause," *New York Herald Tribune*, May 19, 1937, 2.

148 William E. Leutchtenburg, *The FDR Years* (New York: Columbia University Press, 1995), 223. On the effects of congressional initiatives to curb judicial review generally, see Tom Clark, *The Limits of Judicial Independence* (New York: Cambridge University Press, 2010). For the view that the switch was driven by factors internal to the Court, see Barry Cushman, *Rethinking the New Deal Court* (New York: Oxford University Press, 1998). For an effort to reconcile the "external" and "internal" explanations for the switch, see Laura Kalman, "The Constitution, the Supreme Court, and the New Deal," *American Historical Review* 110 (2005): 1052.

149 National Labor Relations Board v. Fansteel Metallurgical Corp., 306 U.S. 240 (1939).

150 United States v. Carolene Products Co., 304 U.S. 144, 147, 149, 154, 155, 152 (1938).

151 Ibid., 152n4. The Court had the opportunity to reconsider the complaint of Carolene Products, but it remained unsympathetic. Justice Stanley Reed seemed to open the door a crack for a constitutional challenge by denying that Congress had suppressed filled milk "merely because it competes with another such article" of commerce. Congress needed at least a fig leaf of a public purpose, but the barrier to judicial examination of that fig leaf was high, for Congress was "beyond attack without a clear and convincing showing that there is no rational basis for the legislation; that it is an arbitrary fiat." Carolene Products Co. v. United States, 323 U.S. 18, 31–32 (1944).

152 National Labor Relations Board v. MacKay Radio & Telegraph Co., 304 U.S. 333, 347–348 (1938).

153 National Labor Relations Board v. Stowe Spinning Co., 336 U.S. 226 (1949).

154 Guaranty Trust Co. v. Henwoord, 307 U.S. 247, 258 (1939).

155 Sunshine Anthracite Coal Co. v. Adkins, 310 U.S. 381, 394 (1940). See also Federal Power Commission v. Hope Natural Gas Co., 320 U.S. 591 (1944); Bowles v. Willingham, 321 U.S. 503 (1944); Baltimore & Ohio Railroad Co. v. United States, 345 U.S. 146 (1953).

156 Berman v. Parker, 348 U.S. 26, 32 (1954).

157 Guessefeldt v. McGrath, 342 U.S. 308, 319 (1952).

158 Ibid., 329.

159 National Labor Relations Board v. Jones & Laughlin Steel Corp., 301 U.S. 1 (1937).

160 Cushman, *Rethinking the New Deal Court*, 209.

161 United States v. Darby, 312 U.S. 100, 123 (1941).

162 "Justice Robert Jackson, Memo on Wickard (1942)," in Gillman, Graber, and Whittington, *American Constitutionalism*, 1:453.

163 Wickard v. Filburn, 317 U.S. 111, 125 (1942).

164 See, e.g., Cleveland v. United States, 329 U.S. 14 (1946) (punishing polygamists who traveled across state lines); United States v. Sullivan, 332 U.S. 689 (1948) (punishing a pharmacist who purchased and then repackaged and relabeled drugs for local sale); United States v. Kahriger, 345 U.S. 22 (1953) (requiring gamblers to acquire a federal license and pay a punitive tax).

165 Lorain Journal Co. v. United States, 342 U.S. 143 (1951).

166 Woods v. Cloyd W. Miller Co., 333 U.S. 138, 144 (1948). The Court admitted that "the question whether the war power has been properly employed" was "open to judicial inquiry," but it emphasized that the congressional judgment on such matters was entitled to "respect." Ibid.

167 Sunshine Anthracite Coal Co. v. Adkins, 310 U.S. 381, 398, 400 (1940). See also United States v. Rock Royal Co-op, 307 U.S. 533 (1939); Opp Cotton Mills v. Administrator of Wage and Hour Division, 312 U.S. 126 (1941); Pittsburgh Plate Glass Co. v. National Labor Relations Board, 313 U.S. 146 (1941).

168 National Broadcasting Co. v. United States, 319 U.S. 190, 226 (1943).

169 Hirabayashi v. United States, 320 U.S. 81, 92 (1943). See also In re Yamashita, 327 U.S. 1 (1946).

170 Yakus v. United States, 321 U.S. 414, 424, 425 (1944). See also Board of Governors of Federal Reserve System v. Agnew, 329 U.S. 441 (1947).

171 United States ex rel. Knauff v. Shaughnessy, 338 U.S. 537, 542 (1950).

172 Carlson v. Landon, 342 U.S. 524, 543 (1952).

173 Tot v. United States, 319 U.S. 463 (1943).

174 See United States v. Cardiff, 344 U.S. 174 (1952) (finding that a provision of the Federal Food, Drug, and Cosmetic Act was not sufficiently clear in giving notice to those potentially subject to criminal sanction).

175 United States v. Lovett, 328 U.S. 303 (1946).

176 Schneiderman v. United States, 320 U.S. 118, 120 (1943).

177 Ibid., 132, 144, 158.

178 Bridges v. Wixon, 326 U.S. 135, 148, 154, 147, 156 (1945). See also Wong Yang Sung v. McGrath, 339 U.S. 33 (1950).

179 Ex parte Endo, 323 U.S. 283, 299, 302 (1944). See also Duncan v. Kahanamoku, 327 U.S. 304 (1946).

180 United States v. Congress of Industrial Organizations, 335 U.S. 106, 121 (1948).

181 Tenney v. Brandhove, 341 U.S. 367, 376 (1951).

182 Collins v. Hardyman, 341 U.S. 651, 662 (1951).

183 United States v. Five Gambling Devices, 346 U.S. 441, 449 (1953).

184 Korematsu v. United States, 323 U.S. 214, 216 (1944).

185 United States v. Miller, 307 U.S. 174 (1939).

186 National Labor Relations Board v. Virginia Electric & Power Co., 314 U.S. 469, 477 (1941). See also International Brotherhood of Electrical Workers, Local 501 v. National Labor Relations Board, 341 U.S. 694 (1951).

187 National Broadcast Co. v. United States, 319 U.S. 190 (1943).

188 Associated Press v. United States, 326 U.S. 1, 20 (1945). See also Lorain Journal v. United States, 342 U.S. 143 (1951).

189 United Public Workers of America v. Mitchell, 330 U.S. 75, 96 (1947). See also United States v. Harisss, 347 U.S. 612 (1954).

190 American Communications Association v. Douds, 339 U.S. 382 (1950); Dennis v. United States, 341 U.S. 494 (1951).

191 David A. Yalof, *Pursuit of Justices* (Chicago: University of Chicago Press, 1999), 42.

192 See Bernard Grofman and Timothy J. Brazill, "Identifying the Median Justice on the Supreme Court through Multidimensional Scaling: Analysis of 'Natural Courts' 1953–1991," *Public Choice* 112 (2002): 55; Lawrence Baum, "Membership Change and Collective Voting Change in the United States Supreme Court," *Journal of Politics* 54 (1992): 3; Jeffrey A. Segal, Lee Epstein, Charles M. Cameron, and Harold J. Spaeth, "Ideological Values and the Votes of U.S. Supreme Court Justices Revisited," *Journal of Politics* 57 (1995): 812.

193 John Kenneth Galbraith, *The Affluent Society* (New York: Houghton Mifflin, 1958); Lizabeth Cohen, *A Consumers' Republic* (New York: Vintage, 2003); Ronald Inglehart, *The Silent Revolution* (Princeton, NJ: Princeton University Press, 1977).

194 Pendleton Herring, "On the Study of Government," *American Political Science Review* 47 (1953): 972.

195 Richard Nixon, "Remarks of Vice President Nixon, Civic Auditorium, Albuquerque, NM, October 11, 1960," American Presidency Project, http://www.presidency.ucsb.edu/ws/?pid=25344; Harry Truman, "St. Patrick's Day Address in New York City, March 17, 1948," American Presidency Project, http://www.presidency.ucsb.edu/ws/?pid=13131.

196 Gunnar Myrdal, *An American Dilemma* (New York: Harper & Row, 1944), 1:3, 4.

197 William Howard Taft, "The Supreme Issue," *Saturday Evening Post*, October 19, 1912, 81.

198 Edward S. Corwin, *Constitutional Revolution, Ltd.* (Claremont, CA: Claremont Colleges, 1941), 111; Felix Frankfurter, *Mr. Justice Holmes and the Supreme Court* (Cambridge, MA: Harvard University Press, 1938), 51; Alpheus Thomas Mason, *The Supreme Court, Palladium of Freedom* (Ann Arbor: University of Michigan Press, 1962), 178.

199 Whittington, *Political Foundations*, 117–119.

200 Lucas A. Powe, *The Warren Court and American Politics* (Cambridge, MA: Harvard University Press, 2000), 214. See also Howard Gillman, "Party Politics and Constitutional Change: The Political Origins of Liberal Judicial Activism," in

The Supreme Court and American Political Development, ed. Ken Kersch and Ronald Kahn (Lawrence: University Press of Kansas, 2006); Michael J. Klarman, "Rethinking the Civil Rights and Civil Liberties Revolutions," *Virginia Law Review* 82 (1996): 1; Mark Tushnet, "The Warren Court as History: An Interpretation," in *The Warren Court in Historical and Political Perspective*, ed. Mark V. Tushnet (Charlottesville: University of Virginia Press, 1993).

201 This is not to say that the Warren Court spent no time building on the themes of the Roosevelt Court. The Court emphasized, for example, that Congress possessed a sweeping power of eminent domain to engage in redevelopment projects and could extend labor regulations to state and local government employees. Berman v. Parker, 348 U.S. 26 (1964); Maryland v. Wirtz, 392 U.S. 183 (1968).

202 Michael J. Klarman, "Rethinking the Civil Rights and Civil Liberties Revolution," *Virginia Law Review* 82 (1996): 1; Michael J. Klarman, "The Racial Origins of Modern Criminal Procedure," *Michigan Law Review* 99 (2000): 48.

203 Bolling v. Sharpe, 347 U.S. 497, 499 (1954).

204 Heart of Atlanta Hotel, Inc. v. United States, 379 U.S. 241 (1964); Katzenbach v. McClung, 379 U.S. 294 (1964).

205 *Katzenbach v. McClung*, 301, citing Wickard v. Filburn, 317 U.S. 111, 127 (1942).

206 South Carolina v. Katzenbach, 383 U.S. 301, 307 (1966). See also Katzenbach v. Morgan, 384 U.S. 641 (1966).

207 Jones v. Alfred H. Mayer Co., 392 U.S. 409, 413 (1968).

208 Kinsella v. Krueger, 351 U.S. 470 (1956). In the 1950s roughly half a million dependents accompanied servicemen abroad. By the time the Court first ruled on the issue, more than 2,000 civilians had been tried by court-martial under the UCMJ provision. Brittany Warren, "The Case of the Murdering Wives: *Reid v. Covert* and the Complicated Question of Civilians and Courts-Martial," *Military Law Review* 212 (2012): 141.

209 Memorandum from Justice Stanley Reed to Justice John Marshall Harlan II, quoted in Warren, "Case of the Murdering Wives," 170.

210 Reid v. Covert, 354 U.S. 1 (1956).

211 United States ex rel. Toth v. Quarles, 350 U.S. 11 (1955).

212 United States ex rel. Kinsella v. Singleton, 361 U.S. 234 (1960); Grisham v. Hagan, 361 U.S. 278 (1960); McElroy v. United States, 361 U.S. 281 (1960). In another case, the Court chose to construe a provision of the predecessor to the UCMJ narrowly to disallow court-martial jurisdiction over a soldier imprisoned in the United States and charged with killing another inmate in 1949. Although peace treaties with Germany and Japan had not yet been formally signed at the time of the murder, the Court refused to attribute to Congress an intention to maintain military authority in a context that was "destructive of civil rights." Lee v. Madigan, 358 U.S. 228 (1959). Eventually, the Court ruled that even active service personnel who commit crimes against civilians while on a pass should be tried in civilian courts. O'Callahan v. Parker, 395 U.S. 258 (1969).

213 Perez v. Brownell, 356 U.S. 44, 57 (1958). The Court had earlier upheld a 1907 statute that specified that American women take the citizenship of their husbands for the duration of the marriage. MacKenzie v. Hare, 239 U.S. 299 (1915).

214 Trop v. Dulles, 356 U.S. 86 (1958).

215 See Kennedy v. Mendoza-Martinez, 372 U.S. 144 (1963).

216 Schneider v. Rusk, 377 U.S. 163 (1964).

217 Afroyim v. Rusk, 387 U.S. 253, 268 (1967).

218 Jencks v. United States, 353 U.S. 657, 681 (1957).

219 On Red Monday, see Elizabeth J. Elias, "Red Monday and Its Aftermath: The Supreme Court's Flip-Flop over Communism in the Late 1950s," *Hofstra Law Review* 43 (2014): 207; Arthur J. Sabin, *In Calmer Times* (Philadelphia: University of Pennsylvania Press, 1999); Walter F. Murphy, *Congress and the Court* (Chicago: University of Chicago Press, 1962), 100–106; Powe, *Warren Court*, 93–102.

220 Yates v. United States, 354 U.S. 298, 329 (1957).

221 Watkins v. United States, 354 U.S. 178, 195, 187 (1957). See also Quinn v. United States, 349 U.S. 155 (1955); Emspak v. United States, 349 U.S. 190 (1955).

222 Murphy, *Congress and the Court*, 188.

223 Kent v. Dulles, 357 U.S. 116, 130 (1958).

224 See Sabin, *In Calmer Times*, 186–208; Murphy, *Congress and the Court*, 127–243; Powe, *Warren Court*, 99–102; C. Herman Pritchett, *Congress versus the Supreme Court* (Minneapolis: University of Minnesota Press, 1961).

225 Barenblatt v. United States, 360 U.S. 109, 128, 133 (1959).

226 Sabin, *In Calmer Times*, 206; Elias, "Red Monday," 222–224; Bernard Schwartz, "Felix Frankfurter and Earl Warren: A Study of a Deteriorating Relationship," *Supreme Court Review 1980* (1980): 119–120.

227 See Powe, *Warren Court*, 143–156; Fleming v. Nestor, 363 U.S. 603 (1960); Wilkinson v. United States, 365 U.S. 399 (1961); Braden v. United States, 365 U.S. 431 (1961); Communist Party of the United States v. Subversive Activities Control Board, 367 U.S. 1 (1961); Scales v. United States, 367 U.S. 203 (1961); Killian v. United States, 368 U.S. 231 (1961).

228 Whittington, *Political Foundations*, 118.

229 Aptheker v. Secretary of State, 378 U.S. 500 (1964).

230 Lamont v. Postmaster General of the United States, 381 U.S. 301 (1965).

231 United States v. Brown, 381 U.S. 437 (1965).

232 Albertson v. Subversive Activities Control Board, 382 U.S. 70 (1965).

233 United States v. Robel, 389 U.S. 258 (1967); Schneider v. Smith, 390 U.S. 17 (1968).

234 Marchetti v. United States, 390 U.S. 39 (1968); Grosso v. United States, 390 U.S. 62 (1968); Haynes v. United States, 390 U.S. 85 (1968); Leary v. United States, 395 U.S. 6 (1969); United States v. United States Coin & Currency, 401 U.S. 715 (1971).

235 International Association of Machinists v. Street, 367 U.S. 740, 790 (1961).

236 Ibid., 806.

237 Eastern Railroad Presidents Conference v. Noerr Motor Freight, Inc., 365 U.S. 127, 137 (1961).

CHAPTER 7. CONGRESS AND THE CONSERVATIVE COURT

1 Earl Warren, *The Memoirs of Earl Warren* (Garden City, NY: Doubleday, 1977), 303.

2 Lucas A. Powe Jr., *The Warren Court and American Politics* (Cambridge, MA: Harvard University Press, 2000), 424; William G. Ross, "Attacks on the Warren Court by State Officials: A Case Study of Why Court-Curbing Movements Fail," *Buffalo Law Review* 50 (2002): 483.

3 See Gregory A. Caldeira, "Neither the Purse nor the Sword: Dynamics of Public Confidence in the Supreme Court," *American Political Science Review* 80 (1986): 1209; Roger Handberg, "Public Opinion and the United States Supreme Court, 1935–1981," *International Social Science Review* 59 (1984): 3; Walter F. Murphy and Joseph Tanenhaus, "Public Opinion and the United States Supreme Court: A Preliminary Mapping of Some Prerequisites for Court Legitimation of Regime Changes," *Law and Society Review* 2 (1968): 357.

4 Tom S. Clark, *The Limits of Judicial Independence* (New York: Cambridge University Press, 2011).

5 John Massaro, "LBJ and the Fortas Nomination for Chief Justice," *Political Science Quarterly* 97 (1982–1983): 603; Keith E. Whittington, *Political Foundations of Judicial Supremacy* (Princeton, NJ: Princeton University Press, 2007), 221–222.

6 Nancy Scherer, *Scoring Points* (Stanford, CA: Stanford University Press, 2005); Mark Silverstein, *Judicious Choices*, 2nd ed. (New York: W. W. Norton, 2007); Jonathan P. Kastellec, Jeffrey R. Lax, Michael Malecki, and Justin H. Philips, "Polarizing the Electoral Connection: Partisan Representation in Supreme Court Confirmation Politics," *Journal of Politics* 77 (2015): 787; Neal Devins and Lawrence Baum, "Split Definitive: How Party Polarization Turned the Supreme Court into a Partisan Court," *Supreme Court Review 2016* (2016): 301.

7 Vincent Blasi, ed., *The Burger Court: The Counter-Revolution that Wasn't* (New Haven, CT: Yale University Press, 1983); Mark V. Tushnet, *A Court Divided* (New York: W. W. Norton, 2005); James F. Simon, *The Center Holds: The Power Struggle Inside the Rehnquist Court* (New York: Simon & Schuster, 1995). For more partisan assessments, see Cass R. Sunstein, *Radicals in Robes* (New York: Basic Books, 2005); Mark R. Levin, *Men in Black* (Washington, DC: Regnery Publishers, 2005).

8 Thomas M. Keck, *The Most Activist Supreme Court in History* (Chicago: University of Chicago Press, 2004).

9 For one overview, see Keith E. Whittington, "Taking What They Give Us:

Explaining the Court's Federalism Offensive," *Duke Law Journal* 51 (2001): 477; Keith E. Whittington, "The *Casey* Five versus the Federalism Five: Supreme Legislator or Prudent Umpire?" in *That Eminent Tribunal*, ed. Christopher Wolfe (Princeton, NJ: Princeton University Press, 2004).

10 Donald H. Zeigler, "The New Activist Court," *American University Law Review* 45 (1996): 1367.

11 Planned Parenthood v. Casey, 505 U.S. 833 (1992); "Symposium: The End of Democracy? The Judicial Usurpation of Politics," *First Things* 67 (November 1996): 18.

12 Christopher Wolfe, introduction to *That Eminent Tribunal*, 1–2.

13 See Keith E. Whittington, "The Least Activist Supreme Court in History? The Roberts Court and the Exercise of Judicial Review," *Notre Dame Law Review* 89 (2014): 2221.

14 Keenan D. Kmiec, "The Origin and Current Meanings of Judicial Activism," *California Law Review* 92 (2004): 1441; Craig Green, "An Intellectual History of Judicial Activism," *Emory Law Journal* 58 (2009): 1195.

15 John F. Dillon, "Address of the President," *Annual Report of the American Bar Association* 15 (1892): 211; Ronald Dworkin, *Freedom's Law* (New York: Oxford University Press, 1996), 364.

16 See Whittington, "Least Activist Supreme Court," 2221–2223.

17 Keck, *Most Activist Supreme Court.*

18 On Rehnquist in particular, see Keith E. Whittington, "William H. Rehnquist: Nixon's Strict Constructionist, Reagan's Chief Justice," in *Rehnquist Justice*, ed. Earl Maltz (Lawrence: University Press of Kansas, 2003).

19 Mark Tushnet, "Foreword: The New Constitutional Order and the Chastening of Constitutional Aspirations," *Harvard Law Review* 113 (1999): 68–69.

20 See Whittington, "Least Activist Supreme Court," 2241–2248.

21 The dissents in cases upholding legislation are not fully representative of the pent-up pressure for activism, however. Some of those dissents are based primarily on nonconstitutional grounds. That is, the dissenting justices might agree that Congress's action is constitutionally valid but would rule on some other grounds for the party raising constitutional claims. Moreover, those dissents reflect disagreement only on the cases that are actually on the docket. It is possible that a different lineup of justices would have accepted a different set of cases to review, so it is possible that some additional, unobserved pressure for judicial activism would have been apparent in the votes if the Court's docket were different. It is notable that in the Roberts Court, there has been a sharp decrease in the number of cases in which the Court affirms the decision of a lower court upholding a federal statutory provision against constitutional challenge. It is possible that the conservative justices have declined to take such cases if they believe they lack the votes to reverse those decisions and invalidate the laws. If Kennedy's replacement provides a critical fifth conservative vote, more of those

cases might find their way onto the Court's docket for argument and decision. See also Benjamin Johnson and Keith E. Whittington, "Why Does the Supreme Court Uphold So Many Laws?" *University of Illinois Law Review* 2018 (2018): 101.

22 Of course, the composition of the Court is not the only moving part in this equation. Legislators might change their behavior as well. If the conservatives on the contemporary Court have been relatively deferential because state and national legislatures have been relatively conservative, then a leftward turn at the polls could wake up the slumbering conservative judiciary. There has been a great deal of Democratic legislating in Congress and the state legislatures since the 1980s, yet the conservative justices have been tapping the brakes on statutory invalidations. Perhaps the continued polarization of the two major parties will draw Democratic legislatures further and further away from the constitutional comfort zone of a consistently conservative Roberts Court.

23 Mark Tushnet, "The Burger Court in Historical Perspective: The Triumph of Country Club Republicanism," in *The Burger Court*, ed. Bernard Schwartz (New York: Oxford University Press, 1998).

24 See Keith E. Whittington, "The Burger Court, 1969–1986: Once More in Transition," in *The United States Supreme Court*, ed. Christopher Tomlins (New York: Oxford University Press, 2005); Whittington, *Political Foundations*, 222–226.

25 Richard M. Nixon, "Conversation with Newsmen on the Nomination of the Chief Justice of the United States, May 22, 1969," in *Public Papers of the Presidents: Richard Nixon, 1969* (Washington, DC: Government Printing Office, 1969), 389.

26 Shapiro v. Thompson, 394 U.S. 618 (1969).

27 Graham v. Richardson, 403 U.S. 365 (1971).

28 Davis v. Richardson, 342 F. Supp. 588, 593 (D. Conn. 1972); Richardson v. Davis, 409 U.S. 1069 (1972). See also Jimenez v. Weinberger, 417 U.S. 628 (1974).

29 U.S. Department of Agriculture v. Murry, 413 U.S. 508 (1973); U.S. Department of Agriculture v. Moreno, 413 U.S. 528 (1973). See also United States v. Clark, 445 U.S. 23 (1980).

30 *Moreno*, 534.

31 Rostker v. Goldberg, 453 U.S. 57, 65 (1981).

32 Schlesinger v. Ballard, 419 U.S. 498 (1975).

33 Frontiero v. Richardson, 411 U.S. 677 (1973); Weinberger v. Wiesenfeld, 420 U.S. 636 (1975); Califano v. Goldfarb, 430 U.S. 199 (1977); Califano v. Silbowitz, 430 U.S. 924 (1977); Califano v. Westcott, 443 U.S. 76 (1979).

34 See, e.g., Selective Service System v. Minnesota Public Interest Research Group, 468 U.S. 841 (1984) (upholding the withholding of financial aid from male students who did not register for the draft); Schweiker v. Wilson, 450 U.S. 221 (1981) (upholding the consideration of institutional Medicaid payments in calculating Social Security benefits); United States Railroad Retirement Board v. Fritz, 449 U.S. 166 (1980) (upholding the "grandfather" provision of the 1974 Railroad

Retirement Act); Fullilove v. Klutznick, 448 U.S. 448 (1980) (upholding contracting set-asides for minority-owned businesses); Harris v. McRae, 448 U.S. 297 (1980) (upholding the Hyde Amendment, limiting the use of federal funds for abortion services); Califano v. Boles, 443 U.S. 282 (1979) (upholding the restriction of "mother's insurance benefits" to mothers who were at one time married to the wage earner); Fiallo v. Bell, 430 U.S. 787 (1977) (upholding immigration restrictions on alien natural fathers of illegitimate citizen children); United States v. Antelope, 430 U.S. 641 (1977) (upholding a federal enclave murder statute on tribal lands); Mathews v. Castro, 429 U.S. 181 (1976) (upholding the restriction on divorced wives receiving Social Security benefits).

35 Chief of the Capitol Police v. Jeannette Rankin Brigade, 409 U.S. 972 (1972), affirming without opinion Jeannette Rankin Brigade v. Chief of Capitol Police, 342 F. Supp. 575 (D.D.C. 1972); Flower v. United States, 407 U.S. 197 (1972).

36 Blount v. Rizzi, 400 U.S. 410 (1971); Bolger v. Youngs Drug Products Corp., 463 U.S. 60 (1983).

37 *Bolger*, 69. See also Lowe v. Securities and Exchange Commission, 472 U.S. 181 (1985).

38 Federal Communications Commission v. League of Women Voters of California, 468 U.S. 364 (1984).

39 Ibid., 387.

40 Buckley v. Valeo, 424 U.S. 1 (1976).

41 Richard Nixon, "Veto of a Political Broadcasting Bill, October 12, 1970," in *Public Papers of the Presidents: Nixon*, 837.

42 *Buckley*, 14.

43 Ibid., 16; United States v. O'Brien, 391 U.S. 367 (1968).

44 *Buckley*, 19–20.

45 Ibid., 242, 261, 263, 265.

46 Lucas A. Powe Jr., "Mass Speech and the Newer First Amendment," *1982 Supreme Court Review* (1982): 275–279.

47 Ibid., 252.

48 Federal Election Commission v. National Conservative Political Action Committee, 470 U.S. 480, 521 (1985).

49 Federal Election Commission v. Massachusetts Citizens for Life, Inc., 479 U.S. 238 (1986).

50 *Buckley*, 120–142.

51 Gerald Ford, "Statement on Signing the Federal Election Campaign Act Amendments of 1976," in *Public Papers of the Presidents*, 2:457.

52 Elliot Levitas, *Congressional Review of Agency Rulemaking: Hearings before the Subcommittee on Rules of the House*, 97th Cong., 1st sess. (1981), 245.

53 William P. Rogers, "Authority of Congressional Committees to Disapprove Actions of the Executive Branch," *Opinions of the Attorney General* 41 (1957): 300.

54 Immigration and Naturalization Service v. Chadha, 462 U.S. 919, 951 (1983). See

also Process Gas Consumers Group v. Consumer Energy Council, 463 U.S. 1216 (1983); U.S. Senate v. Federal Trade Commission, 463 U.S. 1216 (1983).

55 See Barbara Hinkson Craig, *Chadha* (Berkeley: University of California Press, 1988); Louis Fisher, "The Legislative Veto: Invalidated, It Survives," *Law and Contemporary Problems* 56 (1993): 273; Jessica Korn, *The Power of Separation* (Princeton, NJ: Princeton University Press, 1996); David E. Pozen, "Self-Help and the Separation of Powers," *Yale Law Journal* 124 (2014): 1.

56 Bowsher v. Synar, 478 U.S. 714, 722 (1986).

57 Oregon v. Mitchell, 400 U.S. 112 (1970).

58 *Fair Labor Standards Amendments of 1973: Hearings before the Senate Subcommittee on Labor*, 93rd Cong., 1st sess. (June 7, 1973), 243.

59 Ibid., 499.

60 *Fair Labor Standards Amendments of 1973*, Sen. Report No. 93-300, 93rd Cong., 1st sess. (July 6, 1973), 26.

61 Maryland v. Wirtz, 392 U.S. 183, 197, 198–199 (1968).

62 National League of Cities v. Brennan, 406 F. Supp. 826, 827, 828 (D.D.C. 1974).

63 National League of Cities v. Usery, 426 U.S. 833, 842, 852 (1976).

64 Ibid., 856.

65 Garcia v. San Antonio Metropolitan Transit Authority, 469 U.S. 528, 572 (1985).

66 Ibid., 580.

67 U.S. Civil Service Commission v. National Association of Letter Carriers AFL-CIO, 413 U.S. 548 (1973).

68 United States v. 12 200-Foot Reels of Super 8mm Film, 413 U.S. 123, 130 (1973).

69 Marshall v. United States, 414 U.S. 417 (1974); Parker v. Levy, 417 U.S. 733 (1974); Federal Communications Commission v. Pacifica Foundation, 438 U.S. 726 (1978); National Labor Relations Board v. Retail Store Employees Union Local 1001, 447 U.S. 607 (1980).

70 Federal Energy Regulatory Commission v. Mississippi, 456 U.S. 742, 775 (1982); Equal Employment Opportunity Commission v. Wyoming, 460 U.S. 226, 251 (1983).

71 William H. Rehnquist, "The Notion of a Living Constitution," *Texas Law Review* 54 (1976): 706, 695.

72 Whittington, "Rehnquist," 12.

73 William Bradford Reynolds quoted in David G. Savage, *Turning Right* (New York: John Riley & Sons, 1992), 9.

74 White House report quoted in David A. Yalof, *Pursuit of Justices* (Chicago: University of Chicago Press, 1999), 153.

75 *Nomination of William H. Rehnquist to Be Chief Justice of the United States: Report from the Senate Committee on the Judiciary*, 99th Cong., 2d sess. (1986), 82, 30.

76 See Steven M. Teles, *The Rise of the Conservative Legal Movement* (Princeton, NJ: Princeton University Press, 2010); Amanda Hollis-Brusky, *Ideas with Consequences* (New York: Oxford University Press, 2015).

77 Philip Shenon, "Meese and His New Vision of the Constitution," *New York Times*, October 17, 1985, B10.

78 Lane Kirkland quoted in Earl M. Maltz, "Anthony Kennedy and the Jurisprudence of Respectable Conservatism," in Maltz, *Rehnquist Justice*, 141.

79 It is no surprise that one conservative columnist in the 1990s instructed the next conservative president, "Be damned sure you are putting a Scalia clone on the bench and not another Kennedy." Don Feder quoted in Martin Garbus, *Courting Disaster* (New York: Henry Holt, 2002), 198. Even more emphatically, "No More Souters" became a rallying cry of the religious Right. Bush's gamble on a stealth nominee turned into a "fiasco." Frederick S. Lane, *The Court and the Cross* (Boston: Beacon Press, 2008), 94.

80 The story is much the same when it comes to the invalidation of state laws. See Whittington, "Least Activist Supreme Court," 2243–2251.

81 Tushnet, *Court Divided*, 35.

82 Hollis-Brusky, *Ideas with Consequences*, 56 (emphasis omitted).

83 Scalia once cast himself as a "faint-hearted originalist," and it is telling that Thomas is frequently praised by conservatives for being "unafraid." Antonin Scalia, "Originalism: The Lesser Evil," *University of Cincinnati Law Review* 57 (1989): 864; Douglas Kmiec quoted in Hollis-Brusky, *Ideas with Consequences*, 56. On Thomas's "fearless originalism," see also Randy E. Barnett, "Scalia's Infidelity: A Critique of Faint-Hearted Originalism," *University of Cincinnati Law Review* 75 (2006): 7.

84 Thomas has been in the majority in 73 percent of cases invalidating a federal statutory provision, to Ginsburg's 60 percent. Ginsburg was much more likely, however, to be in the majority in cases striking down a state or local law. Whittington, "Least Activist Supreme Court," 2243–2251.

85 See Keith E. Whittington, "Dismantling the Modern State? The Changing Structural Foundations of Federalism," *Hastings Constitutional Law Quarterly* 25 (1998): 483.

86 Cornell W. Clayton and J. Mitchell Pickerill, "What Happened on the Way to Revolution? Precursors to the Supreme Court's Federalism Revolution," *Publius* 34 (2004): 85; J. Mitchell Pickerill and Cornell W. Clayton, "The Rehnquist Court and the Political Dynamics of Federalism," *Perspectives on Politics* 2 (2004): 233.

87 Pickerill and Clayton, "Rehnquist Court," 238.

88 Herbert Wechsler, "The Political Safeguards of Federalism: The Role of the States in the Composition and Selection of the National Government," *Columbia Law Review* 54 (1954): 543; John C. Yoo, "The Judicial Safeguards of Federalism," *Southern California Law Review* 70 (1996): 1311.

89 See, generally, Hollis-Brusky, *Ideas with Consequences*, 93–146.

90 Eric N. Waltenburg and Bill Swinford, *Litigating Federalism* (Westport, CT: Greenwood Publishing, 1999); Paul Chen, "The Institutional Sources of State

Success in Federalism Litigation before the Supreme Court," *Law and Policy* 25 (2003): 455; Paul Nolette, *Federalism on Trial* (Lawrence: University Press of Kansas, 2015).

91 Yalof, *Pursuit of Justices*, 143–144.

92 Whittington, "Taking What They Give Us," 505–507.

93 "Justice Robert Jackson, Memo on Wickard (1942)," in Howard Gillman, Mark A. Graber, and Keith E. Whittington, *American Constitutionalism*, 2nd ed. (New York: Oxford University Press, 2017), 1:453.

94 On congressional deliberation after the New Deal, see J. Mitchell Pickerill, *Constitutional Deliberation in Congress* (Durham, NC: Duke University Press, 2004); Donald Morgan, *Congress and the Constitution* (Cambridge, MA: Harvard University Press, 1966).

95 United States v. Lopez, 514 U.S. 549, 557, 561 (1995).

96 United States v. Morrison, 529 U.S. 598, 616 (2000); *Lopez*, 567.

97 It is of note that Justice Ginsburg wrote for a unanimous Court, holding that a statute that made it a federal crime to burn any "property used in interstate or foreign commerce or in any activity affecting interstate or foreign commerce" could not be read to apply to a private home, in part out of concern about running afoul of the strictures laid down in *Lopez* against federalizing "a paradigmatic common-law state crime." Jones v. United States, 529 U.S. 848, 857–858 (2000).

98 Gonzales v. Raich, 545 U.S. 1 (2005).

99 Gregory v. Ashcroft, 501 U.S. 452, 457 (1991).

100 New York v. United States, 505 U.S. 144, 175 (1992).

101 Printz v. United States, 521 U.S. 898 (1997).

102 Chisholm v. Georgia, 2 U.S. 419 (1793).

103 Hans v. Louisiana, 134 U.S. 1 (1890).

104 Hoffman v. Connecticut Department of Income Maintenance, 492 U.S. 96 (1989); Seminole Tribe v. Florida, 517 U.S. 44 (1996); Alden v. Maine, 527 U.S. 706 (1999); Florida Prepaid Postsecondary Educational Expense Board v. College Savings Bank, 527 U.S. 627 (1999); College Savings Bank v. Florida Prepaid Postsecondary Educational Expense Board, 527 U.S. 666 (1999); Kimel v. Florida Board of Regents, 528 U.S. 62 (2000); Board of Trustees of the University of Alabama v. Garrett, 531 U.S. 356 (2001); Federal Maritime Commission v. South Carolina State Ports Authority, 535 U.S. 743 (2002).

105 Civil Rights Cases, 109 U.S. 3 (1883).

106 Employment Division Department of Human Resources of Oregon v. Smith, 494 U.S. 872 (1990).

107 City of Boerne v. Flores, 521 U.S. 507, 529 (1997).

108 Cutter v. Wilkinson, 544 U.S. 709 (2005); Nevada Department of Human Resources v. Hibbs, 538 U.S. 721 (2003); Tennessee v. Lane, 541 U.S. 509 (2004); United States v. Georgia, 546 U.S. 151 (2006).

109 The Court used due process concerns to limit federal statutes in a number of cases, but the issues were rarely of substantial public interest. See, e.g., Brock v. Roadway Express Inc., 481 U.S. 252 (1987); Granfinanciera S.A. v. Nordberg, 492 U.S. 33 (1989); Chauffeurs, Teamsters & Helpers Local 391 v. Terry, 494 U.S. 558 (1990); Feltner v. Columbia Pictures, 523 U.S. 340 (1998); Immigration and Naturalization Service v. St. Cyr, 533 U.S. 289 (2001); Zadvydas v. Immigration and Naturalization Service, 533 U.S. 678 (2001).

110 Texas v. Johnson, 491 U.S. 397 (1989). See Whittington, *Political Foundations*, 139–143; Robert Justin Goldstein, *Burning the Flag* (Kent, OH: Kent State University Press, 1996).

111 United States v. Eichman, 496 U.S. 310 (1990).

112 Sable Communications of California Inc. v. Federal Communications Commission, 492 U.S. 115 (1989).

113 Reno v. American Civil Liberties Union, 521 U.S. 844 (1997).

114 Denver Area Educational Telecommunications Consortium Inc. v. Federal Communications Commission, 518 U.S. 727 (1996).

115 United States v. Playboy Entertainment Group Inc., 529 U.S. 803 (2000).

116 Ashcroft v. Free Speech Coalition, 535 U.S. 234 (2002).

117 Legal Services Corp. v. Velazquez, 531 U.S. 533, 548 (2001).

118 Rubin v. Coors Brewing Co., 514 U.S. 476 (1995); Edward J. DeBartolo Corp. v. Florida Gulf Coast Building and Construction Trades Council, 486 U.S. 568 (1988). See also Boos v. Barry, 485 U.S. 312 (1988); Greater New Orleans Broadcasting Association Inc. v. United States, 527 U.S. 173 (1999). The justices were divided in less familiar ways in some commercial speech cases. United States v. United Foods Inc., 533 U.S. 405 (2001); Thompson v. Western States Medical Center, 535 U.S. 357 (2002).

119 Gomez v. United States, 490 U.S. 858 (1989); Public Citizen v. U.S. Department of Justice, 491 U.S. 440 (1989).

120 Clinton v. City of New York, 524 U.S. 417 (1998).

121 Morrison v. Olson, 487 U.S. 654 (1988).

122 Mistretta v. United States, 488 U.S. 361, 413, 412 (1989).

123 Pickerill, *Constitutional Deliberation*, 31.

124 I refer to the Roberts Court as it behaved through 2018. The Roberts Court also continued the Rehnquist Court's trajectory of deciding only a few cases striking down state laws. See Whittington, "Least Activist Supreme Court," 2241–2242.

125 Johnson and Whittington, "Why Does the Supreme Court Uphold," 101.

126 Apprendi v. New Jersey, 530 U.S. 466 (2000); Blakely v. Washington, 542 U.S. 296 (2004).

127 United States v. Booker, 543 U.S. 220 (2005).

128 Pepper v. United States, 562 U.S. 476 (2011).

129 Peugh v. United States, 133 S. Ct. 2072 (2013).

130 Johnson v. United States, 135 S. Ct. 2551 (2015); Welch v. United States, 136 S.

Ct. 1257 (2016). See also Shepard v. United States, 544 U.S. 13 (2005); Sessions v. Dimaya, 138 S. Ct. 1204 (2018).

131 *Punishing Depictions of Animal Cruelty: Report of the Committee on the Judiciary on H.R. 1887*, H. Rpt. 106-397, 106th Cong., 1st sess. (October 19, 1999), 5.

132 United States v. Stevens, 559 U.S. 460, 472 (2010).

133 Matal v. Tam, 137 S. Ct. 1744 (2017).

134 Agency for International Development v. Alliance for Open Society International, 133 S. Ct. 2321 (2013); Sessions v. Morales-Santana, 137 S. Ct. 1678 (2017).

135 United States v. Alvarez, 132 S. Ct. 2537, 2557 (2012).

136 *Stolen Valor Act of 2013: Report from the Committee on the Judiciary*, H. Rpt. 113-84, 113th Cong., 1st sess. (May 20, 2013), 4.

137 Hamdi v. Rumsfeld, 542 U.S. 507 (2004).

138 In *Rasul v. Bush*, 542 U.S. 466 (2004), the same six-justice majority held that even noncitizens held in Guantanamo Bay were entitled to a judicial hearing. In *Hamdan v. Rumsfeld*, 548 U.S. 557 (2006), a narrower majority held that Congress had not expressly authorized the use of military tribunals to provide hearings for the detainees; thus they should have access to civilian courts.

139 Boumediene v. Bush, 553 U.S. 723 (2008).

140 Esmail v. Obama, 639 F.3d 1075, 1078 (2011).

141 Bill Clinton, "Statement on Same-Gender Marriage, September 20, 1996," in *Public Papers of the Presidents*, 2:1635.

142 Bill Clinton, "The President's News Conference with Chancellor Helmut Kohl of Germany in Milwaukee, May 23, 1996," in ibid., 1:809.

143 P.L. 104-199, 110 *Stat.* 2419 (1996).

144 Lawrence v. Texas, 539 U.S. 558, 578, 585, 590 (2003).

145 Goodridge v. Department of Public Health, 440 Mass. 309 (2003).

146 "Statement of the Attorney General on the Litigation Involving the Defense of Marriage Act, February 23, 2011," https://www.justice.gov/opa/pr/statement-attorney-general-litigation-involving-defense-marriage-act.

147 United States v. Windsor, 133 S. Ct. 2675, 2691, 2692, 2693 (2013).

148 Ibid., 2696, 2709.

149 Barack Obama, "Statement on the United States Supreme Court Ruling on the Defense of Marriage Act, June 26, 2013," in *Daily Compilation of Presidential Documents*.

150 Obergefell v. Hodges, 135 S. Ct. 2584 (2015).

151 Free Enterprise Fund v. Public Company Accounting Oversight Board, 561 U.S. 477 (2010). By contrast, the liberals won a symbolic and somewhat surprising victory in striking down a conservative-backed measure to name Jerusalem as part of Israel on the passports of Americans born in that city. Although the conservative justices generally favored presidential power in foreign affairs, in this, they emphasized the division of authority between the legislative and executive branches in regulating foreign affairs. Zivotofsky v. Kerry, 135 S. Ct. 2076 (2015).

152 George F. Will, "Unlawful Health Reform?" *Washington Post*, November 19, 2009, A27.

153 Ian Millhiser, "Pelosi Dismisses Tenther Reporter: 'Are You Serious?'" *Think Progress*, October 23, 2009, https://thinkprogress.org/pelosi-dismisses-tenther -reporter-are-you-serious-9cfb4272d15/.

154 United States v. Lopez, 514 U.S. 549, 560 (1995).

155 James B. Stewart, "How Broccoli Landed on the Supreme Court Menu," *New York Times*, June 14, 2012, A1.

156 National Federation of Independent Business v. Sebelius, 567 U.S. 519 (2012).

157 South Dakota v. Dole, 483 U.S. 203 (1987).

158 Most notably, Ohio chose to opt in to Medicaid expansion, and as a result, Republican governor John Kasich became an active opponent of Obamacare repeal. Dan Zak, "Spurning the Party Line," *Washington Post*, January 5, 2016. See also Keith E. Whittington, "'Our Own Limited Role in Policing Those Boundaries': Taking Small Steps on Health Care," *Journal of Health Politics, Policy and Law* 38 (2013): 273.

159 Roberts took even more heat for a later decision salvaging a key provision of Obamacare. King v. Burwell, 135 S. Ct. 2480 (2015); John Gerstein, "Conservatives Steamed at Chief Justice Roberts' Betrayal," *Politico*, June 25, 2015; Adam Liptak, "Angering Conservatives and Liberals, Chief Justice Roberts Defends Steady Restraint," *New York Times*, June 27, 2015, A13; Shikla Dalmia, "How John Roberts' Obamacare Apostasy Helped Conservatives Crush Obama's Environmental Overreach," *The Week*, June 29, 2015.

160 P.L. 89-110, 79 *Stat.* 437 (1965).

161 South Carolina v. Katzenbach, 383 U.S. 301, 328–329 (1966).

162 P.L. 109-246, 120 *Stat.* 577 (2006).

163 Northwest Austin Municipal Utility District Number One v. Holder, 557 U.S. 193 (2009).

164 Shelby County, Alabama v. Holder, 133 S. Ct. 2612, 2618 (2013).

165 Ibid., 2618–2619.

166 Ibid., 2621, 2624.

167 Ibid., 2632.

168 Ibid.

169 Barack Obama, "Statement on the United States Supreme Court Ruling on the Voting Rights Act, June 25, 2013," in *Daily Compilation of Presidential Documents*.

170 Buckley v. Valeo, 424 U.S. 1 (1976).

171 Federal Election Commission v. National Conservative Political Action Committee, 470 U.S. 480 (1980); Federal Election Commission v. Massachusetts Citizens for Life Inc., 479 U.S. 238 (1986); Colorado Republican Federal Campaign Committee v. Federal Election Commission, 518 U.S. 604 (1996).

172 David M. Primo, "Public Opinion and Campaign Finance: Reformers versus

Reality," *Independent Review* 7 (2002): 1086; William G. Mayer, "Public Attitudes on Campaign Finance," in *A User's Guide to Campaign Finance Reform,* ed. Gerald C. Lubenow (Lanham, MD: Rowman & Littlefield, 2001).

173 George W. Bush, "Letter to the Senate Majority and Minority Leaders on Campaign Finance Reform Legislation, March 15, 2001," in *Public Papers of the Presidents,* 1:244.

174 *Cong. Rec.,* 107th Cong., 1st sess. (March 29, 2001), 5038.

175 George W. Bush, "Statement in Signing the Bipartisan Campaign Reform Act of 2002, March 27, 2002," in *Public Papers of the Presidents,* 1:503.

176 McConnell v. Federal Election Commission, 540 U.S. 93 (2003).

177 Ibid., 264.

178 Ibid., 286.

179 Ibid., 248.

180 Federal Election Commission v. Wisconsin Right to Life Inc., 551 U.S. 449 (2007).

181 Ibid., 507.

182 The language derives from a Thurgood Marshall opinion upholding a Michigan campaign finance law, in which he argued that the state had a compelling interest in restricting corporate expenditures on political messages in order to ensure that the amount of political speech "reflect[s] actual public support for the political ideas espoused by corporations." Austin v. Michigan Chamber of Commerce, 494 U.S. 652, 660 (1990). In dissent, Scalia thought this doctrine meant that "virtually anything the Court deems politically undesirable can be turned into political corruption—by simply describing its effects as politically 'corrosive,'" which is fundamentally at odds with the principles outlined in *Buckley.* Ibid., 685.

183 Davis v. Federal Election Commission, 554 U.S. 724, 741 (2008).

184 Citizens United v. Federal Election Commission, 558 U.S. 310, 337, 339 (2010).

185 Ibid., 469.

186 McCutcheon v. Federal Election Commission, 134 S. Ct. 1434, 1448 (2014).

CONCLUSION

1 Robert A. Dahl, "Decision-Making in a Democracy: The Supreme Court as a National Policy-Maker," *Journal of Public Law* 6 (1957): 279.

2 Thomas Jefferson quoted by Anna Harvey, *A Mere Machine* (New Haven, CT: Yale University Press, 2013), xvii. Jefferson's hope was that a judge would be machine-like in dispensing justice "equally and impartially," rather than giving in to the all-too-human temptation to act on the "eccentric impulses of whimsical, capricious designing man." Thomas Jefferson to Edmund Pendleton, August 26, 1776, in *The Papers of Thomas Jefferson,* ed. Julian P. Boyd (Princeton, NJ: Princeton University Press, 1950), 1:505. In her study of the politics of judicial

review, Harvey uses the metaphor to characterize a Court "systematically and predictably deferential to elected branch preferences."

3 See, e.g., Keith E. Whittington, "'Interpose Your Friendly Hand': Political Supports for the Exercise of Judicial Review by the United States Supreme Court," *American Political Science Review* 99 (2005): 583; Mark A. Graber, "James Buchanan as Savior? Judicial Power, Political Fragmentation, and the Failed 1831 Repeal of Section 25," *Oregon Law Review* 88 (2009): 95; Barry Friedman and Erin Delaney, "Becoming Supreme: The Federal Foundation of Judicial Supremacy," *Columbia Law Review* 111 (2011): 1137.

4 For a more sophisticated analysis reaching similar conclusions, see Tom S. Clark and Keith E. Whittington, "Ideology, Partisanship and Judicial Review of Acts of Congress, 1789–2006" (working paper, 2011).

5 Howard Gillman, *The Votes that Counted* (Chicago: University of Chicago Press, 2000), 7.

6 "Brutus, No. 11," in Howard Gillman, Mark A. Graber, and Keith E. Whittington, *American Constitutionalism*, 2nd ed. (New York: Oxford University Press, 2017), 1:57–58.

7 "Brutus, No. 12," in ibid., 58.

8 Alexander Hamilton, "The Federalist, No. 78," in ibid., 61.

9 See Barry Friedman, "The History of the Countermajoritarian Difficulty, Part Three: The Lesson of *Lochner*," *New York University Law Review* 76 (2001): 1383.

10 Alexander M. Bickel, *The Least Dangerous Branch* (Indianapolis: Bobbs-Merrill, 1962), 1, 16, 17.

11 Barry Friedman, "Mediated Popular Constitutionalism," *Michigan Law Review* 101 (2003): 2596; Stephen M. Griffin, "Judicial Supremacy and Equal Protection in a Democracy of Rights," *University of Pennsylvania Journal of Constitutional Law* 4 (2002): 281; Mark A. Graber, "Constitutional Politics and Constitutional Theory: A Misunderstood and Neglected Relationship," *Law and Social Inquiry* 27 (2002): 209; Ilya Somin, "Political Ignorance and the Countermajoritarian Difficulty: A New Perspective on the Central Obsession of Constitutional Theory," *Iowa Law Review* 89 (2003): 1287; Scott E. Lemieux and David J. Watkins, "Beyond the 'Countermajoritarian Difficulty': Lessons from Contemporary Democratic Theory," *Polity* 41 (2008): 30; Allison M. Martens, "Reconsidering Judicial Supremacy: From the Counter-Majoritarian Difficulty to Constitutional Transformations," *Perspectives on Politics* 5 (2007): 447; Keith E. Whittington, "The Power of Judicial Review," in *The Oxford Handbook of the U.S. Constitution*, ed. Mark Tushnet, Mark A. Graber, and Sanford Levinson (Oxford: Oxford University Press, 2015), 387.

12 Bickel, *Least Dangerous Branch*, 17.

13 United States v. Carolene Products Co., 304 U.S. 144, 152n4 (1936).

14 L. A. Powe Jr., "Does Footnote Four Describe?" *Constitutional Commentary* 11 (1994): 197.

15 Ibid., 210.

16 Leslie P. Goldstein, *The U.S. Supreme Court and Racial Minorities* (New York: Edward Elgar Publishers, 2017), 4.

17 Ibid., 400.

18 This is George Hoar's characterization of the US Senate. For more detail, see Keith E. Whittington, "Sober Second Thoughts: Evaluating the History of Horizontal Judicial Review by the U.S. Supreme Court," *Constitutional Studies* 2 (2017): 97.

19 Alexander Hamilton, "No. 78," in Alexander Hamilton, James Madison, and John Jay, *The Federalist Papers*, ed. Clinton Rossiter (New York: Mentor, 1961), 468; Bickel, *Least Dangerous Branch*, 58, 239.

20 See Cass A. Sunstein, *One Case at a Time* (Cambridge, MA: Harvard University Press, 2001).

21 Ng Fung Ho v. White, 259 U.S. 276 (1922).

22 Wong Wing v. United States, 163 U.S. 228 (1896).

23 Rasmussen v. United States, 197 U.S. 516 (1905).

24 United States v. Phelps, 33 U.S. 700 (1834).

25 Burgess v. Salmon, 97 U.S. 381 (1878).

26 Monongahela Navigation Co. v. United States, 148 U.S. 312 (1893).

27 Reynolds v. M'Arthur, 27 U.S. 417, 435 (1829).

28 Fairbank v. United States, 181 U.S. 283, 312 (1901).

29 United States v. Hvoslef, 237 U.S. 1 (1915); Thames & Mersey Marine Ins. Co., Ltd. v. United States, 237 U.S. 19 (1915); A. G. Spalding & Bros. v. Edwards, 262 U.S. 66 (1923).

30 Blodgett v. Holden, 275 U.S. 142 (1927); Nichols v. Coolidge, 274 U.S. 531 (1927).

31 Benner v. Porter, 50 U.S. 235 (1850).

32 Coyle v. Smith, 221 U.S. 559, 580 (1911).

33 Buckley v. Valeo, 424 U.S. 1 (1976).

34 United States v. Windsor, 133 S. Ct. 2675 (2013).

35 Legal Services Corp. v. Velazquez, 531 U.S. 533 (2001).

36 United States Department of Agriculture v. Murry, 413 U.S. 508 (1973).

37 Marshall v. Barlow's, 436 U.S. 307 (1978); Aguilar v. Felton, 473 U.S. 402 (1985).

38 Boumediene v. Bush, 553 U.S. 723 (2008).

39 Immigration and Naturalization Service v. Chadha, 462 U.S. 919 (1983); Clinton v. New York City, 524 U.S. 417 (1998); Shelby County v. Holder, 133 S. Ct. 2612 (2013).

40 Reno v. American Civil Liberties Union, 521 U.S. 844 (1997).

41 Keith E. Whittington, *Political Foundations of Judicial Supremacy* (Princeton, NJ: Princeton University Press, 2007), 208–210.

42 United States v. Eichman, 496 U.S. 310 (1990); Peter Hanson, "Flag Burning," in *Public Opinion and Constitutional Controversy*, ed. Nathaniel Persily, Jack Citrin, and Patrick J. Egan (New York: Oxford University Press, 2008).

43 Hosanna-Tabor Evangelical Lutheran Church and School v. Equal Employment Opportunity Commission, 565 U.S. 171 (2012).

44 Califano v. Goldfarb, 430 U.S. 199 (1977); Jimenez v. Weinberger, 417 U.S. 628 (1974).

45 Leary v. United States, 395 U.S. 6 (1969).

46 United States v. Stevens, 559 U.S. 460 (2010); Blount v. Rizzo, 400 U.S 410 (1971); Flower v. United States, 407 U.S. 197 (1972).

47 Trop v. Dulles, 356 U.S. 86 (1958). See, e.g., Ruth Ellen Wasem, "Trump Administration Now Has Naturalized Citizens in Its Sights," *The Hill,* July 17, 2018.

48 James R. Rogers, "Information and Judicial Review: A Signaling Game of Legislative-Judicial Interaction," *American Journal of Political Science* 45 (2001): 84; Keith E. Whittington, "Legislative Sanctions and the Strategic Environment of Judicial Review," *International Journal of Constitutional Law* 1 (2003): 451–454.

APPENDIX: IDENTIFYING CASES OF JUDICIAL REVIEW

1 Legislative Reference Service, *The Constitution of the United States—Analysis and Interpretation* (Washington, DC: Government Printing Office, 1952), 1241. This volume was a radically revised version of an earlier document: Legislative Reference Service, *The Constitution of the United States, Annotated* (1923). The earlier document included its own list of "acts of Congress Declared Unconstitutional by the Supreme Court." That list included forty-three cases but notably left out the *Dred Scott* case, which is widely regarded as a canonical instance of judicial review.

2 The editors claimed they dropped those cases in which the statutes "were not held unconstitutional in their entirety and therefore inoperative," but only their "application to specific factual situations . . . was held to be prohibited by the Constitution." Legislative Reference Service, *The Constitution of the United States—Analysis and Interpretation,* rev. ed. (Washington, DC: Government Printing Office, 1964), 1401.

3 See Nicholas S. Zeppos, "Deference to Political Decisionmakers and the Preferred Scope of Judicial Review," *Northwestern University Law Review* 88 (1993): 296.

4 See especially Mark A. Graber, "Naked Land Transfers and American Constitutional Development," *Vanderbilt Law Review* 53 (2000): 73.

5 Thus, when the Department of Justice relies on the provisions of the Sherman Anti-Trust Act to bring legal action against the E. C. Knight Company for creating a monopoly over the production of refined sugar, the scope of congressional authority is at stake. When a federal district judge issues constitutionally flawed jury instructions or a customs official searches an office without a proper warrant and collects evidence, the scope of congressional authority is not at issue. Since many of the constitutional restrictions built into the Bill of Rights are

aimed primarily at judges and executive branch officials rather than Congress, a great deal of the Court's elaboration and application of civil liberties against the federal government is not included in the data set. At a relatively early date, for example, Congress passed the Tucker Act of 1887, which expanded the jurisdiction of the Court of Claims to hear all monetary claims against the federal government founded on the Constitution. One effect of the Tucker Act was to largely convert constitutional takings cases under the Fifth Amendment from challenges to congressional authority into challenges to judicial interpretation of the statute.

6 See, e.g., Kilbourn v. Thompson, 103 U.S. 168 (1881) (limiting the contempt power of legislative inquiries); National Labor Relations Board v. Canning, 134 S. Ct. 2550 (2014) (determining that pro forma legislative sessions are sufficient to preclude use of the presidential power to make recess appointments). These boundaries are permeable across cases and over time. The treaty-making power, as such, is distinct from the legislative power of Congress, but treaties may give rise to related statutes and constitutional questions about congressional authority to pass such statutes. For a significant part of its history, Congress actively legislated for territories and the District of Columbia (and thus invited constitutional disputes over the limits on congressional legislative authority), but once day-to-day governance is delegated to a territorial legislature or a city council, many such questions are no longer framed in a way that implicates the constitutional limits on Congress itself. See, e.g., Dunphy v. Kleinsmith and Duer, 78 U.S. 610 (1870) ("From the provisions of the organic law . . . it is apparent that the Territorial legislature has no power to pass any law in contravention of the Constitution of the United States"); Mullaney v. Anderson, 342 U.S. 415 (1952) ("We cannot presume that Congress authorized the Territorial Legislature to treat citizens of States the way States cannot treat citizens of sister States. Only the clearest expression of Congressional intent could induce such a result. It is not present. . . . [The territorial legislature] was granted no greater power over citizens of other States than a State legislature has.").

7 Instances of lower courts striking down an act of Congress are *almost* always appealed to the US Supreme Court, but even in such appeals, the Court's decision might not directly address the substantive constitutional question.

8 The search included various combinations of keywords that reflected federal legislation (e.g., "Congress," "federal w/2 government," "national w/2 government") and constitutional review (e.g., "constitution!" "unconstitution!" "invalid," "void," "no w/2 power") until no new additional cases could be located. One benefit of a full text search is that it includes not only the judicial opinions themselves but also the reporter's headnotes and syllabus and (for earlier periods) a transcription of the lawyers' arguments. A relevant term would frequently appear in one part of the text (such as the opinion itself) but not in another (such as the headnotes). Although variations on "Congress" and "constitution!"

captured most of the cases, a significant number (including some on the CRS list) escaped such a search. The headnotes were a particularly unreliable guide to whether constitutional review had occurred in the nineteenth century.

9 See, e.g., Embry v. United States, 100 U.S. 680 (1880) ("We have had no difficulty in reaching the conclusion that the appellant is not entitled to recover. The important constitutional question [of whether Congress can restrict the president's power to remove an executive official] which has at times occupied the attention of the political department of the government ever since its organization, and which was brought to our attention in the argument, is not, as we think, involved."); Lewellyn v. Frick, 268 U.S. 238 (1925) ("We do not propose to discuss the limits of the powers of Congress in cases like the present."); The Martha Washington, 16 F. Cas. 871 (1860) ("Every question involving the constitutional power of the general government is important, and there can be scarcely any one more so than this. . . . Although this question must be decided, I think it cannot be in the present case, and the courts of the United States are not in the habit of volunteering their opinions when they are not called for."); United States v. Apel, 134 S. Ct. 1144 (2014) ("The Court of Appeals never reached Apel's constitutional arguments, and we decline to do so in the first instance.").

10 See, e.g., City of Cleveland v. United States, 323 U.S. 329 (1945) ("Little need be said concerning the merits. . . . Congress may exempt property owned by the United States or its instrumentality from state taxation in furtherance of the purposes of the federal legislation. This is settled by such an array of authority that citation would seem unnecessary [but providing citations]."); California v. United States, 320 U.S. 577 (1944) ("We have disposed of the only serious question raised. The numerous other questions call for only summary treatment. . . . It is too late in the day to question the power of Congress under the Commerce Clause to regulate such an essential part of interstate and foreign trade as the activities and instrumentalities which were here authorized to be regulated by the Commission, whether they be the activities and instrumentalities of private persons or of public agencies. *United States* v. *California*, 297 U.S. 175, 184–5."); National Labor Relations Board v. Fruehauf Trailer Co., 301 U.S. 49 (1937) ("The questions relating to the construction and validity of the act have been fully discussed in our opinion in *Labor Board v. Jones & Laughlin Steel Corp.*, 301 U.S. 1 [1937]. We hold that the principles there stated are applicable here.").

11 The restriction on cases that simply cited existing precedent excluded a small number of substantively unimportant cases. Especially given that the Court did not have discretionary jurisdiction for much of its history, the goal was to exclude legally trivial cases that simply reaffirmed what is reflected elsewhere in the data set without establishing new constitutional rules.

12 On saving constructions, see, generally, Emily Sherwin, "Rules and Judicial Review," *Legal Theory* 8 (2000): 299; Adrian Vermeule, "Saving Constructions,"

Georgetown Law Journal 85 (1997): 1945. On as-applied versus facial invalidations, see Richard H. Fallon, "As-Applied and Facial Challenges and Third-Party Standing," *Harvard Law Review* 113 (2000): 1321. Cf. Matthew D. Adler, "Rights against Rules: The Moral Structure of American Constitutional Law," *Michigan Law Review* 97 (1998): 1.

13 Mark A. Graber, "The New Fiction: *Dred Scott* and the Language of Judicial Authority," *Chicago-Kent Law Review* 82 (2007): 187. Cf. Ashwander v. Tennessee Valley Authority, 297 U.S. 288, 346 (1936) (Brandeis, J., concurring).

14 See, e.g., Bond v. United States, 134 S. Ct. 2077 (2014) ("Because our constitutional structure leaves local criminal activity primarily to the States, we have generally declined to read federal law as intruding on that responsibility, unless Congress has clearly indicated that the law should have such reach."); Atascadero State Hospital v. Scanlon, 473 U.S. 234 (1985) ("We . . . affirm that Congress may abrogate the States' constitutionally secured immunity from suit in federal court only by making its intention unmistakably clear in the language of the statute."); United States v. Bass, 404 U.S. 336 (1971) ("We will not be quick to assume that Congress has meant to effect a significant change in the sensitive relation between federal and state criminal jurisdiction . . . [and therefore employ] a requirement of clear statement."); United States v. Rumely, 345 U.S. 41, 46 (1953) ("Whenever constitutional limits upon the investigative power of Congress have to be drawn by this Court, it ought only to be done after Congress has demonstrated its full awareness of what is at stake by unequivocally authorizing an inquiry of dubious limits.").

INDEX

Numbers in italics refer to pages with figures or tables.